The Correspondence of Sarah Morgan
and Francis Warrington Dawson

THE CORRESPONDENCE

OF

Sarah Morgan

AND

Francis Warrington Dawson

WITH SELECTED EDITORIALS

WRITTEN BY SARAH MORGAN

FOR THE

Charleston News and Courier

Edited by Giselle Roberts

The University of Georgia Press

Athens & London

The publication of this book is supported in part by a grant from the Watson-Brown Foundation, Inc.

© 2004 by the University of Georgia Press
Athens, Georgia 30602
All rights reserved
Designed by Louise OFarrell
Set in 11.5/14 Fournier by Graphic Composition, Inc.
Printed and bound by Thomson-Shore
The paper in this book meets the guidelines for
permanence and durability of the Committee on
Production Guidelines for Book Longevity of the
Council on Library Resources.

Printed in the United States of America
08   07   06   05   04   C   5   4   3   2   1

Library of Congress Cataloging-in-Publication Data

Dawson, Sarah Morgan, 1842–1909
The correspondence of Sarah Morgan and Francis Warrington Dawson, with selected
editorials written by Sarah Morgan for the Charleston News and Courier / edited by
Giselle Roberts.
p.   cm. — (The publications of the Southern Texts Society)
Includes bibliographical references and index.
ISBN 0-8203-2591-0 (alk. paper)
1. Dawson, Sarah Morgan, 1842–1909—Correspondence. 2. Dawson, Francis
Warrington, 1840–1889—Correspondence. 3. Couples—South Carolina—
Charleston—Correspondence. 4. Charleston (S.C.)—Biography. 5. Charleston
(S.C.)—Social life and customs—19th century. 6. Charleston (S.C.)—Social
conditions—19th century. 7. Women—Southern States—Social conditions—19th
century. 8. Sex role—Southern States—History—19th century. 9. Family—
Southern States—History—19th century. 10. Southern States—Social conditions—
1865–1945. I. Dawson, Francis Warrington, 1840–1889. II. Roberts, Giselle, 1974–
III. News and courier (Charleston, S.C. : Daily) IV. Title. V. Series.
F279.C453A242 2004
975.7'91503'092—dc22   2004001263

British Library Cataloging-in-Publication Data available

For Glenn, with love

CONTENTS

ACKNOWLEDGMENTS

This book has been a joy to work on, made all the more delightful by the host of friends and colleagues who taught me that the journey can be just as wonderful as the final destination.

The Francis Warrington Dawson I and II Papers are held at the Rare Book, Manuscript, and Special Collections Library at Duke University, thousands of miles away from my home in Melbourne, Australia. Without the expertise and enthusiasm of research services librarian Elizabeth Dunn, this project would have been a difficult one, indeed. Elizabeth spent countless hours helping me decipher difficult words and references, following up questions, and locating papers and photographs. Her support and encouragement inspired me to look forward to the day when I could present her with this book and thank her for her contribution and her friendship, both of which are nothing short of exceptional.

Family and local historians, librarians, and scholars all over the United States generously shared their research with me, making the task of finding challenging references an achievable one. Special thanks to Jewell Anderson Dalrymple (Georgia Historical Society), Laura Edwards, Robert Janosov, Charles Joyner, Heidi Kuglin, Joseph Matheson, Cindy McClay, Ann Miller, Elisabeth Muhlenfeld, Gregory Stoner (Virginia Historical Society), and Dell Upton. Robert Conte kindly sent me a copy of his beautiful book on the Greenbrier and, with the assistance of Laura Smith, scanned the image of White Sulphur Springs that appears in this book. Emily Clack and Eunice Barkes, descendants of Sarah Morgan Dawson's sister, Eliza, provided me with valuable information on the LaNoue family. Morgan Potts Goldbarth, a descendant of Sarah's brother James, shared her family history and collection of previously unpublished photographs. I am grateful for her generosity and friendship. Ingrid Barker kindly translated French for me and never tired when I asked her for help on "just one more" word or phrase.

More than ten years ago, Charles East's edition of Sarah Morgan's Civil War diary provided my introduction to American history. I thank him for doing a brilliant job and setting such a high scholarly standard for me to meet. He has shared his research and his time, read and commented on papers, and offered me advice and support. It has been a great privilege to be the recipient of his expertise, so generously given.

Michael O'Brien, chair of the Editorial Board of the Southern Texts Society, has also been an instrumental—and inspirational—force in the publication of this book. Since my initial proposal, he has worked tirelessly on redraft after redraft, challenging me to sharpen my analysis and providing me with an education in the craft of editing. His professionalism, honesty, and encouragement have improved the book in many ways. I feel very fortunate to have had such a capable editor. I also thank the Southern Texts Society for its enthusiasm regarding my original proposal and its timely suggestions. Nancy Grayson, editor-in-chief at the University of Georgia Press, has also made the publication process a pleasure. I thank her and all the staff at the University of Georgia Press for their support. Special thanks to managing editor Jennifer Reichlin and copyeditor Ellen Goldlust-Gingrich for their expertise and assistance.

At La Trobe University, John Salmond and William Breen have been the finest mentors anyone could wish for. Over many pleasant lunches at the Staff Club, they listened patiently to my fears and frustrations and celebrated my successes. This book would not have been possible without their steadfast faith in me, which sustained me more than they may know. Warren Ellem's wonderful classes on the Civil War and Reconstruction nurtured my interest in American history, and I thank him for being a fine teacher and mentor with the rare talent of making the past come to life.

Jenny Alexander and Erin Gook have been the truest and best friends, offering me support and encouragement every step of the way. So too have Fran, Marie, and William Fenamore of New York, whose hearts are at least as big as the beautiful city they call home. I love them all dearly.

My parents, Ron and Tricia Myers, and my sister, Nerissa, spent many dinners looking at photocopies of Frank and Sarah's letters in an effort to work out what were then indecipherable words. My mother read drafts and always knew just the right thing to say after I had spent a frustrating day searching for references—and found none. My father's intelligence and true creativity have always been my source of inspiration.

And finally, I thank my husband, Glenn, whose good humor, honesty, and love have been the most precious gifts of all. He, along with our cats—

Abby, Katie, and Jermima—remind me daily that the present is just as important as the past.

Parts of the introduction appear in Bruce Clayton and John Salmond, eds., *Lives of Struggle and Triumph: Southern Women, Their Institutions, Their Communities* (Gainesville: University Press of Florida, 2003). I thank both editors for their permission to republish and for their valuable comments and suggestions.

INTRODUCTION

Francis Warrington Dawson fell in love with Sarah Morgan in January 1873 and spent the rest of the year trying to win her hand in marriage. Their courtship was highly unconventional, reading more like an epic novel than, as Frank put it, the story of "a very ordinary man & a very lovely woman."[1] He was a thirty-two-year-old Englishman living under a nom de guerre who had fought for the Confederacy and later settled in South Carolina, where he became editor of the *Charleston News*. She was a thirty-year-old Confederate belle who was living as an unwelcome guest in her brother's household near Columbia. When the two met in the winter of 1873, Frank was mourning the recent death of his wife, while Sarah was still grieving the life she had lost as a result of war and defeat.

The correspondence of Frank Dawson and Sarah Morgan provides a window into relationships, family, class, and gender in the postwar South. The couple's relationship came to encompass both the personal and the professional: Frank loved Sarah, and in an attempt to free her from her unhappy existence, he convinced her to accept a position on the editorial staff of the *News*. Writing to secure her independence and support her mother and nephew, Sarah's editorials provided an intimate portrait of her personal journey as she searched for new ways of living in the postwar world.

Sarah Morgan is most well known for her acclaimed Civil War diary, first published in 1913 and most recently edited by Charles East in *Sarah Morgan: The Civil War Diary of a Southern Woman*. Her six-volume journal chronicles the life of an articulate, passionate, and intelligent young woman from Baton Rouge, Louisiana. By locating her own story within a grand narrative of war, Sarah left a legacy that has helped historians to examine southern women's varied wartime experiences and the ways in which these women rebuilt their lives and identities during Reconstruction. This process, along with its long-term effects, has become one of the most contentious issues in southern women's history. Was the Civil War a watershed event? Did it prompt women to embrace new opportunities, or did it force them to rebuild their lives in the shadow of a conservative feminine ideal?

An earlier generation of historians argued that the Civil War "provided a springboard" from which women leaped into a world "heretofore reserved for men." Recent scholarship has revised this interpretation, suggesting that the wartime experiences of elite southern women led them to "invent new selves designed in large measure to resist change" rather than to embrace it. While emphasizing the ways in which postwar life fostered women's involvement in the social reform movement, these historians conclude that "everything had changed, and nothing had changed." In the postwar South, ladies may have entered the public arena, but they continued to cling to the preexisting racial and class hierarchy as they looked for ways to assert their status in a world without wealth or slaves.[2]

While the scholarly debate has centered on the watershed aspect of the war, historians have only just begun to examine how elite women invented new selves in its aftermath. Much of this recent academic work has focused on an analysis of the ways in which domesticity emerged as a site for the reconstruction of the elite southern identity. LeeAnn Whites contends that the reassertion of a conservative model of femininity was inextricably tied to the resurrection of elite southern masculinity. To rebuild demoralized soldiers, she argues, women subordinated themselves within the domestic sphere to become the "last legitimate terrain of domination" for their men. In so doing, women's sense of self became firmly attached to their domestic and familial roles.[3]

Laura Edwards provides a variation on this theme, arguing that elite southern women fashioned an ideal of domesticity and used it as a mechanism for asserting their status. By attending to the needs of their husbands and children, "putting well-prepared meals on the table, banishing dirt and dust, selecting tasteful interior decorations, and maintaining a cheerful, supportive atmosphere," southern ladies reconstructed their identities as "worthy women." Further, they used this framework to distinguish themselves from African American and poor white women, whose economic status prevented them from attaining the exalted domestic ideal.[4] As Edwards notes, the domestic reconstruction of elite white womanhood was most successfully achieved through marriage, which usually facilitated the establishment of a new household and granted women the status of wife and mistress of the home. In this environment, wives could attend to their homes and children while deferring and submitting to their husbands.

By centering their analysis on married women, scholars have paid far less attention to the experiences of women who fell outside the categories of wife and mistress. Sarah Morgan's postwar journey provides a new perspective on these themes by telling the story of how one single, adult, financially dependent woman rebuilt her elite identity through employment rather than marriage. Trapped as an unwelcome guest in her brother's household, Sarah Morgan used her secret career as a writer to free herself from the shackles of dependence. Although her editorial work provided her with the means to attain a home of her own, writing also forced Sarah to grapple with her understanding of the single white woman's place in the postwar community, in which the antebellum ideals of marriage, submission, and gentility were often pitted against women's employment and independence.

Frank and Sarah's letters focus on the process of rebuilding one's identity in a world where there was no longer a definitive hierarchy or way of being. Frank's British heritage safeguarded him from this crisis, but he experienced it secondhand through his personal and professional relationships with Sarah, who struggled to reconcile her antebellum socialization in the southern feminine ideal with the realities of life in postwar South Carolina. The autobiographical content of Sarah's editorials informs and problematizes this journey while turning outward the overwhelmingly inward gaze of the correspondence, providing a woman's perspective on the American South in the grip of Reconstruction. Sarah's commentary on the plight of elite society, the presence and influence of carpetbaggers, and the status of women and freedpeople provides a candid and revealing portrayal of the way one southern lady viewed the world she inhabited even as she struggled to find her place within it.

A Confederate Belle

Sarah Morgan spent her girlhood in training for a world that disappeared with the coming of war. Born in New Orleans, Louisiana, on February 28, 1842, Sarah was the seventh child of Judge Thomas Gibbes Morgan and Sarah Hunt Fowler Morgan. Thomas, who was born in New Jersey in 1799, had moved to Baton Rouge in the 1820s to pursue a career in law. After the death of his first wife, he met Sarah, a northern-born woman who had been raised by her guardian, George Mather, on his sugar plantation in St. James Parish, Louisiana. The couple married in 1830 and moved to the Crescent City, where Thomas worked as a collector for the Port of New Orleans and

Sarah raised their eight children: Lavinia, Eliza Ann, Thomas Gibbes Jr., Henry Waller Fowler, George Mather, Miriam Antoinette, Sarah Ida Fowler, and James Morris Morgan.

In 1850, the family relocated to Baton Rouge, where Thomas served as a district attorney and later a district judge. The Morgans became well known and highly respected members of the community, often described by locals as the "proud Morgans" or the "aristocrats of Baton Rouge." Like most professionals in the city, their lifestyle was comfortable and genteel, not opulent. Thomas, Sarah, and the children occupied a handsome two-story home on Church Street with wide galleries that provided some relief from the oppressive Louisiana summers. Like most of their neighbors, the Morgans were slaveholders, owning eight slaves who worked as domestic servants.[5]

The landscape of Baton Rouge and its surroundings provided the backdrop for Sarah's socialization in the edicts of the southern tradition. Like most elite young women, Sarah received education and training that would later allow her to fulfill the important duties associated with marriage and motherhood. Under the tutelage of her mother, her sisters, and a collection of female relatives and friends, Sarah was instructed in temperament, piety, fashion, social graces, and manners. After "ten short months at school," she spent her days at the family home studying French and the classics, playing her guitar, and enjoying the company of family and friends.[6] Socialized within a world dominated by family, household, and community, Sarah was also educated in the complexities and nuances of the southern hierarchy, which used race, class, and gender to construct relationships and identities. Elite white men such as Thomas Gibbes Morgan dominated this hierarchy by governing politics, business, familial relationships, and the household. At the other end of the scale, the Morgan family's slaves were relegated to positions of legal, economic, and social inferiority.

Sarah Morgan enjoyed the privileges bestowed on her by her race and class, but like her mother and sisters, she was bound to respect the head of household, whose position as master, husband, and father reinforced his power and authority. In a society governed by reciprocal obligations, women deferred to men and in return received protection and respectability. Sarah, like most women, accepted her place in this model. She supported the notion of reciprocity, citing her parents' marriage as successful in part because of their ability to fulfill their designated roles. "I want to think all marriages as happy, all husbands as indulgent and kind, all wives as mild and submissive as father and mother," she wrote in May 1862, "I look for no more beautiful model." As a young lady, Sarah revered the image of her father as the benevolent patriarch and looked for these qualities in a husband. "My lord and master must be . . . the one that, after God, I shall most venerate and respect," she declared. "Woe be to me, if I could feel superior to him for an instant!"[7]

The Civil War destroyed many of the physical, emotional, and ideological structures that had governed Sarah's antebellum life in Baton Rouge. As the trumpet of war sounded in early 1861, Sarah lost a brother, Henry (Harry), to another code of honor, the duel. Grief-stricken by the senselessness of the affair, which had taken place because a man named James Sparks called Henry a liar, Sarah nevertheless lauded her brother's bravery and his commitment to family honor. "Courage is what women admire above all things and that he possessed in the most eminent degree," she wrote. "Months after he died, passing a group of gentlemen in New Orleans, Jimmy [another brother] heard them mention Harry's name, and one said 'I saw him when he stood up, and I saw him fall, and I never saw as brave a man.' 'That is the way with all the men of that family; they are as brave as can be, and those girls are not an inch behind them' returned another. No! there never was a braver man than Harry."[8]

Sarah was left to endure the tragedy without the sustaining influence of her brothers, Gibbes and George, who had offered their services to the Confederate army. Just one day before Henry's death, twenty-three-year-old George had departed with the First Louisiana Volunteers for Norfolk, Virginia, where he joined Gibbes, a second lieutenant with the Seventh Louisiana Infantry. At home, a combination of grief and anxiety soon wore down Sarah's health. Overcome by exhaustion, she spent weeks languishing on her daybed, rising only from her invalid state for carriage rides to the graveyard. "So tired, that it seemed as if only Death could rest" her, she glimpsed Judge Morgan's "anxious distressed face" and found the will to recover. "[I] then felt the pain I suffered was nothing to what he felt on seeing me in that state," she recalled, "and I tried to get strong for his sake." Sarah's battle to regain her strength was met with a bitter victory, when, in November 1861, her father died after a severe asthma attack. "All that made our home happy, or secured it to us, was gone; a sad life lay before us," she wrote. "My heart failed me when I remembered what a home we had lost, but I could thank God that I had loved and valued it while I had it, for few have loved home as I."[9]

One tragedy followed another. As Sarah mourned the loss of her father and brother, the Union army continued to make strong advances in the Mississippi region. By April 1862, David Glasgow Farragut had captured New Orleans, and the citizens of Baton Rouge anxiously anticipated the imminent arrival of Federal troops. "There is no word in the English language which can express the state in which we are all now, and have been for the last three days," Sarah wrote excitedly in April 1862. "I believe that I am one of the most self possessed in my small circle of acquaintance, and yet, I feel such a craving for news . . . that I believe I am as crazy as the rest, and it is all humbug when they tell me I am cool."[10]

Alone and afraid, Sarah confronted a daunting and unfamiliar social landscape that left Confederate men out of the equation. "O my brothers, George, Gibbes and Jimmy, never did we more need protection!" she cried, "where are you?" Terrified by her vulnerability, Sarah resorted to carrying about a bag filled with hairpins, starch, embroidery, and combs, with the collection "crowned by [her] dagger." In May 1862, she used her diary to record a warning to any Yankee who attempted to "Butlerize—or brutalize" her. "And if you [Yankees] want to know what an excited girl is capable of," she declared, "call around, and I will show you the use of a small seven shooter, and large carving knife which vibrate between my belt, and pocket, always ready for use." Days later, Sarah was perturbed by her transformation from a genteel young lady into a bloodthirsty Confederate. "I, who have such a horror of bloodshed, consider even killing in self defense murder, who cannot wish them the slightest evil, whose only prayer is to have them sent back in peace to their own country, *I* talk of killing them!" she cried, "for what else do I wear a pistol and carving knife?"[11]

Confused and a little daunted by her new wartime role, Sarah fantasized about dispensing with "useless" femininity. Glorifying her brothers' honor and highlighting the irrelevance of her upbringing in her current predicament, Sarah described women as "useless trash . . . of no value or importance to ourselves or the rest of the world." "What is the use of all these worthless women, in war times?" she questioned. "I dont know a woman here who does not groan over her misfortune in being clothed in petticoats." Within the pages of her diary, Sarah dreamed about donning breeches and slaying Yankees. On one desperate occasion, she even attempted to try on her brother's suit. "I advanced so far as to lay it on the bed, and then carried my bird out—I was ashamed to let even my canary see me," she wrote, "but when I took a second look, my courage deserted me, and there ended my first and last attempt at disguise." Sarah had already reflected on the changed state of wartime femininity. "Pshaw! there are *no* women here!" she scoffed. "We are *all* men!"[12]

Yet like her beloved Confederate soldiers, Sarah and the other civilians of Baton Rouge could do little to prevent the occupation of their city. Within days of the Federal attack, Sarah, her mother, and her sister, Miriam, were forced to abandon their home for safer quarters in Clinton, Louisiana. After a brief visit through enemy lines to collect papers, clothes, and family treasures, Sarah never saw her Church Street home again. Months later, an acquaintance described the destruction of the Morgan estate. "It was one scene of ruin," she commented after hearing the report. "Libraries emptied, china smashed, sideboards split open with axes, three cedar chests cut open, plundered, and set up on end; all parlor ornaments carried off—even the alabaster Apollo and Diana that Hal [Henry Morgan] valued so much."[13]

When Sarah Morgan lost her home, she lost more than just the physical facade: she also lost the foundation on which she had built her identity as an elite young lady. Stripped of the security of her Church Street life and set adrift in a world turned upside down by war, Sarah regarded her homelessness as an assault on her femininity. "O my home, my home!" she lamented. "I could learn to be a woman there, and a true one, too. Who will teach me now?" Inhabiting a sparsely furnished one-bedroom apartment in Clinton, Sarah viewed her prospects with trepidation. "I look forward to my future life with a shudder," she confided in her diary in July 1862. "Why, if all father has left us is lost forever, if we are to be pennyless, as well as homeless, I'll work for my living. How I wonder? I will teach! I know I am not capable, but I can do my best. I would rather die than be dependent, I would rather die than teach. There now, you know what I feel! Teaching, before dependence, death before teaching. My soul revolts from the drudgery."[14]

A buggy accident spared Sarah from a life of teaching. In November 1862 she was thrown from a horse and spent months incapacitated by a back injury. "Ah me! how much more cheerfully I would have borne the breaking of an arm!" she remarked while writing in a "horizontal" position on her sickbed. "Spare me my feet! Merciful Father let me walk once more! Anything, save a helpless cripple!" Some doctors speculated that she might never walk again, but under the care of General Albert Carter and her sister-in-law, Lydia (the wife of Gibbes Morgan), Sarah made a partial recovery at the Carter plantation in East Feliciana Parish. The assault on the Confederate stronghold at Port Hudson by Federal troops in July 1863, however, forced the Morgan women to make a final desperate exodus to occupied New Orleans, where they joined the household of Sarah's half-brother and Unionist sympathizer, Judge Philip Hicky Morgan. While in his home, she received news of the death of her brothers, Gibbes and George, in February 1864. "Dead! dead! Both dead!" Sarah cried at hearing the news. "O my brothers! what have we lived for except you? We who would so gladly have laid down our lives for yours, are left desolate to mourn over all we loved and hoped for, weak and helpless; while you, so strong, noble, and brave, have gone before us without a murmur. God knows best. But it is hard—O so hard!"[15]

Confederate defeat brought little relief to such a thoroughly devastated family. Instead, the war's end only reminded Sarah of all she had lost. Despite her years of waiting and praying, Gibbes and George would not be among the tired, dejected Confederate soldiers who made their way back to New Orleans. "Since the boys died I have constantly thought of what pain it would bring to see their comrades return without them," Sarah conceded tearfully, "to see families reunited, and know that ours never could be again, save in heaven. Last Saturday the 29th of April, seven hundred and fifty paroled Louisianians from Lee's army were brought here—the sole survivors of ten regiments who left four years ago so full of hope and determination. On the 29th of April 1861, George left New Orleans with his regiment. On the fourth anniversary of that day, they came back; but George and Gibbes have long been lying in their graves—George far away in desolated Virginia."[16]

The war had also stripped Sarah of her home, possessions, and slaves—everything that had previously defined her status and her membership in Louisiana's urban elite. Further, the conflict had robbed Sarah of her intended life as a young southern lady, forcing her to become a woman without the fancy-dress balls and beaux that had characterized a belle's rite of passage. Her wartime refrain—"Better Days Are Coming"—now seemed but a cruel delusion. "My life is sad, and dark, and dreary, it rains, and the wind is never weary," she wrote on a cold September day in 1866. "Within and without it is unutterably gloomy. *Can* I bear my life? Why yes! with God's help, I could bear a sadder one! Yet how perfectly repugnant—!"[17]

Without an independent fortune, Sarah spent the late 1860s as a dependent in Philip Morgan's household. In May 1872, she, her mother, and her nephew, Howell (of whom Sarah had assumed custody after his father's death and his mother's remarriage), moved to South Carolina to make their home with Sarah's younger brother, James Morris Morgan. James had served as a midshipman in the Confederate States Navy and had subsequently served as a captain in the Egyptian army. James returned from Egypt and settled in South Carolina, where he purchased Hampton Plantation, located on the Congaree River four miles below Columbia. The property, spanning several thousand acres, contained a new house and a "huge barn capable of stabling a hundred animals." "The place is immense, and may some day regain its former value," Sarah wrote to Lydia. "At present, it is all rather rough."[18]

Sarah and her mother moved to South Carolina with the intention of making Jimmy's new house a home. At the outset, the domestic arrangements seemed perfect. With the arrival of his mother and sister, James could devote his complete attention to planting cotton, rebuilding his masculinity through hard work that would later translate into earned wealth.[19] In turn, the Morgan women had charge of their own household, giving them a sense of autonomy that they had not enjoyed since their antebellum days in Baton Rouge. As mistresses of Hampton, Sarah and her mother fulfilled the postwar domestic ideal, creating a happy, inviting home; cooking; cleaning; and providing James and Howell with the love and moral guidance that only women could bestow. "This is my path in life," Sarah remarked, "the adopted mother of some orphaned child, and the housekeeper at the hearth of some widowed, or bachelor brother."[20]

In early 1873, however, James Morgan married Gabriella Burroughs, throwing Sarah's congenial domestic arrangements into disarray. The new Mrs. Morgan was eager to establish herself as mistress of Hampton and did not take kindly to the presence or the well-meaning advice of the former managers. Within weeks of her arrival, Gabriella set up her own domestic regime, and Sarah and her mother found themselves relegated to the position of unwanted guests. Deprived of their domestic autonomy and assigned auxiliary roles within the household, Sarah and her mother experienced a demoralizing shift in their understanding of their dependence. As active and important members of Hampton, Sarah and Mrs. Morgan had regarded the arrangement as reciprocal: they submitted to James, worked within his household, and received protection and respectability in return. As guests in another woman's home, however, they were unable to fulfill their end of the reciprocal arrangement or to participate in the fulfillment of the domestic ideal. Consequently, their dependence was accentuated. No longer regarded as contributing members of the household, Sarah and her mother were cast into the role of economic dependents, compelled to live off

James and Gabriella's charity. Sarah and her mother now "stood a little aside, . . . being in but not of the domestic world."[21]

Sarah, who had once vowed that she would rather die than be dependent, found the new arrangement intolerable. Charged with Howell's care and education, Sarah also worried about her ability to provide for the child in a household where she possessed no authority or financial independence. Depressed and discouraged by her sister-in-law's efforts to evict her from Hampton, Sarah turned to Frank Dawson for assistance.[22]

A Newsman

The Civil War left Sarah Morgan with a legacy of grief and dependence. For Frank Dawson it had a binary effect, freeing him from the ties and obligations of the Old World and allowing him to embrace a successful career in the United States. Born in London on May 17, 1840, Austin John Reeks was the first child of Mary Perkins Reeks and Joseph Austin Reeks. Joseph was a member of one of the oldest Catholic families in England, with a proud heritage tracing back to the War of the Roses. In accordance with family tradition, Joseph graduated from the college of Saint-Omer in France and returned to England to marry in 1837. Joseph and Mary Reeks had three children, Austin, Joseph, and Teresa, before Joseph Sr. lost the family fortune in a string of bad investments on the wheat market in the 1840s. He made several unsuccessful attempts to regain his money, ultimately leaving his children to forge their way in the world without the benefits of wealth or education.[23]

Austin Reeks bore the legacy of his father's poor decisions. Bereft of the funds required to obtain a higher education in London or France, he tried his hand at writing and penned at least one moderately successful play. Austin struggled to earn a living from his craft until 1861, when he boldly resolved to put down his pen and sail across the Atlantic to fight for the Confederate States of America. "I had a sincere sympathy with the southern people in their struggle for independence, and felt that it would be a pleasant thing to help them to secure their freedom," he recalled years later. "It was not expected, at that time, that the war would last many months, and my idea simply was to go to the South, do my duty there as well as I might, and return home to England. I expected no reward and wanted none, and had no intention whatever of remaining permanently in the Southern States."[24] When the css *Nashville* docked in Southampton in November 1861, Austin presented himself to Captain Robert B. Pegram and begged for permission to join the crew. Pegram consented, and a jubilant Austin returned to London to inform his parents of his departure to the United States.

Joseph and Mary Reeks did not respond favorably to the news of their son's daring Confederate adventure. Joseph was enraged by Austin's plan, declaring that his impulsive actions threatened to dishonor the family name. If the boat was captured, Joseph argued, Austin would be hanged as a pirate, not a belligerent. Joseph's outburst did little to sway his son's determination to fight for the Confederacy. Instead, Austin resolved that if he were to die at sea or on the battlefield, he would do so under his own name. After some consideration, he chose Francis Warrington Dawson: Francis after his patron saint, Francis of Assisi; Warrington after his relations, the Warrens; and Dawson after his soldier uncle, Captain William A. Dawson. In January 1862, the newly minted Dawson presented himself to Captain Pegram in full sailor's regalia. "I wore a blue woolen shirt open at the neck," Dawson recalled, "a black silk handkerchief, with ample flowing ends, tied loosely around the neck; blue trousers, made very tight at the knee and twenty-two inches in circumference at the bottom, and on my head a flat cloth cap ornamented with long black ribbons." His work commenced on February 2, 1862, when the *Nashville* departed Southampton and set sail for North Carolina.[25]

If Frank had envisioned a thrilling voyage filled with Confederate camaraderie, he was sorely mistaken. As Captain Pegram and his associates retired to their comfortable quarters, the overdressed Dawson was left to make his acquaintances with a crew of eight weathered seamen who "represented almost as many different nations." "There was an Irishman, and a Belgian, a North Carolinian and a Swede, a fat Cockney Englishman and a Frenchman, a Scotchman and a Spaniard," he remarked indignantly. "I found them to be mean, treacherous and obscene." After an unpleasant dinner and a bout of seasickness, Frank settled into life on the *Nashville*. With his "experience in nautical affairs . . . confined to sailing miniature yachts on the Serpentine in Hyde Park," the new recruit was "not worth [his] salt," according to the boatswain, who ordered Dawson to take charge of only the most basic duties—scouring the deck, polishing the brass work, sweeping, emptying the spittoons, and shoveling coal. Frank's diligence was later rewarded with a regular shift as a lookout. "There I had the pleasantest hours that I knew on the *Nashville*," he wrote. "It was quiet and still. I was far removed from the bickering and blackguardism of the crew, and could indulge myself freely in watching the varied hues of the dancing waters, broken now and again by a shoal of porpoises, or by the brief flight of the flying-fish as they darted from the wave in the effort to escape from their pursuers. But all this was not conducive to keeping a sharp lookout."[26]

The *Nashville* arrived in Morehead City, North Carolina, on February 28, 1862, less than one month after its departure from England. "For the first time I realized my isolated position," Frank commented. "There was no home or friends for me; nothing but doubt and uncertainty, yet I had confidence that with time, faith and energy, I might accomplish what I desired." Upon his arrival in the United States, Frank was appointed a master's mate in the Confederate navy. After preparing a report on the *Nashville*'s voyage for Captain Pegram, Frank was sent to Richmond, Virginia, and "assigned to duty on a floating battery lying in the James River." "I was not satisfied with myself, and saw no prospect of accomplishing anything as long as I remained in the Navy," he recalled. Frank's time in Richmond served only to lure the Englishman from Virginia's waters to its bloody battlefields. "McClellan's army was close to Richmond, and one fine morning, at the end of May, the battle of Seven Pines began," he wrote. "I obtained leave of absence, and, armed with a navy sword, hastened down to the field, arriving there about night-fall. The first troops I fell in with at the front belonged to a Georgia regiment, the Eighth Georgia, I think; and I asked to be permitted to take a musket and go in with them as a volunteer, the next morning. Next morning came, but the fight did not, and I trudged disconsolately back to Richmond."[27]

Captivated by "exhilarating and imposing" images of "gleaming bayonets," "waving flags, the rumbling of the artillery, and the steady tramp of the men," Frank immediately resigned his naval position and enlisted as a private in the Purcell Battery, which was attached to Field's Brigade, A. P. Hill's Division. In August 1862 he was commissioned a first lieutenant of artillery. "Do you not feel proud that I have been so honored?" Frank wrote to his mother. "How many years must a man serve before he can obtain such a position in the British Army! It is only 3 months and a few days since I landed in this country! I was at once appointed an officer in the navy, resigned this, and now hold a higher [and] better rank in the Army." With Pegram's guidance and support, Frank had attained professional credibility and social acceptance within Virginia's most select circles—a feat, he acknowledged, that would have been impossible in his native England. Relishing his rise from Britain's middle-class margins to the apex of southern society, Frank seized on every opportunity to inform his parents of his new-found prestige. "I am very highly thought of here; pardon the apparent ego-tism of the remark," he wrote with pride. "I have a troop of wealthy and influential friends here who will do anything for me. Mr. Raines of whom I have spoken to you before has even expressed a wish to adopt me as a son. I have no hardship of any consequence to endure, money I can command whenever I require it."[28]

Frank continued to climb in rank and favor among Virginia's command-ing forces. After his promotion, he became an assistant ordnance officer of the I Corps of the Army of Northern Virginia, where he was appointed to the rank of captain in April 1864. Frank held this position until October 1864, when he was ordered to take charge of ordnance for Fitzhugh Lee's cavalry division. Frank served in this capacity until the end of the war. From 1862 to 1865, he participated in military encounters at "Mechanicsville, Sec-ond Manassas, Fredericksburg, Gettysburg, Chattanooga, Knoxville, the Wilderness, Spotsylvania, North Side James River, the Valley of Virginia, and Five Forks." He was wounded on three occasions and was briefly incar-cerated at Fort Delaware after being taken prisoner by Federal troops in September 1862. Every experience, hardship, battle, or loss only affirmed Frank's commitment to and respect for the Confederate army. "A military life suits me perfectly," he wrote to his mother in November 1862, "although we have to undergo many hardships."[29]

Contrary to his original plan, Frank did not return to England in April 1865. While he greeted the war's end with "worldly possessions" consisting of "a postage stamp and what was left of a five dollar greenback that a friend in Baltimore had sent," Frank saw fresh opportunities in the South he had grown to love. "I am more and more convinced that the old country is not the place for a young man," he wrote to his father in May 1865, "and I think that I can be of more assistance to you here than I could be at home."[30]

Frank contemplated managing a friend's plantation in Virginia but finally accepted a position on the staff of the *Richmond Daily Examiner*, where he worked as a local reporter for Henry Rives Pollard. Describing the fiery ed-itor as "a queer character; not without ability, but lazy, vain and dissolute," Frank found himself assigned to the "unpleasant position" of "advisor and best man for Pollard in his principal rencontres," many of which were a re-sult of the "careless . . . statements he made affecting any one's reputation." Dodging bullets instead of writing stories, Frank nevertheless found time to make acquaintances with Bartholomew Rochefort Riordan, a senior reporter at the *Examiner*. Born in Fairfax County, Virginia, Riordan had graduated from Mount St. Mary's College in Maryland in 1858. In 1859, he had worked on the staff of the *New Orleans Delta*, later moving to Charleston to accept a position as managing editor of the *Mercury*. A clubfoot prevented Riordan from offering his services to the Confederacy, and he ran the newspaper until the evacuation of Charleston in February 1865.[31]

Riordan quickly became Frank's mentor at the *Richmond Examiner*, nurturing the Englishman's talent with advice and encouragement. "Mr. Riordan and I were . . . on very good terms," Frank remarked. "We slept in one of the rooms at the *Examiner* office, in which we worked, and took our meals together at Zetelle's restaurant." During their evening meals, Riordan "broached . . . a plan for starting a cheap and popular newspaper in Charleston, South Carolina. He said that the Charleston newspapers were very slow and old fashioned, and that there was a fine field for a new and bright paper. This he had thought for a long time, but had not taken any steps to give the project shape, because he had not found the right sort of man to go into it with him. He was pleased to say that I was just the man he was looking for, and that he was quite sure that he and I could make the paper successful. The whole of the details of the prospective newspaper were carefully discussed."[32]

Without the necessary funds or ready opportunities, Frank and Riordan's newspaper idea seemed more like a pipe dream than a business strategy. In 1866, both men lost their jobs after the Federal Military Authority suspended the *Examiner* for "cleverly satirizing" the Union soldiers occupying the city. Frank joined the staff of a rival paper, the *Richmond Dispatch*, while Riordan worked briefly in Washington before returning to Charleston to work on the staff of the *Courier*. By November 1866, Frank Dawson joined his friend in South Carolina and accepted a position as an assistant editor at Robert Barnwell Rhett's *Charleston Mercury*. Within months, Frank and Riordan devised a plan to purchase the *News*, a small, unimpressive Charleston newspaper that had lagged far behind its competitors since its establishment in August 1865. With the financial backing of Benjamin Wood, editor and proprietor of the *New York Daily News*, Riordan, Dawson, and Company purchased the *Charleston News* in October 1867. Frank and Riordan suddenly found themselves "owners of one-third of a newspaper which had a *bona fide* circulation of twenty-five hundred, or three thousand, copies daily, with debts amounting to nearly $20,000, and property consisting of two very old presses, a broken down engine, and a suit of badly worn type." "But we were very cheerful about it," Frank remarked, "and our confident expectation was that, in about five years, we should be able to retire from newspaper work, in part, and live at our ease on the property we had accumulated."[33]

Riordan and Dawson's *News* made its debut on October 28, 1867. Riordan took charge of business matters, securing advertising and balancing the books, while Frank emerged as the paper's charismatic editor with a fresh approach to Charleston's postbellum problems. In a war-ravaged state still lamenting the loss of its Confederate cause, Frank called for the industrialization and agricultural development of the South, coining the popular slogan "The Mills Must Come to the Cotton." "Respect for ourselves and our fathers requires us to reverence the past," he wrote in February 1869, "but we cannot rebuild the fallen structure, and it would be simply foolish [of] our people to spend the fleeting years of opportunity in lamentation; let us help rear it, and make it better if we can."[34]

Frank and Riordan brought the *News* back from the brink of financial ruin. Riordan's business savvy and Frank's enthusiasm and literary flair greatly contributed to the paper's newfound popularity. By August 1872, the *News* had crushed its rival, the *Charleston Mercury*, and relocated to 19 Broad Street, the building formerly occupied by Southwestern Railroad Bank. Situated in the heart of Charleston's business district, Riordan, Dawson, and Company now boasted that the *News* "formed without exception the most elegant and valuable and the best arranged newspaper establishment in the Cotton States."[35]

As the outspoken editor of Charleston's leading newspaper, Frank emerged as an influential commentator on the city's political and economic affairs. He became a respected member of the Hibernian and St. George's Society and served on numerous committees, including the Chamber of Commerce and the county and state Democratic committees. His ties to Charleston, however, were not merely professional. Shortly after his arrival in South Carolina, Frank had met Virginia Fourgeaud, the daughter of Celena and Eugene Fourgeaud, the Charleston agent for the South Carolina Railroad. After a brief engagement, the couple married on May 1, 1867, and set up house in a wing of the Fourgeaud home at 8 Rutledge Avenue. Their married life was short-lived, however. After a long battle with consumption (tuberculosis), Virginia died on December 6, 1872.[36] In deep mourning, Frank left Charleston in January to visit his wartime friend, James Morris Morgan. When he returned from his trip, he wrote his first letter to James's sister, Sarah.

The correspondence of Frank Dawson and Sarah Morgan began in January 1873 and ended in October of the same year, when Sarah arrived in Charleston. There are no surviving letters written by Sarah during the initial months of the correspondence, though an almost complete set of Frank's letters provides a lens through which to view Sarah. The correspondence between the couple is complete for July through October.

Frank Dawson's letters to Sarah Morgan began as an unconventional love story. Writing on mourning stationery from the Broad Street offices of the *News*, Frank regarded Sarah as his salvation, a "Guardian Angel" whose morality and "strong right hand" led him to "betterment." "*You* can bring anything from me," he declared, "more, at least, than [any] other mortal can, & I, under your hand, were capable of harmonies of usefulness which no other touch can waken. You are the complement of my life; its crown & completeness, & so, time shall show."[37]

Frank believed that his love had fostered a strong spiritual connection with Sarah. Only days after his return to Charleston, he wrote of having visions of his new love while in the midst of "the dullest & most prosaic of work; balancing my books." "Instantly I became filled with your presence; your voice was in my ears, I could see your pure face, it seemed that you were around & above me," he wrote. "I felt then that you must, at that hour, be thinking of me; perhaps praying for me." Still carrying out the mourning rituals of a recent widower, Frank found himself eulogizing his dead wife in one paragraph and declaring his love for Sarah in the next. After purchasing a number of portraits and cartes-de-visite of Virginia from a leading Charleston photographer, he sent a framed copy of one of the best pictures to Sarah so that she might have "an idea of what [Virginia] was two or three years ago." "My poor wife's photograph lies next to your ribbon, next to my heart," Frank commented, "so there is no rivalry there."[38]

In the postbellum tradition of the self-made man, Frank regarded earned wealth and professional success as essential prerequisites to the new code of masculinity, but even these achievements "remained incomplete without a wife and home." Sarah was indeed his "crown," for without her, Frank believed that he lacked the moral compass to fulfill the ideal of "virtuous manhood" or the reason "to do more than [his] duty." After purchasing the *Courier* in April 1873 and consolidating it with the *News*, Frank declared that even this momentous achievement, which placed him at the helm of one of the most influential newspapers in the United States, could not compare with the fulfillment of his personal desires. "Without you I do not care to live," he wrote only a week after the *News and Courier*'s debut. "Here are all these people envying me, flattering me, congratulating me, & what not; while I know that I would, so gladly, renounce everything they value for the kind words & loving looks of just one little somebody at Hampton. It is no choice either between newspaper name or public fame, and personal happiness. Without the last I shall not have the first. Mark it!"[39]

A succession of florid letters and marriage proposals did little to convince Sarah, who remained dubious about the constancy of Frank's love and the propriety of his lavish attentions. Like many elite southern women, Sarah found herself torn between her idealization of woman "in perfect subjection to man" and the ways in which she had seen this antebellum ideology crushed under the insurmountable weight of war. Willing female dependence had exacted a high price in a wartime landscape devoid of men, resources, or substantial government support, and the harsh postbellum environment confirmed women's reluctance to again "celebrate helplessness." Sarah, like many women, had suffered the consequences of embodying the southern feminine ideal. Submission had rendered her dependent on a string of men who could not or would not fulfill their responsibilities to provide and protect. Her father, Thomas, and her brothers, Henry, Gibbes, and George, had died, and her brother, James, had offered her a demeaning place in his household. Sarah's personal struggle with this reality played itself out in her relationship with Frank, in which she both encouraged and repelled his advances. Often dismissing his overtures as nothing more than a passionate but fleeting "winter romance," thirty-year-old Sarah refused to consider marriage to a recent widower as an appropriate resolution to her personal unhappiness. The painful legacy of love and female dependence made it almost impossible for her to relinquish her miserable position at Hampton for a marriage bound by even more stringent forms of legal and social subordination.[40]

Frank was aware of Sarah's unhappy plight, and when he visited Hampton in late January, he made her a rather unconventional proposal. The couple had often talked about political issues, and in one conversation, Sarah had likened the fate of the people of Louisiana to that of Andromeda, a Greek mythological figure whose father had chained her to a rock and left her to be devoured by a sea monster. Frank was suitably impressed by Sarah's analogy and implored her to write an editorial for his newspaper.

Sarah initially refused the offer but was eventually won over by the editor's insistence. "Very well, Captain Dawson, but I shall make my own conditions," she explained. "I shall write that for you exactly as I spoke it, but I refuse to take the trouble to re-read it because I don't consider it worth it. As I finish each page, I shall throw it away—on the floor. If you choose to go down on your knees to pick up the pages, that's your own affair—only since nobody is to know I have written it, on getting back to your office, you shall recopy the whole in your handwriting and destroy my original so it shall be thought you wrote it yourself."[41]

Frank consented to Sarah's demands, and "The New Andromeda" appeared in the *News* on March 5, 1873. "This is indeed inauguration day," Frank wrote to Sarah on the eve of her debut, "the inauguration for you, let us pray, of a new career—one for which you have full capacity and in which you will do even more good for others than for yourself." The event marked a turning point in Sarah's life. At Hampton, she too had become an Andromeda-like figure, chained to the rock by her economic dependence and her inconsequential role in the household. Sarah's new position at the *News*—where she was contracted to write one social article and two general pieces per week— provided her with an income, allowing her to reclaim power over her future and her identity as an elite southern woman. She kept her writing an "inviolable secret" from everyone except her mother and sister, aware that "receiving money for toil" was sure to offend both her brother's masculinity and his honor. In a world bereft of slaves, willing female submission had, after all, helped to rebuild the lives of defeated southern men. Sarah's career and quest to stand on her own financial feet struck at the heart of James's postwar identity as the master of Hampton and of his dependents.[42]

Sarah had her personal genteel sensibilities to consider as well. While women's employment could be incorporated into the domestic ideal, women most often went to work out of necessity, not choice. In the postwar South, hard times compelled many elite women to enter teaching, take in sewing, or run boardinghouses. Not surprisingly, writing emerged as the most attractive option for well-read, literary-minded ladies who looked to the success of Augusta Jane Evans as evidence that southern respectability—and even wealth—could be attained by endeavors made of pen and ink. Busily writing poems, short stories, letters, or novels after finishing domestic chores, most women who attempted to write scratched out at best a meager living for their prodigious efforts. There were, however, enough exceptions to the rule to offer some hope to aspiring women writers. Augusta Jane

Evans, perhaps the most successful nineteenth-century southern novelist, wrote a series of best-sellers, including *Macaria; or, Altars of Sacrifice* and *St. Elmo*. North Carolinian Frances C. Fisher published more than thirty novels, including *Valerie Aylmer*, under the pseudonym Christian Reid. Mary Bayard Clarke followed a different career path, working as both a writer and editor of *Southern Field and Fireside*, while Eliza Jane Poitevent took over the editorial management of the *New Orleans Picayune* after the death of its editor—her husband. Sarah was certainly part of this privileged group, yet she remained ambivalent about her claim to the "mantle of authorship." She feared the social and familial repercussions of her decision and worked closely with Frank to preserve her anonymity at all costs.[43]

More importantly, Sarah's secrecy about her career meant that she was not obliged to expend her income maintaining the status quo at Hampton. Instead, she placed some of her money into a bank account under the name "Mr. Fowler," invested a portion of her wages in stocks, and began to plan for the day when she and her mother would be able to set up a home of their own.[44] To achieve this domestic ideal, Sarah was compelled to revise her understanding of southern femininity, revoking her complete submission to James by exercising her autonomy and seeing herself as an economic provider rather than an unwanted dependent. Sacrificing deeply held beliefs and risking her relationship with her brother, Sarah embarked on a new path in an attempt to rebuild her elite identity and attain her vision of the domestic ideal.

Like most upper-class southern white women, Sarah found the transition to paid employment—along with the secrets and lies—both physically and emotionally exhausting. Despite her efforts to conceal her work, family and friends soon began to gossip about the steady stream of books, papers, and letters that made their way from the offices of the *News* to Hampton. Sarah had already declared her unwillingness to accept Frank as her husband, and James Morgan soon voiced his disapproval at what he considered scandalous and improper behavior. When a tearful Sarah informed Frank that his visits to Hampton must stop, he grew concerned at the possible termination of their friendship. "I beg that you will let me write to Jemmie to define my position & yours," he wrote anxiously. "We understand each other thoroughly . . . & as our 'business relations!' compel me to write to you often, & you to write to me, there ought not to be any looming difficulty to make our work the harder." "It is the old story of South & North again," he added. "We ask to be let alone, don't we?"[45]

James Morgan, however, was right—Frank and Sarah's relationship was highly unconventional. It was neither strictly personal nor professional but rather a complex mix of business and pleasure. Sarah's editorial work created a binding association with Frank, and Frank used this aspect of their relationship to pursue his most personal designs. "Business letters" were laced with romantic overtures, and regular trips to Hampton were justified in terms of "editorial meetings." Frank sent Sarah his favorite books and papers for "writing purposes" as well as alcohol and tonics to improve the health of his "fair contributor." Their relationship—set within a professional framework—allowed Frank to pursue Sarah for months and share intimacies that far exceeded what James Morgan and other southerners considered acceptable or appropriate.

At Hampton, Sarah was left to negotiate her way through a minefield of social propriety and secrecy. Dodging James's stern comments, she found it increasingly difficult to fulfill her professional obligations to the *News* without attracting further censure from her disapproving brother. With little time to devote to her work, Sarah often found herself dashing off articles ten minutes before the arrival of the mail train. Plagued by feelings of professional inadequacy, she soon regarded her newspaper work as a disagreeable necessity that drained her already fragile health. Fearful that Sarah's "modest opinion of [her] own powers" might compel her to "march from the field of literature before the fight has fairly begun," Frank spent much of his time encouraging his temperamental new writer. "You are, unhappily, in a condition in which it is necessary for you to exert to the utmost the talent which God has given you," he wrote. "I know too well how much it pains you to write anything for any eye to see, and I would not press you to continue, only that what you have already done proves that you can do every thing, and more, that I predicted of you." Frank urged Sarah to consider her newspaper work as a grand expression of her moral influence as a woman, giving her a voice that allowed her to reach far beyond the confines of Hampton and into the community of which she was a part. "Your influence is no longer confined to your own house: hold," he lectured her. "You have it in your power to preach to a larger congregation than Beecher & Spurgeon command, and with words as much loftier, and thoughts and aims as much purer, than theirs, as the nature of woman is higher than that of man."[46]

Sarah remained unconvinced of her ability to "do good to [her] people" through her work at the *News*. Her personal circumstances, however, compelled her to persevere with her writing endeavors. During 1873 she penned more than seventy editorials on topics ranging from euthanasia to boring people, depression, cremation, and mothers-in-law. Frank initially scanned the papers and periodicals for topics but soon encouraged Sarah to build up her own repertoire of themes. "Watch events in Louisiana & Spain & send your comments whenever there is an important change in the situation," he instructed her. "You will gradually, in this way, accumulate subjects with which you are familiar, and will have no trouble in giving your two general articles (as well as the Saturday) a week. Whenever I see a good point to be made I will tell you; but hunt up as many as you can for yourself."[47]

Frank reiterated the importance of brevity but gave Sarah the scope to explore any issue, "ethical, literary, financial or political." "Let yourself run riot, & do not use the curb," he declared. "I have no idea of abandoning you to your own devices, & will give the themes which I come across for you, but I want to teach you to walk alone, not to keep you in leading: strings, & therefore urge you to watch for & take up anything that will make an effective article or paragraph." Sarah responded with an eclectic range of articles and editorials. She wrote about the alleged separation of the marquis of Lorne and Princess Louise of Britain, the murder of a young girl by her jilted lover, marrying a deceased wife's sister, the introduction of the plea of insanity, the influence of people's names on their character, pocket money for children, funerals, mourning rituals, and "fashion gossip for Charleston ladies."[48]

Frank also urged Sarah to move beyond the literary boundaries of "frills and furbelows" to write pieces on domestic and international politics, topics that were not common in women's public utterances of the period. After Sarah wrote her first piece, examining carpetbagger rule in Louisiana, Frank sent her copies of the South Carolina and U.S. constitutions and encouraged her to keep "acquainted with the condition and progress of every matter of public consequence." Sarah initially submitted pieces based on journal articles and newspaper clippings supplied by Frank. Her editorial "A Booth to Let In Vanity Fair," for example, drew on Thomas Buckle's *History of Civilization in England* and an article from *The Nation* on the Spanish Republic. "Just read what both say," wrote Frank in a letter he enclosed in the package, "and work up the subject in your own dear way." Sarah's editorials on international politics largely came about as a result of this closely directed editorial process.[49]

Still, Frank soon encouraged his new writer to explore her own political standpoint. "You have not touched politics yet," her wrote to Sarah in April,

"& I should like to see you armed at every point." Sarah responded with a limited yet insightful series of editorials on domestic politics that bore the hallmark of her elite, conservative upbringing. As a young girl, she had "abhorred politics" and disapproved of women "meddling" in men's affairs. While she had always doubted the sustainability of southern independence, her patriotism for the Confederacy never faltered through war and defeat. Even after demoralized Rebel troops had made their way home, Sarah defiantly refused to surrender her belief in a cause that her brothers had fought—and died—to protect. "I . . . pray never to be otherwise than what I am at this instant," she wrote in June 1865, "a Rebel in heart and soul, and that all my life I may remember the cruel wrongs we have suffered." Sarah's ardent belief in the principles of southern nationalism defined her commentary on postwar politics. In her editorials she passionately championed the cause of the "men, women and children silently enduring the suffering entailed upon them by the strife of [northern] politicians," whose corruption and desire for retribution had left the South in a political and economic "death swoon." Freedpeople, she argued, were nothing more than "political tools" in the northern quest for "tyrannous oppression." Sarah likened the appointment of "the worst of blacks" to public office to a form of white "slavery which far exceeds that from which the negroes were freed." "It is unreasonable and unwise," she declared, "if not a crime against Nature, to subject an enlightened race to the domination of a class who have not been fitted for the work of government by either birth or education."[50]

Public degradation, however, did not amount to personal dishonor. In Sarah's editorials, "Northern adventurers" and "ignorant negroes" may have scrambled their way to public office, but their ephemeral claim to power was no match for an "enlightened race" that possessed the "intelligence" and foresight "to restore peace and fortune to the Polands of the South." A fitting end to this terrible episode, Sarah remarked, would be the welcome retirement of President Ulysses S. Grant "to his cabbage-beds in the West," leaving the South's "rightful leaders" to govern their land with "experience, intelligence and integrity."[51]

Sarah made a limited yet valuable contribution to the political pages of the *News and Courier*. Passionate about issues but not overly interested in the intricacies of the American political machine, she found her work on politics particularly challenging and time-consuming. When her health began to deteriorate, Sarah limited herself to shorter pieces such as "Paradox," which added "another string to [her] bow" without breaking it completely.

Keenly aware of his contributor's ill health, Frank soon abandoned his original plan and proposed an alternative series of articles on the "deadly sins & cardinal virtues, as it were." "You need training in the habit or routine of writing for the press," he gently reminded Sarah, "& the things I suggest, while admirable for us, would be easier to you, just now, than politics & the like." Debates on constitutional principles, Frank realized, would have to be put aside until Sarah's health and well-being improved.[52]

Frank was right—Sarah certainly preferred to write about social issues. Her most poignant pieces, however, were not on sin and virtue, as Frank had proposed, but on the postwar condition of southern womanhood. Unlike other elite ladies, who confided their life experiences to diaries or close friends, Sarah had the benefit of a very public genre—editorial writing—in which to safely explore the injustices of her world and to imagine alternatives without the fear of familial or social reprisals. Her editorials on women covered a range of issues, including "The Use and Abuse of Widows," "Old Maids," "The Property of Married Women," "Work for Women," "Suffrage-Shrieking," "Age," and "The Natural History of Woman." In examining these and Sarah's other writings, scholars have described her as anything from a feminist to a "newly born woman and a budding . . . deconstructionist." Many have failed to contextualize Sarah's writing, assessing her later, more radical views on motherhood and society alongside the editorials she wrote as a thirty-one-year-old single woman.[53]

Sarah's writing career spanned the 1870s, and her views on women and society certainly changed over time. On one level, as E. Culpepper Clark has argued, her "essays were lectures to Frank on the dangers of marrying Sarah Morgan." The editorials she wrote were also autobiographical on another level. Her work from 1873 highlights the set of challenges that confronted young, single, elite, white women in the postbellum South. In particular, Sarah spoke candidly of the plight of Confederate belles, who had sacrificed their traditional rite of passage during the Civil War only to find that southern defeat brought with it far more devastating consequences. Lacking homes, possessions, finery, or men for courting, most young ladies were unable to resume their genteel prewar lives. Like Sarah, many also faced the prospect of an unmarried existence, since numerous potential suitors had died for the cause and others had returned home maimed in body or spirit. From this band of poor, dejected, sometimes dependent soldiers, young ladies often searched in vain for suitable husbands while subjected to the same pressure to marry from family and friends.[54]

During the war, Sarah had reflected on the possibility of never realizing her intended role as wife and mother. Accepting spinsterhood as her likely fate, she planned out a single life with a close friend: "Marie and I say to each other almost daily with an emphasis that makes it almost ludicrous 'We will never, never marry.' Every one laughs at us, and prophesies that before another year has elapsed we will recant our vow at the altar. Never! We speak knowing what we say, and firmly resolved (at present) to carry out our resolution." Refraining from discussions about finances, Sarah and Marie preferred instead to devote their time to imagining their fine home in the Pyrenees, where Sarah laid claim to a room with a view of the magnificent sunsets. "We shall have a fine library in which our days shall be quietly spent, and certain hours shall be devoted to making clothes for poor people, and embroidering for our army of neices [*sic*] and nephews," she related. "What blissful, happy, quiet days we will spend! . . . And the secret of such bliss as this quiet life would be, is to be found in the motto to be inscribed above the door 'No gentlemen or children admitted.'" Sarah's vision of single blessedness was popular among antebellum women of the Northeast and among well-to-do ladies in the southern cities of Charleston and Savannah, Georgia. This vision stressed a "desire to pursue autonomy, to explore the self, to expand intellectual and personal horizons, and to serve God and the community through the development and application of individual talents and abilities." In the urban enclaves of the antebellum South, notes Christine Jacobson Carter, elite single women married their familial obligations to a lifestyle encompassing society, mobility, friendship, education, and benevolence. An "unmarried woman could surround herself with friends and acquaintances, fill her social calendar, and throw herself into a myriad of benevolent organizations, church activities, and charitable causes."[55]

Yet as Sarah's adolescent daydream suggests, the cult of single blessedness rested on financial comfort, if not wealth, and only well-off women could fully reap these rewards. The hardships and turmoil of life in the defeated South often produced an alternate version of spinsterhood, epitomized by the "dreaded, lonely, [and] sad existence" of the old maid. While Confederate widows were regarded after the war as true sacrificial patriots, single, financially dependent women like Sarah were often reviled as "old maids," a "withering epithet" that, she noted, "blasts a hardly matured woman at twenty-five." Sarah felt the scorn of her new title and devoted much of her editorial writing to the plight of the old maid. "The most poignant as well as the most universal anguish is that produced by the terror of increasing years," she wrote in "Age." "Certainly no other iron enters so deeply into the soul of woman. . . . To be pronounced *passée* is more terrible to a woman than a good kicking is to a man. Insult can be avenged, but how may one resent the awful imputation of Age?"[56]

While Sarah acknowledged that even "Sweet Sixteen shudders at the thought of being converted into a French participle," *passée*, the widow, "that adder of men among women, is attractive, surrounded, irresistible at thirty, forty, fifty—yea, when past, by a quarter of a century, the age when the unmarried woman begins to read neglect and contempt in the manners of those around her." Sarah argued that widows perpetuated the poor condition of old maids by "sinking the most indifferent men" with natural magnetism and irresistible charms. "O for a law to abide by the vote of unmarried women on the question of enforcing the Hindoo Suttee, among the nations prolific of widows!" she declared. "And, if that be too flaming an advertisement of their perils and charms, O for a decree, like that of the Medes and Persians which altereth not, that no widow shall marry until the last girl has perished."[57]

In another editorial, Sarah addressed the "scarcely veiled . . . contempt" that marked the status of the old maid. This stigma, she noted, had existed in the antebellum South and persisted in the postbellum period despite the physical and emotional legacies of war and defeat. In a world where elite femininity and the domestic ideal were epitomized by marriage and motherhood, single adult women without independent fortunes or households of their own were often viewed as failures or, worse, as economic burdens who taxed the financial stores of frugal postwar households. Sarah argued that the adult woman's single status eclipsed all else, defining her identity and relegating her to the fringes of community life. "It is doubtful whether civilization will ever advance so far that the name Old Maid will cease to bring a smile of contempt to human lips," she wrote. "While the idealized Mother is glorified by poets for tending her puny babies in her self-inflicted nursery, it is Old Maids like Miss Dix, Miss Nightingale and Miss Faithful who go about, bringing God's sunshine into darkened places, raising the fallen, loosing the prisoner's bands, and preaching Hope and Charity to men."[58]

Sarah constructed single womanhood as an honorable choice, far "superior" to the "infinite number of foolish virgins [who] prefer marrying men unworthy of a good woman's respect to facing the jibes and sneers of their mating and mated associates." "Put it to the vote a year, a month, a week after marriage and how many women would secretly black-ball their choice!" she boldly proclaimed. "At least the Old Maid has no sickening conviction that only the name of a husband's love is hers. . . . She has no fear for the future; for, at the worst, her destiny is in her own hands, and she is not chained to a dead hope and a living despair. Shall we laugh at the multitude of Old Maids, or cry, Heaven help the Wives!" By depicting single life as a noble choice rather than an unfortunate state imposed on second-rate maidens, Sarah's views drew on northeastern beliefs that lauded women who remained unmarried "not because of individual shortcomings but because they didn't find the one 'who could be all things to the heart.'" In Sarah's reading, the spinster was no longer "an oddity in a culture" that celebrated domesticity but "a highly moral and fully womanly creature" whose devotion to honorable ideals set her apart—and above—the "mated" women chained to "unworthy" but available candidates.[59]

Sarah also urged single women to recognize their agency. Using her position at the *News and Courier,* she wrote editorials on the importance of employment and self-support as an alternative way for adult single women to serve and honor the family unit. "The efforts making in the North to open a wider field of labor for women, cannot be too highly praised," she argued in "Work for Women." "There are tens of thousands of delicately nurtured women, pining in want and in enforced idleness, to whom the possibility of earning a support for themselves, or for those dependent on them, would be an inconceivable blessing," "In the North," she noted, "numbers of women find employment in factories, shops, libraries and ticket offices." In the South, however, women had only been "developed as rare exotics for the ornament of refined homes."[60]

With the coming of war and defeat, Sarah argued that these "helpless" southern belles had been "thrown as ruthlessly as broken flowers on the stones of an unsympathetic world." Convinced that even the most honorable gentleman would be "glad" to see his "most cherished" kin at work, Sarah called for an end to the "prejudice" that "shuts [the woman] out from work she could do, perhaps better than the man to whom the preference is given." Instead of languishing, Sarah urged old maids and women in similar circumstances to contribute to the domestic ideal by working outside the home, thereby enhancing their status as worthy and contributing members of their families and communities. In so doing, such women would become active participants in the quest for the domestic ideal instead of "sad-eyed, unwelcome dependents" often regarded as a drain on familial prosperity.[61]

Sarah's liberal comments on employment were made on the grounds of postwar necessity, not woman's rights. Sarah argued that there was a sharp division between the northern "chimera" of woman's rights and woman suffrage and the honorable cause of offering "means of self-support to that host of respectable mendicants who are ashamed to beg." Sarah reserved only contempt for "suffrage shriekers," who, through their "ravings," "injured" the call from "worthy women" to advance their sphere of "practical usefulness." "Woman suffrage is, of course, sheer nonsense," she proclaimed. "Shall maid and matron claim and exercise the privilege of electing the right woman to the wrong place[?] They will triumphantly prove themselves capable of blundering as systematically as the average male voter."[62]

Defeat may have thrown ladies into gainful employment, but for Sarah, the war had not altered the proper state of relations between men and women. Despite her own inability to defer and submit, Sarah still cherished the belief that "woman's proper sphere was to be in perfect subjection to man," irrespective of her contribution to the economic well-being of the family unit. Women's employment was often necessary to ensure the attainment of the domestic ideal. Suffrage, she believed, offered no such advantages. In her editorial work, Sarah sought only to reposition the adult single woman within her household and community, to grant her alternative ways to enhance her position, and to give her the tools to move from the margins of postwar life to the center. Equality with men was never part of this vision. Instead, Sarah Morgan offered readers an ideal of the way life should be, a vision in which women's work outside the home was accepted as a valued contribution to the domestic ideal that rebuilt rather than destroyed the single woman's identity. Sarah's vision, however, was far from her own reality. Employment may have offered the opportunity to attain the domestic ideal, but Sarah's ambivalence about her career meant that it never became a central part of her postbellum identity. Like Mary Kelley's literary domestics, Sarah struggled to reconcile the inherent contradictions between her domestic life and her roles as a "public figure, economic provider, and creator of culture."[63]

The Springs Correspondent

Sarah Morgan's editorials created a sensation in Charleston, exciting widespread speculation about the author's identity. "There is much anxiety here to know who is writing the social articles," Frank wrote excitedly in March, "they are doing The News good. Persons now read our editorials who never read them before." Despite her resounding success, the demands of newspaper work, combined with the volatile environment at Hampton, soon wore down Sarah's health. In June, Dr. Benjamin Taylor diagnosed Sarah with gastritis, an inflammation of the stomach lining. Alarmed by her deteriorating condition and fearful of the repercussions of a "long hot Summer at Hampton," Frank urged Sarah to consider taking a trip "to some quiet Springs for a month." "You are going on so handsomely in your new career that I want you to do the best that is in you," he continued, "& that best cannot be had unless you are more composed in mind and stronger in body." Refusing his proposal "on the score of want of means," Sarah compelled her suitor to pursue a professional course of action. Within days, Frank appointed her the *News and Courier*'s official "undercover" correspondent for the season at West Virginia's White Sulphur Springs, the preeminent summer retreat for the southern elite. Frank proposed that Sarah could both furnish the paper with social articles on the guests, activities, and accommodations and benefit from the healing properties of the Springs, which were reputed to alleviate the effects of numerous diseases, including "chronic rheumatism, neuralgia, jaundice and scurvy." Once again, the personal and professional dimensions of their relationship came into play. Frank alleviated the suffering of his beloved Sarah by employing her as a social correspondent. He also purchased fashionable items for her wardrobe to hasten her departure to the Springs. In turn, Sarah gratefully accepted these otherwise improper advances by placing them within the framework of "business relations."[64]

The trip was a resounding success. In mid-June, Sarah and her mother arrived at "the White," an Eden where the domestic ideal was downplayed and antebellum conceptions of gentility and social networking revived downtrodden elite identities. For the "homeless" Morgan women, who felt sure that Gabriella Morgan would never allow them to return to Hampton, White Sulphur Springs provided the ideal environment in which to rebuild their identities as the aristocrats of Baton Rouge. For decades, planters, professionals, politicians, and even presidents had flocked to the "breezy hills of Virginia" to escape the oppressive and unhealthy conditions that prevailed in the South between June and August. Gathering at White Sulphur Springs, elite southerners affirmed their status through unceasing rounds of balls, visiting, and excursions to the springs. Visitors promenaded through carefully manicured gardens, gazed at the majestic mountains, and marveled at the "four-story, four-hundred-foot-long hotel" adorned with "arcades, columns, and porticos." Even after the war, when economic necessity had curtailed many luxuries, young ladies still tripped gaily across the ballroom floor in a setting that evoked the old ways of life, not the hardship and struggle that characterized the new. "After a long and weary search for a terrestrial Paradise, I have, at last, discovered the original site of the garden of Eden," Sarah wrote with delight.[65] Surrounded by cultivated society, belles, balls, sumptuous dinners, and attentive and deferential black attendants, Sarah exhibited her gentility through her fashionable new wardrobe and by reestablishing social networks, which had always been regarded as essential prerequisites for membership in the southern elite.

As she resurrected her identity on her family name and antebellum status, Sarah's time at White Sulphur Springs exposed her personal struggle to reconcile work with her cultured upbringing, a theme on which she had barely touched in her editorials on women's work. Employment had furnished Sarah with a trip to the Springs and provided the requisite funds for fashionable attire. As she remarked in a letter to Frank, "no song, no supper!" "Mine earns breakfast & dinner in addition," she added. "I scarcely touch any of them, but it is reputable to have meals, you know, & my pen alone can earn them for me in future. Depend upon it, there is no service of the brain you can demand of me that I shall not be glad to give, even unto the whole of my kingdom."[66]

At the same time, Sarah faced the alarming prospect that if her work became publicly known, her status as a proud Morgan would be overshadowed by her sensational identity as a correspondent. As Charlene M. Boyer Lewis has noted, antebellum families used their time at the Virginia Springs to "compete with members of their own group for a top place in the springs hierarchy." Sarah's letters indicate that the hardships of postbellum life had done little to dampen the social aspirations of many elite southerners, who looked to affirm their status by ostracizing "undesirable" or "unworthy" individuals from their select group. Sarah feared that if others learned of her work as an "undercover correspondent," the result would be a scandal that would terminate her interlude with society, leaving her with nothing but the pity of her peers. She never considered the possibility that they would admire her literary talent or that the notoriety might even enhance her reputation. Instead, Sarah "pleaded inability" when curious guests asked "why [she] did not write for the papers." When a woman approached Sarah one night after dinner and inquired about whether she "had written some very clever letters for a Southern newspaper," Sarah emphatically denied the allegation, thereby telling her "first deliberate falsehood." "She persisted it was a great compliment," Sarah related in a letter to Frank. "I could not see it. . . . I shall continue to resent the charge."[67]

Anxious and self-conscious, Sarah found herself in limbo, caught between the safe Morgan identity she cherished so dearly and the new southern womanhood she idealized in her editorials but could not embrace as her own. She remained strongly ambivalent about her writing, terrified by the thought of being discovered even as she warmed to the compliments bestowed by a couple who strolled past her room while discussing the merits of an accomplished "lady correspondent." By the end of the season, the gossip and innuendo had become almost too much for Sarah to bear. "I cannot doubt that my 'official capacity' is freely whispered about," she admitted. "I see people pointing me out at dinner. Day before yesterday four tables had me under inspection at once. . . . I grow sick to see men peeping at me over other people's shoulders, & hear them whisper something inaudible, but which I choose to interpret 'Correspondent.'" "Perhaps it had to be," she added, "but it makes me miserable."[68]

While she called for old maids to revoke their secondary status and rebuild their identities through "worthy" occupations, Sarah continued to struggle with meanings of work and gentility. One may have facilitated the other, but for Sarah, the legitimacy of her elite identity was grounded on her acceptance as a member of fashionable society, not as an employed correspondent. "I think I would be overwhelmed with shame if I was published," she admitted. The example of others did little to sway her position. Her friendship with Hetty Cary Pegram, the widow of a Confederate soldier who became the respected principal of a Baltimore girls school, indicated that work, gentility, and membership in the exclusive Springs society could coexist. Although Sarah admired these qualities in her friend, she could not accept them as her own. Instead, Sarah used her work to rebuild her postwar identity within an unstable antebellum framework of southern refinement.[69]

Sarah left White Sulphur Springs in August. After visiting George Morgan's grave at Orange, Virginia, Sarah, Frank, and Mrs. Morgan traveled to Greenville, South Carolina, where the women spent a month at a boarding-house operated by Mary Ware. The sojourn marked a time of reflection and transition. White Sulphur Springs had indeed awakened Sarah to new possibilities, and shortly thereafter she informed Frank of her decision to move to Charleston. Free from a humiliating existence at Hampton, Sarah now saw an exciting life opening up before her, filled with family, friends, and of course, Frank. After months of hard work, Sarah finally reclaimed the domestic ideal, a place of her own where she could nurture her gentility while discreetly pursuing her career. Feelings of hope and anticipation spilled over into her writing. "I give you carte-blanche in writing more confidently than ever before," exclaimed Frank in September, "because there is a better tone in your articles—the unconscious expression of the new birth which is dawning for you as it has dawned for me. . . . Perhaps the change may be expressed thus: A year ago you were dead, & content to remain so. Now you regret that you died, and wonder whether there can be a resurrection. . . . the stone age is nearly over."[70]

While Charleston was a certainty, Sarah soon concluded that a love affair with Frank was not. After months of deliberation and confusion, Sarah entreated her editor to think of her only as "a sister & friend." She accepted Frank's personal assistance regarding the arrangement of suitable accommodation in Charleston but refused all other proposals. The work that had granted Sarah financial security now rendered marriage to Frank a choice, not a necessity. Single life, it seemed, was far more palatable when it no longer smacked of dependence. The prospect of a life and home in Charleston gave Sarah the strength to abandon the reviled image of spinsterhood with which she had lived at Hampton and to replace it with the independent, worthy ideal she had envisioned in editorials such as "Old Maids." Sarah joined an earlier generation of northeastern women, along with a band of fellow Charleston ladies, who rejected marriage in favor of autonomy.[71]

While Frank may have hoped that a professional alliance would foster feelings of love on Sarah's part, he had always been grimly aware that Sarah's work—and growing sense of independence—might lead to his romantic downfall. "The old bird who teaches her young ones to use their feeble wings knows, if she knows anything, that the first use made of them by birdie will be to fly away from her," he remarked not long after Sarah's editorial debut. "So it will be with me & thee. I am teaching you to do without me, although I know that, without you, the brain & energy I have will count for nothing." Overwhelmed by the effects of a financial crisis, Frank grew withdrawn and disconsolate at the news that "all my labor to win your love has been miserably in vain." He responded by "suppress[ing] everything beyond what a brother would say" and venting his emotional distress through professional—and cutting—critiques of Sarah's work and in particular of her "disposition to make sweeping general statements, which are not . . . borne out by the facts." In a final letter written before her departure to Charleston, Sarah urged a heartbroken Frank to "keep a brave heart, & all will be well."[72]

While Frank may have doubted the likelihood of Sarah's assurances, he met her and her mother in Columbia. They visited briefly with James, and then Frank accompanied the women to Charleston, where Sarah and her mother achieved their long-anticipated dream, moving into their own apartment in Gadsden House on Meeting Street. With their "entire store for housekeeping" consisting of "silver forks & spoons, & five linen sheets," Sarah devised "a thousand means of employing every dollar I can earn" to attain a pleasing elite household. Nevertheless, the Morgan women rejoiced at inhabiting their own home. Although Sarah may have struggled to reconcile work with elitism, she could not deny that employment had provided her with the requisite funds to establish a home of her own where she could finally marry her gentility and newfound sense of self-worth with the postwar domestic ideal.[73]

The correspondence of Sarah Morgan and Frank Dawson illustrates what Laura Edwards has described as "gendered strife and confusion." In the postwar South, meanings of race, class, and gender were contested and negotiated. Men and women were forced to fashion new identities out of old ideals and postwar necessity and in so doing were also forced to negotiate their relationships with one another and the society of which they were a part. Sarah struggled to reconcile her antebellum socialization with the demands of the new southern world. She expressed these struggles in her letters to Frank and looked for answers in her writing. Frank and Sarah's relationship was founded on this negotiated territory, where old ideals were married with postwar reality.

1. Dawson to Morgan, August 5, 1873, Dawson Papers.
2. For earlier interpretations that regard the Civil War as a watershed for southern women, see Scott, *Southern Lady;* Simkins and Patton, *Women;* Massey, *Bonnet Brigades.* For recent interpretations, see Rable, *Civil Wars;* Faust, *Mothers;* Whites, *Civil War;* Edwards, *Gendered Strife;* Edwards, *Scarlett.*
3. Whites, *Civil War,* 132–59.
4. Edwards, *Gendered Strife,* 107–44; Edwards, *Scarlett,* 182–85.
5. S. M. Dawson, *Sarah Morgan,* 70; for an account of Sarah Morgan's early life, see xv–xx.
6. Sarah received far less formal education than did most of her peers. See S. M.

Dawson, *Sarah Morgan*, 290, 136–37. On women's education in the antebellum South, see Farnham, *Education;* Jabour, "'Grown Girls, Highly Cultivated'"; Stowe, *Intimacy and Power*, 142–53.

7. S. M. Dawson, *Sarah Morgan*, 80, 60–63. On reciprocity between men and women, see Cashin, *Our Common Affairs*, 10; Burton, *In My Father's House*, 128; Faust, *Mothers*, 6.

8. S. M. Dawson, *Sarah Morgan*, 38–39; see also 22–26, 45–46, 53–55.

9. Ibid., 56, 22.

10. Ibid., 47–48.

11. Ibid., 76, 150, 77, 51, 65.

12. Ibid., 77, 166–67, 65.

13. Ibid., 233.

14. Ibid., 435, 153.

15. On Sarah's buggy accident, see ibid., 333–37, 339; on the deaths of Gibbes and George, see 597–602. On the Morgan family's observation of mourning rituals, see Schoonmaker, "As Though It Were unto the Lord."

16. S. M. Dawson, *Sarah Morgan*, 610.

17. Sarah Morgan diary, September 10, 1866, vol. 5, Dawson Papers. On the wartime experiences of young Confederate women, see Roberts, *Confederate Belle*.

18. For a full description of Hampton, see Morgan, *Recollections*, 316; Sarah Morgan to Lydia Carter Morgan Purnell, May 16, 1872, Dawson Papers.

19. For an examination of the postwar ideal of southern masculinity, see Edwards, *Gendered Strife*, 121–29.

20. S. M. Dawson, *Sarah Morgan*, 282.

21. O'Brien, *An Evening When Alone*, 3.

22. S. M. Dawson, *Sarah Morgan*, 153.

23. Clark, *Francis Warrington Dawson*, 10–11; Logan, "Francis W. Dawson," 1–8. I have drawn heavily on Logan's and Clark's work to compile this biographical sketch of Frank Dawson. See also Logan, "Francis Warrington Dawson."

24. Clark, *Francis Warrington Dawson*, 11–12; F. W. Dawson, *Reminiscences*, 3.

25. Clark, *Francis Warrington Dawson*, 13–14, 15–16; F. W. Dawson, *Reminiscences*, 8.

26. F. W. Dawson, *Reminiscences*, 10–11, 26.

27. Ibid., 29, 33, 43, 45.

28. Ibid., 47, 187, 193.

29. Clark, *Francis Warrington Dawson*, 17; F. W. Dawson, *Reminiscences*, 190. On Frank's military career, see Reeks, "Catholic Soldier"; Logan, "Francis W. Dawson," 8–38.

30. F. W. Dawson, *Reminiscences*, 146; Frank Dawson to Joseph Reeks, May 30, 1865, in Logan, "Francis W. Dawson," 39–40.

31. F. W. Dawson, *Reminiscences*, 153–58. Bartholomew Rochefort Riordan never used his given name but preferred to be called by his surname. For biographical information on Riordan, see Clark, *Francis Warrington Dawson*, 21; Logan, "Francis W. Dawson," 61–62; Sass, *Outspoken*, 58.

32. F. W. Dawson, *Reminiscences,* 157–58.

33. Ibid., 173–74; Logan, "Francis W. Dawson," 41–64; Clark, *Francis Warrington Dawson,* 21–22.

34. Clark, *Francis Warrington Dawson,* 30; Logan, "Francis W. Dawson," 63; *Charleston News,* February 24, 1869, in Logan, "Francis Warrington Dawson," 20.

35. *Charleston News,* September 2, 1872, in Logan, "Francis W. Dawson," 83–84.

36. Logan, "Francis W. Dawson," 77. On the marriage of Frank Dawson and Virginia Fourgeaud Dawson, see Logan, "Francis W. Dawson," 75–76; Clark, *Francis Warrington Dawson,* 22.

37. See Dawson to Morgan, January 27, 22, 31, February 9, 1873, Dawson Papers. On the relationship and subsequent marriage of Frank Dawson and Sarah Morgan, see Logan, "Francis W. Dawson," 85–106; Clark, "Sarah Morgan and Francis Dawson."

38. Dawson to Morgan, January 19, February 15, 11, 1873, Dawson Papers.

39. Edwards, *Gendered Strife,* 122–29; Dawson to Morgan, April 3, 17, 1873, Dawson Papers.

40. Faust, *Mothers,* 251.

41. Logan, "Francis W. Dawson," 99–100. Warrington Dawson (Frank and Sarah's son) related this story to Logan.

42. Dawson to Morgan, March 4, 16, 1873, Dawson Papers. Sarah began her career as a writer for the *Charleston News.* In April, Riordan, Dawson, and Company bought the *Charleston Courier* and merged the two papers. On the idea that women's work outside the home damaged the reputation of the head of household, see Edwards, *Scarlett,* 177, citing the example of Gertrude Clanton Thomas, whose husband, Jeff, initially would not consent to her working because "to have his wife work for wages announced his own failure to provide for his family. It symbolized how far down in the world he had come."

43. On the association between employment and downward social mobility, see Rable, *Civil Wars,* 279, 282; Faust, *Mothers,* 81; Peterson, *Family, Love, and Work,* 120–21. On the incorporation of employment into the domestic ideal, see Edwards, *Gendered Strife,* 142. On women writers in the South during the Civil War and Reconstruction, see Faust, *Mothers,* 153–78; Rable, *Civil Wars,* 282–83; Scott, *Southern Lady,* 119–21; Censer, "Changing World"; Crow and Barden, *Live Your Own Life.* Writers such as Sherwood Bonner, who left her husband and child in 1873 to pursue a career as a writer in Boston, represent the more unconventional women of this profession. See McAlexander, *Prodigal Daughter.*

44. Dawson to Morgan, March 18, April 1, 1873, Dawson Papers.

45. Dawson to Morgan, April 1, 2, 1873, Dawson Papers.

46. Dawson to Morgan, March 7, 18, 16, May 15, 1873, Dawson Papers. In her work on literary domestics, Mary Kelley argues that feelings of professional inadequacy were a result of the "female experience of intellectual restriction, frustration, and belittlement," which "denied them a secure sense of their intellectual capacities, undermined their intellectual self-respect, and withheld intellectual self-confidence" (*Private Woman, Public Stage,* 104). Arguing the benefits of

Sarah's "moral influence" on the readers of the *News and Courier* became one of Frank's regular means of encouraging Sarah to continue writing. He drew on ideology that argued that women were morally superior to men. See, for example, Lebsock, *Free Women*, 51, 143; Weiner, *Mistresses and Slaves*, 55–56; Stevenson, *Life*, 41. Zsuzsa Berend, "The Best or None!'" notes that single women in New England used these ideas to justify their entrance into the paid workforce.

47. Dawson to Morgan, March 16, 1873, Dawson Papers.

48. Dawson to Morgan, March 14, 18, 1873, Dawson Papers. See appendix for a full list of Sarah's editorials.

49. Dawson to Morgan, March 16, 5, 1873, Dawson Papers; "A Booth to Let in Vanity Fair," March 13, 1873.

50. Dawson to Morgan, April 15, 1873, Dawson Papers; S. M. Dawson, *Sarah Morgan*, 611; "The New Andromeda," March 5, 1873; "Whites and Blacks," May 12, 1873. For Sarah's adolescent views on politics, see S. M. Dawson, *Sarah Morgan*, 73–74, 121–22, 142.

51. "Whites and Blacks"; "The Third Term," April 29, 1873.

52. "Paradox," April 25, 1873; Dawson to Morgan, March 18, May 15, 1873, Dawson Papers.

53. In her study of American novelists, Anne Goodwyn Jones argues that writing fiction allowed women to cast their voices through a "mask" that made it possible for them to avoid "either the literal alienation of physical departure or the psychological alienation of selflessness or madness" (*Tomorrow*, 24; see also Faust, *Mothers*, 178). Scholars differ considerably in their interpretations of Sarah's diary and writings. Mary Katherine Davis argues that Sarah's work was "a reaction against chivalry, the code of honor, Southernism; not a positive assertion of female equality" ("Sarah Morgan Dawson," 5). Charlotte Telford Breed contests this thesis and describes Sarah as a "new Southern lady" who was motivated by the "diametrically opposed" forces of southernism and feminism ("Sarah Morgan Dawson," 3). In her more recent study, Clara Juncker contends that Sarah Morgan emerged from the Civil War "a newly born woman and a budding Louisiana deconstructionist" ("Behind Confederate Lines," 7). Charles East, who edited the most recent edition of Sarah's wartime diary, disputes all these viewpoints, arguing that Sarah never joined the "forces of the women's rights movement, but remained the independent she always was." He contends that her personal conflict between feminism and Southernism was "never resolved" (S. M. Dawson, *Sarah Morgan*, xxxviii). See also Cann, "A Most Awful and Insoluble Mystery." E. Culpepper Clark, biographer of Frank Dawson, examined Sarah's writing within the context of the couple's relationship. See Clark, "Sarah Morgan and Francis Dawson." See also Logan, "Francis W. Dawson," 85–106. Historians have frequently cited an undated essay, "Comment on the Role of Women as Childbearers," as evidence of Sarah's feminist perspective. However, there is no evidence in the document or in the correspondence to suggest that this essay was written in 1873.

54. Clark, "Sarah Morgan and Francis Dawson," 14; Rable, *Civil Wars*, 270; Roberts, *Confederate Belle*, 165–80.

55. S. M. Dawson, *Sarah Morgan*, 548; Chambers-Schiller, *Liberty*, 1; Carter, "Southern Single Blessedness," 10. See also Lebsock, *Free Women;* Broussard, "Female Solitaires."

56. Carter, "Southern Single Blessedness," 10. On the construction of Confederate widows as sacrificial patriots, see Gross, "'Good Angels'"; "The Use and Abuse of Widows," March 10, 1873; "Age," June 21, 1873.

57. "Age"; "The Use and Abuse of Widows."

58. "Age"; "Old Maids," March 15, 1873.

59. "Old Maids"; Berend, "'The Best or None!'"; O'Brien, *An Evening When Alone*, 3. See also Chambers-Schiller, *Liberty*, 12.

60. "Work for Women," April 15, 1873.

61. Ibid. Sarah's comments on work were not unusual for the time. Indeed, she may have been influenced by editorials and letters that appeared in the *New Orleans Daily Picayune* in the late 1860s. See Schuler, "Women." Sarah was a resident of New Orleans in the late 1860s, and it is likely that she read or heard about these letters and editorials.

62. "Work for Women"; "Suffrage-Shrieking," May 20, 1873; "Two Hundred and Fifty Dollars for a Vote," April 4, 1873.

63. Morgan to Dawson, July 29, 1873, Dawson Papers; Kelley, *Private Woman, Public Stage*, 111.

64. Dawson to Morgan, March 16, May 18, 20, 1873, Dawson Papers. Sarah's health had been fragile since 1863, when she was thrown from a buggy (S. M. Dawson, *Sarah Morgan*, 333–37). For a comprehensive history of White Sulphur Springs, see Conte, *History;* Lewis, *Ladies and Gentlemen.*

65. Dawson to Morgan, June 9, 1873, Dawson Papers; Lewis, *Ladies and Gentlemen*, 27; "The Eden of the South: Summer at the White Sulphur Springs," June 26, 1873. On the unhealthy conditions that prompted many southerners to visit the Springs, see Lewis, *Ladies and Gentlemen*, 60. Sarah wrote eight pieces on the season at the Greenbrier (see appendix).

66. Morgan to Dawson, August 8, 1873, Dawson Papers.

67. Lewis, *Ladies and Gentlemen*, 152; Morgan to Dawson, August 5, 15, 1873, Dawson Papers.

68. Morgan to Dawson, August 1, 17, 1873, Dawson Papers.

69. Morgan to Dawson, August 1, 1873, Dawson Papers.

70. Dawson to Morgan, September 10, 1873, Dawson Papers.

71. Morgan to Dawson, September 14, 1873, Dawson Papers; Chambers-Schiller, *Liberty*, 1.

72. Dawson to Morgan, April 14, September 28, 22, 20, 1873; Morgan to Dawson, October 1, 1873, Dawson Papers.

73. Morgan to Dawson, September 16, 1873, Dawson Papers.

EDITORIAL NOTE

The Francis Warrington Dawson I and II Papers held at the Rare Book, Manuscript, and Special Collections Library at Duke University (cited throughout as Dawson Papers) contain more than 190 letters written by the couple in 1873. I have selected 80 letters that provide a representative sample of the correspondence. The majority of these letters are included in their entirety. Some documents, however, have been edited, mostly to avoid excessive repetition. For example, Frank often detailed his travel plans in consecutive letters to Sarah, and if a minor change was necessary, he rewrote the entire schedule. Other omissions relate to Frank's letter-writing conventions. After writing a principal letter to Sarah he would often add on a number of lengthy postscripts, which appear as letters in their own right with dates, times, and salutations. Bracketed ellipses [. . .] at the beginning, middle, or end of a letter indicate the omission of part or all of these additional "letters" or of other material.

I have preserved inconsistencies in the correspondence, including variations in spelling and punctuation, and irregularities in capitalization. I have, however, replaced Frank and Sarah's use of "+c" and "+" with the more conventional "&c" and "&." I have lowered raised letters, so that "M^r" and "M^{rs}" appear as "Mr." and "Mrs." and "7th" appears as "7th." Spelling mistakes have not been corrected, and where the mistake is only a minor one, I have refrained from using *sic*. More substantial mistakes are annotated. On occasion, I have inserted a missing word to clarify the meaning of a sentence. I have also inserted approximate dates for all undated letters. This information has been enclosed in square brackets. All days and months in the datelines have been edited to avoid abbreviations; thus, "Thurs" becomes "Thursday" and "Apl" becomes "April."

I have preserved the general layout and paragraphing with one exception. Frank often left a large space to indicate the end of a paragraph and began a new topic on the same line. In these cases, I have placed the new paragraph on a new line. All paragraphs have been indented. All underlined words or phrases appear in italics except where Frank underlined his name in closing a letter, and cancellations have been ignored.

I have attempted to identify all the people, places, and quotations mentioned in the correspondence and editorials by consulting family and local histories, court records, land records, newspapers, census material, maps, city directories, concordances, dictionaries, and databases. Where a reference is not included, I have been unable to make an identification. A list of frequently mentioned people is included for easy reference.

Perhaps the most difficult issue I faced when editing these documents was how to approach the gap in Sarah's correspondence, which spans January to June 1873. Sarah may have destroyed this correspondence, along with a diary she kept during the late 1860s–70s: "I regret having destroyed these half glimpses of the most awful period in my life," she wrote in 1896. "Nothing else would have accounted for the blessedness of my married life, and my adoration of my husband."[1]

Frank's letters to Sarah largely bridge the gap in the correspondence. Frank centered much of his writing on Sarah and made a point of responding to the issues she had raised in her letters. Thus, the absence of some of Sarah's correspondence has not silenced her voice. Through Frank's words, Sarah emerges as an elite woman grappling with the postwar meaning of her life. While using her writing as a means to attain financial independence and a home of her own, she struggled with the notion of employment, battled frequent bouts of depression, and strove to be a good mother to her nephew, Howell. In a world where marriage had assumed even greater importance, Sarah did not use Frank's love as an easy way out of her difficult position at Hampton. Her anguish, her doubts, her depression, and her resolve are all reflected in Frank's writing. Consequently, readers will still get a clear picture of both correspondents and the development of their personal and professional relationships. Further information can also be found in the short explanatory notes between letters.

Sarah's editorials on the postwar South are also an inextricable part of Frank and Sarah's correspondence. Each genre informs and contextualizes the other, allowing comparison between Sarah's private thoughts to Frank and the public rhetoric of her editorial writing. On many occasions, Sarah used her newspaper work to explore her most intimate thoughts about family, femininity, and society. Comparing genres provides unique insight into Sarah's struggle to reconcile her antebellum socialization with the realities of her life in postwar South Carolina. In many cases, there is an intriguing disparity. Sarah's articles on women's employment, for example, resonate with the confidence and resolve that she was unable to embrace in her career as a writer. Similarly, Sarah's scathing comments on the irresistible charms of the widow are problematized by her decision to tell new acquaintances that she was a widow. Because the editorials reveal the complexities of Sarah's postwar journey, I have integrated them into the correspondence. I have organized her editorial work under four major themes—women, family and relationships, politics, and society—and have inserted them in two blocks following chapters 2 and 6. An appendix provides a chronological list of Sarah's published work for 1873.

1. Sarah Morgan Dawson diary, "1896," vol. 6, Dawson Papers.

LIST OF
FREQUENTLY MENTIONED PEOPLE

Virginia Fourgeaud Dawson	Frank's first wife
Alcée Louis Dupré (Louis)	Miriam's husband
Miriam Morgan Dupré	Sarah's sister
Eugene and Celena Fourgeaud	Virginia Fourgeaud Dawson's parents
Gabriella Burroughs Morgan (Ella)	James Morgan's wife
George Morgan	Sarah's brother who died in Virginia during the Civil War
Howell Morgan	Sarah's nephew, son of Thomas Gibbes Morgan Jr. and Lydia Carter Morgan Purnell
James Morris Morgan (Jimmy, Jim, Jem)	Sarah's younger brother
Sarah Hunt Fowler Morgan	Sarah's mother
Lydia Carter Morgan Purnell	Howell's mother
Bartholomew Rochefort Riordan	Frank's business partner
Francis Holmes Trenholm (Frank)	son of George and Anna Trenholm
George Alfred Trenholm	father of James Morgan's first wife, Helen Trenholm Morgan
William Trenholm	son of George and Anna Trenholm

The Correspondence of Sarah Morgan
and Francis Warrington Dawson

A Winter Romance

January–February 1873

Frank Dawson was a widower of less than six weeks when he wrote his first letter to Sarah Morgan—on black-bordered mourning stationery to signify his recent loss. The practice, though widely adopted by grieving nineteenth-century families, provided Sarah with an unsettling reminder of the impropriety of her admirer's attentions. Frank was aware of "Miss Sarah's" reservations and downplayed all romantic overtures in favor of an appeal to spiritual enlightenment. Drawing on popular ideology that hailed women as the keepers of morality, Frank declared that Sarah was his beacon of hope and righteousness and that only her "strong right hand" could lead him to "betterment." Any repulsion of his advances, he warned, would force him to take his "first step on the broad road which leads to destruction." "I do dread succumbing to some terrible temptation," he wrote, "if you put me away like a garment which has served a purpose."

Frank's letters provide a candid portrait of the social quandary in which many widowers found themselves. Caught between mourning and court-ship rituals, Frank often eulogized his late wife in one letter and then declared his love for Sarah in the next. He sent photographs of Virginia to Sarah and wrote to her about the portrait he had commissioned of his "dead love." He told Sarah of his desire to maintain his rooms "exactly as they were before Virginia died" and lay Sarah's "knot of ribbon" next to his late wife's picture. "There is no rivalry there," he assured her.

None of Sarah's letters from this period survive. While she tested Frank's resolve by dismissing his feelings and instituting a "four letter rule" (writing one letter for every four of his), her actions indicate that the attraction may not have been entirely one-sided. Sarah answered Frank's letters, advised him on business as well as spiritual matters, and gave him small tokens of friendship. She also encouraged his visits to Hampton and accepted gifts such as books, periodicals, and newspapers from New Orleans.

ↀↂↀ

On January 15, 1873, Frank wrote his first letter to Sarah from his residence at 8 Rutledge Avenue in Charleston, the family home of his in-laws, Eugene and Celena Fourgeaud.

Charleston[1]

January 15. 1873

My dear Miss Sarah;

I wrote you a long letter last night, but I was so miserable that I thought I had better sleep on it. This is the result—for better or for worse, in the words of a service which a lady never reads. I found my business in a very satisfactory condition, with mountains of dry work to be done. "Home," as it is called, is inexpressibly dreary. Enough of me!

I have sent you some New Orleans papers and to-day I have sent by Express the second volume of Middlemarch, the French Revolution, & Valerie Aylmer.[2] What can I say of Middlemarch, except that I shrink now from reading more than we read together. The Carlyle you will, of course, read leisurely. With Lamartines' Girondins & the Tale of the Two Cities,[3] it will give you a vivid understanding of the causes and excuses of the crimes committed in Liberty's name. (My hand trembles fearfully. Why is it that even writing to you affects me so?) Valerie Aylmer I almost feared to send you, after reading over its last chapters. But if it teaches you to be happy, the rest matters little. The book about Westminster Abbey I have kept with the hope of explaining it to you myself when, by God's mercy, your woeful Southern trip is put aside or happily over. How I wish that I could say something to cheer your loneliness, but I dont know how. Those days at Hampton's[4] were amongst the happiest of my life & so shall remain. The pines are as plainly seen as when I last looked upon them, & there is a wealth of meaning in their gray lights & dreamy shadows. Of this be certain: You have sealed me with your seal, and, God willing, you shall never be ashamed of me. Proud of me you will not be: you may, in some new happiness, forget all about me, but you live, & will live, as freshly & tenderly to me as when you were quietly saying that winter as well as summer romances must fade away. You see, I fancy I am at Hampton's again. Would that I were! For me you have abundant work to do, if you care to do it. As you determine I shall linger in the

plain or breast the mountain height. Do as you will with me, and ask anything except that I forget you. Do write to me if you may, & as kindly as you
can. I am not well in mind or in body, but my head is clear & the fumes of
Columbia are gone never to return. Give my love to your dear Mother &
brother & to Howell.[5] And for you I pray, that Our Lady may keep you &
watch over you now & always. This is the best (of what you have not) that
can be given you by your poor servant.

F.W.Dawson

1. Frank wrote this letter to Sarah on mourning stationery. Letters dated January
   19, 22, 27, February 10, 18, 1873, were written on the same stationery.
2. George Eliot, *Middlemarch* (1871–72); Thomas Carlyle, *The French Revolution:
   A History* (1837); Christian Reid [pseud.], *Valerie Aylmer; A Novel* (1870).
3. Alphonse de Lamartine, *Histoire des Girondins* (1847); Charles Dickens, *A Tale of
   Two Cities* (1859).
4. Hampton, formerly owned by General Wade Hampton (1818–1902), was the
   home of Sarah's younger brother, James Morris Morgan (1845–1928). It was located on the Congaree River, four miles below Columbia, South Carolina. Sarah
   and her mother, Sarah Hunt Fowler Morgan (1807–74), moved to Hampton in
   May 1872 and were still living with James at the beginning of 1873. In his memoirs, James recalled the living arrangements: "My mother and sister occupied the
   second story of the frame house, and there was only one staircase leading from
   the wide hall to the upper chambers, and in that hall was kept burning a kerosene
   swinging lamp on account of my mother being nervous. My bedroom was on the
   lower floor" (*Recollections*, 345).
5. Sarah's nephew, Howell Morgan (1863–1952), the son of Sarah's older brother,
   Thomas Gibbes Morgan Jr. (Gibbes)(1835–64) and Lydia Carter Morgan Purnell (1836–1915). Gibbes enlisted in the Confederate army in June 1861, was captured by Union troops in 1863, and died at Johnson's Island Prison, Ohio, on January 21, 1864. In his memoirs, Howell Morgan noted that Sarah had adopted him
   after his mother's marriage to George W. Purnell. "Mr. Purnell, after much per-
   suasion, agreed to give up Howell to the Morgans, and was taken by [Sarah] with
   her mother, to her brother Jimmie's home in South Carolina, 1872" (Howell
   Morgan Memoir, 19, Sarah Morgan Dawson and Family Papers).

♔

*Frank's friendship with Sarah invited comment from Charleston business
magnate George Alfred Trenholm, an acquaintance of Frank's whose
daughter, Helen, had been married to James Morgan before her death.
George remarked on the peculiarity of Sarah's single status, indicating that
it was a topic of discussion among the Morgan family and friends.*

My dear Miss Sarah;

I have just written to James and said to him that I should write to you to: morrow, but to-day is better, because nearer, and I write at once.

Since I wrote to you I have seen Mr. Trenholm[1] who spoke very warmly about you. As a warning to me I suppose, he said that there was a quasi-engagement between you and "a Col Hill",[2] at which I smiled surprise. He also said that he was astonished that so "charming and accomplished" a lady should not have been "gobbled up" long ago. I told him that I supposed it was because you did not want to be "gobbled." I have, also, seen "sweet William", who made a very happy little speech at the Chamber of Commerce the other day, reported in The News of Saturday.[3] He hopes to be in Columbia in time for the reception. Please do not say anything about poor me to Col Trenholm. What you think of me, good & bad, keep for yourself. You know that I am speaking now only of what society: talk you might indulge in; but even that would pain me. Do not be shocked at this request. I am strangely sensitive, in whatever concerns you & me.

Is it not a sad thing to feel that what we most desired to say has been left unsaid? That is my case. I know that I was talking incessantly while with you, and yet it seems now that I said nothing. You gave me so many new thoughts and ideas, of which you were & are the centre, that I have as much to tell you now, as if I had really left Hampton's for good on the morning when you insisted on telling me not to come back again. One thing chère amie [dear friend], you will be glad to hear. I have gained one victory over myself. It was a hard fight, beginning last night & ending this morning, but I won—won, when all else failed, by remembering what you had said, what counsel you had given, what you expected of me, what pain it would be to you if I were a castaway. Thank God & you! And now I beg of you to send me word what your plans are, where and when you are going. I want to know where you are, and I want within a month to see you again, if only for an hour or two. Let me have one more talk with you, &, if you so wish, I will then unmurmuringly go out into the night. And you will have read "Middlemarch" and "Valerie Aylmer," and we shall have so much to talk about. Do not deny yourself and me this happiness; there is not so much pleasure in our path that we need pass around what is right before us.

Is there, or not, some strange link between you and me? Last Thursday night at 9 or 10 o'clock I was engaged in the dullest & most prosaic of work;

balancing my books. Instantly I became filled with your presence; your voice was in my ears, I could see your pure face, it seemed that you were around & above me. I felt then that you must, at that hour, be thinking of me; perhaps praying for me. It was so sweet a thought, & for an hour or more, while the spell was upon me, I was perfectly happy. Was it chance, or was it as I believe? I ought to stop now, but I am so near to you in spirit that I could keep on for ever.

I had already told you that I found things in a satisfactory condition in a business way. The result of the year is far better than I expected. The portrait of my wife[4] (a porcelain type) which I had ordered is finished. It is a beautiful piece of work & I do wish that you could see it. Of "home" news I have none, except that my mother-in-law emerged from her retirement to-day,[5] went to church and took her place at the head of the table. Otherwise, no change. I am as lonely as ever, except when thinking of you, but my head is straight and my aches and pains have well: nigh vanished.

And now Good: Night. You have known many who loved you, but I fear not to say that no one has had for you or for any woman a purer or more un-selfish affection than that which animates

Faithfully yours

F.W.Dawson

NB Please give my love to your Mother & Howell

1. George Alfred Trenholm (1807–76), a Charleston merchant who operated a successful fleet of blockade-running steamships during the Civil War. He became secretary of the Confederate treasury in 1864. James Morgan married Trenholm's daughter, Anna Helen Trenholm, on November 16, 1865, but she died in 1866, leaving a ten-day-old daughter, Emily, who was adopted by the Trenholm family. Sarah was well acquainted with the Trenholm family and spent considerable time with them when she traveled to South Carolina for James and Helen's wedding. "It is no hard task to be happy, surrounded by this lovely family," she remarked during her visit. "Among ourselves we sing, laugh, and play games to our hearts content" (Sarah Morgan diary, August 27, 1865, vol. 6, Dawson Papers).
2. Colonel James Davidson Hill (b. 1842) of New Orleans. On October 10, 1866, Sarah commented, "This is the man Jimmy says even now he wished me to marry, above all others. So does Miriam; so do they all" (Sarah Morgan diary, vol. 5, Dawson Papers).
3. Colonel William Lee Trenholm (1836–1901), son of Anna and George A. Trenholm. After graduating from South Carolina College in 1855, he traveled to England to further his father's business interests in Liverpool. With the outbreak of war, he returned to South Carolina and helped organize the Rutledge Mounted

Riflemen. He served as lieutenant and captain of this company and subsequently became a lieutenant colonel. After the war, William became heavily involved in Charleston's commercial affairs. The article to which Frank refers was "The City License Law," *Charleston News,* January 18, 1873.

4. Virginia Fourgeaud Dawson (1844 or 1845–1872). Frank met Virginia not long after his arrival in Charleston, and in a February 1, 1867, letter to his mother, he described her as "22 years of age, a fervent Catholic, very handsome and accomplished, a charming singer, a polished woman, and a devoted and affectionate child" (Clark, *Francis Warrington Dawson,* 22). The couple married on May 1, 1867, but Virginia died of consumption less than six years later.

5. This was probably the first public appearance by Celena Fourgeaud, forty-eight, since her daughter's death.

Charleston S.C.

Wednesday January 22. 1873

I have just received your letter of Sunday, and it makes me feel so bright and happy, so much better able to do my work as you would have it done, that I begin my answer at once. But, to begin with, there is something awfully wrong with your mailing arrangements, & I can't help wondering how long my letter of Sunday last to you was on the road.

So you thought that I had closed the door; thought so, for a minute or two perhaps. You may try to persuade yourself that every impression fades, but I shall be one of the exceptions to the rule. The circumstances were peculiar; such as, if you had been different or I had been different, could not have happened as in a life: time, & if you & I had been in different case it would not be as it is. But why should I try to persuade you of what you must know, & if you do not fully know time will convince you. You tell me that what you can do you will do, & that, if it depends on you I shall not linger in the valleys. And you say also you will only answer my letters when sure of doing me good. What you can do is, by your constant encouragement and sympathy, to keep my chariot out of the slough & enable me to cleanse the mire from the wheels. You can keep me from wrong, and lead me into right. You can bring me out of the depths and place me on the heights. But my nature is peculiar. I require a steady & lasting pressure in the upward direction. Leave me to myself & I shall not mount up, for ambition will die the death. You have told me that I can do good to my people. The measure of that good rests with you. Do not think that I am shifting responsibility from my shoulders to yours. That is not my way. I mean that my dead love is nothing without my living love; that a word from you has more power than a world of buried hopes & fears. Now then can you give me your strong right hand? Just now you can only (& how much it is!) do this: Let me see you occasionally and answer my every letter. It does not rest with you to decide whether your letters will do me good. I know that they will. Write to me, tell me when I may hope to see you—that is, say where you will be a week or two weeks hence. And then you need not dread that I shall fall; and if I do, I shall, your hand being held out, rise instantly again. Never was there a man more open to the influence of woman. Your influence is all for the pure & true. What might be the influence of some other? And I do dread succumbing to some terrible temptation, if you put me away from you like a garment which has served a purpose. Is it not a new experience to you? That I, who have often led, should feel an intense content in having you to lead me. Again I say that you can make of me what you will, there is plenty of material, but I must see you and hear from you. [. . .]

Do you know that I cannot bear to resume the reading of Middlemarch. It ended for me with the last word I read to you. As for Valerie: Let me have the opportunity of reading it to you. And this brings me to the result of my pondering this long day. I cannot explain myself clearly in a letter without seeming to say too much or too little. The threads are too badly tangled for me to unravel them alone. There is some business to attend to in Columbia next week. If by going there I can see you I shall go; if not my partner[1] will go and I shall stay here & fume. My plan is to leave Charleston on Wednesday or Thursday next, go to Columbia, and ride out at once to see you. I know you well enough to be able to say that I can understand that Jimmy will not care to have any visitors, and I know that you will not have any room to spare. I should therefore stay with you as late as I could, and then go back to Columbia or Charleston. Your part of it is this: to write to me at once and say whether I may come and can come, & I will by return mail let you know when to expect me. Should you deem it best I could perhaps wait until the week after next. You must in this, as in so many other things, tell me what to do. Remember that I go to see you and to have a long talk with you. After that I can be content to write. Without that I cannot. I am and shall be like wax in your white hands. And I will promise to be "a good boy" for ever if only you will allow me to see you again.

I have not forgotten what day this is.[2] God grant it may all turn out well; nor do I forget that this will probably reach you when you are surrounded by your dear old Charleston friends. But I no more fear that they will make you think less of me than you should fear that time place & the world will make me think less of you. You have begun the good work & must finish it. Would that I could say to you here what I know of myself, but when we meet I will strive to unbosom myself, shock you however much I may. Tell me then frankly what is the situation at Hampton, & do not forget that I, who would give my right arm to be with you, await your reply. This letter is incoherent I know, though one strain runs through it all. You are convinced that I am safe for to-day & to-morrow; you can make my life all to-day & to-morrow. And more! You can bring out of me, as you did in Hampton, powers I did not know that I possessed, and teach me to use them for the elevation, enlightenment and purification of the people.

I must stop now. I am half-ashamed of writing so much. Give my love to your Mother & Howell & Jimmy, and say whatever pretty thing you think of for me to Mrs. Morgan—the bride.[3]

How earnestly, nay! tearfully, do I implore the Father of All to shower his mercies & richest blessings upon her who is all the world to this poor wanderer

F.W. Dawson.

1. Bartholomew Rochefort Riordan, thirty-two.
2. Probably the marriage of James Morgan to Gabriella Burroughs. This was Frank's first reference to Gabriella as a "bride." In his memoirs, James Morgan wrote, "I married Miss Gabriella Burroughs, a granddaughter of former Chancellor William Ford DeSaussure, the head of an old Huguenot family. . . . My wedding took place some months before that of my sister" (*Recollections*, 344).
3. Gabriella Burroughs Morgan, daughter of Eliza G. DeSaussure Burroughs (1812–95) and Henry K. Burroughs, M.D. (1809–51), and the second wife of James Morgan.

⁀⊃€⁀

Sarah did not react favorably to Frank's overt declarations of love and wrote to him in an effort to discourage what she often described as his "ephemeral" feelings for her. Shocked and dismayed by Sarah's comments, Frank responded by subtly shifting the emphasis from the romantic to the spiritual.

Charleston S.C.
Monday Night. [January 27, 1873]

My dear Miss Sarah;

I should not write to you so soon after the receipt of your letter which came to me to: night, only that I fear I have failed miserably in what I had desired to do. It was my hope & intention to bring as much brightness as I could into your lonely life. I knew that the influence which you exerted over me would be for my good, and faithfully have I done what you bade me. This was & will be some satisfaction to you, for you have told me so. And what you have done once you can always do again. I hoped, besides, to cheer you by reading to you, by talking with you, by writing to you, by doing whatever man may to secure the well: being and content of a pure and candid woman. For a time I succeeded, I think. It was not (strange as it may seem) my purpose to write to you of my own feelings towards you. What I wanted, & all that I intended, was to let you see that you had done me good, & I do not know any better way of comforting so sweet a friend than by showing her that, even in the isolation of which she speaks, she has been able to heal a bruised spirit, solace an aching heart and give tone to a failing will. I did not, nor do I, presume upon your kindness. Yet with all my trying I have pained you, made you uneasy, undone whatever good I was doing. This must not be. If I feel more I shall strive to say less. And do not I entreat you think any other thing than this: that you are my Guardian Angel to whom I look up for guidance such as only woman can give. Do not let what I say in this note wound you for I am trying so hard to say what you might wish me to say. Hold all the rest in abeyance, and think of me as you did on the sad morning when I parted from you.

I will not go to Columbia this week. But, God willing, I will leave Charleston on Wednesday night February 5, & shall be at the Pump[1] very early Thursday morning. I shall try to read Middlemarch that we may talk about it, & we can, maybe, read Valerie together. Please send the indispensable Levy to the Pump to meet me.

Give my love to your Mother & Jemmy & to his bride if she will allow me to say so affectionate a thing to the wife of my old friend. I suppose the "whirligig of time"[2] will bring things aright, but I confess that I feel in the "Marianna moated-grange"[3] mood to:night. Think of me as kindly as you can & À Jeudi [Till Thursday]!

F. W. Dawson

1. The location where the train stopped to deliver mail or visitors to Hampton.
2. "Thus the whirligig of time brings in his revenges" (Shakespeare, *Twelfth Night* 5.1).
3. "There, at the moated grange, resides this dejected Mariana" (Shakespeare, *Measure for Measure* 3.1). Mariana was Angelo's rejected lover as well as the subject of Tennyson's "Mariana" (*Poems, Chiefly Lyrical* [1830]).

*Frank visited Hampton and again proposed to Sarah, and again she re-
fused. Sarah did, however, confide in Frank about her personal unhappiness and her increasingly uncertain future in South Carolina, both of which
had been brought on by her brother's marriage to Gabriella Burroughs.
Sarah remarked that if she could afford to do so, she would like nothing
better than to travel to Provence, France. In a bold declaration of love,
Frank conveyed his desire to make Sarah's wish a reality. This letter also
reveals Frank's liberal views on the position of women, which differed considerably from Sarah's belief that a lady's place was "in perfect subjection
to man."*

Charleston S.C. February 9th, 1873[1]
Sunday Night

I have only been away from you a few hours, my darling, and already I am
fleeing to you for consolation; asking you, with the music of your words, to
charm away my sadness, as Annot Lyle banished the gloom of the fierce
highlander you wot of with the music of her harp.[2] Now I know how unutterably wretched I should have been had you sent me away, sorrowing, at the
moment, that friday evening, when you and I turned our faces from the
crimson glories of the setting sun. And why am I so sad? This house de-
presses me, dear! I was greeted very kindly, but the shadow will rest upon
me, until by talking to you, as now, I can scourge it away; not a cloud which
has a tempest in its bosom, but a cloud which veils the light. Let me speak to
you as frankly as I did twenty four hours ago, &, as usual, about me.

At my office things look rather blue; business bad & money short. It was
high time that I returned; the more so as I see a narrowness creeping over the
paper which is very foreign to my ideas of its policy. But think of it! they expected me to remain at Hampton until Monday night & then go over to Augusta. I lost two days with you by doing what I felt was right to be done. But
I have asked Mr. Riordan to try to go to New York.[3] He sees no reasons for
hurrying. I see many; one of which (not to be named) is that I have no hope
of seeing you again until after his return. In New York too he will see if I can
sell my interest in my paper; a step preliminary to Provence; yet it is always
Provence to me where you are, a land of brightness & content, rich with the
purple grape whence is drawn the wine of happy living. To: morrow I shall
speak to Mrs. Fourgeaud about the arrangement of my rooms; I will do it
gently. And now (see how I wander!) for that stray passage in Middlemarch,
which I have just found: Vol 1.390. It was this "beauty-repose" this "sub-

missiveness of the goose, as beautifully corresponding to the strength of the gander" of which you were speaking. But *I* say there is repose in strength not in weakness. A strong brain must rest upon a strong brain; a fertile mind upon a fertile mind. How stable is a pyramid when standing upon its apex? Is there more repose upon the point of a pin than upon a massive column? Talleyrand, you know, said (It was either Talleyrand or Metternich) I am perfectly happy with my wife—Elle est si bête [She is so foolish].[4] And this is what you thought best for me! A chaining to a corpse; a living in vacuum. Ah, sweetest! my wife must be what you are—all that I am, & more. Have I convinced you?

I have thought to: night of what your pure face and lofty brow reminded me. It was a picture, I think, of Petrarch & Laura.[5] She on a pedestal, palm branch in hand, eyes uplifted, draped in sheeny white, an image of physical beauty & intellectual symmetry, an epic woman. He by her side, conscious of his power, but looking up to her for the inspiration & guidance of his life. So is there a subtle relation between the artist and the material with which he works. The one must correspond to the other. A Paganini[6] may draw linked sweetness from one string, but his power is limited by the capacity of the mellow Cremona or Stradivarius[7] over which that string passes. *You* can bring anything from me; more, at least, than [any] other mortal can, & I, under your hand, were capable of harmonies of usefulness which no other touch can waken. You are the complement of my life; its crown & completeness, & so, time shall show. Sweetest & best! deal with me tenderly, & think of me as kindly as you can. This dearest, is *one* letter; you understand. And, when the welcome words from you shall come, tell me, at least, that you did not think less of me this morning when we parted than you did when we parted the first time in the same hallowed place; poetized by your presence; consecrated by your smile. Darling! the dullness is exorcised now. I am going to work; late as it is. May God Almighty bless you always. I kiss my little knot of ribbon[8] & wish you a sweet good: night, beloved!

F.W.Dawson.

1. Years later, Sarah wrote at the top of this letter, "Can it be possible he remembers it was 'No' eternally? Yet how could he forget? I might as well think I forget, myself." Sarah also dated the letter.
2. Annot Lyle charmed highlander Allan M'Aulay with her musical talent in Sir Walter Scott, *The Legend of Montrose* (1819).
3. The *News* was heavily backed by financial interests in New York. Benjamin Wood, editor and proprietor of the *New York Daily News,* was a silent partner in the newspaper.

4. Charles Maurice de Talleyrand-Péigord (1754–1838), French diplomat; Prince Klemens von Metternich (1773–1859), Austrian statesman. Sarah later used this quotation in "Very Young America," May 10, 1873 (see chap. 4), attributing the phrase to Talleyrand.
5. Petrarch (Francesco Petrarca) (1304–74), Italian poet who fell in love with a woman named Laura, who inspired much of his romantic work.
6. Niccolò Paganini (1782–1840), Italian classical violinist.
7. Italian violinmakers.
8. Sarah had given Frank one of her ribbons as a token of friendship.

Letter No2:

Charleston Monday February 10th[1] [1873]

Good Morning! dearest.

I am so worked down to-day that I have hardly time to scratch a word in time for the evening mail. I spoke to Mrs. Fourgeaud saying: "I do not like to speak of these things, but it would be very pleasant to me to have my rooms arranged exactly as they were before Virginia died. The furniture &c which you now have I had used during the whole of my wedded life, & it is dearer to me than any that I could buy or you could give." She made no answer & I said no more. What the outcome of it will be I cant tell; but it is the first time that I have expressed to her a positive desire to have something done.

I went this morning to the photographer's & find that the second portrait of my dead love (for me) is beautiful as a work of art and excellent as a likeness. Some of the cartes-de-visites[2] were ready, but they are so poor, comparatively, that I will not send you one until the second lot are ready, when you shall have the best of them all. I hope to send you some New Orleans papers by the morning mail, & in a day or two will send you Edwin Drood.[3] The shawl &c were sent to Mr. Trenholm's this morning.

What should I do without you; tell me! All my life centres in you & I prattle of the small things which make up so much of living as freely as of the great events which give form & character to our lives. How deeply should I thank God that he has allowed me to know you, which is to love you; for the sun now has a brighter light & the sky a deeper blue. The whole world seems truer & better, & this pilgrim, instead of lingering in the depths, is breasting the healthy difficulties of existence, with his eyes fast fixed on you. Whatever else may fail, believe always in the devoted & unselfish love of

Francis Warrington Dawson!

1. Frank numbered his letters as a result of Sarah's "four letter rule." Sarah dated this letter.
2. Small photographs the size of visiting cards.
3. Charles Dickens, *The Mystery of Edwin Drood* (1870).

෪

As their relationship developed, Frank increasingly discussed his business interests with Sarah and often solicited her advice. In the following letter, Frank informed Sarah of the impending sale of the Charleston Courier, *a rival of the* News.

Letter No3.

February 11th [1873][1]

Cherie [Dear]! it is between two and three o'clock Tuesday morning and I have been at work without interruption since nine o'clock yesterday morning. The only halt I had was in scrawling a few words to you which (Letters 1 & 2) went off by Monday evening's mail. Am I tired? I was, but am not now. Writing to you, my dearest, is the only rest & comfort I have. Take that away, and what would be left? So I mean to write a few words to you every day or night; & send them off in batches so as not to frighten you. In reading this you will begin to realize what an infliction your poor servant is likely to be. Mr. Riordan, my partner, is completely bouleverse [distressed]. He has discovered to-day that there is a combination in Charleston, consisting of two Bank presidents, one Cresus[2] of a merchant, and a stray lawyer, to buy up our old rival The Courier & crush out The News by sheer weight of money. Their main reason is that The News is unreasonably independent, and cannot be wheedled or brow: beaten into grinding any private axe. I am not a bit scared. Much money & little brains will not overcome some means and lots of brains. (Modest!) But then poor Riordan has no Provence to dream of & no Sarah Morgan to love, and write to, & strive to be worthy of. That is the difference. Whatever the new combination is it cannot seriously hurt us as long as I have my health, a clear head and a hopeful heart. And, perhaps, you might guess upon whom that depends! [. . .]

This is enough for my part of me! What have you done this magnificent day? Have you read and worked, sewed and sowed? Would that I could read to you while you elaborated your (to-be) charming robe. But, perhaps, you have been catechizing yourself; wondering whether you had done me harm or good. Oh! why will you not leave all that to time to determine. It is goodness, it is almost perfect happiness, it is manhood & worthily doing my duty. That to me is knowing you. The devotion of a lifetime could not be return enough for what already you have done for me. (Before I forget: I saw Col Trenholm to-day who enquired, it seemed, rather anxiously about your health. I told him that you looked bright, & that I had seen you tripping gaily across the lawn on Saturday night. At which he appeared to be much relieved.) I have so much more to tell you, but I shall write again to: morrow & say new things of this same love. Do, sweetest & best, take good care of your precious health. Remember how much depends on you & is bound up in you. And do not forget that it is nobler to live doing God's work than to die with that work undone. I have kissed my little ribbon again, & with all my heart & soul and strength wish you pleasant dreams & a happy awakening, beloved as thou art.

Frank.

1. Sarah dated this letter.
2. Croesus, the last king of Lydia (ca. 560–ca. 546 B.C.), described as the richest man in the world.

Two o'clock Thursday Morning,
February 13. 1873.

What shall I call you, dearest? I would call you mine, but we are not yet in Provence! These four days that I have written to you, you have looked into my heart of hearts as you looked in my face when I met you last at Hampton, & surely you have seen there that, since I parted from you, I have been a "good child," have done no evil thing & thought nothing wrong. This you must know, but it will be pleasant for you to hear me say so; I say *hear* me, for I fancy that you can now, that you are dreaming may be, [and] hear what I say. I have been as abstemious as an anchorite. My only trouble is in my separation from you whom I value more than all the world besides. You told me these impressions would fade. Does it seem so now? You have thought of me, with mingled feelings, these long days of absence, & you have never been absent from my thoughts. What I do fear is that I may tire you with my letters, because I am having all the talking to myself & this must be so until you write to me. You promised that you would write once for every four letters of mine. The third and fourth letters were sent you to-day, & you will not make me sick with hope deferred. Sarah Morgan never does less than she says she will, and generally does more. It is strange to me, even now, that you should have so absolute a control over me. You can do any thing with me & I, knowing this, come to you with the confidence of a child: For you give me a childlike feeling, protecting me from harm and encouraging me to good. Others may live and grow in stature without you. I can not. Be with me & there is no height to which I cannot reach. Leave me, and the dull round of duty will consume my life. What, with you, I can do for the benefit of my fellows must, without you, remain undone. But, my sweetest, I am talking almost sadly, if so lovingly, let us speak of Heine.[1] It is too late to: night for me to give you any idea of his character; so you must take three of his short poems to excite your curiosity. The first is that which I have often repeated to you:

> Thou'rt like a lovely floweret,
>   So void of guile or art,
> I gaze upon thy beauty,
>   And grief steals o'er my heart.
>
> I fain would lay, devoutly,
>   My hands upon thy brow,
> And pray that God will keep thee
>   As good and fair as now. [. . .]

I must stop, darling. Nothing new to-day except the good news that when I came home to-day I found that my rooms were returned to their old state. I am sure it is good for poor Mrs. Fourgeaud & it is very sweet to me.

This letter will not go until friday, by which time I hope to hear from you; to rest my eyes where yours have been, to place my hand where yours has been, and hear in your own sweet word what I know will, at once, soothe my soul and strengthen my spirits. May Our God bless you! my dear one. Good, good, night:

F.W.Dawson

1. Heinrich Heine (1797–1856), German poet. This excerpt comes from Heine's "The Homecoming," *Book of Songs* (1827; trans. 1846). Frank copied more of Heine's writings for Sarah, including some of his prose.

*After consultations with Riordan, it was decided that Frank would make
the business trip to New York. Sarah realized the conflict between newspaper ownership and Provence, and on the eve of Frank's departure, she
questioned him on the plausibility of selling his interest in the* News. *The
"Provence Plan" was consequently abandoned.*

Charleston[1]

February 18. [1873] Midnight

And is your letter which I received to-day to be my good: bye, my God:
speed? I fear so, &, indeed, it gave me a very far: away feeling. This you shall
explain to me in your own sweet way, when I come back. I am going farther
from you, and am glad; because the farther in the end will bring me nearer.
Was that the philosophy of your letter, dearest? Never mind, we will speak
of those things later. One or two points I will at once clear up.

As to Provence: It is clearly and unquestionably to my pecuniary interest
to retain my share in The News. It gives me a salary of about $3.000 a year,
besides the increase in value of the share, & the prospective profits in the
way of dividends. Were I to sell out, what I should realize would probably
give me $1.000 a year only—nothing beyond. Why then did I speak of sell-
ing? Because you said you would like to go to Provence. That was enough
to determine me. I had rather remain here, but whither you go I will go, &
your people shall be my people.[2] An active life I always desire, and usually
have; & whatever I do, good or bad, I do with all my might. I know that I am
in the right place to do good, & that what I have done is all earnest of what
I might do. Why then did I speak of retiring with you to Provence? Because
I cannot live worthily without you; because, without you, I cannot walk the
long path; because, without you, brain and energy will first sleep and then
fail. There is no evidence of a dehumanizing influence, on your part, in this
fact. You have done much for me; you have led me through the first circles
of the "Inferno."[3] Your every influence has been for my benefit, & knowing
this I place my life at your feet for you to tread it out if you will. Though I
never saw you again, what you have said and written would remain graven
on my soul to the last; yet without you I shall never climb higher. Who can,
without hope & love? Not a man like me; not a man who cares very little for
success for itself, and very much for what it is to others. The laurels I should
win would crown your fair head not my humble brow. The Courier combi-

nation does not weigh one iota with me. Let me keep my health and brains and I can break any of their rings, whether gold or iron! But here you come in again. It may be that I shall soon be wishing for a sudden end to a sad career. Ah! Well.

I am glad to see that you have given up your matrimonial schemes in which Miss Fisher figured. You are very severe in your criticism, although, strictly speaking, rigidly just. More of that when I see you.[4]

Thanks for your advice about the printing presses and folding machine. What a sweet child you are to watch over me so. And it made me laugh very heartily when, an hour after the sunshine came in, Mr. Riordan asked me to see if I could not buy a stereotyping machine in New York. Only $100. [. . .]

One word as to yourself and myself and I have done—I have much work to do to: night. I regret that your house affairs are still entangled, but I am very happy at the thought that you will be where I can see you—for some time to come. And, besides, as long as you can remain there Hampton is the best place for you; provided always that you have recreation, some little excitement & not too much introspection.

As to myself: it is very sweet to be praised by you, but I am doing nothing to deserve it in remaining here. It appears to be the right thing & is, therefore, a pleasant thing—that's all. And now I am coming to the end of your letter and of mine. What do you vouchsafe me? That when we get to Heaven you will like me very much. Like me there, dearest, and love me here. Give me some bit of Heaven to light my way. I am very lonely when your face seems averted. But I dare not follow out this strain of thought! Du Courage [Have Courage]! Shall I not see you soon again! I will write to you from New York on Saturday, & will telegraph to Jemmie when to expect me in Columbia. I am putting off the evil moment just as though I were standing by you. However, it must come. Good: bye then, dearest sweetest and best. Remember that I am always, always, thinking of you, that I have no wish or plan separate from you, that I love you with a strength beyond my poor power to express & revere you more than I love you. At least wish me "a safe journey & a quick return" when this comes to you, & do deal with me gently. I can no more. I kiss your hands, again. And once more Good: bye:

F. W. Dawson

1. At the top of the page Frank noted, "An eleutheromaniac is a person crazy on the subject of liberty—what I should call a freedom: shrieker."

2. "And Ruth said, Intreat me not to leave thee, or to return from following after thee: for whither thou goest, I will go; and where thou lodgest, I will lodge: thy people shall be my people, and thy God my God" (Ruth 1:16).

3. Dante Alighieri, "Inferno," *The Divine Comedy* (completed 1321).

4. Sarah may have been referring to Frances C. Fisher (1846–1920), who had published *Valerie Aylmer* under the pseudonym Christian Reid. Frank had loaned Sarah a copy of this novel in January.

A New Career

March–April 1873

Frank Dawson made his business trip to New York. On his return home, he visited Sarah at Hampton, where domestic arrangements had changed significantly since his previous visit. James Morgan's new wife, Gabriella, had become mistress of the estate, and Sarah and her mother had found themselves relegated to the margins of domestic life. Dependent on her brother for financial assistance, Sarah grew increasingly depressed by her powerlessness to change an untenable situation.

Frank was aware of Sarah's plight and convinced her to accept a position on the editorial staff of the *Charleston News*. Employment, he argued, would provide her with the funds she required to leave Hampton and set up a household of her own. Drawing on notions of spiritual enlightenment (which he had also used to construct his personal relationship with Sarah), Frank explained that her "new career" should be viewed as a grand expression of her moral obligation to others. "You have it in your power to preach to a larger congregation than Beecher & Spurgeon command," he declared. "And with words as much loftier . . . than theirs, as the nature of woman is higher than that of man."

Yet as Frank's letters reveal, Sarah struggled to embrace her career as a writer. On one hand, she yearned for the financial independence that only her work could provide. On the other, she viewed writing for money as a degrading assault on her gentility. Battling feelings of inadequacy and depression, Sarah could not accept her editorial work as a legitimate foundation on which to build her postwar identity. Still, she persevered, aware that remuneration for her efforts provided her with the best opportunity to attain the domestic ideal and furnish her nephew with the education he required.

On March 5, 1873, Sarah Morgan made her writing debut in the News *with "The New Andromeda." The piece examined the political turmoil that had erupted in Louisiana after the highly fraudulent election of 1872 prompted both the Republican and Fusion candidates to claim victory. Republican William Pitt Kellogg was finally seated as governor after receiving official recognition from President Ulysses S. Grant. Frank and Riordan were delighted with Sarah's "maiden effort" and contracted to have her write two general articles and one editorial (or "Saturday") per week. Sarah's work was published anonymously. Only Frank, Riordan, and Sarah's mother and sister were aware of her professional association with the* News. *On the eve of her newspaper debut, Frank wrote Sarah a congratulatory note, which he enclosed with a proof copy of her editorial.*

Charleston:
Tuesday: March 4. [1873]

My dear Sarah

This is indeed inauguration day: the inauguration for you, let us pray, of a new career—one for which you have full capacity and in which you will do even more good for others than for yourself. I send you, dearest, a proof of your Louisiana article; your maiden effort. Let it encourage you, when you see it in the columns of The News of to-morrow, to continue the work so well begun. You owe this to yourself, to those about you & to the good God who gave you the eminent talent you possess.

Lest you might be embarrassed by want of paper, I send you a small supply for editorial work by mail at once. If you divide the slips longitudinally, you will find them of a convenient size.

I have forgotten to say aught about myself. I am at my desk again; already counting the days that must pass before I may hope to see you.

Good: bye & God bless you:

Yours affectionately
F.W. Dawson

The New Andromeda, March 5, 1873

It is not necessary to harp upon the claims of warring factions in Louisiana. What this paper thinks of the contending parties stands upon the record. But there is a question and an issue higher than platforms and higher than sectional animosity—the welfare of the people of Louisiana, the supreme law of patriot and statesman. This demands that some measure of protection and encouragement be given to those who so patiently bear the yoke that binds them to plough through their own hearth-stones.

What is the case of Louisiana to-day? How can civil government be maintained where its very form and essence are matters of hot dispute? And while each party is convinced that it surely is "the people," and that with that party "wisdom shall die,"[1] the State lies moribund. Fusionists and Kellog-gites,[2] like Hogarth's physicians, tear each other's coats and put out each other's eyes![3] In the domain of the blind the one-eyed are kings. And, per-haps, among the completely blind the one eye would be more powerful and far-seeing than our unconscious, clear vision. But it is not written in any Gospel or Vedas that the blind shall lead those who see! And what have we here? Hundreds of thousands of men, women and children silently endur-ing the suffering entailed upon them by the strife of politicians. Their burden only changes to be increased. Chastised by whips; now they are scourged by scorpions.[4] Even the remedies of law, the universal refuge of oppressed souls, are in abeyance. With unsettled courts and most uncertain judges, the only assurance the people can have is, that the decisions of one judge will be reversed by the other—not always a pleasant process for those who are the first to win their cause. With taxes at a fabulous rate, and prop-erty assessed at threefold and fourfold its value, at the caprice of the asses-sor, real estate may well go begging and fail to find a purchaser. The planter, uncertain of the future and without capital, is unable to carry on his opera-tions. The merchant, restricted in means and cautiously curtailing his ven-tures, finds his business seek other channels. The grand railroad enterprises which promised a world of benefit to the State, and which gave employment to thousands of hardy laborers, are at a stand still. The hearts of men fail them for fear, and, looking for the things that must come upon them, even the most "truly loyal" are shaken in their faith in the wisdom of a govern-ment which can calmly contemplate such havoc—so wanton a loosing, in these days of so-called peace, of the dogs of horrid war.[5]

In this condition stands Louisiana; a new Andromeda[6] chained to the rock; her only garments tribulation and anguish; bound motionless by giant Selfishness. For her there is not even the hope that the swelling of the waters shall rescue her from the grasp of the dragon. There she lies, in her death swoon.

For the deliverance of Andromeda the gods sent Perseus. In all Olympas, where our fumaceous Jove[7] reclines among his thunderbolts, can no Perseus be found, wise, and bright, and pure enough, to rescue a perishing sister?

1. "And Job answered and said, No doubt but ye are the people, and wisdom shall die with you" (Job 12:2).
2. The Fusion ticket in Louisiana's 1872 election comprised members of the Reform and Democratic Parties. John McEnery (1833–91) was nominated as the party's candidate for governor, running against Republican William Pitt Kellogg (1831–1918). Grant recognized Kellogg as the victor, and he served until 1877.
3. William Hogarth (1697–1764), artist. Sarah alludes to his composition *Consultation of Physicians, or Company of Undertakers,* a satirical representation of the medical profession.
4. "And now whereas my father did lade you with a heavy yoke, I will add to your yoke: my father hath chastised you with whips, but I will chastise you with scorpions" (1 Kings 12:11).
5. "Cry 'Havoc!' and let slip the dogs of war" (Shakespeare, *Julius Caesar,* 3.1).
6. In Greek mythology, Andromeda was the daughter of Cepheus and Cassiopeia, the king and queen of Ethiopia. Andromeda was chained to a rock and left as prey for a sea monster, which had been sent to Ethiopia after Cassiopeia declared that Andromeda was more beautiful than the Nereids. Perseus, the son of Zeus and Danae, rescued Andromeda and married her.
7. Jove (Jupiter), the supreme god in Roman mythology. He punished the people by sending lightning and thunder to earth.

Charleston
Wednesday March 5 [1873]

My dear Sarah;

I have sent you a big parcel by Express to-day. It contains: 1. The Worcester's dictionary, which, upon the whole, I think is better than Websters.[1] 2. A batch of paper for your editorial articles. Have you pencils? 3. A box of writing paper and envelopes. As it was cheaper to buy the box which cost $1.50 I took that instead of buying a dollar's worth. I have charged the 50 cents difference to your account. 4. A frame and stand for my wife's picture, & some "insides" for your sister's picture. They cost me nothing. 5. The volume of Buckle, and an article from The Nation on the Spanish Republic.[2] Just read what both say, and work up the subject in your own dear way. Take room enough to say what you think. I can make two articles of it if necessary. 6. The State constitution. You need not read the acts—take only the constitution and ordinances. The U.S. constitution I will send in next package. I find that "the Seven Dolours" is by Father Faber.[3] It will be lent to me, and by me to you.

Now for the good news: My friend Mr. Riordan is "a grave and silent man." Last night he asked me what progress I had made in my wooing. I told him, None! He said: ["]I am an impartial observer and judge this matter without feeling and I tell you that, if you keep in the same mind (and I believe you will) you will marry Miss Morgan." You see, dear, that you might as well make up your mind to face the inevitable, hard as it may be.

Your article I carefully concealed last night & Riordan saw nothing, & heard nothing of it until it was in print. This morning he said very coolly: "Your friend Miss Morgan is a very clever writer; especially if, as I suppose, that was her first piece of newspaper work." I modestly suggested that I might have done it myself; whereupon I was snubbed. I told R that I could not tell him anything about the article; but he insisted on saying so many sweet and encouraging things about your dear self that he fairly stirred my heart with gladness. Indeed, as a practical suggestion, he said: "the best thing is to look out for subjects & send them to Miss Morgan." This, you mind, is what I proposed to do.

And now, my darling, I must leave you for a little while. Words are wanting to express my love for you, & my thankfulness that there lies open before you a path of credit & well: doing.

By: the: way I saw Col Trenholm for a moment this morning, who saluted me, in the most matter of fact way, with the question: "How did you leave every one at Hampton?" Your name was not mentioned. It is clear that in his view whenever I am not in Charleston I am at Hampton; which, as you know, is wide of the truth. I have not been with you three weeks in two months.

Sometimes I fear that you will think so much of your editorial work that you will think nothing of me, but I can love for both & the kindness of your eyes as you bade me good: bye is one of the sweetest of my memories.

Ask your dear Mother, with my love, whether she is not proud of her daughter. Will it compromise you to kiss her for me? Give my love to the bride & to Jemmie, to whom I am now about to write. Is it to make a formal proposal for your hand? I am awfully busy; things otherwise very well. They had not even used the $500 I sent from New York. Again, Good Night & sleep well, dear Angel.

Yours affectionately
F.W. Dawson

1. Joseph Emerson Worcester (1784–1865), a New England lexicographer, published the *Comprehensive Pronouncing and Explanatory Dictionary of the English Language* (1830), which became the chief rival of the work of Noah Webster (1758–1843). Webster and Worcester had different philosophies, with the latter adhering more closely to usage in England.

2. Henry Thomas Buckle, *History of Civilization in England,* 2 vols. (1857–61); "The Spanish Revolution," *The Nation,* February 20, 1873, 129–30. Sarah used this material to write "A Booth to Let In Vanity Fair," March 13, 1873, which drew on Buckle's theories to examine the political unrest in Spain.

3. Frederick William Faber, *The Foot of the Cross; or, The Sorrows of Mary* (1853–60).

Charleston S.C.

March 7. 1873

Midnight

My dear Sarah;

These two days I have been a little uneasy about you; wondering whether you would think as well of your article on Louisiana as I do, and wondering, besides, whether your letter, with the second article, will really come tomorrow. I constantly fear that your modest opinion of your own powers may, for the moment, prevent you from pushing on, and I tell you, in advance, that I shall not abandon the contest until you have proved yourself & won the fight. There are few women who have any sense & fewer still who have the qualities of mind & heart which enable one to write well. You have, by nature and by cultivation, the qualities which have enabled many in the like condition to preach a new Gospel of Peace & Love, & to do, besides, the plain substantial literary work which will strengthen your flight & justify you in laboring a part of your time for ends which cannot be reached in a day or year. For your motto take the burly Danton's

"L'Audace! de l'Audace, toujours de l'Audace!"[1]

Or its prototype in the Faerie Queene

"Be Bolde! Be Bolde! Be ever Bolde!"[2]

And remember that, as you charge me to be good & pure because you believe in me, so do I charge you to continue & persevere in writing because I believe in you. My love for you is not greater, dearest, than my faith in you, now & always.

About myself I have little to say except that I am grumbling because it will be many weeks before I can again hold sweet converse with you. All manner of little things are conspiring to keep me here, & I suppose that the end of it will be that I shall wait until my patience is exhausted and then desert—to Hampton. One thing you did teach me. Many men pass their lives without knowing what they are worth. I know my worth to five cents! Which five cents, with a dainty little ring attached, is very near the heart whose every pulsation is a wish & prayer for you. "Dunna forget, Love!" who I belong to. I am yours to do with as you will. And you have already made me so gentle and considerate in my dealings with every one that I see some surprise upon many a face. Bless you! for all you have done. I sent you, last night, some papers; also a Saturday Review and a Nation. Whenever there is anything which to me seems especially worth reading, or writing up, I will mark the article for you. There will be a book or two for you ere long. With this I send you the Vesper hymn of which I spoke to you. I think you could easily set it to some simple melody—if you like it that is. Did you read about George Eliot in to-days News?[3] Good: night, darling; I would that I were with you.

F.W Dawson

1. "De l'audace, encore de l'audace, et toujours de l'audace" (Boldness, again boldness, and ever boldness). This phrase is attributed to French statesman and revolutionary figure Georges-Jacques Danton (1759–94), who used it in a 1782 speech to the Legislative Assembly in Paris.
2. "Be bolde, Be bolde, and everywhere, Be Bold" (Edmund Spenser, *The Faerie Queene* [1596], 3.11).
3. "The Author of Middlemarch," March 7, 1873.

ఁ౦౿ఁ

Sarah's position at the News *required her to maintain a constant dialogue with Frank, and books, newspapers, and periodicals sent from Charleston began to arrive regularly at Hampton. Unaware of Sarah's career as a writer, family, friends, and neighbors began to question the propriety of her relationship with a man she declared she had no intentions of marrying. Alarmed and upset by the gossip and innuendo, Sarah asked Frank not to visit her again.*

Office of the Charleston News
Charleston, S.C., Saturday, [March 7, 1873]

My poor darling; Your letter pains me beyond expression, but I am not powerless to help you. For myself I care very little, when your Peace is at stake.

If you do not desire to see me you shall not, because what I wish is of little moment in comparison with your repose. But if you will see me, no living man & no thing shall keep me from you. Upon one point my mind is made up. You should not be exposed to this trouble again—on my account. Leave that to me. And Our God knows that I never loved you so tenderly and devotedly as at this moment, when you are enduring sorrows which I can share without, for the moment, leaving. There is a silver lining to the cloud. Your paper on Widows is the best article from an inexperienced writer which has passed through my hands. It needs no revision whatever, & will be printed on Monday as it stands. What we think of it, in a business sense, will be said by Mr. Riordan who, of his own volition, writes to you to-day. I pledge you my word, as a gentleman, that my judgement is not biased by any feeling for you, & that his judgement is as cold as though you were an aged hack of whom he had never heard. By your writing, after three months or so, you can support yourself & your mother. That is the least. And now, my precious one, have courage. There will be a crown for all these crosses. Remember that I am ever with you, ever praying for you, even if I do not see you in the body, & for Christ's sake do not think less of me or say that we must not meet again. I dare not write more now. May God help you!

F.W. Dawson.

ⵊϽℂⵒ

Sarah's editorial, "The Use and Abuse of Widows," which was published in the News *on March 10, 1873, "excited great talk" in Charleston. The piece addressed the "perplexing" question: "What can be done with widows?"—those "treacherous" women who, according to Sarah, waged "war on maidens" in a desperate attempt to snare the "most indifferent men." Sarah's unique style and hard-hitting humor heightened speculation regarding the identity of the paper's new writer. Frank was delighted by the public conjecture.*

Office of the Charleston News.

Charleston, S.C., Wednesday [March 12] 1873

[. . .] I find that your article on Widows has excited great talk here & I write to tell you so. The "Widows", new & stale, abuse it with characteristic virulence & declare that worse can be said of Widow*ers*. The men think it rare fun & like Oliver call for more.[1] Do then let your next article (for Monday week) be upon Widowers or Bachelors.[2] We must keep up the fire. And do not forget what I said about the novel.[3] However weary you may be, however lonely & desolate, the better this working with the brain will be for you. It will be a sharp tug at first, but it will bring its reward. Do not give up your writing. We rely on you. And bear in mind (especially outside of the social articles) to say no more than you have to say. Three short articles are better than two long ones. Variety is the spice of newspaper life. Can't you write something about the maiden "all for Lorne."[4]

I say naught of myself; save that I am always with you, & most when you suffer. God help us both!

F.W. Dawson

1. "Please, Sir, I want some more" (Charles Dickens, *Oliver Twist* [1838]).
2. "Bachelors and Widowers," March 22, 1873 (see chap. 4).
3. Sarah also wrote book reviews for Frank, but none appear in her scrapbook for this period.
4. Frank was referring to Princess Caroline Alberta Louise (1848–1939), a daughter of Queen Victoria (1819–1901) who created an uproar in 1871 when she wed John Douglas Sutherland Campbell (1845–1914), marquis of Lorne and later the ninth duke of Argyll. Campbell served as Canada's governor-general from 1878 to 1883. Sarah wrote a short article on the princess, "The Maiden All for Lorne," which appeared on March 19, 1873.

❧

Success did little to boost Sarah's self-confidence. Instead, she admitted that her editorial work was nothing more than a painful assault on her gentility. Frank replied with words of encouragement and practical suggestions on the art of newspaper writing.

Charleston:

Sunday Night March 16/73

I am now about to answer your "line"; as a few hours ago I said that I would do.

I know too well how much it pains you to write anything for any eye to see, and I would not press you to continue, only that what you have already done proves that you can do every thing, and more, that I predicted of you. You have exceptional advantages, in the inviolable secrecy which will be maintained about your writings, until you shall desire it to be known. You are, unhappily, in a condition in which it is necessary for you to exert to the utmost the talent which God has given you. It is in your power to help your poor friend by giving him more time for other matters of pith & moment. Above all, while exercising healthfully your mind, you are making yourself ready to place your seal upon the face of the time & do good to your people. With these considerations before you, you cannot doubt what your duty is. As you nobly say, you owe it to yourself "to strive to succeed", & the striving will assuredly bring you a fruitful success. You have made a better beginning, and more progress in a short time, than any writer that I know. As you can see, your articles need barely any changing, & less and less as each succeeds the other. You must go on. But it is best for you to find yourself up for the work. It is not pleasant to read for business, instead of for amusement, but you must keep yourself acquainted with the condition and progress of every matter of public consequence. This you can do by the papers I send and by the Columbia & Charleston papers. Watch them & seize upon anything that strikes you. For example, you have written upon Louisiana and upon Spain & upon "Killing no Murder."[1] Watch events in Louisiana & Spain & send your comments whenever there is an important change in the situation. Likewise as to the murder business. You will gradually, in this way, accumulate subjects with which you are familiar, and will have no trouble in giving your two general articles (as well as the Saturday) a week. Whenever I see a good point to be made I will tell you; but hunt up as many as you can for yourself. One suggestion I will make: Be chary of speaking, in your general articles, of the Deity. Newspaper readers are accustomed to see newspapers treat the topics of the day from the material rather than the moral stand: point. Uphold the moral right & denounce the moral wrong; avoiding as far as practicable any personal reference to God. Let us strive to keep His name Holy. And do not fear to be short, as I have said before. Your article on Lorne is excellent (though not as good as the Murder article) but the report about Louise seems to be untrue & I must adapt it to the new deal.[2] There is much anxiety here to know who is writing the social articles; they are doing The News good. Persons now read our editorials who never read them before. Will you, then, desert your friends?

I am very, very glad that you will stay at Hampton for the present & I hope that you will carry out your plans of going to Clermont.[3] Will I visit you there? Indeed, I will; gladly, there or anywhere. Some time next month, please God, I shall certainly see you, & if you have changed quarters before then you must tell me how to get to your new resting place. It grieves me sadly to hear that you are physically no better. I hope, so hard, that you will improve now that the worst is over, & that your mind will be occupied with your work. Do not fail to tell me what progress you make in improving your strength. Go out every day, if you can, for a few minutes, & I know very well which way I would have you walk. Have courage! There is work for you to do. And to do it worthily you need your full bodily force. Rest assured that I will endeavor not to make your burden heavier to bear.

About myself I hardly know what to say. I came down to Charleston resolved to root out my love for you, or so diminish it that I might think of you, and speak to you, only as a dear friend. I have well: nigh broken my heart in the endeavor, & love you more passionately & devotedly than ever before. You cannot know what it costs me to write to you coldly as I do when my whole being is melted in tenderness, & every tender & endearing word that the soul of man has conceived is trembling on my lips. And I cannot help praying Our Father that I may continue to love you more and more, for without my love for you I should soon become a hissing and reproach[4] to whomsoever cares for me. I know this even better now than when I parted from you. Do not, however, mistake me. My every promise to you has been more than kept. There has been no backsliding. Why? Because, of my love for you. I do not say this to attach any responsibility to you. Reject my love as often as you will, you cannot make me cease to love you. Do not wish that you could. When you succeeded in that I should already have taken the first step on the broad road which leads to destruction. I am writing just as I would talk to you. Bear with me! I am brave enough, I know, when there is no cloud between us, & patient enough when there is anything to do for you. There, deal with me gently.

Hitherto (since I left you) you have sent me bare scraps of letters. Answer this one freely & frankly. I will then, if you bid me, try to go back to business letters to you & say nothing of myself.

Give my love to your Mother & to Jemmie & his wife. Good: night & may God bless you.

F. W. Dawson.

1. "Killing No Murder," March 17, 1873, reported on the murder of an elite girl by a jilted admirer. Sarah used the murder to denounce the southern code of honor. "The justification of murder is the popular creed that men hold in their own hands the redress of all their imaginary or actual injuries," she wrote. "'Honor' asserts that the Creator, who has proclaimed that vengeance belongs to Him, and that He will repay, is too tardy in fulfilling His promises to satisfy arrogant, spirited man. What marvel is it then that the boy, who hopes soon to claim a place in the exalted order of mature men, should be eager to attest his fitness for promo-

tion by displaying an utter disregard for other's lives, and a jealous solicitude to secure, at any price, his own selfish aims?" Sarah became a critic of dueling after her brother, Henry, died in a duel in New Orleans in 1861 (S. M. Dawson, *Sarah Morgan*, 5–11).

2. In "The Maiden All for Lorne," Sarah reported on the news that the "Marquis of Lorne and the Princess Louise had separated on the convenient plea of 'improbability of temper.'" Frank revised the article by adding that the story was "probably false."

3. Clermont was a plantation located on Granny's Quarter Creek in Kershaw County, South Carolina. It was built by Colonel Henry Rugeley (fl. 1775), one of the leading Tories in South Carolina, and around 1820 was purchased by Daniel Louis DeSaussure (1796–1857), who lived there with his family until 1846, when they moved to Camden. Civil War diarist Mary Chesnut (1823–86) commented that Eliza G. DeSaussure Burroughs was living in "the old DeSaussure house" in the 1860s, but it is unclear if she was occupying the home in 1873 (*Mary Chesnut's Civil War*, 389).

4. "And I will persecute them with the sword, with the famine, and with the pestilence, and will deliver them to be removed to all the kingdoms of the earth, to be a curse, and an astonishment, and a hissing, and a reproach, among all the nations whither I have driven them" (Jeremiah 29:18).

Charleston March 18. 1873

Your letter of the 17th which reached me this morning was particularly welcome, because it indicates that you are acquiring confidence in yourself, & no longer think of marching from the field of literature before the fight has fairly begun. Most of what I had to say upon this subject was contained in my letter of Sunday night. You will always have my advice & criticism, whatever they may be worth, but some of the verbal changes which I would suggest to be made, & do make, in your articles cannot be explained in writing. If you will be good enough to read the articles as they are printed, you will see what I mean. Do not allow your favorite Carlyle[1] to lead you into an involved style: Keep to a stern simplicity. Southey's Life of Nelson,[2] by the way, is about the purest English that I know. In your Saturday articles & all articles upon like topics, however, let yourself run riot, & do not use the curb. I have no idea of abandoning you to your own devices, & will give the themes which I come across for you, but I want to teach you to walk alone, not to keep you in leading: strings, & therefore urge you to watch for & take up anything that will make an effective article or paragraph. The short bit about Widows[3] to-day is good; so is the Sisters in Law,[4] but some of my ideas about marriage, as you know, differ from yours, & would it be right for me to give advice which I do not heed myself? I may cut out one or two sentences for that reason. Strike out boldly & you will soon learn to swim. Indeed, I have the sad conviction that you will soon be able to do without my help.

I enclose something about Japan; about female clerks, (their increase in numbers is one good point in the Federal administration); about the woman who wanted to hang for Foster;[5] also an article which might suggest a Saturday essay on chronic Growlers or Grumblers. You had better get up something on France; that will be another string to your bow. I gave your message to Riordan who was amused, & is evidently convinced that he does get the worth of his money. No receipt (formal, I mean) is needed, as the little sum is regularly charged to Mr. Fowler[6] (or any other *man?*) on our books. Let me know, however, that the remittances reach you.

What a pleasure your Mother's pleasure must have been to you. That is something worth living for, & I dont know anywhere a little woman who can please as many persons as you can. Halte La [Stop There]! Do not allow the magnitude of your income to lead you into extravagance. I suppose that you will soon take an interest in the price of diamonds and the current quotations of Point d'Alencon.[7]

I sent you to-day, by Express, a Paris Guide book (the one I brought from England) with a map of the City; also Bagehot's Physics & Politics which, I think, you will like; also, my pet Lamb's old English dramatists, which you must read at leisure & tell me about; also, Bread & Cheese & Kisses; also, the Constitution of our fathers & some other patriotic pabulum which you are expected to digest.[8] I sent you, besides, copies of all your published articles. You had better keep them. If you have any objection to this, Ask your Mamma.

I am glad that Col Dupré[9] is going to Europe; & do not object to the baby, if it will be as accommodating as that good little Howell is, & will not interrupt your work.

Do not think that I am tending towards extravagance or more extravagance, because I sent you some stamped envelopes. Yesterday I resigned from the Hibernian Society, & as the anniversaries come round I propose to do the same thing with other societies to which I belong.[10] In truth, I am growing more into myself, & shutting *me* up closer, every day, & the only real pleasure I have now is writing to you, & receiving letters from you! This brings me to myself again; a highly unpleasant subject. I do not know that I can add anything to what I said on Sunday night. Certainly, I could not, even in jest, blame you for anything. I do not conceal my one great trouble from you. It is as well known to you as to me. I suppose my old hopefulness will come back, one of these days; how soon does not depend on me.

Now, for savage criticism! You say "If your guide book &c I *would* like to borrow it." Should not the *would* be *should*? To me it is as wrong to say "If you come &c to:morrow, I *will* have ten cents," when you mean "shall" have; the idea being of time, not of volition.

I was introduced to: day to Mr. Ervington Hume. He is very much of a Britisher, but seems to be a very pleasant fellow, with a penchant for meridional ale (or be: ah) & oysters. I have a bad head: ache & must bid you a sweet Good: Night. Give my love to your Mother, & thank her for her message.

F.W.Dawson:

1. Thomas Carlyle (1795–1881), a British historian and essayist.
2. Robert Southey, *The Life of Nelson* (1813).
3. "The Economic Aspect of Widows," March 19, 1873 (see chap. 3).
4. "Marrying a Deceased Wife's Sister," March 21, 1873.
5. "Liberty of Conscience in Japan," April 4, 1873, which reported on "the special edict ordering the toleration of Christianity throughout Japan; "Work for Women," April 15, 1873 (see chap. 3); "Remember!" March 26, 1873, which reported that a woman had offered to hang in place of William Foster, who had been convicted of murdering Avery Putnam in New York in April 1871.
6. Mr. Fowler (Sarah's mother's maiden name) was the name that appeared on Sarah's paychecks.
7. A delicate needlepoint lace often referred to as the queen of laces.
8. Walter Bagehot, *Physics and Politics* (1872); Charles Lamb, *Specimens of English Dramatic Poets* (1808); Benjamin Leopold Farjeon, *Bread and Cheese and Kisses* (1873).
9. Sarah's brother-in-law, Alcée Louis Dupré, who married Miriam Morgan (1840–98) in 1866. The couple had two children, Frank Ramsey (b. 1869), who died in infancy, and Lucile (1870–1921), who became an acclaimed violinist. Sarah never approved of her sister's marriage. On June 2, 1866, she wrote, "What I have suffered since Miriam pledged herself to this, is indescribable. I promised Sister and Jimmy to be silent as to my opposition" (Sarah Morgan diary, vol. 5, Dawson Papers). According to James I. Robertson Jr.'s Civil War centennial edition of *A Confederate Girl's Diary*, "Dupré became a brilliant but inebriate Memphis newspaper editor. Because of his over-fondness for drink, Miriam left him through legal separation and rejoined the family in South Carolina" (S. M. Dawson, *A Confederate Girl's Diary*, 466, 313).
10. The Hibernian Society, an Irish benevolent organization established in Charleston in 1801. The society built a hall on Meeting Street in 1840. Frank and Riordan joined the Society on March 19, 1868.

In January, Frank mentioned to Sarah the forthcoming sale of the Charleston Courier. *After lengthy consultations with business interests in New York and South Carolina, Riordan, Dawson, and Company decided to purchase the newspaper and to consolidate the two papers. The* News *and the* Courier *had always been rivals, and upon discovering the identity of the purchasers, the estates of William S. King, Aaron S. Willington, and Richard Yeadon, which owned the* Courier, *did everything in their power to block the sale. At Hampton, James Morgan continued to interrogate Sarah about the nature of her relationship with Frank.*

Charleston April 1. 1873

Bien aimée [Much beloved]:

I am awfully busy to-night & have now to see our lawyer again, and give final instructions to the broker who is to try to spend $10.000 for us to: morrow, but I cannot forgo the pleasure of sending you a few words to "the care of Suber"[1] although my programme was to begin only on Thursday. Remember that every Tuesday, Thursday & Saturday evening at 5. oclock there should be something for you at the Pump.

I beg that you will let me write to Jemmie to define my position & yours. We understand each other thoroughly (you & I, I mean) but I may have led your brother, by my careless conduct, to think that I had been, or am, in some way misled by you. He desires this marriage; & I am sure he will be willing to let me manage my affairs my own way, &, in any case, to hold you blameless. I do think that your dear Mother loves me well enough to be unnecessarily severe to both you & me. I had thought that what I said to her about you would, for once & for all, save you from any misapprehension of your words & motives; & as our "business relations!" compel me to write to you often, & you to write to me, there ought not to be any looming difficulty to make our work the harder. Let us drift with the tide, Chère Amie [Dear Friend]! But do let me write to Jemmie: I will even send you a copy of the letter.

I had a singular chance of picking up your $100 City stock to-day & bought it at once. I will send you a memo of the purchase as soon as the certificate is delivered to me.

I have arranged for the exchange of your Middlemarch, and hope to send you the Shakespeare to H & G[2] to-morrow or the next day.

Your article on Married Women's property was all right. More!!! I enclose copies of "April Fool" & of "Young Couples."[3] Remember, next Saturday—thou slave of the Pen! Paragraph marked A. may suggest something. And do read Susan Dickinson's letter[4] & write something about it. You are not like the women she lectures & you can be as much as her exemplars. Darling! I can do nothing for you unless you continue to help yourself. It must be by your own force & power that you will. I can only give the opportunity, & show where the first blows may most effectively be struck. And remember that *I* know that you can succeed if you *will*. Deserve, then, what I think of you. Do not make yourself ill by doubting yourself, or fearing for me. I have firm faith that our knowledge of each other is for the good of both of us—that it is in the Providence of God! Sweet! I must, though I hate it, bid you good: bye: I shall send you a letter though, by the day train of Thursday. My every thought is with you, & most when you are sad, & need sympathy & help.

Yours always
F.W. Dawson

1. Mr. Suber delivered the mail from the train to the Pump at Hampton.
2. Hope and Gyles, well-known Columbia grocers.
3. "The Property of Married Women," April 2, 1873 (see chap. 3); "April Fool," April 1, 1873, was a satirical piece on the practice of "April fooling" that drew on current affairs; "Young Couples," March 29, 1873 (see chap. 4).
4. Susan Dickinson (1832–1915), a writer and activist for woman's suffrage, wildlife protection, child labor laws, and the improvement of teachers' salaries and working conditions. She published numerous articles in newspapers in Philadelphia and New York. The letter to which Frank refers was not published in the *News*.

Charleston:
April 2, p.m. [1873]

My darling:

Your letter of Tuesday night (just received) is as welcome as flowers in Spring; not only for its assurance that you are still working, which is in itself an earnest of victory, but, also, because of the articles which you enclose. These will serve us well for Friday morning, & will relieve me to-morrow, when the sale of the Courier comes off. À propos, I think there is seriously a chance of our getting that paper, at our price. If so, I pray you do your best to make the "News & Courier" even better than it now is. Do not allow your poor little head to ache so, for then mine aches, & my heart too in sympathy. You have a hard task to fulfill, & my lot is not the easiest in the World; but we can manage to drag through both, if our kind friends will not insist on making us miserable. It is the old story of South & North again. We ask to be let alone, don't we? [. . .]

As only letters on Tues Thsday & Saturday will go to the Pump, & lest any may miscarry please say, whenever you write, what letters of mine you have received since the previous writing. I will do the same.

I am very glad that you like Hume; provided that you dont like him too much, & do please warn your Mother against these Englishmen! They are so persevering.

I am "doing well", chère amie [dear friend]!, as you hope, if it be doing well to do my duty as best I can, and as cheerfully, & thinking of you the while. I have given up smoking in business hours, &, needles being absent so long, feel as fresh as a daisy.

One word my sweet! Mr. Riordan is praising you so desperately that I am growing jealous. Now, he says that you are a woman of "mind." Did he mean mine? He asked how I stood with you. I told him "just the same; only less so." After twelve hours cogitation he told me that what I said on that subject was "conspicuously inexact." which is newspaper English for all L.M: ly:

What mean you by subscribing yourself only my "friend" instead of my "friend ever"? Is it Hume, or humour?

My sweet! I am very much pressed for time; will write you again by Saturday's train—if not before to H & G. Say, that you understand the directions.

Au revoir, then bien aimée [much beloved], & believe in my love for you now & always.

F.W.Dawson

Charleston:
April 3 [1873]
4.p.m

My darling; we have bought that paper for 7.100; $3000 less than I was ready to pay. I am overwhelmed with care. Would to God! that you could be with me. Pray for me! Believe in me! Help me! I have the most serious work that man in this State ever has had. And through it all I feel that my love for you is the one thing that animates me to do more than my duty. I telegraphed to Jem at once (for you) & I hope you will all wish us to succeed. It would take an hour to explain the whole.

Toujours à toi [Always yours]
F.W. Dawson

[. . .] Later!

Dearest! I have just come from my lawyers. The owners of the Courier, anxious to break the sale, object to all the security we offer for unpaid parts. I am now off to make arrangements to pay whole in cash. My blood is up; & they cant whip me. Do your best for me. I rely on you more than ever & Riordan! admits that without you I am a gone somebody.

Always yours

FW Dawson

The certificate for the stock will be ready on Monday.

Charleston[1]

Sunday [April 5, 1873]

My darling: You must do all you can, in every way, for me now. I have a fearful load to carry: with two newspapers on my hands. The most sagacious men here say that we have a fortune, & a grand opportunity, but I feel that it may kill me in the doing of it, and I am not ready for the honors of martyrdom. I will try to write you more fully to: morrow. It must suffice now to say that your Mothers-In-Law[2] is the best article you have given us. Riordan nearly exploded. Good: night, my sweet love! & au revoir. But when shall I see you, now?

1. This letter was written on mourning stationery.
2. In "Mothers-in-Law," which appeared on April 7, 1873, Sarah questioned the "prejudice" against mothers-in-law. "These dragons are not implacable," she wrote. "The prudent man can extract their claws, pare their fangs, and convert them into good beasts of burden for family use."

✧✧✧

The News and Courier *made its debut on April 7, 1873. The proprietors declared that it was their "single aim to give to Charleston and South Carolina a newspaper which shall be the vigilant and untiring guardian of the rights and interests of the people." Sarah's editorial, "Mothers-in-Law," featured on page 2. As the first week's editions rolled off the presses, Frank wrote to Sarah, at last providing her with a full description of the events culminating in the purchase of the* Courier.

Charleston, April 9 [1873] 1.a.m[1]

I have just come home, & I want to talk to you in the old frank way. May I? At least I am unconscious that I have done you any wrong, & if it did pain me acutely that no letter came from you to-night. I do not blame you; & if any thing comes to-morrow to show that you have causelessly deserted me, still I shall not blame you. Well! about this Courier. I had two ideas: one was that it would enable me to make more money; the other was that it would give me more power of doing good & that with your aid I could meet the responsibility worthily. Of course the money part is put first because a certain "gentile donna" [kind woman] insists that she must have two thousand a year, & because there is for me, without her, nor money nor fame. Instantly upon the purchase being made I telegraphed to Jemmie that he might tell you. The next morning I set to work to put my house in order & was overwhelmed by finding that the sellers refused to take, as security for the two thirds of $7.100 to be paid in cash, anything I could give. That friday evening after telegraphing to New York I took a carriage & raced about town for hours from banker to lawyer. Very late, being worn out with fatigue and excitement, I thought I saw my way clear. Not much sleep that night. On Saturday I made new propositions, to be also rejected; more running about. No sleep that night. On Sunday a gleam of light—a few words from you who were still in ignorance of the momentous event. Little sleep, though. On Monday I proposed to pay all $7.100 in cash if they would allow me the interest. Again refusal. Today, however, they have consented to take first mortgage bonds of the S.C. RR as security.[2] These are bought & all ought to be settled in a day or two. Through the five days, besides the anxiety as to money, the pressure of treble work, the preparation of two papers, the multitudinous rearrangements. Only thinking of you kept me up, & yet no word from you, & no help in the way of writing. Par paranthèse [by way of parenthesis] Riordan insisted late at night on holding over the Mothers-in-Law because he wanted the best possible paper on Monday. There is the story. Is it told to inattentive ears? That cannot be. Yet, & I blush to confess it, I have the most absurd ideas about Mr. Hume. I should fear to tell them; they seem so ridiculous; yet they haunt me. [letter incomplete]

Wednesday: 8.a.m.

I arise from dreams of thee—all night dreams, & as sweet & reassuring as could be. An hour or so should prove them true.

Two hours later!

You see that they did come true, my sweet good friend! Thanks for your good words. I will do more mieux [better]! but do try to keep up your spirits.

If you doubt yourself & your power you make me doubt myself. You say that I shall not fail in any but one thing. As to the News & Courier do not expect too much. A strong man can carry 100 or 200 lbs, but can he carry 500? That is what I feel. The work I do may break me down; unless I occasionally have a talk with you as I will. Let me & I will see you for a few hours by May 1st or so. I have no more subjects, except the book. Notice it, & that will count as one article. Dont forget Easter & that Spain & France & England are neglected, besides Louisiana. Your paper work improves steadily. Can you suggest any better way of sending my letters? You seem so long in receiving them when they go to Columbia! I send you to-day the Shakespeare; also the stock certificate, which cannot be sold or transferred without your signature. As to Cecily! I did not mind it, because I knew that you would not have asked me to print something intended as your private moaning.[3] But why have you so changed! Your Saturday's letter was bright as bright could be.

Your sewing machine is all right.[4] Sleep might have been better for you, but the article is better for News & Courier.

I can get you Valentine's Beef[5] at $9 a dozen or $4.50 the half dozen. Will you not take some at that price for *yourself* as well as your Mother? That would strengthen you, & you must, for my salvation if not for your comfort, bear up & be strong.

I enclose a statement of your a/c by which you will see that you owe me twenty five cents & Mr. R will send his usual remittance to-day. May God the Holy Ghost be always with you, best & most devoted of friends! I think I shall write to the Pump nearly every day.

You ever think of your poor servant, & praying that, if what I fear comes true, I may die soon & die in blessing you; wondering whether your letters have miscarried & how many loving letters of mine may lie at H & G for you; wondering all the things which are poisoned whips to scourge us, when those we love do what we do not understand. My good angel, such you are, I have made my heart ache less by talking with you, & if any note from you, or no note, to-morrow bid me put this in the waste basket it will only be one more of the prayers to you which you have never heard. Good: Night. Beloved!

1. In the top left-hand corner of the letter, Frank noted, "I have sent the city-stock to you care of H & G Columbia."
2. Frank was personally and professionally associated with the South Carolina Railroad. Frank's father-in-law, Eugene Fourgeaud, sixty-one, was the Charleston agent for the company, while its president, William Joy Magrath (1817–1902), helped to finance the purchase of the *Courier*.

3. There is no surviving record of this editorial or what it contained. Sarah may have based a piece on a poem, "Cecily," that is contained within her personal scrapbook (Sarah Morgan Dawson Scrapbook, 1853–82, Dawson Papers).
4. "Stitch! Stitch! Stitch!" which appeared on April 10, 1873, examined the plight of women forced to earn a living by sewing (see chap. 9).
5. Valentine's Meat Juice, a popular general tonic, with each bottle containing the juice of four pounds of beef.

Sarah continued to doubt her competency as a writer. Frank's encourage-ment did little allay her fears, and he finally resorted to a "scolding" in an attempt to convince his "fair contributor" to persist in her work "so well begun."

Charleston
April 10. [1873]

Frank Trenholm[1] tells me that he is going to Hampton to-night & I shall ask him to take this to you.

Do not brothers usually scold their sisters? I shall play brother for the nonce and scold you well!

Are the articles which you write intended to please you or please us; & do you or we know best what we want? There is the law & the profits. You give us just the stuff we like; it pays us to take it & we do not mean to allow our fair contributor to escape us because she is not in love with herself. It is not necessary that you should have any opinions as to the value of what you do. It is only needful to have opinions upon the subjects of which you write. Make up your mind what you will say & say it, leaving the rest to us, or to me, if you prefer to phrase it so. And from what you tell me I do not think you take time enough for your work. What business have you to be running a race with the train? You have to write one article every two days; why then should you give yourself only ten minutes for each article?

You have a great work before you; why faint? "*Girl!* there is no such word as fail."[2] And if you coin it for yourself, you do it likewise for me. Read these noble words of George Eliot

It is a vain thought to flee from the work that God appoints us, for the sake of finding a greater blessing to our own souls, as if we could choose for ourselves where we shall find the fulness of the Divine Presence, instead of seeking it where alone it is to be found in loving obedience.[3]

Will you flee, or do you doubt, the genuineness of the appointment? Look over your life, &, if you can see any time when you have had a better opportunity of helping self & neighbor, you may doubt—not before.

Do not give way to feelings of depression: these largely come, believe me, from your low state of health. Exercise & Valentine would soon set you up. I think too you need some of my cheering, & I will give it to you as soon as I can. I have done scolding:

For me! I am most worn out & no present hope of relief. As to business—we have gained 600 subscribers in Charleston this week.

Write to me as often as you can; & believe always that I will try to be what you wish me to be so long as you have any desire in the matter. I hope my important package reached you safely.

À.Dieu!

Mr. Hume has been in & has returned the Bastiat.[4] He says he enjoyed himself immensely, but feels "beastly."

1. Francis Holmes Trenholm (1846–85), son of Anna and George A. Trenholm. In 1865, Francis married Mary Elizabeth Burroughs, the sister of James Morgan's wife, Gabriella.
2. "In the lexicon of youth, which fate reserves / For a bright manhood, there is no such word / As 'fail'" (Edward George Earle Bulwer-Lytton, *Richelieu* [1839], 3.1).
3. George Eliot, *Adam Bede* (1859). Frank had clipped this excerpt from a published piece.
4. Frédéric Bastiat (1801–50), a French journalist and economist. The volume was probably *Sophisms of the Protective Policy*, trans. Louisa S. McCord (1848).

⚜

Bowed by mental and physical lethargy, Sarah persisted with her "writing endeavors." At Frank's request, she penned "Easter Devotions," an examination of the southern woman's preoccupation with Easter Sunday attire that appeared in the News and Courier *on April 12, 1873. In the following letter, Frank described the public's reaction to Sarah's take on fashionable society.*

Monday April 14. [1873]

Somehow I missed your letter of friday at the Post Office last night and only received it this morning.

I hasten to give you some good news. Col Andrews,[1] one of the literati, a man of fine taste came into the office on Saturday & said: "I like the article on Easter. I call that true journalism; instructing & elevating the people, in a good: natured way to which none can object. It will be talked about, Sir! I shall talk about it.'" And he talks as much as any six old women. Upon me the article had a marked effect—the solemn cadence of the closing passages thrilled my very soul & thanks to it Easter day did seem to me a day of Rising: it was the purest worthiest most spiritual day I have had since I last looked upon your sweet pure face. So you see you do good to the individual one as well as to The News & the public. This morning I rode down with Col Trenholm who said: "Captain that was a very nice article on Easter; a very nice article." Do you doubt any longer? I hold it to be established now, beyond peradventure, that you have accomplished the first step; you have proved yourself able, with very little aid from me, to write worthily, by which I mean in a manner worthy of your own talent & the standing of the paper. You will not have me with you very long, maybe, & you must strive now to make the next step—to write so as to need no revision. And the next step will be to write so that any paper in the country will be glad to have your articles. I believe that you can do this in a year, & I say it sadly. The old bird who teaches her young ones to use their feeble wings knows, if she knows anything, that the first use made of them by birdie will be to fly away from her. So it will be with me & thee. I am teaching you to do without me, although I know that, without you, the brain & energy I have will count for nothing.

As your writing is no longer an experiment (witness your brother's own words) I think Jemmie should know what you are doing. It was concealed from him, by my advice, because I would not expose him or you to the possibility of failure, but you have won & I beg of you to let me tell him in my own way when I see him. I can do it so that he will be more proud than ever of you, & if you wish nothing need be said about the $. And telling him will explain why you write to me so often. Now, perhaps, he blames you for it; & I do not wish you to be blamed for anything.

There was no commission on the stock. One of my clerks was selling some & he let me have $100 at the price at which he sold the rest. You & he so saved commission.

I thank you for your counsel about the Courier. We must put our heads together. I want to talk with you; indeed, I am consuming vital force so fast that, coute qu'il coute [whatever the cost] I must have just such rest as you only can give me. I think that I shall leave Charleston for Hampton on either

Thursday night or Friday night & be at Hampton on Friday or Saturday morning. In my letter of Thursday I will tell you positively. You will not ask me to go, & I must go without asking.

I am very proud of you ma bien aimée [my much beloved]: and I am a good boy.

Yours always
F.W.Dawson

Monday Night:

I have just received a sweet note from Sister Miriam which has brought the tears to my eyes & smiles to my lips. How much I had to thank you for; & now how much more!

Good: bye:

1. Colonel Augustus O. Andrews, fifty-four, a commission merchant at Boyce's (North) Wharf in Charleston.

Charleston
Wednesday Eveg April 15 [April 16, 1873]

I wanted to have sent you by this Mail a full account of my plans about the Courier, in order that you might compare notes with me; but I find that it will require more time than I can give to it to-day & must satisfy myself with other things. I enclose two articles which you can work up in any way that to you serves best. One is a purely political article. Write it plainly & practically. You have not touched politics yet, & I should like to see you armed at every point. The Centennial article[1] explains itself.

As to your work: there is little help I can give you and unless (as at Clermont that happy day) I have some text upon which to comment. Generally speaking I think that you are too apt to make general rules for the treatment of particular cases. You will say that *all* do this or that, where it is only the few or the many, as the case may be. Please bear this in mind; remembering that the world is neither *all* good nor *all* bad. For the rest, the rule is simple: Fix your objective point in the mind & get to it by the shortest road. Your Spanish article,[2] for example, was well & logically developed. As, however, you began by speaking of "Natural Selection" it might have been well to point out, in a word, that the success of Alfonso[3] would be the "Survival of the fittest",[4] which I should call a tying of head & tail together; a keeping up of the connection. If I were talking with you I could explain these things better. Remember, also, what Swift said to the young author: "Whenever you have written anything you think particularly fine, strike it out."[5] That is a harsh rule, which will never hurt you, in as much as you never think that anything you write is particularly fine.

I will send you, so as to arrive at the Pump on Saturday morning, or Saturday evening, (most likely the former) some straw: berries which a friend of mine, a market: gardener (not the one who eloped with Dick [Suwitler's?] sweetheart) has promised me. Enjoy them, all of you. You had better send to the Pump for them on Saturday morning, so as to be on the safe side. [. . .]

1. "Wiping Out Old Scores," April 28, 1873, reported on the nation's upcoming centennial celebrations and the role of sectionalism in the festivities (see chap. 9).
2. "The Fight for the Crown," April 16, 1873, speculated on the future of the Spanish republic.
3. Alfonso XII (1857–85), who went into exile after the revolt of the Carlists in 1868 and returned to become king of Spain in 1874.
4. In this article, Sarah drew on the theories of Charles Darwin (1809–82), an English naturalist who devised a theory of evolution commonly known as Darwinism. In *Origin of the Species* (1859), he argued the theory of "natural selection" or "survival of the fittest," contending that the most favorable variations in the reproduction of a species were transmitted to aid in the struggle for survival. Social Darwinists applied this theory to humans.
5. This quotation comes from Samuel Johnson (1709–84) rather than Jonathan Swift (James Boswell, *Life of Samuel Johnson* [1791], April 30, 1773).

Frank made his proposed visit to Hampton. Upon his return, he received a despondent letter from Sarah. After consultations with her sister-in-law, Lydia Carter Morgan Purnell, the decision had been made to send Howell to boarding school at the Home and School of the Holy Communion Institute, an Episcopalian academy in Charleston run by the Reverend Anthony Toomer Porter. Sarah had taken Howell to South Carolina with plans to educate and adopt him, and her editorial work now provided the funds to make this objective a reality. Howell's impending departure nevertheless made her miserable. "I need not tell you that I have decided this matter entirely from the point of view which represented the child's interest," Sarah wrote to Lydia. "At first, it seemed monstrous and impossible. Now, I know that it is best for him. There is no possibility of exaggerating the advantage that is to be derived from Mr. Porter's school. If Howell shows the same good qualities he possesses in my estimation, not only his education, but his fu-

*ture career will be far better than any prospect ever held out to his family."[1]
In the following letter, Frank assured Sarah that she had made the right decision and attempted to allay her fears by offering to act as a father figure
to ten-year-old Howell.*

*In contrast to her home life, Sarah's career went from strength to
strength. Her provocative editorial style prompted a number of Charleston
writers to pen articles of similar style and content. Poet George Herbert
Sass, a regular contributor to the* News and Courier, *tried his hand at a
piece titled "Flirtation," which appeared in the* News and Courier *on
April 19, 1873. Sarah was bemused by the article and responded with an
April 25 rebuff, "'Flirtation': A Lecture to Flirts and an Incidental Indictment on the Courier for Coquetting," in which she dismissed Sass's approval
of such "innocent" behavior, declaring that "flirtation is as innocent—as
murder." "Flirting robs the heart of freshness," she added, "youth of bloom,
the person of dignity, and the character of its integrity." She signed the piece
"Fossil Remains."*

No5.

Charleston

April 24 [1873]

My poor darling:

I grieve so much that this new trouble about Howell should have come upon
you, but, believe me, when the first wrench is over, it will be better for him
and for you. On the one hand he will be putting himself in a position that will
enable him, when we elders are dead, to support himself. You, without him,
will be able to do more towards supplying his little needs until he can take
care of himself. As you now are, each, my sweetest, stands in the way of the
other. Neither will lose the love for the other; & you know that Howell will
have me to talk with & advise with, as a sort of big brother, whenever he has
holiday. It is for the best, darling. But think of this! You cannot do what you
wish to do for Howell, unless you increase your bodily strength. In refusing
to eat, & to take the Valentine, which would give you new life, are you not
sinning against him, as well as against yourself? What you will not do for
me, will you not do for your Mother (I nearly called her "Mother" without
the pronoun) & for Howell? I leave it to your conscience, not your inclination! You ask me whether I am not tired of these frequent letters. I live in
you; in seeing you & hearing of you. That is the answer. And I will not quar-

rel with you, my love, for you need more than ever all the tender consideration I can show you. Would to Heaven we were engaged: it would be a happy thing for both of us. You shall not be "crushed out"; unless by your own hand. I am strong enough for two.

As to the articles: the reply to "Flirtation," & the "Young America"[2] are as bright & fresh as this summer weather, and as true as your dear self. I struck out one sentence from the reply, lest it might betray you. The Euthanasia[3] I will keep until I see you, which shall be within two weeks! As I know you will be busy I shall resign myself to no letter for some days, but do write soon. I shall write every day. Make some temporary arrangement for procuring my letters after Howell's departure. I can fix it with Mr. Suber as soon as I can get up. I hope the cake arrived safe; for it ought to be some consolation to you to know that there is one somebody always thinking of you, & praying for you.

So much, I have written immediately on the receipt of your letter. I may write a few words more this evening.

·   ·   ·

Such fun! Herbert Sass[4] has been here & we have told him that he is to be scarified in the evening paper. He is crazy to know who the writer is, & says there is no one here except James Lowndes[5] & the "professionals" who can write anything. Your secret is safe. Sass is made to believe that we dont know much about it ourselves, & that the work is done by a man who is trying to write like a woman. He does not know that the Saturday articles are by the same hand.

For your next Saturday article, give us "Social Bores"[6] unless you have something on the sticks, & do let me have it by to-night week. I must halt again.

·   ·   ·

Thursday night
I have had to: night what seems to me a happy thought. There is no need of hurrying Howell's departure for a few days, it being determined he shall go, & some one ought to come down with him. If you say so: I will be at Hampton on Saturday week May 3 and when I come down on the next day will deliver Howell (right side up with care) to whomever you say. This seems to me a splendid arrangement for all of us. Send me your determination about it.

I send you some papers with a N.Y. Times which may give you some subjects.

I fairly broke down about 3 oclock Wednesday morning. When I tried with my head to write one thing my hand wrote another. It was more funny than pleasant. Be brave, darling, & confident! If you are not as good a boy as I, it is because you will not take that Valentine for me, while I do anything for you. Good: bye, sweetest!

1. Sarah Morgan to Lydia Carter Morgan Purnell, April 28, 1873, Dawson Papers.
2. "Very Young America," May 10, 1873, examined American parenting practices (see chap. 4).
3. "Euthanasia," May 22, 1873.
4. George Herbert Sass (1845–1908), a writer and poet who published under the pseudonym Barton Gray.
5. James Lowndes (b. 1835), a Charleston lawyer.
6. "Bores," May 17, 1873.

Friday [April 25, 1873]

Your article on "Young America" was given to the printers this morning for to-morrow's paper, when Mr. Sass came in with his reply to your letter.[1] I told him I would print it on Monday, but he pleaded so hard that I finally consented to insert it tomorrow as a Saturday article. One reason was that you will be so busy with Howell as to need as much leisure as I can give you. So, next Saturday is provided for, unless you write something about Social Bores so superlatively good that I shall not hold it over. I enclose a proof of Ss article. I told him it was only a lame apology, but it is very well, & kindly, done. He can't make out where the letter came from; nor will he.

I have bought almost $2000 of presses and type this morning. Your head is so clear that I heartily wish I could talk over these complicated money matters with you. When can I?

The fault of your article on Euthanasia was not "over righteousness" per se. It was the lugging of theology into a question which can be argued upon practical grounds and upon the grounds of general morality which includes every religion. Be as moral in writing as you are in fact! It is not needful to support your position by texts. Let the propositions speak for themselves.

You ask me if I am not weary of your communications. Might I not more reasonably ask if you are tired of mine. In that I love you, there is reason why *I* should dwell with infinite pleasure upon every word that falls from your lips or comes from your pen. You tell me that you do not love me, & why should you care to read these rambling screeds of mine? But you can do good, and so can I; & most when together. Let then nothing come between us.

It pains me, dearest, to hear you say that you distrust yourself. Why should you? Have you not had encouragement enough? Remember this, however. You can not continue to improve in your work unless you purge out every morbid feeling. Can you expect to win, if you believe yourself predestined to defeat? My sweet love! you add so much to your difficulties, by encouraging gloomy thought. And, one of these days, I shall really give you a good scolding, which would be, as you know, a very serious matter! I hope you will take my advice about Howell. But do what you think best. At all events let me know when the child comes. And now, my dearest, good: bye again. Keep up your heart, be of good cheer, have faith in yourself as well as in the God of the Fatherless, & believe that if I do not do all you would have me do it is because I know not how, until you teach me.

Yours always

F.W. Dawson[2]

1. George Herbert Sass, "Flirtation Once More," April 26, 1873.
2. On the last page of this letter, Frank wrote the following notes:
   I dont know what the flavor *means*.
   There is no Express Messenger on Sunday; so my next will not *reach the Pump till Monday ev'g*.
   How's your supply of Edl paper?

Friday Night:

11.30 p.m [April 25, 1873]

I have already to-night sent off a letter to the Pump, and I will let this go to H & G.

Judge Bryan[1] has just left the office. You know him to be something of a big: wig in literature if not on the bench. In the course of conversation he asked me whether we would have anything more about Old Maids & Widows and the like. I told him that we would. He then said that he should like to know who was the writer of those articles. I rejoined: Why? do you want to tar and feather the unfortunate? He said: ["]No! indeed; they have attracted, and deservedly, a great deal of attention, as possessing much merit; and if it is not a secret I should very much like to know who wrote them." I told him that it was a profound secret.

And now, sweet child, that I have given you this crumb of comfort, while it was hot, I will contentedly go on with my work.

Yours always

F.W. Dawson

1. Judge George S. Bryan (1809–95) was one of the leaders of the Whig Party and the antisecession movement in South Carolina. In 1866, he became the presiding judge of the U.S. District Court of Charleston, serving in this position for twenty years. On April 1, 1868, he granted U.S. citizenship to Frank.

After reading the state and federal constitutions, Sarah wrote "Wiping Out Old Scores," an editorial on the upcoming U.S. centennial celebrations and the role of sectionalism in the festivities. Fearing that Sarah might not have correctly "apprehended" some of the political theories, Frank wrote the following letter explaining the sensitive relationship between the states and the federal government.

Saturday night
April 26. [1873]

No7.

Bien aimée [Much beloved]: I shall not mail this until to-morrow night, and I hope you will receive it on Monday evening to assure you that not an hour passes that I am not thinking of you and planning for you.

1. In reading your little article on the Centennial celebration, which appears on Monday, I find evidence, I think, that you do not apprehend correctly the theory of our govt, or that you have gone over to the centralizationalists. You speak of the states as *fractions* of a *unit*, or parts of one common whole. This would be correct in speaking of a county in a State as related to the entire State, but is incorrect when applied to a state as related to the United States. This country is not a nation of individuals, but a nation of States. The States, not individuals, are the subjects. The constituent elements are separate and distinct States; & the Federal or U.S. govt has no powers but those conferred on it by the states in the constitution, all powers not so conferred being expressly reserved to & by the States. This theory in its extreme form justifies secession; *ie* a breaking up of a voluntary association or copartnership of equals. In its most moderate form, as defined by the U.S. Supreme Court last week,[1] it forbids any interference with the domestic concerns of the states. I mention this now to set you thinking, & because I am not willing for you to seem to be in the dark while I can give you a rush-light.

2. I had a chat to-night, for the first time in months, with that "funny little Mrs. Cay"[2] who soon said something about my visits to Columbia. To which, without blushing, I rejoined: that I did not go to Columbia but to Mr. Morgan's, that it was just like home, that I could come & go & do as I pleased. Next, I was asked who were there: whereupon after eulogizing Jemmie & his wife & your Mother I took up that most interesting subject S.M. of whom, personally & mentally, I said as many laudatory things as I could think of. This silenced the enemy, who, however, said very naively that she thought you were in La all this time.

3. Do not fear that your "rabid views" of marriage, as expressed to my venerable friend, will "suppress any proposal that might have been in store" for you. I have asked you to marry me a good many times already, & I expect to ask you several times more before you are wearied into saying Yes! It is not, therefore, necessary to answer your question: "How shall I stand maidenhood?" God bless you darling, & a sweet Good Night.

1. *The Butchers' Benevolent Association of New Orleans v. the Crescent City Live-Stock Landing and Slaughter-House Company*, 83 U.S. 36. The *News and Courier* had reported on this decision. "The Louisiana Legislature granted a New Orleans Company the exclusive right to slaughter cattle," it stated. "The butchers resisted the powers conferred by the charter, as in violation of the provisions of the thirteenth and fourteenth constitutional amendments. The Supreme Court of Louisiana decided in favor of the company, which decision is affirmed by the Supreme Court of the United States" ("State Rights," April 23, 1873).
2. Mrs. A. E. Cay, thirty-six, was Eugene Fourgeaud's sister. She lived within the household of Edward Lafitte, fifty-eight, a Charleston merchant.

⁂

In late April, Howell Morgan left Hampton to attend the Home and School of the Holy Communion Institute in Charleston. Sarah wrote to Frank, expressing her sadness at the loss of her child.

No8

Sunday April 27 [1873]

My Darling! I grieve too much that you should be so sad to write you any of the cheering words you need. Howell will miss you sorely, but your pain will be worse, because longer, than his. The child will have the edge of his sorrow taken off by companionship with boys of his own age, who will take the old: manishness out of him, & prevent him from growing old too soon. And, think of it, if he makes a bright man of himself as he can, he may one of these days, when you also are in Charleston, come into harness on that News & Courier about which we both think so much. One lesson I do draw from what you say about him; viz, that you show that you have, as I knew that you had, one of the most loving & tender hearts that ever beat in woman's breast. Your affectation of coldness never deceived me. I know that you love the child, and I shall love him for your sake. I do not mind your calling yourself a widow, if you like it. You know, dear, that I take you as you are, without looking back. Nor can you tire me by speaking of yourself; the dearest subject on earth to me.

I will hunt up that letter! & key. No answer from Mrs. Dupré yet, but I have two copies of Appleton's Journal by mail to-night containing an article by Col Dupré on Colorado,[1] which I take as an indication that the good gentleman is not very mad, whatever "Sister Miriam" may be.

You may expect me at 5 oclock Saturday morning, unless something goes wrong down here. Do warn poor Jemmie! I am bothered awfully, awfully! Say to Jem's wife that I feloniously misappropriated her "Valerie Aylmer", & will bring it penitently back. I did not discover my mistake until I looked in her copy for something that I did not find. Keep your courage dear! That is the best way to make me work aright. Thanks for Grant![2]

Yours always

F.W. Dawson

1. L. J. Dupré, "Glimpses of Colorado," *Appleton's Journal: A Magazine of General Literature* 208–9 (March 1873): 368–71, 399–402.
2. "The Third Term," April 29, 1873, reported on speculation surrounding President Grant's aspirations for a third term (see chap. 9).

Charleston:

Tuesday April 29 [1873]

5.30 p.m.

I have just come back from a visit to your child! Mr. Gadsden,[1] the principal of the Home & School, caused Howell to be hunted up & brought in to the room where I was. It would have pleased you to hear the child's shriek of delight & to see his smiles. As to looks: he is clean, rosy, & as neat as ninepence. As to spirits: he says he is not homesick & does not mean to be. Mr. Gadsden told him he must take a prize next year, & Howell said "I'll try!" Who can [ask] more? Howell only entered to-day & his bed or bunk, or whatever they call it, is not assigned to him, so that I did not see his quarters. The boys are allowed to go out on friday afternoon & evening, and on Saturday evening. I have made an appointment with Howell for 4.30 p.m next friday. Mr. Gadsden tells me that Howell has a pleasant companion of his own age, Louis Lee Zimmer,[2] the son of an old (big German) acquaintance of mine. Louis speaks German, & he & Howell are expected to become poly glots. Howell sends his love & a kiss to you, and his grand: mother. (& all the rest of the family understand) He has written to you, and sent, or given, the letter to Mrs. Frank Trenholm.[3]

Goodbye I am very busy.

Always yours
F.W. Dawson

1. John Gadsden (1833–1902) served as principal of the Institute from 1867 to 1885.
2. Lewis L. Zimmer, ten, was the son of Lewis Zimmer Sr., forty, and Virginia Zimmer, twenty-seven. According to the 1880 census, the family lived in Spartanburg County, South Carolina.
3. Mary Elizabeth Burroughs Trenholm was the sister of James Morgan's wife, Gabriella.

↬ THREE ↫

Women

Editorials by Sarah Morgan

Sarah Morgan may have made her writing debut with an editorial on southern politics, but her essays on women created a sensation among readers of the *News and Courier*. Her second published piece, "The Use and Abuse Of Widows," caused such a stir in Charleston that Frank urged his correspondent to write on similar topics. "We must keep up the fire," he remarked with enthusiasm.

Sarah followed with a string of articles, including "Old Maids," "The Economic Aspect of Widows," "Work for Women," and "Age." Much of this work addressed her life experience as a single, adult, elite, white woman of the postbellum South. "Old Maids" and "Age" reflected thirty-one-year-old Sarah's search for a purpose and identity outside the prevailing stereotypes of the southern belle and lady. Similarly, "The Natural History of Woman" revealed Sarah's long struggle to reconcile intellect—and later journalism—with the southern feminine ideal.

Sarah's editorials also provide further insight into the complexities and contradictions that embodied her quest to rebuild her identity. Like the writings of nineteenth-century women novelists who used fiction as a mask to imagine new landscapes and social alternatives, Sarah's work provided her with a safe realm in which to explore and deconstruct femininity, marital status, and age.[1] Comparing Sarah's published work with her personal correspondence to Frank provides a window into her vision for "a new school for woman" along with the reality of her life in South Carolina.[2] "Work for Women," for example, uncovers an interesting dialogue between the personal shame Sarah associated with her career and her public espousal of a legitimate place for women in the workforce. Similarly, there is an intriguing disparity between Sarah's scathing critique of widows and her decision to tell new acquaintances that she was a widow, rather than an unmarried woman. In this way, Sarah's editorials provide a rare glimpse into her most intimate dreams and ideals. Frank and Sarah's correspondence shows how these dreams were played out against southern conventions and postwar reality.

1. Jones, *Tomorrow*, 24.
2. S. M. Dawson, *Sarah Morgan*, 579–80.

"The Use and Abuse of Widows" caused an uproar in Charleston and heightened speculation about the author's identity. "The 'Widows' new & stale, abuse it with characteristic virulence," Frank remarked on March 12. "The men think it rare fun & like Oliver [Twist] call for more."

The Use and Abuse of Widows, March 10, 1873

In this utilitarian age, the problem of the Widows must strike the practical mind as one of Nature's secrets, unrevealed, yet as indisputably existent as the Ozone which was breathed for thousands of years before it was analyzed. In a period when the object of all classes, from the political economist to the rag picker, is to secure the greatest possible good with the least possible waste—when the monopoly of any common blessing is not advocated by the most despotic—when no law exists limiting the capacity of each stream to turning a single mill—when the very dust is sifted, sorted, classified and utilized, well may the profound mind, when not absorbed by questions of exhausted coal mines and vanishing forests, be appalled by the more perplexing suggestion, "What can be done with widows?"

Nature would intimate that they should be husbanded, as her forces are. And what widow would raise a dissenting voice? But still the question would present itself—What were they made for? To assert that they are providential institutions for the encouragement of the manufacture of crape and bombazine, is a narrow view of their mission; to assert that they were made as a scourge for their sex, is a popular, but perhaps prejudiced belief. What then is their secret? Unveiled, they stand Sphynx-like as ever. The eagle wing for swiftness; the lion claw for power; inscrutable, mysterious, towering over men. O for a chemist to analyze their component parts, that the secret proportions may be revealed to the wondering! O for some Medea[1] to entice them into a rejuvenating cauldron, and there reduce them to a phosphate that shall cause the more tender flowers to spring into stronger life! O for a law to abide by the vote of unmarried women on the question of enforcing the Hindoo Suttee,[2] among the nations prolific of widows! And, if that be too flaming an advertisement of their perils and charms, O for a decree, like that of the Medes and Persians which altereth not,[3] that no widow shall marry until the last girl has perished.

Yet such is the paralysis that results from long neglect of acknowledged evils, that it is safe to predict that even this appeal will remain unanswered; that widows, even in the dog-days, will be at large, unchained and unmuzzled; and that winter will not find them placarded "dangerous" like the less treacherous ice. Waging war on maidens, sinking the most indifferent men, the crimes of these pirates will still be attended by a great profit, like that of the widow of Sarepta.[4] And even the Bible does not encourage the belief that Elisha replenished the oil can of any famishing maiden. Her cake, if she had one, remained dough, while the widow's baked.[5] But while the whole evil is not to be eradicated, the oppressed might be relieved by fixing an age beyond which widows shall cease to be dangerous. The unbiased mind may well be struck by the withering epithet "old maid," which blasts a hardly matured woman at twenty-five, while the widow, that adder of men among women, is attractive, surrounded, irresistible at thirty, forty, fifty—yea, when past, by a quarter of a century, the age when the unmarried woman begins to read neglect and contempt in the manners of those around her.

A Turk meditating in a graveyard (probably on the uncertainty of widows) was struck by the manoeuvres of a closely veiled woman, who was kneeling by her husband's tomb, fanning, fanning, earnestly, unflaggingly. Even a soul that had slipped off the bridge of Al Serat could not fail to be refreshed by so steady a breeze. Venturing to inquire into the reason of so unparalleled a devotion, he learned from the lady that she had made a vow not to marry until the mortar had dried on her husband's grave. And Petronius[6] tells of a widow, distracted with grief, who entered the cave with her husband's corpse, resolved there to perish. A soldier, guarding seven bodies hung on trees, abandoned his post to console her, being touched by her despair. He succeeded so well, that when the reviving widow heard his cry of horror that he must forfeit his life for one of the bodies which had been stolen in his absence, she proposed to fasten that of her husband in its place; and, as a widow generally carries out her designs, she assisted him in the ghastly work.

Since all fables have morals, and this, if it be a fable, appears perfectly destitute of any, the most obvious deduction is that widows know that it is not good to live alone, and with a dexterity born of long experience, practice what they preach. Cold impartiality asks why should not girls have an equal chance in the matrimonial race? Let the unmarried see to it, and make the Uses and Abuses of Widows the grand Woman's Rights and Social Equality questions of the day.

1. In Greek myth, Medea was a sorceress who fell in love with Jason and used her magic to help him obtain the golden fleece. After he deserted her, she killed their two children. Medea's cauldron and magic herbs were reputed to restore youth.
2. Suttee is a Hindu practice in which widows commit suicide on their husbands' funeral pyres.
3. "Now, O king, establish the decree, and sign the writing, that it be not changed, according to the law of the Medes and Persians, which altereth not" (Daniel 6:8).
4. Luke 4:26.
5. Elijah requested a "morsel of bread" from the widow of Sarepta. When she baked him a small cake with her last stores of meal and oil, she was promised that henceforth her "meal shall not fail" or her "cruse of oil fail" (1 Kings 17:9–16).
6. Petronius (d. ca. A.D. 66) was a Roman satirist. Sarah is referring to one of his most famous pieces, "The Widow of Ephesus," from his *Satyricon*.

✦❉✦

As a young girl, Sarah Morgan had dreamed of becoming an old maid. "I mean to be an old maid myself," she remarked, "and show the world what such a life can be." On July 24, 1862, she wrote in her diary, "It shocks me to hear a woman say she would hate to die unmarried. If I had my choice of wretchedness on either hand, I would take it alone; for then I only would be to blame, while married, he *would be the iron that would pierce my very soul. I can fancy no greater hell."[1] Even as an adult, Sarah refused to consider a hasty marriage to Frank as an alternative to the unhappy domestic relations she endured at Hampton. "Old Maids!" confirmed her commitment to single life as preferable to marriage "without love but actually with aversion."*

Old Maids! March 15, 1873

It is doubtful whether civilization will ever advance so far that the name Old Maid will cease to bring a smile of contempt to human lips; even to those whose roses are already fading in the ill-defined twilight of the dreaded limbo of women. The young and the wedded may laugh gracefully; but Lord help the woman who feels that she too must join in the cuckoo cry, or herself be classed among the neglected and forsaken.

There is exquisite humor in "bombazine assumed in grief and perpetuated in economy."[2] We laugh unrestrainedly; though the rusty folds be the symbol of a buried love, and the token of a poverty from which there is no resurrection. It becomes wondrous touching, however, when the inky garment is stuffed with widow's bones. The original weeds may have been donned for an incarnation of Satan, whose exodus left the mourner under the impression that the millennium had begun for her alone; yet they possess a sanctity, a pathos with which neither sorrow, nor holiness, nor suffering can invest those of the Old Maid.

Does any one know the typical Old Maid? Is she not as mythical as the English "Yankee" or the American "John Bull?" That she is like

"Sweet bells jangled out of tune"[3]

is the kindest thing that is ever said of her. And yet is there anything more common than wrangling wives and impatient mothers? Does any one believe that the class whose chief weakness is a love for cats and canaries, are moved to bang little innocents, as tender mothers are privileged to do? But these can be forgiven because they have husbands, and the law of reprisals exists among all nations in a state of war, provided they can find foes of whom they can take advantage. Maternal love, the vaunted, is pure selfishness, if traced to its source. The fiercest animals possess it in a greater degree than woman. While the idealized Mother is glorified by poets for tending her puny babies in her self-inflicted nursery, it is Old Maids like Miss Dix, Miss Nightingale and Miss Faithful[4] who go about, bringing God's sunshine into darkened places, raising the fallen, loosing the prisoner's bands, and preaching Hope and Charity to men. Strange that she who devotes her life to her own interest, hoping for a return in kind, should be more honored than the one who feasts the lame, the halt and the blind, and sits by a blackened hearth, content with the crumbs which fall from emptied dishes, and looking for no wine until she shall drink it fresh from the vintage at the marriage feast of eternity!

Grace Darling was an old maid when she saved seven sailors from the raging Atlantic.[5] Charlotte Corday was unwed when Marat received his bath of blood.[6] Rosa Bonheur is half a century old.[7] Joanna Baillie and Hannah More were very old maids.[8] It was the Maid of Orleans, not the wife or mother, who led the French to victory.[9] Had the heroine of Saragossa been married she would have lingered by the cradle side, papspoon in fist, instead of hastening to the ramparts to hurl shot and shell at the besiegers.[10] Good Queen Bess was an old maid, with red hair.[11] Nevertheless, it is a "reproach" to be an Old Maid! That is the universal cry. Yes! thanks to those who have been trained in the creed which those words express, and who are debarred from marriage by an exceptionally hard fate. Without the dignity and self-respect to extend themselves quietly and decently on the gridiron until they are broiled into a dish fit to be set before the king, they must frisk and kick until—torn, singed, half-dressed and wholly anomalous—they escape from the hands of the executioner and mince across the coals rejoicing that *they* are not yet dished as Old Maids. There is sublime moral heroism in accepting the situation. None but superior souls can do it gracefully. An infinite number of foolish virgins prefer marrying men unworthy of a good woman's respect to facing the jibes and sneers of their mating and mated associates. O women who seek this so-called "respectability," can you, do you, believe it decent to marry not only without love but actually with aversion? Is it more reputable to marry a man for *his* money, than to catch *your* fish with a golden hook?[12] Is it "proper" to marry John because Thomas is not available? Is not the loveless marriage the real reproach; a harder lot than that of an Old Maid who buries the love God denies and walks silently the appointed way, satisfied that He chose for her? Henri Quatre was a brave King, but, somehow, his glory fades before his own declaration,

"*Paris vaut bien une messe!*"[13]

There are some to whom religion is worth more than Paris and the world besides; especially if that religion, with its fundamental truths, inculcate the observance of the moral and social laws of delicacy and pure taste.

All women cannot marry. Witness, the seventy thousand majority of Nature's "last best gifts to man" in Massachusetts alone! For them no perennial Leap year blooms; and if it did no male stick presents itself for them to drape themselves around. But Dame Nature is not wholly obdurate. Even among the army of the unwed, grim and silent as the ghosts that haunt the Stygian lake in default of the obolus which shall secure their passage to Hades,[14] (alas! how significant!) it may well be doubted whether any have reached, by compulsion, that bourne from which no maiden returns. Every woman has her opportunities of marriage; perhaps, not always with the one she would desire or accept. But there would not be as many unaccountable marriages if the mania for asking were not as common among men as ill-assorted matches are among women. The vast disproportion between the forces of rejectors and rejected is balanced by the disposition of man to solicit many maidens; restricted only by the law which limits him to one wife at a time, or to as many as he can successively dispose of within a legitimate period.

Put it to the vote a year, a month, a week after marriage and how many women would secretly black-ball their choice! Yet these same wives, smiling in ghastly faintness to conceal some hidden stroke, will scoff at Old Maids who have no one to marry. At least the Old Maid has no sickening conviction that only the name of a husband's love is hers. She has no shrinking perception that irreproachable sherry can produce an obfuscation of intellect similar to that which "Old Rye"[15] shall cause. She has no terror of the marital lion roaring for a retarded meal, or growling over an over-done roast. She has no fear for the future; for, at the worst, her destiny is in her own hands, and she is not chained to a dead hope and a living despair. Shall we laugh with the multitude of Old Maids, or cry, Heaven help the Wives! Woman's best protector is not the individual man, but the opinion of other men in the mass. But for this, there would be an irresistible luxury in hitting one's wife. The day that this bond of terror and sympathy is dissolved, up go the switches and down goes woman's security.

And the Old Maids, the angels with disjointed wings and moth-eaten feathers, denied the courtesy of men and the consideration of women— what shall compensate them for the loss of so great a reward as the suffrages of the world on the question of their respectability? On earth they can hope for nothing; but let us trust that it will be with them as with the poor relations who, as Holmes[16] thinks, shall be pardoned much in the next world in consideration of their position in this, and that Beelzebub[17] himself will be moved to say to the humble-minded spinster, who presents herself as only fit for obscurity: "Go up higher, friend. Brimstone and fire can offer no new pain to one who has borne the title of Old Maid."

1. S. M. Dawson, *Sarah Morgan*, 175, 548–51.
2. "Appearing as if it began as a piece of mourning and perpetuated itself as a bit of economy" (Oliver Wendell Holmes, *The Professor at the Breakfast-Table* [1860]).
3. "Now see that noble and most sovereign reason, / Like sweet bells jangled out of tune and harsh" (Shakespeare, *Hamlet*, 3.1).
4. Dorothea Dix (1802–87), a pioneer in the movement for specialized treatment for the mentally ill, also known for her work as superintendent of Union war nurses during the Civil War; Florence Nightingale (1820–1910), an English

nurse regarded as the founder of modern nursing; Emily Faithful (1835–95), a British advocate of women's employment who in 1857 established a London printing firm with a predominantly female staff.

5. Grace Darling was the daughter of lighthouse keeper William Darling. On September 7, 1838, she helped to rescue survivors from the wrecked ship *Forfarshire* off England's Northumberland coast.

6. Marie Anne Charlotte Corday d'Armont (1768–93), a French royalist sympathizer who stabbed Jean Paul Marat (1743–93) in his bath to avenge his attacks on the Girondists.

7. Rosa Bonheur (1822–99), a French artist renowned for her paintings of animals.

8. Joanna Baillie (1762–1851), an English poet and dramatist; Hannah More (1745–1833), an English writer, poet, and playwright.

9. Joan of Arc, the Maid of Orleans (1412–31), a French national heroine.

10. Augustina Zaragoza, remembered for her bravery when Zaragoza, Spain, was besieged by France during the Peninsular War of 1808–9.

11. Queen Elizabeth I of England (1533–1603).

12. A Latin proverb.

13. King Henry IV of France (1553–1610). In 1593, he abjured Protestantism with the remark, "Paris is well worth a Mass."

14. Hades was the world of the dead, named after the ruler of the underworld. The obolus was the coin that was placed in the mouth of the dead to pay Charon's fee for ferrying them across the Styx to Hades.

15. Whiskey.

16. Oliver Wendell Holmes (1809–94), an American author and physician.

17. Philistine god known as the Lord of the Flies and often associated with Satan.

꙱ꙮꙪ

Frank encouraged Sarah to follow up her Saturday editorials with articles on similar topics. After the success of "The Use and Abuse of Widows," Sarah pursued this theme in one of her shorter weekday submissions.

The Economic Aspect of Widows, March 19, 1873

"It is proposed, in Alabama, to exempt all widows from taxation whose property does not exceed ten thousand dollars in value."

—Devourers of the substance of widows and babes will please take notice that a brevet of ante-celestial bliss is about to be conferred upon them. The widow who labors for daily bread and unruly children deserves exemption from any additional tax on either capital or patience. But if the law wishes to perfect its benevolent scheme, it should impose a special tax on all widows who have more than ten thousand dollars, to be applied to the relief of the innumerable horde of destitute mothers and maidens. There may not be enough *esprit de corps* to prompt a voluntary subscription; but the double luxury of widowhood and an independent fortune, might well command a liberal sum, especially if assessed at the price at which the taxpayer values her lone self.

෴

In the following piece, Sarah reported on the emergence of property rights for women. State law in the United States had originally adopted the British common-law concept of coverture, under which a woman's property and earnings passed to her husband upon marriage. Women's rights activists Susan B. Anthony and Elizabeth Cady Stanton contested the law in the 1850s and 1860s, but many southern states did not revise their statutes to expand the property rights of women until after the Civil War. As Suzanne Lebsock has noted, southern politicians enacted these reforms in a desperate attempt to save their holdings in the aftermath of war and defeat.[1] Sarah regarded the new laws as an opportunity for women to fulfill a "higher duty" to their husbands by safeguarding them from the "consequences of misfortune."

The Property of Married Women, April 2, 1873

The Legislature of Kentucky has passed a law providing that a woman shall not be held responsible for debts contracted by her husband. This is an evidence of the steady liberalization of opinion on the Woman question. Some years ago the Republican Legislature of South Carolina secured absolute protection to the property of married women. It is gratifying to see a Democratic body adopting, even incompletely, the same wise measure. And it is to be hoped that other governments will follow the good example.

It is in England that women have been most exposed to oppression. There the law gave the husband unlimited control over his wife's property or earnings. The lower classes suffered more severely from this, as they were not likely to meet with that forbearance which "upper-tendom" could hope to receive. But even in England protection is now afforded to property acquired after the wife has been deserted by her husband.[2] A law has further been suggested of a "limited liability" partnership in marriage, which approaches the American idea of justice.

A true wife would gladly give all she owns to save her husband from the consequences of misfortune, or of an error repented of too late. It is simply her duty to make any sacrifice for that purpose. But where the generosity of a woman only lends fuel to the flames, it becomes a higher duty to refuse the means of reckless waste, in order to save her husband when he can no longer help himself. She who thus denies him the opportunity of inflicting hopeless poverty on herself or her children is more noble than the wife who weakly yields, and afterwards deplores her loss.

The late concessions on the part of lawmakers, recognizing the necessity of protecting the interests of the weaker sex, prove that the true doctrine of Woman's Rights—the right of doing as she will with her own—is obtaining favor among men. It is certain that women have the power in their own hands, and if they desire a wider field they have only to prove themselves capable of filling worthily that to which they are now confined.

1. Lebsock, "Radical Reconstruction."
2. Divorce and Matrimonial Causes Act (1857).

⟨ℑℭ⟩

Sarah Morgan had personal knowledge of the plight of thousands of women whose wartime misfortune compelled them to earn a living in the postbellum South. Her editorial "Work for Women" became part of a larger dialogue on the issue. Indeed, Sarah may have been influenced by a series of articles that appeared in Louisiana newspapers in the late 1860s. In a letter published in the New Orleans Daily Picayune *in 1869, a female reader urged men to leave clerking positions "for their less fortunate and more numerous sisterhood of spinsters, widows and girls" who otherwise remained "a burden to their friends, their families and themselves."[1] Similar themes appear in Sarah's editorial, which argued for a "larger field of honorable, useful labor" for all those "sad-eyed, unwelcome dependents" too "ashamed to beg." In "Work for Women," Sarah looked to the ideal, a place where a woman's self-worth was not destroyed by employment. Her letters, describing the shame she associated with her own career, indicate the reality.*

Work for Women, April 15, 1873

The efforts making in the North to open a wider field of labor for women, cannot be too highly praised. It is an example the South will do well to follow. There are tens of thousands of delicately nurtured women, pining in want and in enforced idleness, to whom the possibility of earning a support for themselves, or for those dependent on them, would be an inconceivable blessing. Poverty, to man sharper than a serpent's tooth, pierces woman even more cruelly. No man need suffer if he is willing to lay aside all false pride. When all else fails he can dig ditches or drive a dray. But the physical organization of woman excludes her from these last resorts. And public prejudice, strengthened by her habitual dislike of all discipline, shuts her out from work she could do, perhaps better than the man to whom the preference is given.

As cooks, laundresses, chambermaids and waiters, the uneducated class can earn a living. In the North, numbers of women find employment in factories, shops, libraries and ticket offices. In the South, to be a seamstress or a governess is the only alternative left open to indigent respectability. Ladies advertising their capability of teaching five languages, music on half a dozen instruments, willing to instruct boys in the humanities of life, and girls in the requirements of society, and do the family sewing besides, are hardly thought entitled to a pallet in the nursery.

Women have so long wilted in dark places that their woes and wants have become as vague and as unreal as the nursery tales, which called forth tears in childhood, but cannot now be remembered. Half educated, or presenting only a brilliant surface of froth, thousands of these helpless creatures, developed as rare exotics for the ornament of refined homes, are thrown as ruthlessly as broken flowers on the stones of an unsympathetic world. There they take the chances of being picked up by some pitying hand, or of being deliberately crushed under some boorish foot. The dead leaves of the forest give as little concern. They are made to perish. Myriads will replace them. Let them make way for a brighter, fresher growth.

There is no greater bore than a female dependent. Some men still cling to the ancient prejudice of woman's sanctity, and maintain that she is desecrated by labor. But few are the enthusiasts who would not quietly see that sacred being slowly perish, if it was needful to insure their own comfort. Receiving money for toil is deemed a disgrace. A few will zealously endeavor to feed the expiring flames on family altars; but the light is flickering out on every hearthstone. There is scarcely a man who, in his secret heart, would not be glad to see the most cherished friend, aunt, cousin, niece, or sister earning her own living independent of his assistance. He would only stipulate that the scene of her labors should be removed from his sight, and that he should be spared public comment. Perhaps, the relief to the oppressed recipient of charity would be even greater than that afforded to the reluctant benefactor.

The North is in advance of the South in these liberal movements. Bearing the reproach of giving birth to such chimera as Woman's Rights and Woman Suffrage, it can also claim the honor of having offered means of self-support to that host of respectable mendicants who are ashamed to beg.

The most modest and retiring may hail the promise of a day when the equality of the sexes will be established on the true basis of equal remuneration for equal services. It is an excellent feature in the government at Washington that a large number of its clerkships are bestowed on women. Such positions require little beyond the masculine virtues of attention, system and punctuality. Few men are at first qualified for the offices they assume; and women, with their ready tact and happy imitative faculty, can acquire the necessary knowledge even more readily than the average man.

Some wise women in New York, with minds as liberal as their means, have formed an insurance company whose policies, offices, clerkships and agencies are all to be held by women. There is no reason why this scheme should not prove successful, and encourage the formation of other companies. Thus a still larger field of honorable, useful labor may be opened to the sad-eyed, unwelcome dependents who figure as skeletons at almost every board.

1. Schuler, "Women." Sarah was a resident of New Orleans in the late 1860s, and it is likely that she read or heard about these letters and editorials. When she moved to South Carolina, she continued to receive a regular supply of newspapers from Louisiana.

꒳

As she aged, Sarah began to contemplate her society's obsession with youth. In a world where the belle ideal was surpassed only by marriage and motherhood, Sarah bore the brunt of two "withering epithets": old and maid. In the following editorial, she explored "age" and the ramifications of her own Confederate bellehood, which forced her to "resign even the reputation of youth" for a "blank" existence.

Age, June 21, 1873

The most poignant as well as the most universal anguish is that produced by the terror of increasing years. Certainly no other iron enters so deeply into the soul of woman. Friends, lovers, husbands and children, may be replaced as naturally as maimed crabs and lobsters develope new claws. Youth alone cannot be duplicated. The feminine mind is incapable of conceiving happiness beyond it; impressed as woman is by the scarcely veiled masculine contempt for those who have passed the early dawn of life. It is a strange paradox that extreme youth suffers more acutely than old age from this terror. Coquettish seventeen, exciting the envy of her seniors, finds her happiness corroded by the secret regret caused by her advancing years. To herself she seems Methusaleh.[1] To her juniors she appears still more venerable. Sixteen and a half exclaims contemptuously, "That Old Maid! Why the creature is nearly eighteen!" And pale, with vexation at having her own age mentioned, she will exclaim, "I am young, very young!" when she is assailed in turn. No prisoner at the bar feels greater despair as the overwhelming evidence of his guilt is unrolled before him than these poor children feel when confronted with Age.

Novels are responsible for much of this. Heroines beyond seventeen are scarcely admissible. They are selected as much younger as is compatible with other chronological details. Indeed, Time is frequently obliging enough to stand still for their accommodation. Rivals and contemporaries fade away, while the heroine, like Joshua's moon in the valley of Ajalon, stands serenely, at the end of the conflict, just where she stood when the battle began.[2]

Efforts have been made to demonstrate that life possesses some interest, even after the salad days are past, but the charitable laborers have met with no great encouragement. By common consent Life is limited to that brief period during which a girl passes from her mother's nursery into her own. The real life which lies beyond the threshold excites no interest. The duty of the novelist, as the ambition of the woman, is restricted to the scenic effect of withdrawing from the stage. White satin and tulle close the vista. Wretchedness may lie beyond, but the bride has been trained to believe life a failure unless crowned by marriage, and that there is little chance for a proposal after nineteen. To be pronounced *passée* is more terrible to a woman than a good kicking is to a man. Insult can be avenged, but how may one resent the awful imputation of Age? Conceding that immaturity alone is worthy of admiration, what is to become of the unhappy ones who see maturity advancing, ready to stamp them with the sign manual of settled principles and ripened intellect? What weak mind can unflinchingly receive the brand, conspicuous as that of Cain,[3] and inspiring as much repugnance? No marvel that Sweet Sixteen shudders at the thought of being converted into a French participle. *Passée!* A most contemptuous epithet! Rival belles have frequently demonstrated that the words "well preserved," judiciously applied, will blast the prospects of the most imperious beauty.

Neither novelists nor their readers perceive that the conduct and accomplishments of their heroines are perfectly incompatible with their tender age. A middle-aged person, in treating of youth, insensibly imparts to ignorance the sentiments, prudence and dignity only to be attained later in life. The mind and person never mature simultaneously. One is always perfected at the expense of the other. The girl who becomes a belle at fourteen will confound her very admirers by the absurdities of her conduct and conversation. Where the mind is unduly developed, incongruities scarcely less displeasing always exist. Human beings, like fruit, require for their ripening the mellowing influence of time, and the life giving sunshine and storm. If the one proves to be a peach of rarest tints and flavor, and the other a crab apple, he who mistakes the trees need only blame himself. Each one has a tendency to select his own age as the best adapted to an appreciation of life and an understanding of its responsibilities. As time advances, this standard of perfection changes and recedes. The period of perfection invariably corresponds with the age of the speaker.

It is hard to resign even the reputation of youth, if life is to be a blank when youth is passed. There is but one consolation for those who feel this bitterness. That is, that the day must come when their every blooming successor shall, in turn, be pronounced *passée*. Few women have the philosophy to wait calmly for that epoch. They anticipate it eagerly for their friends. The acquisition of wisdom, which outlasts evanescent charms by a life-time, seldom suggests itself as a more worthy pursuit. Women who never heard of Pope adopt his idea that thought is quite as inimical to beauty as time.[4] By annihilating one they hope to conceal the traces of the other.

The surest way to grow old is to dread old age. Furrows of anxiety follow, which would otherwise be the slow work of many years. When once the frantic regret is abandoned, an aftermath of youth remains, which yields a better harvest than the first imperfect grain. But nothing more justly excites ridicule than the affectation of a youth which no longer exists. Each period of life has its natural charm. They only are wise who accept every stage in turn, neither fearing the next, nor regretting the last—intent only on fulfilling the obligations of the present.

There is no more prolific source of falsehood than Age. Worldly men say that the woman who confesses to twenty-five must have either a remarkable degree of fortitude or be very much older. The greatest disadvantage in announcing one's age, is that it is apt to run ahead of time, unless kept constantly before the public. Every one is persuaded that two birthdays a year is a natural allowance for a friend, while finding it difficult to acknowledge one a year for herself. In seven and a half years the gushing creature who confessed to twenty-five will infallibly be proclaimed forty. As none but the most exceptional woman could endure that aspersion, the natural revenge is to add a few years to the age of others, only to keep the balance even.

The suggestion that there is no Time in heaven, reconciles the most worldly woman to the necessity of leaving earth. Sunday after Sunday the Boanerges[5] of the pulpit sees an electric flash irradiating the care-worn faces of his congregation, as he offers this irresistible invitation. Threats and terror may move the vulgar, but the effective argument to draw the mundane soul heavenward is that which touches on the annihilation of Time. Time once passed, there will be no possibility of having one's age exaggerated, or even guessed. No heart-burnings, no jealousy. Expiring Time produces a universal birthday, leaving no measure by which the rest can be reckoned. The soul of woman can conceive no greater bliss than to be forever as young as the youngest, and no older than the oldest. Think of it! Immunity from constantly recurring birthdays! Who can fail to perceive why the "narrow gate"[6] is more attractive to woman than to man.

1. In the Bible, Methuselah was said to have lived 969 years.
2. Joshua was Moses' successor and made the moon stand still during a battle at Ajalon (Joshua 10:12).
3. In the Bible, Cain, the son of Adam and Eve, killed his brother, Abel, in a jealous rage.
4. Alexander Pope (1688–1744), an English poet. Sarah refers to Pope's *Moral Essays: Epistle II—To a Lady* (1731–35).
5. Jesus called St. John and St. James the Boanerges, or Sons of Thunder, for their style of preaching. Sarah uses the term to refer to loud preachers.
6. Matthew 7:13.

꘏

With only "ten short months" of schooling to her credit, Sarah Morgan often lamented what she regarded as her "shocking ignorance and pitiful inferiority." These insecurities plagued Sarah as a young girl and later led to feelings of self-doubt about her competency as a writer.[1] In "The Natu-

ral History of Woman," Sarah tackled the issue of *"women's intelligence,"* or what Frank later described as *"the ethics of foolishness." "I think it is the keenest and wittiest thing you have written,"* he remarked. *"It contains many a hard hit. I shall print it just as it is written, but of course I don't agree in earnest to much that you have said."*

The Natural History of Woman, September 20, 1873

Pope says, "Woman and fool are two hard things to hit."[2] Taken literally, this remark betrays the bachelor, with no larger experience of woman than is derived from the sacred study of a mother. Woman, as represented by Lady Mary Wortley Montague, *was* hard to hit. She was too much for Pope, and hit harder than he could.[3] The line records his own defeat. But to us, whose field of observation is the world, who are surrounded by clouds of women who are amenable to criticism, experience proves that woman and fool are *not* two hard things to hit. We elbow them at every turn. A man cannot touch the chaste brow of his sweetheart without coming in contact with the *rara avis*. He cannot listen to the remarks of his sister without perceiving the connection. He can but feel, when angry with his wife, that woman and fool are so closely allied, that, in striking her, he could kill two birds with one stone. Woman and fool are, then, one and the same. Tangible realities! *Deum Laudamus* [God Be Praised]! Happiness depends on sympathy. What would become of us, bereft of congenial companions? Like a nation of Frankensteins, shall we roam desolate, yearning in vain for kindred spirits to cheer our loneliness?[4] Forbid it Heaven! All praise be to the wise provision that has given, in silly women, helpmeets to man.

"Who is the greatest woman of France?" asked Madame de Staël[5] of the man least capable of appreciating woman or her worth. "She who has borne the greatest number of children," answered Napoleon,[6] whose delicacy and breadth of soul were in inverse proportion to his gigantic ambition. We accept the Napoleonic Code. Men of blessed memory have agreed that women were made merely to become mothers; nothing more. Pre-eminence in Heaven is even promised, by some, to exuberant maternity. Certainly, intellect is not required for that achievement. Indeed, the lower the scale the more prolific the animal. A George Eliot[7] descends to the grave without a child to perpetuate her name; and the meanest creature who haunts her doorstep, puling babe in arms, is, according to Napoleon's rule, a thousandfold her superior.

Why, then, waste intellect on woman, where there is a demand greater than the supply among men? Nature is a severe economist, not to call her a niggard. Whatever she freely bestows, she recalls unless it is freely used. From fish which inhabit subterranean tarns, she withdraws even the rudiments of the eyes for which they have no use. From women whose duties and aspirations are restricted to

"Suckle fools and chronicle small beer,"[8]

she withdraws all save the wisdom necessary for that high and sacred office. Woman, zoologically considered, need never rise above instinct. Man needs the rest. But what becomes of that subtracted fund of intelligence, so conspicuously lacking among certain women? If it has been distributed among certain young men, they guard it so closely that the secret of their wisdom will die with them. Let them beware of the economist Nature, who loses no neglected payment, but ever absorbs neglected and discarded things into her own broad breast.

Wisdom is a man's rightful inheritance. Happy the woman who has just sense enough to keep pins out of her mouth, and who is an authority only on the subject of baby tea. All honor to the woman who cannot read outside her own Bible, and who never consulted the dictionary even for bad words. After all, the best wisdom is that which can conceal ignorance. The great Italian who lived, ate and slept his three score years among his books, knowing the contents of each by a glance at its cover, as we recognize our friends by their faces, is inferior to the woman who never betrays her stupidity. She who can hold her tongue and listen, will acquire a reputation for wisdom more infallible than that of the Delphic Oracle.[9] But who ever saw her? There is scarcely one who will not weakly dribble out to Z all that A has poured in her ear. Bless their weakness! We like them better for that, or for anything which proves their inferiority. Provided *our* secrets are not betrayed, let those of others be published to the world! Mental flaccidity is a potent charm in woman. It fascinates the wise. Only flabby-minded men can tolerate a strong-minded woman. They are usually found coupled together. Philosophers and great men choose their mates from that true type of womanhood, which can neither share nor understand the ambition or pursuits of a husband. A superficial knowledge of Mother Goose is enough for woman, provided she has a turn for housework. There is good reason for the prejudice against learned women. Man was by nature intended for her sovereign.

What becomes of a sovereign when his subjects not only suspect, but know, that he is unfit to dictate to them?

The American boy, especially, is at a disadvantage. His sister has far better opportunities of improvement. Money-making becomes too early the object of his existence to admit of losing time in mental culture. Consequently, the woman who chooses to devote her leisure to study soon surpasses him. She will naturally be regarded as an insufferable usurper. We cannot tolerate the woman who amasses the refined gold we trample under foot, in our haste to secure perishable dross. If a woman has a soul above catnip, it is her imperative duty, figuratively, to drown it in the bowl; literally, to hide it. Nothing is more offensive than superiority, whether implied or felt. Knowledge, shown or suggested, is slavery for a woman. There is no discipline more degrading than the constant suppression of exalted thought and lofty aims. The petty tyranny extends to the least word she can employ. To offend no one by word or deed, she must adopt the colloquial vulgarities in vogue. If they are distasteful, she must not betray it. The pronunciation dictated by ignorance must be followed, or the taunts and ridicule of fools—the most severe penance for intelligent, sentient beings—will be heaped upon her. The plague of flies is nothing in comparison with the comments of fatuous ignorance. The woman who would be friends with the average mankind, must reduce herself to a state of semi-imbecility. If she has sense, she must conceal it. If a man of culture enters the circle, the least appearance of understanding his conversation will annul her previous efforts, and convict her of the ignominy of being a "learned" woman. A learned pig is more respected and admired. Sweet law of sympathy among kindred souls! The earthly pilgrimage would be unendurable without thee!

Who would eat of the forbidden tree of knowledge, paying such a price for its bitter fruit? What man is there who would willingly consort with a Hebrew root, wed a Greek quantity, or take to himself Sanscrit character? Lives there a man who could calmly endure the suspicion that his wife winced at his philological deficiencies, or paled at his grammatical eccentricities? Until man can be elevated beyond the possibility of being rivalled, perish all women who can detect his infirmities!

Woman can be forgiven for moral laxity, physical imperfection, falsehood, treachery, cattishness, or any other feminine trait. But mental equality, or perhaps a shade of superiority, is a crime never pardoned. It is against man and the Bible. "Let the woman learn, in subjection to her husband."[10]

There is no authority to justify her in being capable of instructing him. There is nothing less in demand in the woman-market than brains. There is nothing more injurious to her matrimonial prospects, or destructive of family ties. If woman was created only for man, the less sense she has the more enthusiastic is her admiration of, and the more implicit is her obedience to her lord and master. Suttee immolation is but a feeble expression of the devotion woman can display when her intellectual faculties are systematically neglected. Peace and married happiness depend on submissive ignorance. Long live woman and fool! May they ever continue one and the same!

> "This is fixed as are the roots of earth and base of all;
> Man for the field, woman for the hearth.
> Man for the sword, and for the needle she.
> Man with the head, woman with the heart,
> Man to command, woman to obey;
> All else confusion."[11]

1. For Sarah's girlhood feelings of intellectual inferiority, see S. M. Dawson, *Sarah Morgan*, 290.
2. Alexander Pope, *Moral Essays: Epistle II—To a Lady* (1731–35).
3. Lady Mary Wortley Montagu (1689–1762), English writer. Pope had been an admirer of Montagu's, but they quarreled, and Pope used his poetry to viciously attack her.
4. The monster in Mary Shelley's *Frankenstein* (1818). After being rejected by his creator, Frankenstein wandered the countryside in search of a family.
5. Anne Louise Germaine Necker, baroness de Staël-Holstein (1766–1817), published *Delphine* (1802) and *De l'Allemagne* (1810) and operated a famous Paris salon.
6. Emperor Napoleon I (1769–1821) of France.
7. George Eliot was the pseudonym of English novelist Mary Ann Evans (1819–80).
8. Shakespeare, *Othello*, 2.1.
9. The oracle of Apollo at Delphi was the most famous in ancient Greece.
10. "Let the woman learn in silence with all subjection" (1 Timothy 2:11).
11. Alfred Tennyson, *The Princess* (1847), 5.

FOUR

Family and Relationships

Editorials by Sarah Morgan

Like most elite southern women, Sarah Morgan built her world and her identity around family. She understood herself in relation to others: as a daughter, a sister, a friend, an aunt, and a mother to Howell. These relationships defined Sarah's sense of self and her roles within her family, household, and community. In a postwar world filled with turmoil and uncertainty and in which race and class were no longer clear determinants of status, family membership became something to which to cling.

In 1873, Sarah's personal relationships were in a state of transition. James's marriage to Gabriella had irrevocably altered her relationship with her brother, along with her position in the household. Sarah's guardianship of Howell proved emotionally and financially taxing as she tried to raise the child and provide him with the education he required. And her relationship with Frank, while not yet familial, forced Sarah to confront the complex issues of love and marriage.

When Sarah's home life remained in a state of flux, so did she. What preoccupied her personal life soon came to dominate the editorial content of her published work. For example, Sarah wrote "Bachelors and Widowers" at the beginning of her career, at a time when she questioned the propriety of Frank's attentions so soon after the death of his wife. "Young Couples," an article on love and relationships, followed soon thereafter. Howell's departure to boarding school and Sarah's preoccupation with good parenting culminated in the publication of "Very Young America." And Sarah's disillusionment with her brother, James, prompted her to write "Brothers versus Sisters." Sarah used her writing to look for answers to her personal struggles, and her editorials provide a revealing portrait of her most intimate thoughts and feelings.

Sarah wrote "Bachelors and Widowers" as a follow-up to her sensational editorial on "Widows." Bemused by Sarah's savage treatment of widows, readers of the Charleston News *demanded that the "same caustic and humorous pen" provide a similar vignette of bachelors and widowers, those "useless attaches of society."[1] Frank applauded Sarah's efforts and drew no personal connection between the widowers in her editorial and himself, a widower of three months. Sarah's reservations about the propriety of Frank's love suggest that her concerns may have been embedded within her exaggerated rhetoric.*

Bachelors and Widowers, March 22, 1873

Spartan law decreed that no one should rise up in public places in honor of an unmarried man, no matter how great his age or merit. It was a disgrace to be a Bachelor, and severely was the delinquent made to feel it. Wise people! A nation of heroes, they well understood that domestic discipline is the school for warriors. They knew that the man who could subdue his wife was prepared to conquer or die when the common enemy entered the field.

No Bachelors defended Thermopylae![2] The three hundred would not so resolutely and calmly have met death, but for the certainty that something harder awaited them at home. The two who dared to live were undoubtedly a Bachelor and a Widower who had nothing to fear. They were probably admitted into the ranks of the self-devoted martyrs as reporters who were to transmit their heroism to future ages. Death at Thermopylae rather than life at home, was to be represented as the outgrowth of pure patriotism. It was a delicate precaution, on the part of those husbands, to cover family jars, but one that did not altogether save them from inspection. The secret cause of desperate valor was thus laid bare, and the most severe legislation could not force recalcitrant Bachelors into the traces of the matrimonial harness. Broken down old hacks gave the masonic wink of Danger ahead! while dragging the matrimonial plough with apparent alacrity. So the original outlaws increased; their ranks were strengthened by providentially emancipated Widowers, until, from being the scorn and jest of Society, they became its dictators and kings.

Next to the Widow's office, the greatest sinecure in the gift of destiny is that of a Bachelor or Widower. The latter class alone combines the privileges of a grandfather with the enjoyment of youth. Women adore a Widower. It is not always possible to eat one's cake and have it. And, in this case, there is not only the security of making advances to one who can be claimed as a grandfather in case of defeat, but there is always the possibility of inducing the coy darling to change his changeful mind. Can not Darwin be persuaded to accept the Bachelor as his "missing link?"[3] The Bachelor certainly has no visible connection with the family of man. Isolated, impregnable, yet inviting assault, he maintains his defense, through successive generations, until the wounded and hopeless assailants are compelled to raise the siege and to seek happier hunting grounds. Long past the utmost limit accorded even to Widows, the Bachelor shoots up like Jack's bean stalk, or a century plant, calling the attention of the world to his youthful bloom. According to his own account, a Bachelor or Widower is a ravening lion among women. Each has a private cave where the bones of more or less than eleven thousand virgins are blanching in secret. Unhappy victims to their own persistency, and to his unfortunate capacity for requiting human love, none pities them more than he. However unattractive, each is convinced that the women are crazy about him, and that, like Mrs. Winslow's Soothing Syrup,[4] the biggest babies cry most loudly for him.

There is a certain humiliation in receiving the universally imparted confidences of senile youth. The philanthropic heart is moved to schemes for their amelioration or eradication. If the latter is decided on as the safer plan, the tribe need not be put to death; insensibly as that of Levi,[5] it may be made to disappear. Taxation, as the people of the South know to their cost, is the surest method of annihilation. Suppress the race by imposing a tax on derelict Bachelors and Widowers, to be devoted to the support of Old Maids and unenterprising Widows. Let them pay a fixed sum to each of those in whose breasts they have excited delusive hopes. Then we shall hear less boastings of their conquests. Their devotion will be less general. There will be a marked decrease in the annals of hand-squeezing and of paternal applications of dyed moustaches. We shall see fewer startling illustrations of Balaam's beast—face to face with an angel, and talking like an ass.[6]

On Widowers the law should press less severely. They have already thrown a sop to Cerberus;[7] possibly, have thrown several. Verily they deserve some consideration. The best evidence of their appreciation of women is, that few of them have ever taken a wife without applying for more of the article when the first supply was out. At least once in his life the Widower has the satisfaction of knowing that every woman's heart is throbbing for him. He is too well disciplined to betray the consciousness that the palpitation is produced by lawful speculations and eager anticipations of his next choice. Trained to consideration for the feelings of others, and inured to business habits, he affects to look upon the agitation as a natural consequence of a rise in the market, totally unconnected with personal hostilities.

We commend both Bachelors and Widowers to mercy. Soon the hour of retribution will knell. The Amazons of the North will ere long conquer the ballot-box and bind with the law the unappreciative wretches who decline more graceful fetters. Let gentle voices plead that moderate fleecing may suffice for the punishment of these venerable lambs. Somewhere in your gardens, O more modest maidens, prepare a plat for the moral cultivation of these wild flowers of civilization! Nourish them! Dig them! Tend them! Even if they fail to produce flowers fit to deck your charms, they may serve to redeem some hopeless ground. The barren fruit tree was suffered to stand to the last. And even should these graceless stalks die without giving sign of improvement—

> "Lay them in the earth,
> And from their fair and unpolluted flesh
> May violets spring!"[8]

1. "Bluffton and the Bachelors," *Charleston News*, March 24, 1873.
2. In 480 B.C., the Persians defeated the Spartans at Thermopylae.
3. In one of his most famous theories, Charles Darwin argued that there was a "missing link" in the evolution of monkeys to humans.
4. A medicine containing high doses of morphine that was reputed to alleviate the suffering of teething babies.
5. In the Bible, Levi, the son of Jacob and Leah, was the founder of one of the tribes of Israel. After the Israelites took possession of the land promised to them by God, it was divided into territories and allotted to different tribes. The Levites formed the priesthood and so did not receive territory of their own (Deuteronomy 18:1).
6. Balac, king of Moab, entreated Balaam to come and curse Israel. Balaam was permitted to make the journey on the condition he obey God's commands. As he traveled, Balaam's ass exhibited signs of anxiety, and Balaam hit the animal for his disobedience. God gave the ass the gift of speech, and the ass told Balaam of his cruelty. Balaam suddenly saw an angel, the object of the ass's distress, and was told by the figure that the ass had saved Balaam's life (Numbers 22:22–34).
7. In Greek myth, Cerberus, a multiheaded dog with a tail of snakes, guarded the entrance to Hades.
8. Shakespeare, *Hamlet*, 5.1.

Sarah Morgan wrote "Young Couples" while struggling to make sense of her personal and professional relationships with Frank. Many of the themes that appear in this piece, however, were reminiscent of ideas she had expressed in her wartime diary. "Women who look to marriage as the sole end and object of life are those who think less of its duties," she wrote in May 1862, "while those who see its responsibilities, and feel its solemnity, are those who consider it by no means the only aim and purpose of life. The first think their destiny is fulfilled, they have nothing to do in future but to kill time; the second, feel that the real trial of life has now commenced, and take up their burden with an humble, self-mistrusting heart, looking above for help. How few they number!"[1]

Young Couples, March 29, 1873

"Marriage is the sole end for which woman was created." All women must accept that article of belief as containing the sum total of their duty to themselves and man. Men preach it, and urge it on those within their reach. Yet statistics prove that they themselves would rather have it a one-sided affair; since they are notoriously growing cautious and dilatory, not to say averse to marriage. And what heart, however stout, can contemplate without qualms an existence whose pleasure is limited to a St. Martin's Summer[2] of a honeymoon, followed by alternations of tropical storms and Arctic frigidity! Man is not prone to choose darkness and the shadow of death for his abode, while floods of golden sunshine await whomsoever cares to scale the heights. Yet women are seen ready to sacrifice self respect and peace of mind to secure a marriage whose happiness is to wane with the moon; content that there should be no renewal of its splendor. The brighter light that should shine beyond, is forgotten, until chill, awful and rayless as the Arctic midnight sun, it sinks forever in hopeless gloom. Marriage is *not* the end of woman! Where is it accepted with awe, as part of her destiny, it is her new birth in a higher life. And the same training lies before her morally as that which gradually developed her from the helpless, silly, petted baby into the perfect woman. But tell a bride that she must look to the day when unmixed sentimentality will be as fascinating as the babbling of an idiot, and she will indignantly assert that being a helpmeet for man means renouncing every charm and prerogative. No wonder she clings to rhapsodical raving. No wonder she strives to exclude the rational life. No marvel that Sampson lies shorn and feeble, the secret source of his strength cut off by his own Delilah.[3]

Young people, with very little capital or knowledge of the business, rush simultaneously into matrimony and solitude, and consider every interruption to that *tête à tête* of platitudes a moral injury. The repetition of the most simple word causes it to grow strange and unnatural. So isolation and familiarity result in the dolorous experience of Alphonse and Célestine, who, in uninterrupted communion, found defects that had never before been suspected. Alphonse discovered a mole on Célestine's cheek. When he was discourteous enough to mention it, Célestine did not know whether he was referring to her or to her little dog, he squinted so abominably! The mole became a monstrosity, the squint a deformity, until the doctor was consulted. He prescribed a little variety of intercourse, and they were made whole again.

Even on a purely intellectual basis *tête-à-têtes* may become wearisome. Witness Horace Walpole and Mad. Dudeffant.[4] Intellectually enamored, they retired to her chateau to enjoy that communion of soul which the noise of Paris might have disturbed. Walpole, who could certainly talk enough, complained that he was bored to death in a few hours. Before a day had passed they fled apart in mutual disgust. The plaint against *"toujours perdrix"* [always partridge] has a reasonable basis. Some practical man tested it.[5] The victim, who was very partial to partridges, was bound to confine himself to that diet for thirty days. Long before that period had elapsed, he begged to forfeit the money that was to be his reward, loathing partridge as the Israelites did the quail, while the coveted flesh was yet between their teeth.[6]

The grand climacteric and the period of teething are not as dangerous to man as the transition from the lover state into that of husband and wife. Ignoring the fact that union is strength, they are content with its conventional semblance. After the brief period during which love making is endurable, instead of uniting their aims and efforts for one definite object, they find themselves growing only farther apart. She contracts to the size of her nursery, while he expands in a larger life. At last no common interest binds them, save household expenses and the welfare of children. Many have reason to sympathize with the French lady who said: "The first year of my marriage I adored my husband! I could have eaten him! The second year—I regretted that I had not."

"Self-knowledge, Self-reverence, Self-control! These three alone lead man to sovereign power."[7] And these are unattainable to miserable pride and self-sufficiency. And without them marriage must be a purgatory, without hope of transfer. To know one's self would be the sum of human wisdom. To know one's mate would secure happiness. Yet no one claims to have this knowledge, save in a partial, one-sided way. Instead of mutual concessions and earnest endeavors to maintain peace, we have vague suggestions of unrest, and an irresistible tendency to bang the door while living in an edifice whose timbers are as weak as—most resolutions. "Bear and forbear," so universally preached, is at last interpreted as referring to children only. There, all the Law and the Prophets are limited. Yet compassion cannot be denied to the ignorant people who unconsciously incur such risks. The girl has all the orthodox requisites of ringlets, complexion, dainty feet; but her selfishness is not as yet predominant. The lover dances delightfully, has a fine voice, makes love in a bewildering manner; but his temper has not yet had the same advantages of display. Given these two quantities to find the unknown, and the product will be—Trouble. And what is to toil for lovely Rachel; secure her with incredible labor; marry her at last, and wake in the morning to find it blear-eyed Leah—Jacob knows![8]

Man is unquestionably a tyrant; but woman was made for him. Consequently, reasonable submission is a duty. It is hard to live with one who is always right—in his own opinion. The lady is to be envied who closed her doors to the man who was odiously and infallibly correct. But some concessions do not involve conscience; and these will always be made by one who has most self-respect.

> "Thy husband is thy lord, thy life, thy keeper,
> Thy head, thy sovereign; one that cares for thee,
> And for thy maintenance; commits his body
> To painful labor, both by sea and land;
> To watch the night's storms, the day in cold,
> While thou liest warm at home, secure and safe,
> And craves no other tribute at thy hands
> Than love, fair looks, and true obedience;
> Too little payment for so great a debt."[9]

And the woman who has the grace to study this; who has been blessed with a love founded on a rock, and worthy of the temple she will there erect, grows with his growth, ever more exalted, until at last, wholly spiritualized,

> "She set herself to man,
> Like perfect music unto noble words."[10]

1. S. M. Dawson, *Sarah Morgan*, 81–82.
2. Mild weather occurring in late autumn. St. Martin's Day is November 11.
3. In the Bible, Samson loved Delilah, but she aided Samson's enemies by cutting off his hair, his secret source of strength, while he slept (Judges 16:6–19).
4. Horace Walpole (1717–97), English author and fourth earl of Orford, compiled a voluminous correspondence with many famous Europeans, including Marie de Vichy-Chamrond, marquise du Deffand (1697–1780), a French woman of letters whose salon was popular among figures of the Enlightenment.
5. According to Walpole, when a priest rebuked a French king for his infidelity, he forced the priest to eat nothing but partridge to prove that it is possible to have too much of the same thing.
6. After crossing the Red Sea, Moses led the Israelites into the wilderness, where God provided them with quail to eat (Exodus 16:18).
7. Alfred Tennyson, "Oenone," *Poems* (1842).
8. In the Bible, Jacob fell in love with Rachel and made a deal with her father, Laban, to work for him for seven years in exchange for Rachel's hand in marriage. After seven years, Laban tricked Jacob, giving him Rachel's older sister, Leah (Genesis, 29:16–26).
9. Shakespeare, *The Taming of the Shrew*, 5.2.
10. Alfred Tennyson, *The Princess* (1847).

Sarah Morgan spent much of her adolescence helping to raise her nieces and nephews. "Our eldest nieces were born before we were out of babydom, almost," she remarked at age twenty-one, "and every year since has added one to the number, so that there has never been one day out of all these years, that the delicious harmony of an infant's voice has not cleaved our tympanum with its dulcet sounds." One of these children was Howell Morgan, the son of Sarah's brother Gibbes and Lydia Carter Morgan Purnell.[1]

When Sarah agreed to become Howell's legal guardian, she had already formed many of her ideas on parenting. The following editorial, "Very Young America," developed her wartime ideas on parenting practices. "Of the millions of wives and mothers in the world, how many are fit to be either?" she questioned. "It annoys me constantly; I hate to see a state God intended to be so holy and beautiful, degenerate into indifference, bickering and tears in the first, weak nerves and children governed by temper in the second. . . . I know some people who never punish their children unless they are in a temper; I call that brute reasoning. Yet how all theories vanish away, and how all rules are inefficient, where children are concerned!"[2]

Very Young America, May 10, 1873

Disrespect and independence are said to be the crying sins of Young America. But, as few parents take the trouble to exact reverence from their children, and fewer still spontaneously inspire that sentiment, the unhappy little victims of neglect deserve commiseration rather than censure.

When Jack hears his mother complain that he does not mind her, Jack, at the most tender age, intuitively perceives that it is her affair, not his. There is no possibility of ascertaining how soon a child begins to weigh its seniors in the balance, and to find them wanting. A baby in arms will roll its eyes attentively from one disputant to another, and finally hold out its chubby fists and scream for the one in whose favor it has decided. Papa's contempt for mamma's judgement, and mamma's small inconsistencies, are treasured up and faithfully reproduced. Children supposed to be too young to understand family disagreements, never lack the sense to assume an air of unconsciousness that will secure their presence at similar scenes in the future. They compare the opinions of the two parties, and shrewdly conclude that neither is entitled to much honor. As "actions are thoughts ripened into consistency and form,"[3] their insubordination and disrespect are prepared for them by their natural guardians.

If half the trouble bestowed on horses were devoted to the moral culture of children, the whole world would be benefited. Oftentimes the tender parent takes more pains with the dumb animal than with the tender child. A horse's mouth is so sensitive, that one who values him will not jerk the bit. A timid little child, caught up in sudden wrath for some unconscious mischief, is not so gently dealt with. A horse is made vicious by the lash, therefore the rod is reserved for the tender flesh for which Solomon[4] recommended it. Brute force too often takes the place of calm reason, for the sensitive child.

Any girl, fresh from the nursery, believes herself competent to assume the awful responsibility of an immortal soul. Kindly, death claims a large proportion of the doll babies which nature generously provides for the amusement of grown-up children. Still, a large majority of the mothers who retain their toys, are utterly unfit for the duties devolved by their own act upon them. Immature minds, tossed about by caprice, know not the just mean between undue severity and over indulgence. Where impulse takes the place of principle, the child who climbs inopportunely for a kiss, is as unlikely as not to be met by harsh reproof. Angelic forbearance, which encourages wrong-doing, suddenly leaps into exasperation and visits its error on the innocent offender. Sala[5] forcibly observes that where most honey abounds, there, also, will be found most whacks.

The first evidence of maternity is softening of the brain. By motherhood the judgement of the soundest mind is somewhat impaired. It is a cruel wrong, nevertheless, to encourage the formation of parents with no brains at all. Talleyrand had no children, and can be forgiven for the dreary connection which admitted of the remark, *"J'aime ma femme; elle est si bête."*[6] His conscious error is proved by the specious apology, "A clever woman often compromises her husband; a stupid one compromises only herself." This is, perhaps, an advantage to the husband; but the children? Note the sons of such mothers. No man who ever rose above mediocrity was the son of a silly woman. In every man is seen the reflex of his mother's character.[7] Goethe[8] was a most striking illustration of this truth which is sown broadcast in every land.

If the enemies of Young America will but look for the root of the evil, it will be found in the parents chosen by Providence for the juvenile victims to circumstances over which they have no control. It so often happens that children are born to those who marry, that it is scarcely a presumption to treat the cradle as the corollary of the wedding ring. If the contracting parties could calmly weigh the matter, and decide that each is the one whom the other would confidently entrust with the training of the potential child, there would be a new race of heroes among the nations. As it is, the Divorce Court is thronged with parents proclaiming each other unworthy of the office to which they deliberately elected themselves. Perhaps, even the scandal of separation is preferable to the long process of sapping all life from young hearts. When the conflicting views of parents give battle on the debatable ground of the best system of training children, the fair field retains traces of the strife forever. The champion swearer or the boy drinker will yet be offered a prize in the National Baby Show. Proud papas are training them in divers places. Lips as pure as those of angels are sportively stained with wine. Delighted applause from time to time greets a "good, mouth-filling oath"[9] lisped by a little child.

Swift's[10] suggestion of eating little babies is not a bad one. Many tender little lambs spared by the butcher become tough old rams, fit only for shearing. The gentle "Elia"[11] proved the truth of the adage that the children of old maids and bachelors are the best, when he expressed his preference for children "boiled." Better so than, as hosts of them are served up to the world, underdone and devoid of flavor.

Those who protest against anthropophagy restricted to infants, are recommended to substitute the undesirable parents. Society will lose nothing by it. Figs are not gathered from thistles. Until the market furnishes a better article for family use, we must be content with indifferent fare. But one comfort remains—abusing the cook.

1. S. M. Dawson, *Sarah Morgan*, 548–50.
2. Ibid., 80–81.
3. "By which the aspects of an idea are brought into consistency and form" (John Henry Cardinal Newman, *An Essay on the Development of Christian Doctrine* [1845]).
4. "Withhold not correction from the child: for if thou beatest him with the rod, he shall not die. Thou shalt beat him with the rod, and shalt deliver his soul from hell" (Proverbs 23:13–14). Solomon was the king of the Hebrews.
5. George Augustus Sala (1828–95), a journalist and illustrator.
6. I love my wife; she is so foolish.
7. This concept was the cornerstone of Republican motherhood, which recognized the need to educate women so that they could successfully fulfill their moral role in the household.
8. Johann Wolfgang von Goethe (1749–1832), a German poet, novelist, and scholar.
9. Shakespeare, *King Henry IV, Part I*, 3.1.
10. Jonathan Swift (1667–1745), an English writer and satirist. In "A Modest Proposal" (1729), he argued that famine and overpopulation in Ireland could be solved by eating the country's babies.
11. Charles Lamb (1775–1834), English essayist, most famous for *Specimens of English Dramatic Poets* (1808). Lamb collaborated with his sister, Mary, on several children's books, including *Tales from Shakespeare* (1807). He also wrote a series of essays under the pseudonym Elia.

⁀ƆⱤ⥈

Sarah Morgan had a half-brother as well as four brothers: Philip Hicky Morgan, the son of her father's first marriage to Eliza Ann McKennan; Thomas Gibbes Morgan Jr., who died as a prisoner of war in 1864; Henry Waller Fowler Morgan, who was killed in a duel in 1861; George Mather Morgan, who died in Confederate service in Virginia in 1864; and James Morgan, with whom she was living in 1873.

Sarah idolized her brothers in her wartime diary. "Ah! there are no boys like the Morgan boys," she declared. "Why are not the rest of the men as good, noble and true as they?" Sarah described her youngest brother, James, as "every one's pet at home and abroad." "He is such a brave devil-may-care, generous boy," she added, "likes fun, frolic and danger so well that he would make a jolly old tar."[1]

By 1873, however, Sarah had revised her opinion of James. Disillusioned by his lack of emotional and financial support, Sarah penned "Brothers versus Sisters," a scathing insight into the state of her relationship with her once beloved Jimmy. The editorial also provides a deeper understanding of Sarah's relationship with and views on James's second wife, Gabriella Burroughs Morgan. "Your 'Brothers & Sisters' was admirable," remarked Frank, "but how much pain it must have cost you to write it! It is an article the truth & pathos of which every brother & sister who feels at all must feel."

Brothers versus Sisters, July 12, 1873

"Let every man seek another's, and not his own,"[2] is the one precept of the Bible at which man never cavils, and which he literally obeys, especially as applied to Sisters. His sisters are good enough in their way; woe to the one who should dispute it! But how vastly inferior to the sisters of Tomkins! Now Tomkins holds his sisters in utter contempt, and adores those of Brown. A singular humility leads men to doubt that good can come out of the Nazareth represented by their own family. Even persons who are not remarkable for their modesty, have a latent fund in reserve, which is exercised only in behalf of their relatives.

Another man's sister is the Procrustean measure[3] which dooms girls to suffer the loss of a brother's affection. An attempt at conformity is not only useless, but would be construed into treason. There are brothers to whom the natural roses of a sister are odiously vulgar, if the sister of that other man paints. Collateral ringlets, however graceful, are far inferior in his eyes to the mohair atrocity with which the adored one pads her head. He will crush the exquisite foot of a sister, in his ardor to kneel at the substantial shrine of number seven brogans. How beautiful is a well developed foot on woman! How he dislikes Chinese deformities![4] The only praise many sisters ever receive from brothers, is that which may be indirectly gathered from his laudation of similar charms in another. Let her beware of pointing out her pretensions, however, for her vanity would suffer death on the spot. That other man's sister is only to be rivaled by the sister of still another man.

And yet, to a sister, there is no praise so sweet as that of a brother. To a brother, on the other hand, there is nothing of more supreme indifference than the opinion of a sister. Some brothers resent as an impertinence any remark, whether favorable or dissenting, considering it an evidence of insubordination threatening the dignity and independence of that noble animal, Man. "Snubbing" is a wholesome and effective process devised to repress sisterly demonstrations of any kind. It is as infallible as Babcock's Fire Extinguisher. No home or dignity is safe without it. It is the Lares and Penates[5] enshrined and invoked under countless rooftrees. To make a sister feel her inferiority to persons she may justly contemn, is the self-elected duty of quite a small army of brothers. And yet the roughest fraternal bear is either openly or secretly adored by his sisters. They would gladly devote their lives to concocting unguents and lotions to soothe the proverbial irritation of the growler's scalp.

Occasionally a wife is the unconscious avenger of a sister, whose hidden worth she brings to light by force of contrast. Then, it becomes hard to bow down to one who is only somebody's sister after all. But there is nothing like possession to calm masculine enthusiasm. When a woman is bone of his bone, a man can weigh her as coolly as he does the rest of his relatives, and possibly form a just estimate of her worth. But let no jealous sister hope for promotion even then. More forbearance is practiced toward a selfish, tyrannical wife, than the most inoffensive sister ever received from even a model brother. The impulse to kick the creature that fawns, is irresistible. The exactions of a wife, the injudicious affection of a mother, and the prejudice of a friend, can urge a man to run. But the influence of a sister knows no selfish motive, is never exerted for evil, and seeks only in a brother's behalf the highest good. Where a man consults his sister for any other purpose than to show his disregard for her opinion, he will be found all the better for her counsel.

Hero-worship is necessary for woman. She makes an idol of anything masculine which will suffer her homage. A brother is the first and legitimate object of her adoration. If it ever changes, it is only through his own assiduous efforts to overthrow a faith wearisome from its very blindness. Man knows himself and his fellow man far too well to believe in the sincerity of such admiration. To him it seems exquisite irony, or deliberate falsehood.

He forgets that woman is ignorant of many things plain to his own eyes, that it is her province to invest others with every charm she herself possesses, and that in her sight his very errors are apotheosized. With her love repulsed, trampled upon, and all but shaken, she is still ready to perish in defense of his superiority.

The love of Brother and Sister is surely the best and purest bestowed on man. Whoever has it knows a love that never grows cold, a friend who never betrays, a counsellor in whose words lie safety, and a comforter whose sympathy can sweeten the bitter injustice of the world. Working together, and for each other, one in heart and one in pursuit, the most spiritual influence vouchsafed to man and the most elevating influence extended to woman is that of brotherly love. Strange to say, there is nothing more intolerable to a lover than the usual offer to "love him like a brother." It sounds in his ears like the death warrant of hope. It is sad to mark how many men reject this manna freely given each one, without money and without labor, and to hear them cry out, instead, for that other food which too often brings but sorrow and despair. Man's theory is that happiness lies just the other side of any height that he can attain. Tell him that it is to be found within himself, and in his own immediate circle, and he will either turn sceptic as to its existence there, or sacrifice everything within reach for the doubtful chance of finding it elsewhere.

It is not uncommon to find in this beautiful relationship a feeling akin to that which nourished the hereditary feuds of Montague and Capulet,[6] or Guelph and Ghibelline.[7] There are cases in which it would be cruel injustice to accept the opinion of one member of a family as to the character of the rest. Prejudice and unkindness beget misunderstanding and estrangement. Under steady pressure, man and woman will become precisely what each chooses to believe the other. Natural proclivities avail little. For evil, as for good, faith only is necessary to work any miracle. Remove the evil eye and the true character will reassert itself. Brothers and sisters who have created the wretchedness of their common home, have proved the blessing and life of some new habitation. There is a singular peculiarity about brothers and sisters, in the influence each exerts over the friends of the other. The strongest affection entertained by man for man frequently suffers metempsychosis, if there is a sister in the family. Capital fellow, Jack! *So* glad to see him on the street or at the club! But how one wishes him aboard the Polaris[8] when his sister appears! Celestial creature! how all others pall in comparison! It is only for Jack's sake that one wishes to spare him an unfavorable contrast.

And Jack, dear Jack, yawns afterwards, "Poor Tomkins! you bore him dreadfully. Girls are too conceited. They will put themselves where a fellow is bound to stumble over them, and then hit him when he is down." Once persuade Jack that his friend is to be his brother-in-law, and his affection declines as surely and steadily as the setting sun. He may be civil, nay tolerant, compassionate even; but he cannot repress a secret contempt for a man who would prefer "one of those girls" to himself. He kindly explains that marriage always weakens friendships. To himself, he adds, he never would have cared for Tomkins, if he had known he was to be his brother.

There is no denying that there are more good sisters than good brothers in the world. Almost all sisters secretly long for the approbation of their brothers. No brother ever yet grew melancholy, lacking that of a sister. Few sisters are unworthy of a brother's praise. Still fewer brothers deserve the affection their sisters lavish upon them. The brother who thinks first of his sister is considered a marvel. His fame extends afar. He is a hero whose renown is founded on the prodigies of love and gentleness. The sister whose life is one sacrifice for a brother, is not even thought worthy of mention. It is too common to excite remark. Vanity alone should induce men to secure this transcendent honor, which ennobles him who gives and her who receives. Instead, there are brothers who are ashamed of being thought civil to their sisters. It is a wonderfully good brother who takes his sister to any place of amusement, or to an assembly of any kind. The brother is always there, and generally accompanied, it is true, by a sister; but almost invariably it is the sister of somebody else. If he affects piety, the other man's sister has every facility for walking the church road to heaven, while his own sister runs the risk of being excluded, unless somebody's brother will take her there. Attentions that other young ladies accept without acknowledgement or appreciation, are treasured in memory by a sister through a life time. If dead roses from a brother are not cherished among the treasures of women, it is only because they are not more frequently bestowed. The more shame to those who withhold such trifles, since happiness depends on words and deeds too slight to be recorded, and, the closer the tie, the greater their value.

1. S. M. Dawson, *Sarah Morgan*, 37–40.
2. "Let no man seek his own, but every man another's wealth" (1 Corinthians 10:24).
3. In Greek myth, Procrustes was a son of Poseidon who preyed on travelers by stretching them or cutting off their legs in an effort to fit them in his bed. *Procrustean* describes the attainment of conformity by ruthless means.

4. The Chinese practice of binding women's feet to keep them small.
5. The ancestral gods of a Roman household, usually displayed in the form of small statues near the entrance of a home. The Penates were the guardians of the family larder, and the Lares were guardians of the home in general.
6. The two feuding families in Shakespeare's *Romeo and Juliet*.
7. Opposing political factions in Germany and Italy.
8. *Polaris* was the name of the vessel used in Charles Francis Hall's ill-fated 1871 expedition to the North Pole.

⁂

Since the publication of Carroll Smith-Rosenberg's study on the "female world of love and ritual," historians have often emphasized the strength and endurance of the southern female network, where women "revealed their deepest feelings to one another, helped one another with the burdens of housewifery and motherhood, nursed one another's sick, and mourned for one another's dead." From the cradle to the grave, women were bound together by their life experiences and sustained by their friendships.[1] In her editorial on friendship, Sarah provides a different perspective on these themes by analyzing the superficial "periodic intimacies miscalled Friendship by women," which, she argued, were forever tainted by the adverse "influence of society."

Friends, November 8, 1873

The shrewdest and coldest policy ever announced was, *"Use a friend as if some day he must become an enemy."*[2] No one who is hard enough, and cautious enough, to follow this advice implicitly, will ever regret it. But a generous soul would prefer the pain and disappointment which friends generally feel, to a cruel, mean and selfish security. Friendship is the one blessing without alloy that earth can give. Nothing can supply its place, or equal its calm content. The closest and most beautiful tie between parent and child is simple Friendship. Happy they who know its strength and value! Blood is the weakest of bonds. Friendship gives it tone and power. Family feuds and inveterate aversions prove that Friendship is more than consanguinity.

To talk of "my friends" is as reasonable as to speak of "my wedding rings." Such as it is, a man may own one. But unless he is singularly blessed, he is generally limited to the possession of one in a lifetime. A true friend is as rare as a sea serpent. Every one believes in its existence and has found one, or knows somebody who has captured a score. That is the end of it. Let each man, then, cherish his illusion, and beware of inquiring too closely into the truth of the yarns of those who navigate the sea of life.

In the ordinary acceptation of the term, Friendship is scarcely a desirable relation. Women, especially, have the most imperfect ideas of its nature. With rare exceptions, Friendship among them is as comical as it is with children. The most absurd excesses and unaccountable caprices actuate them both. One moment, toys and sweetmeats cannot sufficiently attest their devotion. The next moment, teeth, nails and tongue are ready to demolish the enemy. The bosom friend of to-day is "that creature" to-morrow. A refusal of a pattern, or an eclipse of the beloved by a full dress demonstration, is amply sufficient. A common admirer will kindle hatred of her dearest Friend in the loving breast of woman. Feminine Friendship has never survived the clash of conflicting interests. Indeed, few men have ever been strong enough to stand the test, and men are undoubtedly the truest and best Friends. If they once rise to the height of understanding the beauty and holiness of Friendship, they are capable of the heroism which is required to preserve it inviolate.

The periodic intimacies miscalled Friendship by women, lack the essential condition of duration. They have no foundation. Caprice builds; and caprice destroys. The very ardor with which they endeavor to identify this "alter ego" with themselves, hastens the inevitable catastrophe. To some expansive young souls, "Secrets" form the sole basis, commerce and proof of Friendship. No secrets, no friend! These exhausted, it is necessary to seek another soul to whom the well-worn subjects will be as good as new. Now the transfer of confidence is as monstrous as bigamy. Hence, the contempt and scorn heaped on each other by women who once were friends.

But, masculine or feminine, how many Friendships are made to last? Looking back after the lapse of a few years, we can not understand the spell which bound us. Either we grow beyond our soul's chosen, or they shrink below us. Which ever it is, the distance is soon perceptible, and is not altogether painful. The charm vanishes, and, with it, the old eagerness and delight. Time, circumstances and development are to blame. Certainly neither party will prove as faithful and agreeable in new combinations as they were to us. Friends of this class are like good worn garments; outgrown and useless, yet still capable of bringing comfort to others who are better adapted to them. It is better to adopt this view, than to indulge in the bitterness which holds that all things change with our humors. Estrangement is a natural phase in almost every connection of life. There is hope of reconciliation for all; save for the treacherous friend. "A reconciled friend is a secret enemy." The truest forgiveness of some grievous wrongs is shown by never coming in contact with the one who inflicted them. True Charity is not the simulation of the trust and cordiality which cannot be renewed; but it is putting the possibility of temptation beyond the reach of the wrong doer.

People are apt to construe passing civilities into something of deeper significance. "The hollow friendship of the world" is then decried, instead of the silly credulity of the dupe. The "world" never pretends to consider "Friendship" more than a conventional name. It signifies merely the intercourse necessary to keep up visiting, gossiping, opera boxes, dinner parties and the rest. It is to be broken without ceremony, when these benefits can no longer be reciprocated. Such "Friendship" is too expensive to be exclusively on one side. The world is no humbug about this, at least. It practices and preaches its doctrine, and, for once, is thoroughly consistent. Unalterable friendship would be an utter bore, could it exist in an atmosphere so inimical to it. Imagine a friend as unalterable as the fit of a bad coat, in shabby genteel pauperism, hanging on the prosperous friend it once commanded! The highest act of Friendship is performed by the world in hustling such a friend back to his legitimate obscurity.

It is only beyond the influence of Society that Friendship can flourish, and then in isolated cases. It requires two exceptional characters. The difficulty is to find these. To make a friend, one must deserve to have one. It is vain to rail against instability and unworthiness which emanate most likely from ourselves.

> "A friend thou hast, and his adoption tried,
> Grapple him to thy heart with hooks of steel."[3]

First be sure it is a Friend. Then forsake all and follow him. For a Friend leads only in the right way.

No sacrifice is too great to make for a Friend. Yet there are obligations, possibly imperative, which, once accepted, will undermine the most perfect trust. "Lose not a Friend for fine gold" is the safe and freely-to-be-interpreted advice of Solomon.[4] The severest test of Friendship is money. To Friends transformed to foes, we owe a reverence of their good name, and respect of the confidence once reposed in us. This is an obligation from which no wrong can absolve us.

Unreserved frankness is fatal to Friendship. Two Friends who undertake to mention to each other every defect they may chance to perceive as marring their general perfection, are on the highway to irreconcilable enmity. No Friendship is strong enough to survive repeated wounds to pride and self-love. The obligation of repeating all the disagreeable things which can be expressed, seems to be the sole understanding some people have of the duties of Friendship. The sooner such a compact is annulled, the better it will be for both sides. Only those who are truly great in character can safely interpose between a friend and his self-will. When a man is bent on ruin, he will prefer ruin to his Friend's advice.

The best Friend a man can have is a sensible woman. The best Friend a woman can have is a man who is not in love with her. There is such a thing as Platonic affection; but it is invariably on one side. The other is ever laboring to change its name and its nature. Hence the just suspicion to which Friendship between men and women is ever exposed. The man who proclaims its truth and beauty most strenuously, will be found, on close observation, to hold that "Platonic affection implies the privileges of a lover, minus the liabilities."

Friendship, unless it tends to moral, intellectual and spiritual elevation, is more to be dreaded than open enmity. Enmity at least has few opportunities of exerting deleterious influences, while Friendship is ever at work, to make or to mar. "Know a man's Friends, and you know the man himself."

To be a true Friend is the highest boon that man need covet. It comprises all that is good and honorable. He who deserves the title has the strongest claims on admiration and respect, whatever his other errors and defects may be. There are questions which greatly complicate the duties and extent of Friendship. The course our Friend insists upon may be the one we feel assured will injure him eventually, and effectually destroy our friendly relations. Arbitration is usually impossible. Pride shuts the door on justice, while we deliberate. The greatest fortitude is required to bear calumny and reproach in silence. But a Friend worthy of the name will strive to endure it, sustained by his knowledge and love of truth. The truest guide, and the most unfailing test of Friendship in all uncertain and perplexing cases, is:

> "This above all! To thine own self be true;
> And it must follow, as the night the day,
> Thou canst not then be false to any man."[5]

1. Smith-Rosenberg, "Female World."

2. "Treat your friend as if he might become an enemy" (Publius Syrus, *Maxim 401*).

3. "The friends thou hast, and their adoption tried, / Grapple them to thy soul with hoops of steel" (Shakespeare, *Hamlet*, 1.3).

4. Sarah may have recalled the phrase "fine gold" from *Song of Solomon*, 5. The meaning of the saying may have come from one or more of the many passages on friendship in Proverbs, some of which are attributed to Solomon.

5. Shakespeare, *Hamlet*, 1.3.

Preparing for the Springs

May–June 1873

Howell Morgan's departure to the Home and School of the Holy Communion Institute left a gaping hole in Sarah's life. Without Howell, Sarah felt "useless" and alone at Hampton. Her editorial work only added to the burden. Instead of giving her a sense of comfort and purpose, Sarah's writing made her feel anxious, and she grew increasingly critical of the pieces she produced. The familial tensions at Hampton compounded her depression and soon wore down her fragile health.

In Charleston, Frank was alarmed by Sarah's poor condition—in particular, by her "carelessness of living & desire to die." Convinced that a change of environment would benefit her considerably, Frank appointed Sarah as the *News and Courier*'s official correspondent for the season at White Sulphur Springs, an opulent and genteel resort located in the Allegheny Mountains, Greenbrier County, West Virginia, on the Virginia border. Boasting a magnificent hotel—the largest in the United States—"the White" restored health and happiness to its guests by providing them with majestic surroundings, fresh West Virginia air, and a regimented prescription of health-giving springwater. Frank was convinced of the resort's innumerable benefits and assisted Sarah with her personal preparations in an effort to hasten her departure to the "breezy blue hills of Virginia." (Frank always referred to White Sulphur Springs as being in Virginia, although the resort was located in West Virginia, which had been admitted to the Union as a separate state in 1863.)

Sarah's impending trip to White Sulphur Springs also provided her with a rare opportunity to nurture her gentility. Using part of her salary, she purchased traveling and morning dresses, a parasol, and other fashionable items, in accordance with the resort's elitist reputation. Still depressed and discouraged, Sarah was unaware that she had taken her first steps on a journey that would revive her health and, more importantly, her antebellum identity as a "proud Morgan."

᠂᠍ᢒᢗ᠍᠂

On May 15, 1873, Frank received a despondent letter from Sarah. Disturbed by her frequent bouts of depression, Frank appealed for Sarah to look at the meaning in her life, as a daughter, a mother, and a spiritual beacon to readers of the News and Courier.

Thursday Night

May 15. 1873

My darling! you ought not to speak of yourself so sadly. Remember that you have told me that your only ailment is your carelessness of living & desire to die, & I cannot understand how it is that you, good & pure as you are, should strive to escape from the work which God gives you & murmur because, for your sake, He does not take you to Himself. You speak of your life as "useless." I know of no life more important or, in its sphere, more useful. In your family you have your Mother & Brother to think of & care for. For your Mother you are able to do what no other person can. Howell is your especial care. What would become of him without your supervision? You know what he was drifting to when you assumed the Protectorate. Again, you have the power to do good by your writing; good not merely to yourself but to thousands of others. That is the difference between the work you *can* do, & the work that other women, in like case, are restricted to. It is not mere bread: winning. Your influence is no longer confined to your own house: hold. You have it in your power to preach to a larger congregation than Beecher & Spurgeon[1] command, and with words as much loftier, and thoughts and aims as much purer, than theirs, as the nature of woman is higher than that of man. Yet you say that your life is "useless." Down on your knees, child! & pray God to teach you that it is the soldier who fights to the end, not him who sticks his head wantonly in the cannon's mouth, who wins & wears the crown. [. . .]

I did not look when I left Hampton, nor do I feel, as if I had "overpowered" any one. You will, I suppose, carry out your threat, and strive to persuade me that *your* stripes & bruises are good for me. Hit me while I am down! One of these days you will be satisfied that your coldness cannot kill my love for you, & then, maybe, you will regret the cuts & thrusts which you often promise and very rarely give. The key to your present conduct is, I suppose, the belief that this passion of mine is an ephemeral affair; too fierce to burn for long. You will see. By the way, if your Mother is really anxious that "the man with the big hands"[2] should try *his* luck, she had better have him invited to Hampton at once as he proposes to go to England next month.

I am very glad that you like the chair. For Heaven's sake! do not attempt to carry it about. If you do you will lose more by that exertion than you gain by sitting in the chair. Make yourself a cushion, & dont forget a small cushion for the hollow of your back when you are very tired.

I am sorry that you missed the "Popular Service."[3] I may be able to send the article. Yesterday I sent you some themes: it is always a feast or a famine, now it is famine. Khiva was all right; also the piano! piano! piano![4] You are getting on very nicely. Rome was not built in a day, remember! The missing Tichborne, I send.[5] You will have seen all about him in the News & Courier. Do not plague yourself by attempting to read through the papers I send. Pick & choose; except where marked. Could you not give, say four hours a day to your work; one hour for writing & three for objective reading. Choose your subjects & read them up. Why can you not give us some thing in the strain of your Easter Sunday article; didactic, but not scriptural? It seems to me that you might write on Selfishness, on Charity, on White lies, on Parsimony, on Prodigality; on the deadly sins & cardinal virtues, as it were. These to be separate from your Saturday articles. You need training in the habit or routine of writing for the press, & the things I suggest, while admirable for us, would be easier to you, just now, than politics & the like. What say you? By the time you had run through them you could do anything:

F. W. Dawson:

1. Henry Ward Beecher (1813–87), a preacher and the brother of author Harriet Beecher Stowe (1811–96); Charles Haddon Spurgeon (1834–92), a Baptist preacher at London's Metropolitan Tabernacle.
2. Ervington Hume.
3. Sarah was probably referring to a service held during the Episcopal Convention in Camden, which took place during the second week of May 1873. The *News and Courier* published several pieces on the convention. At this time, Sarah was absorbed in the trial of George Tupper, who was accused of killing John Caldwell at Pollock's Restaurant in Columbia in September 1872. James Morgan was shot during the incident and testified at the trial. See "The Killing of Caldwell," *News and Courier*, May 10, 1873; Morgan, *Recollections*, 332–39.
4. "Khiva," May 16, 1873, examined the 1873 Russian conquest of a state in southern Uzbekistan; "The Piano Plague," May 16, 1873, reported on the piano-

practicing proclivities of young women that had prompted a French judge to restrict playing to seven hours per household (see chap. 8).

5. "The Tichborne Case," May 8, 1873, discussed Arthur Orton (1834–98), who had impersonated Sir Roger Charles Tichborne (b. 1829), who vanished after embarking on a voyage to South America on a ship called the *Bella*.

Charleston:

Sunday [May 18, 1873]

Your note of the 16th arrived in Charleston yesterday; but as it had evidently been given to the Conductor, & not to the Mail or Express Agent, it passed to Mr. Fourgeaud this morning & only then reached me. For Goodness' sake be easy about your writing. The two articles you enclose are excellent;[1] full of life & freshness; just what we want.

My purpose in writing now is to ask you to do your best in an article intended as a reply to, & comment on, the enclosed letter of "a Georgia girl" which I will not print until Wednesday, so that our article (yours!) may come out immediately afterward.[2] You will feel for her. Be careful not to be too hard on Charleston!

You ask me how good I am & how long do I mean to continue? I have no goodness unless it be goodness to keep my word to you, & to think of you, dream of you, plan for you & hope & pray for you now & always. That will continue as long as this life continues & be born again with more force & purity in the next. How can it be "sweet comfort" for me to hear that you are "ghastly & forlorn"? You do not pale for me; it is not my indefinite absence which makes you sad. Nor would I have you so, on any account. My one object is to make you happy, & unless I believed that to marry me would make you happy, I would put myself out of sight very quickly & trouble you no more. It does not please me to hear that you are suffering, dear; just the reverse. This is a mere business letter; you will have your regular letter on Tuesday.

Do not think, my life, that I meant to be harsh in scolding you on friday about your weariness & hopelessness. I would do anything to save you from pain, but what I said was right & true & it was best to say it. Do not blame me.

Yours always

F. W. Dawson

I have reopened this letter twice & lost six cents, because I feared that something in it might, in your depressed condition, seem unkind. Believe, then, that I intend nothing of the sort. D . . .

1. "Blue Laws in 1873," May 19, 1873, reported that a New Haven boy had been fined by the town council for playing ball on Sunday; "Suffrage-Shrieking," May 20, 1873 (see chap. 9).
2. The "Georgia girl's" letter, "The Sin of Being Natural," appeared in the *News and Courier* on May 21, 1873. In it, she sought advice on what she described as her "greatest fault"—the sin of being "natural" in society. Sarah responded with "Society and Propriety," May 24, 1873 (see chap. 8).

⁂

Frank's thirty-third birthday prompted him to reflect on the past year and look toward the coming one with renewed hopes of winning Sarah's hand in marriage.

At Home: Sunday Night

May 18. 1873

Bien Aimée [Much Beloved]; I intended to write to you a cheery comforting letter, but it is not in me. There was yesterday, my birth-day, a sort of moral accounting day, next door to judgement day & worse than New Years day; a day, in fine, when what has been left undone is every thing, and what has been done counts for nothing. If I could look over the record of the Angel these last 365 days, I fear it would be a sad tale for me to read. In some respects I fear that this last year, or the first nine months of it, has been as bad as any in my chequered life. You know that I am not a Saint, but I like to feel that I am going higher, not lower, & I could not feel that until a few months ago, & not now always. Indeed, when you stretched out your hand to save me I was trembling on the brink of temporal and eternal ruin. This was one useful act of your "useless" life! But now this life of mine is very dreary; always is, when I am away from you, and know not when I shall see you again. I am like the traveller in the long tunnel; there is light behind me, and light before me; but I have gone too far to see the one, and not far enough to behold the other. Is there light ahead for me? Yea! beloved, & for thee. And I shall try to deserve you, my pure of heart! Try to be worthy of you, & to convince you (as you are not convinced now) that you and yours could safely cast your lot with mine; that with me the sensitive plant would never have cause to fold its quivering leaves. If I could only write to you, or talk to you, one tithe of the tenderness I feel for you, it would convert you at once to my way of thinking, Miss Morgan! But I am treading on dangerous ground. Nevertheless, giving you credit for your honesty of thought &

word, would you not feel that you had lost something that belonged to you if you lost my love? Would it not be strange if no word of affection ever passed my lips? Would it not be saddening if there were no letters to look for at the Pump, these Summer days? Put it how you will, & upon what footing you will, I am *something* in your life; more, perhaps, than you know. And, par paranthèse [by way of parenthesis], your letters, sweet as they are, are not as sweet as they used to be. I write you lots about newspaper matters and articles & the rest, but I do not, for that, give you less of general letter writing. Your letters, on the contrary, are nearly full of "newspaper." And I hate newspapers; especially one called the "News and Courier." You think more of the newspaper than you do of me. That is patent. Sarah! have you forsaken me for that vile sheet? Have I nursed a viper to sting me; or more correctly, have I bought a keg of ink to be blacked in the face with? Is newspaper type, a type of woman: kind, or any other kind, or more than kin and less than kind. At all events it is the nature of type to make "an impression," which is more than I can do. You see, my sweet sweet child, that the mercury is rising by this gossiping. Now, about yourself. I dread the long hot Summer at Hampton for you and your Mother. It will exhaust you, and, as I have a literary lien upon You, I insist that you shall be kept in full health. I demand my pound of flesh; 17 oz to the lb. Mens sana in corpore sano![1] Can not you & your Mother go to some quiet Springs for a month, towards the end of the Summer? The Cherokee Springs in Spartanburg County S.C. will open soon. The waters are equal to the Va White Sulphur, the charge will be moderate, & there will be no crowd of fashionable fools to make fine dresses & things needful. I think that $80 at the outside would cover your expenses (with your Mother) for a month, including travelling &c You could very well afford that if, as I believe, it helped to reestablish your health which, as you know, depends very much upon surrounding circumstances. Dont say No! in haste. You are going on so handsomely in your new career that I want you to do the best that is in you, & that best cannot be had unless you are more composed in mind and stronger in body.

Do you remember my promising you a Canary? Three of the little featherless wretches are now blinking at the moon in the attic, & Mrs. Fourgeaud, to whom I spoke long ago, informed me to-day that the best of the three (in looks & singing) was for me. Which is, for you. I suppose the thing will be ready to travel in a few weeks. How shall I send it? Do you understand their treatment & have you a cage?[2]

The end! I have written you a long letter & not about business, and I insist that you drop the shop, for once, & write me a nice long letter for once instead of the half-sheets, & scraps, you delight in giving me. Send me such a letter as you would have sent before you became a literary Lionne [Lioness]. I will take no refusal. Give my love to your Mother, & Believe me

Yours always (it is so sweet to me to write those words)

F. W. Dawson:

1. A healthy mind in a healthy body.
2. As a child, Sarah had kept canaries, and during the Civil War she was especially concerned about the fate of her bird named Jimmy, whom she was forced to leave behind during the Federal occupation of Baton Rouge (S. M. Dawson, *Sarah Morgan*, 87–88).

꧁ꕥ꧂

At the time Frank was urging Sarah to spend the summer at a resort, Sarah was diagnosed with gastritis, an inflammation of the stomach lining, and the waters of West Virginia's White Sulphur Springs were suggested as an appropriate course of treatment. Frank was delighted with the advice and resolved to send Sarah there as a correspondent for the News and Courier.

Charleston:

Tuesday Morning [May 20, 1873]

My Beloved! your letter in which you speak of Dr. Taylor's[1] advice has just this moment come in. All my firm resolutions not to write except on business have flown away. Is it not strange, Providential I might say, that almost at the moment that Dr. Taylor was ordering you to the Virginia Springs I should have sent off my letter imploring you to go to some place which should have the advantages of those Springs with none of their many drawbacks and inconveniences. You do not refuse to go, except on the score of want of means. That is a difficulty which exists in your imagination only. With your City-stock, & what you will earn before the time comes to go away, you can perfectly well pay your own expenses and those of your Mother, at some quiet place, for a month or more. You need not even sell your Stock. You can give an open power of attorney, and borrow upon the stock about as much as you paid for it; with the option of returning the money within a specified time or of having the Stock sold. You need not do either. Riordan Dawson &Co think well enough of their fair contributor to do for her what they have done, whenever necessary, for every person in their employment; viz, to advance them two or three months pay, whenever it is necessary for them, by reason of sickness or otherwise, to have a larger sum of money instantly than they have in their caisse [cash box]. The only risk to us is that the person to whom the advance is made may grow worse instead of better; & in your case there is no such risk, as Dr. Taylor guarantees you a cure, & that you shall be a "heavier" writer than you are now, which least, in the literary sense only, I strenuously object to. I implore you not to allow any false pride to stand in the way of your recovery. Indeed I am so exercised that I shall be tempted to do something desperate if you refuse. Make any conditions you please. Forbid me to see you, or to speak to you, or to write to you, anything you will; only do not deny us the power of doing what strangers, as a matter of course, are glad for us to do. It is sinful to resign yourself to death, when you have the power to live. It is not manly to shirk the fight with difficulty and danger. Your life is not your own: God gave it to you, &, if you do not do everything you can to preserve it, you will commit suicide as certainly as though you thrust prussic acid down your throat. You say you prepare for death! How? Is it sweet preparation, to resolve not to live? Is not living the only true preparation for dying? I am sick at heart; pained, confused, almost angered. It is impossible for me to reconcile my idea of your duties and responsibilities with your morbid refusal to take the hand which God, in his goodness, holds out to you. It is so wrong of you to speak of "selling yourself"; that would be as wrong as a willing dying. And it cuts me the more, because, poor as I am, you must think (if you really think of it all) of selling your exquisite self to one who is richer than I in money, if poorer in love. See Dr. Taylor, at once; ask him what Springs in South Carolina or Georgia or even in Virginia will do for you. Choose some place where you can, if you like, keep up your work. I know that you will be admired; that, in the gay company, I shall soon be less than nothing to you; but I waive all that, for you are more to me than I am to myself. Finally, if you obstinately decline our offers, I shall write at once to Jemmy & he shall give you at once what funds you require. He has the money, or soon will have. I tell you that you shall not be permitted to kill yourself as you strive to do. Remember too that you will make my love for you a curse to you, if that love prevents you from doing what you otherwise would. Remember, also, that you will soon incur at Hampton, in doctor's bills, as great an expense as that of going to the Springs! That will soon consume your little fund. Why not use it to secure health, rather than merely to alleviate pain. I must stop. I am too much alarmed and excited to write coherently. I have not even looked at your articles. May God help you to decide aright; & if you submit yourself to Him I know, in advance, what your decision will be.

Yours always
F. W. Dawson

1. Dr. Benjamin Walter Taylor (1834–1905), an eminent Columbia physician who graduated from South Carolina Medical College in 1858. During the Civil War, Taylor served as division surgeon of Hampton's Legion before being promoted to the position of medical director of the cavalry corps of the Army of Northern Virginia. After the war, he returned to Columbia to practice medicine.

Tuesday Night [May 20, 1873]

I have been thinking of your affairs all day & my mind is made up. You must go to the White Sulphur & that soon. For years the proprietors, Peyton & Co,[1] have entreated us to send a regular correspondent for the season, & have offered us all manner of inducements in the way of reduced rates. Hitherto we have only paid some one who happened to be there. This year you shall go, with your Mother as chaperone. You will have to send us two letters a week & you will have full swing. It will bring out another phase of your literary ability. You must also do what you can editorially. Of course you will be "incog." I write to Peyton & Co to-night to make the proposition, & see what they will do. You will be paid for your work, & you shall pay every solitary cent that we have to pay. You ought to be off in a couple of weeks. I have the matter so much at heart that I shall plead your cause to you in person, & shall be at Hampton on friday evening or Saturday morning, most likely the former. Do not wait dinner for me. Unless there is some change of programme I will bring my next letter myself. The articles are good—the third can't be printed, you know. Dearest! believe me

Yours always
FW Dawson

1. George L. Peyton, manager of White Sulphur Springs and the Sweet Chalybeate Springs in West Virginia.

૮૪૯૮

On May 21, 1873, Riordan, Dawson, and Company proposed to the management of White Sulphur Springs that "since the consolidation of The News with The Courier, no journal in the cotton states can compare with

ours in point of circulation; and we believe that semi-weekly letters . . .
from your Springs, would be entertaining to our readers and would greatly
benefit you." "We have on our staff an accomplished lady-writer whom we
could send and who could do the work far better than a man," they contin-
ued. "She shall go if the expense is not too great."

Determined that Sarah should go to "the White," Frank helped her to
make the appropriate preparations for a genteel summer in West Virginia.
Unlike the postwar domestic ideal, which reflected social standing through
a clean and harmonious household, visiting the Springs required guests to
affirm their status by adorning themselves in the most elegant fashions.
Lavish yet tasteful attire, impeccable manners, and southern decorum were
essential and basic prerequisites for moving in the most elite circles. Aware
of the importance of outward appearances, Frank rushed around Charles-
ton in an attempt to purchase the materials that would form the staple of
Sarah's Springs wardrobe.

Charleston S.C.

Monday Night [May 26, 1873]

My Love! This is my first experience in shopping, &, while looking as wise
as an owl & as sober as a judge, I have had lots of fun.

1. I send you samples of all the grenadine that can be found, with the price
on each; also a sample of a delaine. I hope some one of them will suit.

2. I find that you can get a travelling suit here ready made. The simple
suits of brown linen, which I should think would do for travelling only, cost
about six dollars. Finer suits, consisting of a Polonaise & skirt, or of an over-
skirt, skirt & basque, cost from $7 to $20. Any of these last, the modiste [fash-
ion adviser] assures me, are good enough to wear as a morning dress at the
Springs. Make up your mind about the grenadine and travelling dress at
once, as you have no time to lose. You can write to me at least by Wednesday night's train. The letter will reach me Thursday morning, & whatever
you order shall be at Hope & Gyles's for you on Friday morning; it will be
safer to send to H & G than to the Pump.

3. Sign your name in full on the back of your City stock (your name as it
is on the Certificate) leaving space enough, above the signature, to write
three or four lines straight across; thus [diagram]. Send me the certificate &
as soon as it arrives I shall have fifty-five or sixty dollars to your credit, upon
returning which you can get your certificate back.

4. I have seen Howell who bids me say he is quite well and perfectly

happy. He had written you each week, but did not know there was a letter box in the school & did not send off his letters. Last Saturday's did go. He tells me that the books used by him in his lower class go, by the rules of the school, to the Principal to be given to other boys, & that he will get nothing for them; he has been to Holmes's,[1] with Mr. Gadsden's sanction, and has bought a new set of books, costing eight dollars. I spoke to him very freely about this & I think there must be some mistake. At all events I think that Howell should not be allowed to contract any debt for any purpose & I advise that you empower me to see Holmes & Gadsden for you, and pay whatever may be due, & give orders at the same time that if Howell wants anything he must come to me for it. I do not want to be officious, but I do want to do for the child what I would do for my own, & what you would do if you were here. Answer!

5. I send you two of my old slates; the smaller might be more useful at the "White" Sulphur.

6. Dont you want a parasol, or sunshade! You can get one of those buff concerns here for from 50 cts to $1.50.

I leave many things to write about. Riordan is satisfied. Keep yourself in light marching order; as you may consider it certain that you will be off within ten days or two weeks. Write up as many social articles as you can in advance so as to take holiday as much as possible at the Springs. My life! What shall I do without you? To: day I have been as contented as a King, because there was something I could seem to do for you: & if, in this letter, I have not told you a thousand times how pure & deep is my affection, you will know, I am sure, that it is only because I have been proving my love by my work. Good: bye, my beloved, & bless you.

Yours always
F. W. Dawson

1. Holmes' Book House, located on the northwest corner of Wentworth and King Streets in Charleston. The proprietor of the store was Francis S. Holmes (1815–82), a professor of geology and natural history. The superintendent of the store was A. Baron Holmes, thirty-nine.

Sarah was pleased with the samples but "grieved" by the thought of imposing on Frank's time. The personal nature of the task may have concerned Sarah, revealing in stark terms the extent to which her professional rela-

tionship with Frank was underscored by affection and even intimacy. In the following letter, Frank assured Sarah that such "commissions" were a welcome addition to his day and hastened her departure to the Springs.

Charleston Thursday April 29 [May 29, 1873]

My Love! you will really grieve me if you think that what little I am able to do for you is any trouble to me. It is the greatest pleasure that I have, to serve you. I am honored by your commands, &, for each thing that you allow me to do, I am the debtor to you for so much happy employment. If then, you think that you owe me anything shew me that you do so by sending me a host of commissions. Would that I knew how to discharge them better.

When I went to Reads'[1] to-night I found that all the blue: stripe was sold save 8 yds. I tried every other principal store & the pattern was not to be had. Time pressed & I feared to send new samples, so I took the nearest pattern I could find. The price was 25 instead of 33, the same quality, and I took 20 yds instead of 16, with the distinct understanding that it should be returned if disliked. Send it back, if you will, and leave the selection of another pattern to me. The white stuff was of two widths, broad & narrow. As you did not say which you wanted I took the broad. The bill will be

20 yds grenadine @ 25cts	5.00
4 " white ? @ 1.10	4.40
	$9.40

It was too late to stop this sum from this week's honorarium; so I will appropriate the necessary sum next week. I sent you some samples of charming summer silk at 75 cts a yd. Why not take one? The parcel was sent off to night to Mr. Suber, and will, I hope, arrive safe. You know how I would admire your blue: grenadine, my love; but *will it not be chiffonnée* [worn-out looking] *by the time that I see it? Answer me that question, without fail!* I should prefer you to buy the travelling dress for yourself. Speak to Jemmie; he will send you into town at any time, because he knows the need of hastening your preparations. The parasol, I shall be only too glad to get for you; but limit me as to price & fix the color. And please dont trouble yourself to "thank" me. I tell you again that it delights me to have something to do for you.

I am afraid I gave you a wrong impression about Howell, whose statement, however, was not very clear. The gist of it was that he had bought the books of Holmes with Mr. Gadsden's approval, Mr. Gadsden holding himself responsible to Mr. Holmes for the bill, which, as Howell naively told me, "could be paid at any time." I think that he has very little idea of the value of money, and the proper plan, of course, is not to allow him to contract any debts, but if anything is really wanted, while you are away, to whom can the child apply, if not to me? You may rely on it that I will not encourage any extravagance; but I want to win his confidence, which he is not disposed to give me, and I fear that your letter to him, revealing what I said, will make him look upon me as a tell-tale, the school: boy's bogy. I still think that you would have done better to authorize me to look into the affair, which I do not feel at liberty to do at present.

I note what you say about the probable removal to Columbia.[2] Do not allow that to trouble you. There is a good God above, & you will not seek vainly for a home, within reach of your work, when you come back, with new health and strength, from the breezy blue hills of Virginia. You will not, cannot fail, in your White Sulphur work. And, if you really want to thank me practically, be Well & Happy! I stop now to read the two articles you enclose, and abuse so unmercifully.

. . .

Why, my sweet, good child, your little article on Russian designs, with two or three verbal infelicities, is a model for imitation, & the Bennett article is awfully jolly. Where did you learn any thing about "Pi." Do you mean that if you cant get pudding you will take pie![3] In sober truth you are surpassing yourself. May Our God, the God of the Fatherless, bless & protect you, purest of women! I am so thankful!

And now, dear life, I must leave myself a corner for whatever may turn up to-morrow. There are so many important things I have to say to you about your journey, your style of work, your return and what comes after, that I hardly know how to write them all. Poor child! I suppose the end will be that you will have to go off without my counsel, & will do better than if you had it. A sweet good: night to you.

NB: dont forget my initials in addressing your letters. These do matter, although the name of the paper (as I said about "the White") does not.

1. J. L. Read and Company, located on King Street, Charleston.
2. James and Gabriella had probably intimated that they planned to move to Columbia for the rest of the year. Sarah was formally told of this plan during her trip to White Sulphur Springs.
3. "The Way to the Water," June 2, 1873, examined the Khivan conquest; "The Last 'Herald' Sensation," May 31, 1873, reported on the alleged romance between James Gordon Bennett (1841–1918), whose father was the founder of the *New*

York Herald, and Danish Princess Thyra. Frank's reference to "pi" is in relation to Sarah's article on Bennett. When discussing the possibility of marriage, she asked, "What kind of mother-in-law will the Queen make? . . . Would she, like other mothers-in-law, attempt to rule the very devil? Without mincing the matter, would the compositors be knocked into 'pi' whenever it suited her taste?"

⸎

After making preliminary arrangements with White Sulphur Springs, Sarah's proposed trip to West Virginia was temporarily canceled when Peyton and Company "changed their minds and refused to make us any concessions." Unwilling to accept the new terms, Frank negotiated the matter while making alternative arrangements for Sarah to visit "another Springs." Within days, however, the White Sulphur management accepted Frank's proposal, and Sarah's trip to West Virginia was confirmed.[1] Frank visited Sarah the weekend before her departure and wrote the following letter on his arrival back in Charleston.

Monday 7.p.m. [June 9, 1873]

My sweet, sweet, Love; I would have given worlds to remain with you to-day; because I saw only too well that you were very much depressed, & needed the encouragement about your work which I only can give you. And I write to you now, not only to express my confidence in you, but to assure you that as soon as you reach the breezy hills of Virginia all your doubts will vanish, and you will be your own brave self, able & ready to give us better work than you dream of & all that I (much as expect) could wish for. I have never deceived you, and would not expose you to even the possibility of failure. Remember that you will have my aid as fully as though I were by your side, & that you cannot fail because *we* (you & I) cannot fail.

The letter from the White Sulphur people is charming. They make a very low rate. They will give you "one good comfortable room, with good accommodations in every respect"; they say they "will be glad to have you" & they "promise to do all in their power to make your time pass pleasantly." Is that not nice? Can you be low: spirited any longer, my darling girl? I telegraph them to-night of your expected departure, & will write them to-morrow. Do, however, be cautious, &, coute qu'il coute [whatever the cost], dont go on Thursday unless you feel that you can stand the journey. No letter from Miriam. I will write again to-morrow. As your dear Mother kissed me to-day for you; you must kiss her for me. Would that I could tell you how infinitely dear you are to me; more so, a thousand times, when you are weak and helpless than when you are bright & gay. And I dont know, even now, whether my love is greater than my pride in you, or than my reverence for you. You are all in all to me; & so shall be for ever. Darling! dont fail to write me good: bye. Your pale, sad face haunts me so.

Yours always
F.W. Dawson

My business & money matters all right.

1. Dawson to Morgan, June 4, 1873, Dawson Papers.

⚬⟩⚬⟨⚬

On the eve of Sarah's departure, Frank dispensed with business matters to compose a sentimental declaration of love. He directed his letter to the News and Courier's *"incog" society columnist at White Sulphur Springs.*

Charleston
Wednesday June 11/73

My Love! I wish that some magician were here to tell me exactly what would please you best, so that I may say it; but I have no magic to help me save that magic of your smile which has taught me so much of peacefulness & content, & that magic of my love for you which has taught me to find "sermons in stones, books in running brooks good in everything!"[1] That magic, such as it is, must serve me for the nonce!

I wonder whether you will really leave Hampton to: morrow, & in leaving it, whether you will carry away with you any pleasant memories. It is a hallowed place to me; the rough granite blocks by the whirling creek; the sylvan throne among the pines; the "long walk," all too short, to the boundary fence; the fallen tree on the hill: side; the quiet little room, with its closed shutters, & the memory of the hours & days of sweet communion with you. Every spot has its sacredness to me, and I cannot help wondering what your recollection and mine will be of the place where, in the sultry August days, we next meet. I shall find you then improved in health, perhaps with a roseate tinge on your ivory cheek. I shall find you full of confidence in yourself, jesting at the fears you now confess, admitting that I have been a prophet for once, & that you could please the public in serving us. And there will be so much to tell, of what you have seen & who, of what you have heard. And how many fresh scalps, dear, shall hang at your belt? Ah me!

This faith I have—that my knowledge of you is for my good, & I pray that it may be for yours. You can make me prouder than ever of you; & you will do it, if you are so careful of your dear self that the body shall not break down and enfeeble the mind. No woman in this country is as thoughtfully pétillante [sparkling] as you, in strength of body, would be.

Mr. Riordan came to the office this morning saying he thought I might want to run up to Hampton again. That cannot be. The News & Courier will be sent to you regularly. Ask for it. If you find being in one room with your Mother in any way unpleasant, say so, & I will have a second room for you. The price they made is so reasonable that we can very well afford this extra charge, if it be essential to your comfort. The "railroad guide" came this morning and I will send it as soon as I hear of your arrival. For an hour or two I must now leave you, my bien aimée [much beloved]!

Evening

It is later now than I thought & I must hurriedly close, in the hope always that this note will only arrive a few hours before you. I have told you all I could think of about the correspondence. Make your letters long or short as suits the subject; write twice a week, & do not fear to write freely & naturally, which is sure to be well. You see that I am so in the habit of lecturing you that I forget myself. I hope you are comfortably quartered, & if your trip does you the good I expect what a happy "girl" I shall be when I meet you. Kiss your mother for me, & believe in the ever: increasing and fervent love of

Yours always

F.W. Dawson

1. "This our life, exempt from public haunt, / Finds tongues in trees, books in the running brooks, / Sermons in stones, and good in every thing" (Shakespeare, *As You Like It*, 2.1).

Thursday Night, June 12 1873[1]

11. p.m.

My darling! This is just the time when you should start from Columbia on your pilgrimage, and you will not blame me if I tell you that I have prayed most earnestly that you may have a safe journey & that the result, in fame and health, may be everything that we desire. But the rain is pelting down, and I think with dread of your weary ride to Columbia, & your waiting there, & your weak condition, and almost blame myself for not persuading you to postpone your departure to Monday, although I know so well that I should not have, even then, the sweet sorrow of again saying good: bye. To: morrow, however, should bring me some tidings of you, and I fancy that had you been too unwell to complete your preparations by to-day, you would have written to me before. My fault, however. You said you would write on Tuesday, and I asked you not to write until Thursday so that I might have your last words. I ought to have begged you to write on both days.

Your name is on the mail list for the White Sulphur, so the inevitable N & C ought to reach you regularly. I will not forget to send you anything of consequence that I come across that will be of service to you.

One thing I am the least bit fearful about. You may not find the weather very bright upon your arrival. Do not let that trouble you, & dont write your impressions until you have a pretty day.

What else can I say, or do, to please you, dear? I know not; though I am constantly thinking of you, repeating to myself your gentle words, conjuring up your purest face, living in the very memory of you. At least you are convinced of one thing, are you not? That your feeble health but makes me love you more, & makes me the more anxious to lavish upon you the wealth of my love. Kiss your mother for me, & so, Good Night, light of my life!

Yours always
F.W. Dawson

1. Frank initially dated the letter May 12, 1873, but Sarah later corrected the month.

ↄ℃ↄ

Sarah became ill and was forced to delay her departure. The news made Frank "miserable."

Office of The News & Courier,
Charleston, S.C. June 14 [June 13, 1873]

Your letter, dated yesterday, only reached me this (friday) evening, and it has made me more miserable than I have been for months, more blue, more desponding, worse Enfin [Still]! Your delay in going does not matter at all. The White Springs people will be suited exactly if you start on Monday. I want you, of course, to begin at once, but the four days will make no difference, if the delay, as it is, is necessary for your recovery of strength. What is it then that pains me? It is this talking about dying when I know that your living is the only thing that makes me live, the only thing that quickens any good thing in me. I do not want you to die for me. You can do me no good when dead. I want you to live; for me, or for somebody else! Only live. But I must not speak to you in this way. You need help & sympathy. Last night I was very uneasy about you, as you will see by the enclosed letter, which I wrote to you at the Springs. Do the best you can; do not let the day of your starting trouble you. Only, for my sake, do make up your mind to be well; do make up your mind to be strong. I can bear your hate, your scorn, your indifference, but your death I cannot bear. The very thought of it makes me so wild that I hardly know what I am doing. Pardon me my incoherence, & believe that if, for once in my life, I cannot write freely and cheeringly it is because I am so sick at heart about you. Your letter is as kind as kind can be, although you do bid me not [to] go to you, and I know how kindly your thoughts were when you wrote, but this does not, to me, make up for this dreadful thing, that you say you will not live. My God! My God! what will become of me. What shall I do!

Your work is nothing. You can do that. It is a mere bagatelle to you. I dont fear any failure there. What I dread is, your dying because you will not live. Is that all you give me?

Never mind about the tickets. Tell Jemmy to get single ones, and to give you the balance, about $30, towards paying the return tickets. Give him the enclosed note. I send you the Railroad Guide and some papers.

Believe me that I desire this letter to be all that you wish it, but I cannot play the hippocrite. All I know is that my life is wrapped up in you, that I adore you, that I had rather have you than the world besides, that I would sacrifice myself, in any way, for you, that with you I am every thing and without you nothing.

Do for God's sake write to me again, the last thing, before you go. Let not the misery last or I shall not last.

Yours in time & eternity

F. W. Dawson

Read the note to J M.M.

You will see by my note addressed to the "White" last night that I hoped you had not gone. Goodbye & may God bless you! D.

༼ༀༀༀ

Sarah recovered from her illness and finally departed Hampton for White Sulphur Springs. On June 22, 1873, Frank received a letter from his correspondent. Sarah and her mother had enjoyed a picturesque trip on the "luxurious cars" of the Chesapeake and Ohio Railroad, which delivered guests and their voluminous wardrobes directly to the resort.

In the following letter, Frank urged Sarah to view her arrival at White Sulphur Springs as a new beginning, banishing thoughts of death and depression and embracing with new determination and vigor the joys of living.

No3.

Charleston; Sunday Night [June 22, 1873]

I wish I could find some *one* word to express the happiness which your letter, received this evening, has given me. *Three* words might do it, and they have been said so often that they may begin to tire even patient you.

I am sure that you will grow strong & hearty if you will only cease to brood over what is gone. You have a chance now to begin a new and useful life. Will you, with Dr. Taylor's solemn words in your ears, refuse to live; for that is what your dying would be? Suicide, nothing less! Remember that there is no difference in God's sight between he who jumps into the waters & he who stands silently on the beach until the waters cover him. You tell me that you are grateful to one who gives you any little pleasure. Show your gratitude by living. This you will do if you wish to serve those who try very hard to serve you. As soon as your letter came, Mr. R telegraphed to bid you not write until you were ready; & to find out how you are. Any telegram from him is, of course, to be taken as a telegram from me. By sending in his name I get the benefit of his free pass as agent of the Associated Press, &, far more important, do not compromise you by connecting my name with yours. Remember, also, that the answer comes free to any dispatch that Mr. R *or I* may telegraph you. In case of any demur tell the operator so.

About your letters. Do not fear! In writing to the N & C you are really writing to me, you know; in as much as I only shall see your letters until I, exacting as I am, feel sure that they are what you would wish. You can write as freely as to me, and leave the rest to me. Pardon me for saying it, but your judgement upon what you write is not safe. Take "Age",[1] for instance, which I enclose. It is a capital article, one of your best; yet you say you are disgusted with it. I know more about these things than you do, and, unless I was confident that you could do what I wish I would not have sent you there. Dear child! dont you know that I will pray for you, that I never enter church or say my prayers without praying for you, that my whole life is a prayer for you. You will succeed, & soon shall laugh at your own misgivings. Remember, also, that there is no imperative need of more than one "Springs" letter a week, unless you choose to write more, provided that you will send us some other matter. By the way, I send you some scraps in an envelope which I asked Mr. R to address, as I thought you might not like to receive two letters in my writing by the same mail. But your letters are awfully long in coming. Thursday's letter reaching me on Sunday evening! Be careful about the waters, & do not fail to see Dr. Moorman.[2] And do not forget to tell me the cost of those tickets & the sum that Jem turned over to you. Business must & shall be attended to.

Your Mother's delight delights me. Do kiss her dear face for me and tell her how glad I am. How fortunate it was that you passed over the Chesapeake RR in the day time. I know that country from Richmond so well; & have tramped all about Waynesboro [Virginia] (where I spent part of the winter of '64) Rockfish Gap, Staunton & Smoots, one of the stations beyond. How glad you must have been, & what would I have given to be with you & witness your pleasure.

Good for the clerks! I am sure you will find them very attentive.

And what news have I to give you? William Trenholm and Frank have besieged me with questions about you, & I had either to say that you had gone to the "White" or tell a story. I did not tell the story.

I have found the prettiest cage there was in Charleston (to my taste) & yesterday I formally transferred "Sweet" to my room. His cage is suspended by a green cord (I could not find *blue*) from the cornice of the big window leading into the piazza, & he has been feasting to-day on figs & sponge cake. I never go into the room, dear! or leave it, without speaking to Sweet! He does not know me yet, & cant sing a bit; but you know what is done with little birds that can sing & wont sing. The poor thing is so young yet. Mrs. Fourgeaud has seven or eight still.

About myself I have very little to say. When I wrote to you on Tuesday I determined to write no more for several days that I might see whether this love for you was a habit or a fancy as you sometimes say. The experiment failed miserably. I have been more absorbed than ever in you. I have punished myself until I feel the grey hairs in my heart, & for it all love you the more. Is it not time to give up these experiments? I have a good deal to do, my own love, & must stop now, but I will write to you again to-morrow if only a few words. And in the meanwhile do not forget that I am always thinking of you, that I share your every trouble, that I have faith in you, & that the whole world besides is nothing in comparison with you to me. But why need I tell you, what you must know so well. Good: bye, dearest, & may God bless and protect you this sweet Sunday Night.

Yours always
F.W. Dawson.

1. "Age," June 21, 1873, examined American society's exaltation of youth (see chap. 3).
2. Dr. John Jennings Moorman (1802–85) began working at White Sulphur Springs in 1838 and became a specialist in using the springwater as a form of health care.

SIX

Feu Follet's Debut

June–July 1873

In the coming weeks, Sarah was captivated by White Sulphur Springs, a place where postwar disillusionment could be momentarily abandoned and the genteel legacies of the Old South revived and celebrated. Comfortably situated in the main hotel, Sarah wrote Springs letters that described the daily pleasures of life at one of the most celebrated resorts in the United States. "The White Sulphur Springs continue to be the enchanted palace of the Fairy tale," she wrote. "Society or isolation can be found here in perfection." Surrounded by elite families, bountiful fare, interesting conversation, and the "unflagging attention . . . of the best servants ever collected together," Sarah and her mother partook in a "summer idyll" of the sort they had not enjoyed since their days in Baton Rouge.[1]

As she renewed friendships with old Louisiana acquaintances, Sarah carefully concealed her writing assignments, which she believed would destroy her newfound status as an accepted member of Springs society. Writing discreetly in her hotel room, Sarah's letters were published in the *News and Courier* under the pen name Feu Follet (Will-o'-the-Wisp).

1. "Beauty and the Beast: A Tale of the White Sulphur Springs," July 1, 1873; "Style at the Springs: The Rush of Visitors to the Greenbrier White," July 23, 1873.

∴❀℃

Delighted as she was by her new surroundings, Sarah lamented her "double life" as a "guest correspondent" and resented having to devote part of her day to her "official duties." She wrote to Frank to tell him so. Shocked by her comments, Frank gently reminded Sarah that her professional "duties" had furnished her with a genteel summer in West Virginia. Only a day

after his declaration that Sarah's death would be "suicide, nothing less!"
Frank also began to regret the severity of his comments. Fearing that his re-
marks would plunge his friend into a state of illness or depression, he spent
the following week in suspense. Hoping to minimize the adverse effects of
his blunt appeal, Frank used the following letter to extend a preliminary
apology to Sarah.

No 4

Charleston:
Monday June 23. [1873]

This is the only paper I have, please excuse it.[1] Your answer to my dispatch
of last night has just come, and it makes me very anxious as it indicates that
you have been ill, and I fear so sorely that I may have been partly the cause.
If so, Forgive me, dear!

In reading over your letter late last night one point struck me which may
not have suggested itself to you. You say that you would be "perfectly
happy," if it were not for your "official duties." Have you thought that those
"official duties" are the means by which you go to the Springs? Your visit
there must do you good, & you say that your Mother is delighted, and, as
these two things are secured to you by your "official duties", you should, I
think, look upon those duties more as blessings than as any thing to be feared
or to stand in the way of your happiness. Then again: there is no possibility
of your failing. In the first place you have already done much more difficult
work, &, with the hints I gave you, there is no serious trouble in what you
now have to do. Again, I stand here ready to help you with all my little experience; so that there cannot be a fiasco unless *you* and *I* together are incapable of writing a letter from a Virginia watering: place to a public which un-
fortunately does not always appreciate the pearls we put before it. By: the:
way, you must make a point on the coolness of the nights, the absence of
mosquitoes & flies, the bountiful fare, the courteous & suave clerks & the
like. Do not fear to lay it on thick. They like it.

Tell me whether Dr. Taylor's letter[2] has reached you; and whether you
have seen Dr. Moorman, & what he says.

You tell me, dear, of your delight in looking at the Blue Ridge & of the
elevation of your thoughts and aspirations. Your letter last night did as much
for me as the mountains did for you. The knowledge that I had been the instrument of giving you & your mother the pleasure you so well described

was an intensely refining happiness to me. I did feel that I had not lived for nothing. Yet I lay awake, tossing about, for I dont know how many hours. The reason of it was that it must have seemed so cruel that I should have written even a suggestion of painful feeling at a moment when you needed so keenly some consideration and encouragement. That letter must have arrived soon after you wrote that which came yesterday. I did not want to write that letter, but my heart was sore and you seemed to have been hitting me when you knew I was down. Again, I ask you to pardon me.

I am sorry that you are sorry that you wrote on Saturday, but I will take good care of the letter. And, mark you! write when you are in the humor, & at no other time. If you are to wear yourself out in writing you had as well have remained at Hampton. We want you to grow well so that we can grind more out of you, &, if you do not gain strength now, what is to become of us next Fall & Winter & all the coming years? I entreat you not to overwork yourself. If you do you will injure us.

There are several things in your letter I should like you to explain, as I do not understand them. But I almost fear to ask. God helping me, I will do what I can.

I do not expect to hear from you to-night so I have written this early; wishing so much I could persuade you, as I fear I never do, of the depth & the constancy of my love.

Yours always.
F. W. Dawson

Do not forget to give my love to your mother:
N.B. Do not scold me, darling, if I telegraph to you occasionally to know how you are. It cannot compromise you, & I love you too devotedly to wait very long without knowing if you are better or worse. If you dont want me to do it, you must find some way to make me love you less, & you have not found that yet. Juste au Contraire [On the Contrary]!

Yours only
F.W.D.

1. Frank and Sarah often wrote on lined editorial paper.
2. Before Sarah left for West Virginia, Frank suggested that she obtain from Dr. Taylor a "sealed memorandum" explaining her medical history, which her mother could use "if by any mishap [she] were compelled to call in a doctor while in Virginia" (Dawson to Morgan, June 1, 1873, Dawson Papers).

No5.

Charleston S.C.

Tuesday June 24. [1873]

I am a firm believer in the life giving power of the Sun, and of fresh air, and I write to you to-night to pray you not to coop yourself up within doors, but to be out in the open air as much as possible. To you the mere looking at those glorious mountains, with their early & late lights and shadows, must be, in itself, a glorious pleasure, & I am sure that your own conscientious spirit will tell you that, being at the Springs, it is your duty to derive as much benefit from them as you can. You speak constantly of doing your duty to us; but you owe a higher duty to yourself, and, besides, as I have so often told you, the one involves the other. As long as you do your duty to yourself; & in the measure of it, you will be able to do your duty to us. A neglect of one must lead to a neglect (through want of power, not will) of the other. I wish I could have a talk with you for a few minutes & I could make this clear.

What on earth is the matter with your mails. It takes 36 hours to go from here to the "White." Yet your letter of Thursday only came on Sunday, & that of Saturday is not here yet—Tuesday night. I confess I am still somewhat blue, and it (the blueness) bids fair to last some seven weeks yet. If you want to make me glad, say that you are growing stronger & are in better spirits.

Good: bye, dearest,

Yours always

F.W. Dawson

୬୨୯୧

As Frank had feared, Sarah responded angrily to his June 22 letter, and he attempted, once again, to explain the context of his "unfortunate" comments.

No 6

Charleston

Wednesday June 25 [1873]

Do you know, dear, I regretted that unfortunate letter the moment it was too late to recall it. I was hurt, I confess. You will remember how hard I had pleaded with you to live, and to determine not to die. I was terribly depressed at the idea of your going away, and not seeing you, & at the thought of the change there might be in you ere I saw you again. Then your letter came; in which you again told me you wished not to live; that you had nothing but a sister's affection to give anyone; that my love was a "misfortune" to you; that I only loved you so because of the "insuperable" difficulty in winning you; that the fever of my love would pass, and turn to hate; that you would soon be no more to me than any other woman. This did cut me to the quick, coming at such a time, but you needed all my consideration, and I ought not to have said a word about it, knowing, as I did, that you could not have intended to pain me. Are you not sometimes so sensitive that a pin would hurt more than a crow-bar? I was so sensitive then that any suggestion of inconstancy on my part hurt me sorely. And surely I have been punished for my wrong doing. I had a week of torture. I knew what manner of letter you would write; how hurt you would be. Forgive me, my darling, will you not? This morning, long after day, I had the sweetest dreams about you that I have ever had, & you know that morning dreams always come true. I took them as meaning that I should have a letter from you this morning telling me how much you were pained, & that the dream was sent to say I was forgiven. In that dream I said to you what has been in my mind these many days. That if, in God's Providence, you do not recover, *I desire then, all the more, to be ever with you that I may soothe your wounded spirit & brighten, as far as I can, the evening of your life.* You know, dear, what a good nurse I am, & you have not seen me under the most favorable circumstances. Tell me that what is painful is forgotten and forgiven, & make me content again.

Your letter is in the printer's hands already.[1] It is capital, admirable. I, even, did not think that you could do so well, and I expected a great deal. It is so funny that you, who can write so, should doubt yourself.

Pray tell me what those tickets cost. Business is Business!

I do hope that your Mother is better; she must think me a brute. And I trust that you have news from Miriam. Her letter has probably miscarried, & if in Abingdon [Virginia] she is in a very healthy place.

I am glad that you have met one of your old N.O. friends. He, of course, will tell others. What are his initials? Mr. R knew several Kennedys in N.O.[2]

What a glorious place the Springs must be. Surely you had a good chance to grow better, and I, by my cruelty, have set you back so far. Do write to Dr. Taylor for that letter, if it has not come. Is your appetite better? I was so worried this morning that I telegraphed to you. I will not do it, so long as I can have good news of you, but you are so far away. I hope for an answer to-day, some time. The mails must be, as you say, upside down, but as I write every day nearly you ought not to be long without news.

The little verses which are enclosed I printed because I thought you would like them.[3]

You say, dear, you hope it will never be in your "power" to pain me again. It will always be in your power, but I will not let you do it. Should any thing be said which would hurt me, I shall feel sure that it was not so meant & will think no more about it. Can you not, my love, do the like for me?

"Sweet" is getting on very nicely, but they tell me that he will not sing for some time yet, as he is only about a month old. What does his mistress think of that?

I have not seen Howell but Frank Trenholm tells me to-day that he [is] "splendid" and enjoying himself "like a colt with the bridle off." I will call on him this week for you.

1.p.m.

My darling: this is better than being at Hampton. I telegraphed you this morning at 10 & have an answer at 1: This beats the "Express." Thank you ever so much, for your good words, which even the wires could not chill. But you will upset the calculations of the telegraph Co if you direct to one name an answer to a dispatch signed by another. "Improving in temper and health." The temper needed no improving. What business has a male brute to trample upon a woman; who is not (is she?) always a camomile (ought it to have an *h*) But that your health is improving. That is a grand and glorious thing, and if it were not so hot (over 90°) & I were not so old, I would make a fool of myself, stand on my head and bang the doors.

Now dearest! in your letter about the Springs you have taken a general view of the situation. In your future letters take up each part in detail, giving me letters to each; to scenery, to lodging arrangements, to diet & feeding the animals, to "the lover at the Springs" (not meaning Mr. Kennedy) to the manner of passing the time, to the ['wry?] faces at the Spring, to the cottages & hotel itself. And dont fear to be "personal" which is the spice of newspaper life. When the first ball comes you must "spread yourself" describe the costumes & give the initials of the persons described. Your "Preston" I suppose is Gen Jn S Preston of this state.[4] I am almost bold enough now to tell you all my dream of early this morning; but I wont. Darling, truest & best, all I love the most, Good: bye &, from my heart of hearts, God bless you.

Yours always,

FW Dawson

1. "The Eden of the South: Summer at the White Sulphur Springs," June 26, 1873.

2. Riordan had spent 1859 in New Orleans working on the staff of the *New Orleans Delta*. Sarah's Civil War diary mentioned a "Dr. Kennedy" and a "Mr. Kennedy" (S. M. Dawson, *Sarah Morgan*, 441, 482).

3. Dawson printed three poems in the *News and Courier*: Christina G. Rossetti, "Rest," June 24, 1873; Arabella Smith, "If I Should Die To-night," June 25, 1873; Edmund Clarence Stedman, "So Near and Yet So Far," June 26, 1873. Sarah clipped Smith's poem for her scrapbook (Sarah Morgan Dawson scrapbook, 1853–82, Dawson Papers).

4. General John Smith Preston (1809–81) owned a sugar plantation in Louisiana but resided in Columbia, South Carolina. A strong advocate of secession, Preston was elected chairman of the South Carolina delegation to the 1860 Democratic Convention at Charleston.

⁂

Sarah's enchantment with "the White" is evident in her first Springs letter, which appeared in the News and Courier *on June 26, 1873, and gave an overview of the exclusive resort and its myriad attractions.*

The Eden of the South: Summer at the White Sulphur Springs, June 26, 1873

The Happy Valley—How the Delightful Days are Spent—Eating, Sleeping and Flirting—The Phenomenal Attendants—Flies and Babies Conspicuous by Their Absence.

[From Our Own Correspondent]

White Sulphur Springs, Greenbrier Co., Virginia, June 21

After a long and weary search for a terrestrial Paradise, I have, at last, discovered the original site of the garden of Eden. If there is any archaeological evidence that that land of pure delight was situated elsewhere, an impartial judgement can only say that Adam and Eve would not have suffered much if the Fall which precipitated them from the first Paradise had thrown them into this one.

possesses some estimable advantages over the original. Here, at least, your stay is a matter of free will. Everything woos you to remain. Life is made so agreeable that you dread risking any change. There are no suggestions of flaming swords to oppose a return. And when a visitor reluctantly resolves to brave the outer world, Mr. and Mrs. Adam find the luxurious cars of the Ohio and Chesapeake Railroad ready to convey them to any desired point, with every facility for the transportation of the voluminous wardrobes which their prototypes never enjoyed.

What did people do with themselves before the White Sulphur Springs were opened? To what pools of Bethesda[1] did invalids resort before these were discovered? It is difficult to believe that those who present themselves here are in search of anything beyond recreation. The worn, haggard faces which arrive to-day are metamorphosed into the bright, eager countenances which greet you on the morrow. The pure, bracing air is tonic enough in many cases. The inert, resigned invalid involuntarily accepts life and strength, and finds both so sweet that the free gift is accepted gladly. Victory over the apathy induced by prolonged suffering, is a triumph reserved for the White Sulphur. It is not even necessary to taste the waters. A magic circle is traced by the Alleghany Mountains. Whosoever is weary of pain and of life has only to cross the mystic boundary to find himself free from one, to be more attached to the other.

IN THE CENTRE OF THE VALLEY

stands the hotel, surrounded by rows of cottages disposed in the most irregular, picturesque manner. Mountains, golden with sunshine or purple with shadow, form the back-ground on every side. Silver mists glide ghost-like along the ascent, while white clouds lay their soft cheeks caressingly on the forest-crowned summit. Imagination can conjure up no more lovely spot.

On arriving at the hotel guests are offered either a room in the house or a cottage. Many prefer the cottages; but each offers such attractions that it is difficult to be resigned to the necessity of occupying only one. There is an irresistible inclination to take both. There is no difficulty in believing that the hotel alone covers more than an acre of ground. The dining-room is said to measure three hundred feet. Before walking half the length one is disposed to multiply the distance by three. The drawing-room is vast enough to accommodate any number of unreasonable lovers, who have some unaccountable prejudice against human proximity. Chaperons can play propriety at a distance, which relieves all parties from the tedium of *Les Bienséances* [The Proprieties]. The ball-room, of corresponding dimensions, occupies the other extremity of the huge building.

THE CELEBRATED SULPHUR SPRING

is about a square and a half from the hotel. No inscription is necessary to identify the spot. Like Job's war horse, it scents the place from afar.[2] About a cubic yard of rock is hollowed out. This forms a basin for the clear, cold, health-giving water. Conscientious people drink it. The less stoical "make believe." His Satanic Majesty alone could relish the draught, and pronounce it equal to "our well"—a compliment country people never vouchsafe to the wells of their neighbors. Passing beyond the Spring, the road leads to the hot and cold Baths.

LIFE BEGINS WITH THE SUN

in this valley. Breakfast lasts from half-past seven to nine. Ladies and gentlemen come in laying aside hats, veils and umbrellas, tokens of early visits to the Spring, or of walks that will follow the morning meal. Every one looks bright and cheerful, gathering around the innumerable tables which form disconnected links of three vast chains. Each face expresses content, and the intention of enjoying life to the utmost. By nine o'clock, the last loiterer has caught up some head-gear and hastened out in the open air. The lawn is a parterre of drifting flowers, dispersing in every direction.

THE POSTOFFICE

is naturally the first resort. The clerk has grown indifferent to the pang of disappointment he inflicts every few moments. But it is quite a study to watch the applicants as they descend from the steps. First, one hurrying off to a secluded place with some carefully secured treasure. Next, another empty-handed and disconsolate. Then a gentleman with more papers than can be conveniently grasped, followed by one seemingly not much edified by a postal card.

Billiards, Ten Pins, or possibly more attractive tete-a-tetes while away the morning. Gentlemen who disdain these pastimes, assemble under the broad piazzas, and enjoy their papers, cigars and discussions, to the envy of the rash youth who has committed himself to less pleasant pursuits. At one o'clock gives notice that in half an hour every appetite will be expected to do its duty from half-past one to three. Those who may have preferred the charms of the siesta and their own society are warned that dinner is about to invest life with fresh attractions. No one dreams of neglecting the summons. Each enters the dining-room with that charming consciousness of conferring as well as receiving pleasant impressions.

Soon after dinner the parlor is deserted. There is an almost universal exodus, walking and driving. The drives are delightful, passing through the most varied scenery. Only the appetite induced by mountain air would reconcile one to returning in time for the 7 o'clock supper. Even the monotony of meeting three times a day at table, does not impress people sufficiently to make them forego the routine. The sun lingering behind the mountains prolongs the twilight glories, and causes inconsiderate youth, as well as its seniors, to disregard Dr. Moorman's caution against night air. Every where people are to be seen realizing their ideas of enjoyment. There is talking, laughing, smoking, walking on the lawn, groups on the interminable piazzas, in the cottages, in the parlors, and around the piano. At last, at such an hour as caprice suggests, sleep is invoked as the only agreeable relaxation omitted from the pleasures of the day.

THE HOTEL IS ADMIRABLY CONDUCTED.

No better arrangements could be made for the enjoyment of the visitors, or for the well deserved renown of the proprietors. The demeanor of the very servants is an additional attraction to the place. They display a solicitude for the comfort of the guests, and an anxiety to anticipate every wish, which would do honor to persons occupying a far higher rank in life. The universality of this sentiment is all the more remarkable, considering the large number of servants employed. The table is unexceptionable. The best of cooks perfects whatever Nature leaves undone. Lack of appetite moves the compassion of waiters who never weary of offering

A SUCCESSION OF TEMPTATIONS,

under which indifference itself eventually succumbs. The only failure yet observed was that of a venerable gentleman in rejecting strawberry icecream. True, he had very much the air of Caesar[4] refusing the imperial crown. He seemed to long to have it forced on him, or even offered once more. But officiousness forms no part of life here. The ineffable glance the patriarch bestowed on the dissolving view of cream, was one to dwell forever in the memory, and remain a warning against inflexibility. As far as even an exacting person can judge, the table at the White Sulphur is deficient only in flies. Every "home attraction" save that, is to be found here. Yet another "home" feature is lacking: As in the first paradise,

NOT A BABY IS VISIBLE

or audible in this Happy Valley. Whether they are born grown-up, or whether considerate mammas leave them on the other side of the mountains, is left to conjecture. The blessed calm is too sweet to be disturbed by any incautious word which might bring down an avalanche of objurgation from those who find in infant voices a music of the future superior, if not akin, to Wagner's.[5]

CHARLESTON SEA BREEZES

pall in comparison with this sweet, bracing mountain air. The thermometer is so little used to exert itself beyond sixty or seventy degrees, that it would "strike" if compelled to labor up to eighty or ninety degrees. On the whole, it rather disdains your thermometer, which tamely submits to scaling the nineties, or even a hundred, as a fair day's work.

THE VISITORS AT THE SPRINGS,

at present, are chiefly from the West and the far North. Baltimore and Washington are well represented, but South Carolinians are yet expected. Every train brings fresh arrivals, constantly increasing in numbers. A gay season is anticipated, and in a week or two the place will be thronged.

Feu Follet.

1. In the Bible, after an angel troubled the waters of the pool of Bethesda, it had the ability to cure the disease of the next person who stepped in (John 5:4).
2. Job 39:19–25.
3. "That all-softening, overpowering knell, / The tocsin of the soul,—the dinner bell" (Lord Byron, *Don Juan* [1819–24]).
4. Julius Caesar (100?–44 B.C.), Roman statesman and general. On three occasions, Caesar refused a kingly crown offered by Marcus Antonius (ca. 83–30 B.C.).
5. Richard Wagner (1813–83), a German composer.

Sarah's sister, Miriam Morgan Dupré, was visiting Virginia, and through a series of letters to Frank, she arranged to meet Sarah and her mother.

Charleston

June 26. 1873

Chère amie [Dear friend]! All my own matters are mixed and muddled exceedingly, yet I feel as merry as a grig to-day. I had the pleasure to send you this morning a telegram to say that I had received a letter from Miriam who, under date of Jne 23, said that she expected to go to Christiansburg, *only 6 miles from you,*[1] on the 25th, yesterday. She seems so glad that she will be able to see you, & you & your dear Mother will be so glad to see her, and I am glad as glad can be, because all of you will be glad. Does not that sound like monosyllabic baby: talk? But the great words of life & death are monosyllables; single ideas; keystones of arches; and why should I not be glad if you are glad? It is only another way of saying that I am the mirror of yourself, & that you cast no shadow on the glass. Strangely enough, I was going to write to you to-day for Miriam's address that I might make some telegraphic enquiries about her. God is good! Will you go to Miriam, or will Miriam go to the Mountain?[2] This brings me to an important point. You must not over: work yourself; & the programme you have marked out leaves no time for sun: baths and fresh air. You must give up one "Springs" letter or the "Saturday" article. I should prefer one letter and one article a week, to two Springs letters; but you must not do both. This is serious talk. I know what thought and time it must take to do work as you are now doing it, and (to use a homely simile, which you must not laugh at) we are not willing to kill the bird which gives the golden eggs. Your first object must be to get well and strong, & one letter and one article a week will be at the rate of twenty oz to the pound which satisfies these N & C Shylocks.

À propos de bottes [Without rhyme or reason], Riordan & I have been fighting as to whether your letter is not better than your social articles. He says he thinks it is. I say I know it is not, because each is incomparable of its kind. Seriously, you have done marvelously well, and you will see by the enclosed that I exhausted all my typographical skill in putting you properly before the public.[3]

Sweet did chirp this morning. Mrs. Fourgeaud says I am too impatient, but proposes to put her best singer as a tutor by the side of Sweet.

What of your blue grenadine and all your war paint? How many scalps?

I am so anxious to see that blue chef d'oeuvre and I know that it will have lost its freshness before I do see it. No matter! if only the soul and heart of she whom I love have gained, from the bright Sun and the mountain air, the freshness which they stole from her robe.

My darling! if you could see right down into the depths of my heart, & know how happy I am when I have the least chance of pleasing you, and how miserable I am when I pain you, then you would never, never, doubt my love, nor think that time or circumstance could make it faint or fail.

As to your programme: My idea is for you to remain two months at the White Sulphur, & go thence to Greenville [South Carolina], (stopping on the way down at Orange C.H)[4] remaining at Greenville until the Fall at least. You can easily go to Christiansburg for a week or two & give us something thence, being careful to retain your room at the White so as to return there. Or you can go to Christiansburg for a week or two after you leave the White Sulphur for good; or both. Tell me what you wish. It is needful that I should write to the Peytons at once, & I want to know, in general terms, what your ideas are.

My blessed saint! *There,* I was going to say, again, how I idolize you, and am wrapped up in you; but you are so weary of it, are you not?

Give my love to your Mother

& Believe me

Yours always

F.W.Dawson

1. Frank was mistaken: Christiansburg, Virginia, is located forty-six miles from White Sulphur Springs, West Virginia. The Christiansburg area was the site of at least two mineral resorts, Alleghany Springs and Montgomery White Sulphur Springs, and Frank may have confused the latter with the better-known West Virginia resort.
2. Frank adapted the proverb, "If the mountain won't come to Muhammad, Muhammad will go to the mountain."
3. Sarah's White Sulphur Springs articles appeared on the front page of the *News and Courier.* Frank used a bold type for the headline and capitalized and centered the opening words of each new paragraph.
4. Sarah and her mother wanted to visit Orange, Virginia, where George Morgan was buried.

No 11

What am I to do with you? When I left the office to-night I sternly resolved that, having written to you already to-day & mailed the letter myself, I would not put pen to paper again, on your account, until to-morrow. Alas! for my frailty. It is only two or three hours later, and I am scribbling away to tell you that I have just finished reading your second Springs letter,[1] & find it so bright & sparkling that I am obliged to sit down & tell you so, without delaying a moment. Does that please you, my love, to have my first impressions in that way. Down goes pen, beloved! I must take a dose of political economy to-night. Good: night, then, & sleep well, sweet Angel!

1. "Beauty and the Beast: A Tale of the White Sulphur Springs," July 1, 1873.

<hr />

As the Morgan women settled into life at White Sulphur Springs, Sarah had time to contemplate her future. Conceding that her return to Hampton was unlikely, she began to ponder "Where is Home?" For most of her life, Sarah had lived within the patriarchal households of her kin: under the benevolent rule of her father in Baton Rouge and within the households of her half-brother, Philip, and her brother, James. She now faced the daunting prospect of heading a household. While she had planned and saved for this outcome, Sarah nevertheless felt apprehensive about the consequences of her decision to leave Hampton. In the following letter, Frank attempted to dispel her fears.

No 15

Charleston

July 4. [1873]

My darling! pardon me for using this paper; it is the badge of your servitude & mine, a badge, by the way, that we willingly wear.[1]

Your sad words "Where is Home?" have been ringing in my ears all day. It would be very easy for me to tell you where I think your Home ought to be, but we must not talk of that to-night. I can, I know, direct the whole of your life as well as a part of it, & the reason that I have been able to do more for you than any other has done is simply this; that my idea, since knowing you, has been to prove my love by deed more than by word, by action as much as by thought of you. I have no greater power than any other gentleman you have known; & I have far less power than most of those who have loved you. This is a digression. My proposal was, that you go to Greenville after coming back from Virginia. The thought was that to go directly to sultry Hampton or red: hot Charleston would take away from you what you had gained under the shadow of the Ridge. You, I know, do not look upon Hampton as a future home. I do not wish you to do so. But there are certain things which ought to be done. Jem is the head of your house. He loves you dearly; no matter what "malefic" influence may be upon him. Now it seems to me that you ought, at once, to tell him what you think of doing (that is, what I have advised you to do, but not mentioning me) and ask him for his advice. This will give him the opportunity of pressing you to go back to Hampton, & will enable you to put your grateful refusal on the simple score of health. Suppose I were to die, darling, & you not my wife! A young man was murdered in Meeting St a few minutes ago, who was as little in expectation of a mortal wound as I am now![2] Keep well, my love, with your brother. It is his right & your duty. Do not allow it to be said by any one that you go to Greenville or elsewhere without Jem's knowledge & consent. He entered cheerfully into your plans for the Springs, & will now do whatever you wish. Pay him the compliment of advising with him. I beg of you to do this in your own winning way. And let me at the same time ask you to write to me as often as you can. That needs no thinking, & I know that you are glad to tell me how happy you are. And if you want to make me feel really jolly tell me that you have a good appetite, & that you sleep about 16 hours out of the 24. Your duty is to yourself, Mark you! Only by caring for yourself can you do your duty to us. Be idle now, that you may work hereafter. It is not worth while for you to do as I am doing; burning the candle at both ends. My lamp wont last very long at this rate; & if you dont love me, what does it matter? Better be with that poor murdered boy whose mother & father are weeping over him to-night! You never will know, in this life, how much I do love you.

Yours always,

F.W. Dawson

1. This letter was written on editorial paper.
2. The *News and Courier* reported this murder the next day ("Murder in Meeting Street: A Young Man Shot and Killed in a Billiard Saloon," July 5, 1873).

My darling:

Mr. W D Clancy,[1] the wit of Charleston, came to the office last night, and talked for an hour about the "essays" which appear in the News & Courier every Saturday. He began by asking whether they were written here or in England, not believing there was any one in the South who could write them. He said "I like them: the man is a genius; a man of original thought. Tell him, 'damn' him! that I congratulate him." Is it not shameful to swear at a man in that way? Clancy did his best to coax out the name of the author, and, as he could not succeed, sent the message I have given. I hope that you are convinced at last that it is believed that a man writes those essays, & that they deserve every bit of the praise that I have given them. The letter from the Springs is superb; the mis: spelling of "Briareus" was due to the devil; it was corrected in the proof.[2]

This is a lovely day and I would give a fortune, if I had it, to be able to leave this place, and gaze with you at the Mountains. There is so much happiness in a silent talk with those whom we love; the unspoken words are more eloquent than those which pass the lips. Do not the theologians say that the prayer which rises directly from the heart, the aspiration which is not clothed in words, is most acceptable to God? I can well believe it; for I know how unworthy of you seem the tenderest phrases I can write, in comparison with the thoughts of you & the loving desire of you, which is hidden in my innermost heart. [. . .]

Do you know, my love, it is more than a month since I last saw you, and, under the most favorable circumstances, it will be five weeks more ere I see you again? The time seems so long. Nothing keeps me up but the knowledge that this separation was for your good, & that you have, by what you are doing, secured for yourself and your Mother a visit to the Virginia Springs every summer! Think of that when you are disposed to take the hue of your favorite hill: tops. There is no fountain of Trevi[3] from which you can drink in Greenbrier, but a deep deep draught of the Sulphur water, taken with Faith, will serve as well. But perhaps next year, or the next, you would prefer to go to Europe! Darling, is Provence so very far away? It is only near when I sleep, and I am sure that you think of nothing but writing letters for "filthy lucre" and of the number of weeks you have to stay!

Why do you not give a pen: and: ink sketch of Dr. Moorman: It would do him good? And now I am going to ask you a question, as frankly as a brother might ask a sister. Your consultations with Moorman and your Mothers illness, together with little expenses you did not count on, must have made a sad hole in your purse. I ask you then to tell me whether you are sure that you have money enough to meet all your expenses until I meet you at Staunton [Virginia]. I charge you to answer this question, dearest, as honestly as it is asked. It may pain you to have me mention such things, but I am "a brute" & you will only find peace in telling me what I ask. Here endeth the lesson in fraternal relations!

I hope to see Howell to-morrow evening. I would have gone up to the School before this, but I am so tired always, & I know that he is quite well.

Give my love to your dear Mother, who is, I hope, much better by this time. You know that she has had many years of trouble and pain which have told upon her constitution, and, at her age, the power of regaining lost strength is not nearly as great as at yours & mine. Happiness & Independence, or anything approaching thereto, will soon restore you both.

Now, Beloved! I must say good: bye once more; praying so for the coming of the moment when my poor eyes may be blessed by the sight of your winsome face.

Yours always
F. W. Dawson

1. William D. Clancy (b. 1835), partner in law firm Whaley, Mitchell, and Clancy.
2. "A Summer Idyll: The Poetry and Prose of Life at the Springs," July 9, 1873.
3. The Trevi fountain is the most famous fountain in Rome.

ஃௐஃ

Sarah's "superb" Springs letter was "A Summer Idyll." Taking Frank's advice, Sarah wrote "freely and naturally," in a relaxed style. The letter provides an interesting vignette of a polished postwar elite, comfortably situated in ordered and elegant surroundings. Former slaves appear not as fellow guests but as an obedient waiter and as an escaped prisoner who is quickly subdued by a competent southern gentleman. Unlike the tired, dejected, and powerless elite in her "Andromeda" editorial, Sarah likened the Springs and its society to an antebellum oasis, replete with the clearly defined hierarchies of race, class, and gender. Perhaps the transformation Sarah saw in those around her was also closely related to her own metamorphosis from an unwanted dependent to a proud aristocrat.

A Summer Idyll: The Poetry and Prose of Life at the Springs, July 9, 1873

Music Hath Charms—The Beginners in the Ball-room—Hotel versus Cottage—The Lover's Walk—Sunset at the Springs—An Anecdote of a Distinguished Beau—The Escape and Capture of a Convict —New Arrivals

[From Our Own Correspondent.]
White Sulphur Springs, July 4.

The band has come and fully justifies all the anticipations of the lovers of music. It is in perfect harmony with the surroundings of the White Sulphur. Could higher praise be given? During the half hour before dinner ladies are distracted from the duties of the toilette by the sweet strains from the lawn. Dinner would be forgotten, but for the wise provision that these

TWO AUTOCRATS OF HUMANITY

shall not interfere with each other. The spiritual music dying away in the mountains, is the signal for the material music of china and silver to begin playing in the dining room. Incredible to relate, there are barbarians who are much more sensible to the melodious combinations of the latter. Before sunset, the band attracts every one to the lawn, which presents the appearance of a rare, variegated flower, with music for the fragrant perfume. About half-past eight, the scene changes to the ball-room. The piazzas and windows are thronged, and many persons love the perils of the highly polished floor and take seats within. But the voice of the charmer, charming never so wisely, has beguiled

FEW DANCES AS YET.

The four or five couples who have been persuaded to break the ice, and open that all-engulfing whirlpool called "The Season," dance remarkably well. The spectators scarcely regret the small number, being well pleased with the advantage of contemplating these at leisure. As usual, everybody seems waiting for everybody else. It is only the pretty feet, which absolutely *cannot* be controlled, which have broken through restraint. The daily arrivals are so numerous and ever increasing that, if confidence depended on numbers alone, timidity would soon be put to flight. There is a rumor that every one is expected and invited to appear in ball-dress this evening, to begin the serious duties which attract so many pilgrims to the White Sulphur. Among less frivolous people, the comparative merits of

HOTELS AND COTTAGES

supersede the exhausted topic of the weather. The Cottagers will not admit that the Hotel has a single recommendation, as a residence compared to their own habitations. The Hotel people cannot be induced to leave it for the boasted Cottages. Evidently every one is satisfied, and each is exactly what it should be. The Hotel, however, thinks it has the advantage when it rains. There is apparently some meteorological connection between the clouds and the dinner bell. Half a dozen times lately the bell-rope has acted like the string attached to a well regulated shower-bath. The first touch turns on the stream. The Cottagers protest that they like it vastly, which still further increases the shower-bath resemblance. Who has not seen blue-lipped, purple-nailed, shuddering forms clinging to the bath-rope, vehemently asserting their actual enjoyment of the torture? When the Cottagers invade the dining-room muffled in waterproofs, over-shoes and umbrellas, Hotel people vainly offer their condolence on their damp, bedraggled condition. Bedraggled? The most infirm and superannuated among them is persuaded that he or she looks like Undine[1] or some other water nixie. They insist that they are in their native element in the rain, and that they are not conscious of moisture. There is even an impression that the White Sulphur showers possess some of the medicinal virtues of its spring.

LIFE IS APPARENTLY AN IDYLL

in those tree-embowered cottages. There is no point of view from which they do not suggest a poem. Sometimes detached, sometimes consolidated, it is difficult to compute their number; but it must be quite large. A cottage is supposed to consist of two rooms, with a long narrow room back of these. But the plan varies considerably. Some have four rooms in front, as Georgia Row; some present innumerable rooms facing the lawn, as Paradise Row; and some are not cottages at all, as Colonnade Row, which is composed of fine brick houses, two stories and a half high. Every building has its indispensable piazza in front; many have one extending around three sides. Georgia Row seems the favorite on account of its proximity to the hotel, facing the ball-room. To the right of this row is the row known as New Cottages. Opposite these Virginia Row sweeps in a crescent, following the road on one hand, and the eastern front of the hotel on the other. Mastlin's Row completes the eastern line going north, resting against a background of the Alleghanies like a cross of pearls set in malachite. On the north, facing the parlor, are Carolina, Tansus and Colonnade Rows. Almost directly opposite the parlor entrance is the cottage once occupied by General R.E. Lee.[2] Facing the grand western piazza of the hotel, Baltimore, Paradise, Louisiana and Alabama Rows are irregularly disposed along the hill side, with the Greenbrier Mountains apparently towering over them. All say

THESE MOUNTAINS BASK IN THE SUNSHINE.

The trees hold out their Briarus[3] arms to catch the darting rays which pierce the shade. The boughs nod and whisper mysteriously to each other of invaded privacy and exposed recesses. As the day passes, a shadow like Doubt gathers around the base, stealing imperceptibly upward. The crest of the mountain still wears a halo of sunshine, and binds the glory on its brow as if to assert its dominion over light forever. But the shadow ever creeping upward, silent as a secret foe, draws an impalpable net over the summit. Enveloped in its meshes, the spirit of the mountain faints in the gloom like captive man. Everywhere darkness deepens and vague awe is king. Hope and light withdraw, apparently never to return. Blackness settles over the mountain, and despair locks it in a rigid embrace. But, as in real life, the light comes when the victim is resigned at last to rayless night. So now—

"Jocund day stands on the mountain tops,"[4] and touching the summit, dispels the gloom.

THE LOVERS WALK

is on the hill, at the back of Baltimore Row. The path is a gentle ascent, typical of what is expected of young ladies who follow it. Winding along the hill side are paths leading upward, downward, around and nowhere. Here the glint of broken rocks; there a mossy throne decked with wild flowers. The clear mountain air is laden with the perfume of pine and faint, unknown odors. The eye turns from charms above to charms below, ever resting on new beauties. Above, the unfathomable abyss of heaven; below, deep ravines leading, who knows where? Spiders are busy in these retreats, spinning the thread to weave dresses which the fairies will wear to-night. Perhaps there is to be a grand ball. Suspension bridges of a single line are thrown from blade to blade of grass, and these indefatigable slaves have already spread countless marquees for the dainty supper-rooms. The new moon promises to shine brightly over the whole.

ON SUCH A NIGHT

as this, young Jessica would be more than justified in preferring the society of Lorenzo, to that of her respected parent.[5] Surely on such a night as this, Dido died o' disappointment when Aeneas fled from her waving wand, leaving her to wear the willow, rather than run the risk of having it worn out across his shoulders.[6] Aeneas "could not see" the storm signals with which his love waved him back to Carthage. He only obeyed the waves which bore him on to Lavinia. How Lavinia bore him, history has not recorded. Probably he bored her. Most likely. They were married.

LE NOM D'UN FOU SE TROUVE PARTOUT![7]

Here, meditation is arrested by a glimpse of various initials carved about trees or a rough seat. On such a date, E.B., among many others, made a fool of himself. L.D. is in close juxtaposition. Are they married? He must have proposed! The man who could resist the impulse in this bewitching spot, is a wretch whom 'twere base flattery to call a villain. It only remains to be stated whether L.D. "found another Ben, whose Christian name was John."[8]

It is only under the influence of this charmed region, that one can fully appreciate the overwhelming emotion of that gallant South Carolinian; the hero of a hundred battles and a thousand hearts. Once, by way of variety, it is rumored that fate threw him here with an unresponding soul. The echo of that eloquent appeal still lingers in the valley, startling the cold-hearted with that cry at a wounded spirit, "If you don't mean sentiment, why the devil did you come?" Echo still murmurs, "why?"

WHY WILL BRIDES FLOCK TO SUMMER RESORTS?

Cupid is surely stupid, as well as blind, to permit such an unfortunate advertisement of the discomforts of matrimony. There is a brand new gloss about them as self-asserting as fresh paint, and almost as objectionable. Every one stares at them, and they seem afraid of everybody. No one dares intrude on their misery. The groom generally wears an air of dejection peculiar to a man who longs for death, who has resolved to die, but who shrinks from the crime of suicide just yet, trusting to a better deliverance. They say this sentiment wanes with the honeymoon, although liable to return afterwards with irresistible and conclusive force. But the first phase of the anguish might be passed in more soothing retirement. In a hotel every one analyzes it without the slightest sympathy for either sufferer, and quite ready to justify any desperate deed which may end the struggle. There was quite

AN EXCITEMENT,

yesterday afternoon, caused by the escape from jail of a negro man. He ran through the grounds of the hotel. The sheriff was in close pursuit, and fired three times at him on the lawn. A stampede followed, every one running to ascertain why others ran. The trampling of the army of waiters was like prolonged thunder, suggesting fire to the timid, as the cause of the panic. A Mr. Stewart arrested the man in his flight, and delivered him to justice in the person of the sheriff. Peace was restored. The band played an air calculated to reconcile the prisoner to his fate, and to soothe the excited feelings of the spectators. Among

THE ARRIVALS THIS WEEK

Are Mr. Corcoran and family, from Washington; Mr. Henry Middleton, of Charleston; Messrs. R.D. Caldwell, S.R. Botts, John Worsham, Mrs. James Alfred Jones and Mrs. Triplet, of Richmond; Mr. James Robb, of New York, and the Hon. C.M. Conrad, of New Orleans.[9]

Feu Follet.

1. Undine was a water pixie who was promised a soul if she married a human.
2. Robert E. Lee (1807–70), Confederate general.
3. In Greek myth, a creature with one hundred arms.
4. "Night's candles are burnt out, and jocund day / Stands tiptoe on the misty mountain-tops" (Shakespeare, *Romeo and Juliet*, 3.5).
5. In Shakespeare's *Merchant of Venice*, Jessica was the daughter of Shylock, a Jewish usurer, who eloped with Lorenzo.
6. In Greek myth, Dido was the queen of Carthage. She fell in love with Aeneas, whose boat was shipwrecked off the coast of Carthage. Dido killed herself when Aeneas left her to continue his journey to Italy, where he married Lavinia, the daughter of King Latinus.
7. One comes across the name of a fool everywhere.
8. "But when he call'd on Sally Brown, / To see how she went on, / He found she'd got another Ben, / Whose Christian-name was John" (Thomas Hood, *Faithless Sally Brown* [1820]).
9. William Wilson Corcoran (1798–1888), a banker and philanthropist who founded the Corcoran Gallery in Washington, D.C.; Henry Augustus Middleton (1793–

1887), a Charleston, South Carolina, lawyer and planter; John Worsham (1839–1920) served in Company F, Twenty-first Regiment, Virginia Infantry during the Civil War and later wrote a book, *One of Jackson's Foot Cavalry* (1912); Mary Henry Jones (d. 1886), the wife of a distinguished Richmond, Virginia, lawyer, James Alfred Jones (1820–94); possibly Nannie J. Triplett, a widow from Richmond, Virginia; James Hampden Robb (b. 1846), a banker and New York state senator (1884–85); Charles Magill Conrad (1804–78), a Louisiana lawyer and politician who served as a representative to the Confederate Congress in 1862–64.

As Sarah and her mother renewed their sense of family honor at White Sulphur Springs, James Morgan prepared to defend his reputation against the insulting remarks of another gentleman. Frank, who was a vocal critic of the southern code of honor, made an impromptu visit to Hampton in an attempt to resolve the dispute between James and another man before it led to a duel. Frank provided a full account of his trip in a letter to Sarah.

20

Charleston
Saturday July 12.[1873]
7. a.m.

I have just come back from Columbia, & will, as I promised, tell you about the trip. Late on Wednesday night I recd a telegram from Jem which I enclose. I took the 6 oclock train on Thursday morning, and went direct to Columbia. Jem was at Hampton; so I chartered a buggy & drove out. The trouble, I found, was this: There was a large party at Jem's on the 4th. Young Trezevant,[1] who stays with Lawrence Taylor,[2] got furiously drunk, and made a disturbance at the stable. Jem went down to stop it, and Trezevant cursed him furiously as "a liar" and "scoundrel," ending by drawing a knife to stab him. D. B. De Saussure,[3] Gen Butler[4] & others say that Jem behaved with almost superhuman coolness, only telling Trezevant he would see him the next day. That day Jem was taken ill. The poor boy had a congestive chill, & was only able to out home on Wednesday; the day he telegraphed me. He told me that he knew he could trust me, and that I would do what I could to avoid trouble. I decided to have a note sent to Trezevant in such way as to give him an opportunity of apologizing. Jem & I took the carriage on Friday (yesterday) morning to go into town to fix this. On the way we met Lawrence Taylor who told Jem that Trezevant was ill; had a high fever; was very penitent, & anxious to make amends. This changed the situation entirely, &, after conferring with D B De Saussure, we resolved to do nothing until after Trezevants recovery, so that he might have full opportunity of making satisfaction, which I am sure he will do. Jem will accept almost any thing, & Trezevant knows he is entirely in the wrong. Therefore, I consider the thing settled! Jem's conduct is worthy of all praise; so every one says. That, darling, is the history of the Hampton trip. Jem looks splendidly, as does his wife. They are alone, & even Mr. Lawrence Taylor is in town. It was a sad trip to me. *I* at Hampton and *you* so far away. I wondered at night whether it was your mosquito bar which covered me; and the night through I was tormented by dreams about you. The whole result is that I am so nervous that, as you see, I can hardly guide my pen. I will do better by and by. And your letter, which met me this morning, was a very sad one too. I did not, I think, make any mistake in numbering the letters, & where two bore the same date they were written on the same day. No 14 was an important letter, as it laid down your itinerary. Be ready to leave the "White" on the 15 or 17 of augt, & I will, if I live, meet you at Staunton & go with you to Orange C.H. The rest will be settled when we meet. I have made enquiries about Greenville, and find it is perfectly practicable for you to live there, until you can come down to Charleston for the winter. If you neither can, nor will, give me aught else; at least give me the happiness of serving you as a brother would. There is no fear that any one will ever see your letters to me. They are enclosed in envelopes, endorsed that the package is to be burned unread. There is only one cheering thing in your letter; viz, that you did, for a moment, wish to live. You can, if you will; but I fear that I have put too heavy a load upon you. You needed rest, & you are eternally writing. Make the most of your time, as I charge you, by my love for you, *not to write a single line for the N & C from Augt 4th to the day of your departure.* Your work is suspended from Aug 4 *until you arrive in Greenville.* I insist on this rest; it is to our interest that you take it. Give me your word that you will take this brief rest! And, indeed, if you do write, after the 4—, I wont print what you write. There! Miss!!! Should there be a big ball between the 4 & 15 I make an exception as to the account of that. I am épuisé [exhausted] & must stop.

Yours always

F.W. Dawson

1. Numerous Trezevants lived in Kershaw and Richland Counties, and it is impossible to know exactly to whom Frank was referring here.

2. Lawrence Whitaker Taylor (b. 1847), the youngest son of William Jesse Taylor (1806–77) and Alexina Jessie Muir Taylor (1811–57). In 1869, Lawrence Taylor married Catherine (Katie) deClemery Burroughs (b. 1848), the sister of Gabriella Burroughs Morgan, so he was James Morgan's brother-in-law.
3. Douglas Blanding DeSaussure (1832–82), the son of Daniel Louis DeSaussure (1796–1857) and Frances Martin DeSaussure (1796–1861). Douglas lived at Clermont during his childhood, was educated at the University of Virginia, and married Martha Lamar Stark of Columbia.
4. General Matthew Calbraith Butler (1836–1909), was a member of the South Carolina legislature. He resigned from this position in 1860 and accepted a captain's commission in the Hampton Legion. He lost his right foot in June 1863 at the Battle of Brandy Station and was promoted to brigadier general in September 1863 and to major general in September 1864. After the war, Butler became a leader of South Carolina's "straight-out" Democratic movement and served in the U.S. Senate between 1876 and 1894.

No 21

Charleston:

July 13. 1873

My dear Love: I forgot to say to you yesterday that I told Mr. Riordan that I thought that you had better take a holyday, on our account as much as your own, for the last two weeks of your stay at the Springs. He agreed with me, and tells me that he has written to you himself. I hope that it was a nice note; such a one as will relieve you of any uneasiness on the score of idleness.

I have thought very seriously of what you said in reply to my advice that you inform Jem of your plans for the future; & I hold to the opinion that it is better to do so. You know that I would not counsel you to do any thing which involved any possibility of humiliation to you; but I think that it is right to say to him that you think of going to Greenville or that neighbourhood for a month or two, so as to give him the opportunity of saying that while he has a home you always have one. I cannot believe that he will fail to do this; because his silence or refusal would prove him unworthy to be your brother or my friend. It is because the issue is so serious, dear, that I urge you to give Jem an ample opportunity of doing what is his duty, & should be his greatest pleasure. At the same time do not understand that I wish you to return to Hampton. I do not think that you would be happy there, and I hope you will never go there to stay; but you ought to have the right to go if you wish to go. I would not have mentioned this matter to you except that it is so important. For the rest my desire is to avoid any topic that can be painful or embarrassing until we can talk every thing over together, and I know that you will let me counsel with you, with the assurance that my one object in life is to make you happy, darling, in your own way. Can I say more? [. . .]

I am very glad that you are so bright and cheerful, but how am I to reconcile that with your sad description of your tired gaunt self. Do you not wish to give me a happy surprise when I see you? You have still a month to be at the Springs, and I feel quite sure that your last two weeks (the idle ones) will do you as much good (and more) as the preceding six. You will be able to watch the mountains all day long, and sleep at night without any haunting dream of letters and articles on the morrow. Will not that be nice? Do try, dear, to be as well as you can; it will give me so much pleasure, & I have none save what comes through you. Much love to your Mother. Do you take sherry or brandy?

> Yours always
> F. W Dawson

> Monday Morning
> July 14. [1873]

23

Darling! You will see by the enclosed that the Boston Globe has copied most of your article on "Mourning."[1] The Globe stands as high as any daily newspaper in America, & as a literary paper stands higher than the leading New York dailies. Your "Brothers & Sisters"[2] was admirable; but how much pain it must have cost you to write it! It is an article the truth & pathos of which every brother & sister who feels at all must feel.

> Yours always
> F.W. Dawson

1. "Mourning," July 5, 1873 (see chap. 8). An edited version appeared in the *Boston Daily Globe* on July 11, 1873.
2. "Brothers versus Sisters," July 12, 1873 (see chap. 4).

> Charleston: July 17. [1873]

No 27!!!

Poor Miriam! I received a letter from her last night, dated July 13. She had gone from one place to another seeking a pleasant spot & landed finally in Christiansburg, of which she speaks very highly. The air is good & the fare is good, but there are no good walks or drives, & there is too much dressing. Altogether I suppose it is a very nice place, & is sure to be so to you who will have the pleasure of meeting your dear Sister there. Miriam had not heard a word of you except through my letters. I wrote to her last night & told her what your plans were. I felt that I could do that as you had given me carte blanche. I hope to meet you at Staunton on the morning of Saturday Aug 16. We will go down to Orange C.H, remain there Sunday & go to Christiansburg on Monday. That will break the trip and save you from fatigue. Let this be considered settled, & say so, & I will so advise Miriam at once.

This morning I received a very sweet letter from Jemmie who asks me to send up Howell to Hampton, by the day train and he will meet him at the Pump. The letter is just as kind as it can be. Jem is quite well, and there is no sign of any difficulty. "Do dont" worry yourself about Howell. He will be well taken care of until you return to S.C., and, in the mean while, we will hold a council of war upon him. I shall take him to the depot myself, on Thursday Friday or Saturday of next week. [. . .]

Charleston:

July 18. [1873]

Bien Aimée [Much Beloved]! I have only a little news to give you to-day. I saw Howell this evening, and have arranged to go to the School, for him, on Wednesday morning next. I will take him to the depot myself, & put him in care of the conductor. I have written to Jemmie to meet Howell at Hampton, where he will arrive at 1. Had the trains run two months ago as they do now, I should have seen you, many a day four hours earlier, at 1. instead of 5. After settling this matter with Howell (I have notified Jemmie to meet him, and will notify the principal) I ice: creamed & caked him, & sent him to school in a car. He says he is very glad to go to Hampton. I have ground out a Saturday for you: tell me honestly what you think of it: I am not afraid of criticism, especially when I am swimming in strange waters.[1]

"Sweet" began to sing to-day. I began to think it a failure. It shall be a very Patti[2] among canaries!

It is not kind of you to tell me you are unwell, and then leave me for days in suspense as to your condition. I have nothing since Sunday, and if I have no news on Sunday night next I shall certainly telegraph.

It is intensely hot here. You will be glad to hear that our new type has come; & the double cylinder press leaves New York to-morrow. We shall strive to don our new dress by the first Monday in August. This is one more reason why I cannot shock you by going to the White. After all I should feel utterly out of place there. I never was much of a society man, and am less so now than ever before. Are you mad with me? Why is it that when I ask you questions which concern me, & must have some interest for you, no notice is taken of them? Give my love to your Mother &

Believe me
Yours always
F. W. Dawson.

1. "Love Letters," July 19, 1873. In this piece, Frank wrote, "As long as men and women love, or think they love, the love letter will be written. Valentines are love letters. And, rightly understood, every tender thought given to the fair woman we love, every thoughtful deed, is an unwritten love letter; speaking not from lip to lip, but direct from heart to heart."
2. Adelina Patti (1843–1919), an Italian opera singer.

Sarah responded immediately to Frank's letter, explaining that she pre-ferred to have Howell remain in Charleston rather than to expose him to the risk of yellow fever at Hampton. She asked Frank to speak with Howell's school and make arrangements for him to board there for the summer. When these plans proved "impracticable," Frank arranged for Howell to stay with the Fourgeauds.

Charleston Monday July 21 [1873]

My dear Love!

I have arranged for Howell to remain in Charleston. Last night I could not say much for the reason that the only plan you suggested had been demonstrated to be impracticable. Before I wrote to you or to Jemmie I saw Mr. Gadsden, and asked that Howell be allowed to remain there during the vacation, on any terms. He said it was impossible, and he could not even promise me the four days of grace that I asked for. That door being finally closed it was useless to try to open it, so I last night, when I went home, had a frank talk with Mrs. Fourgeaud. I told her that Howell's grand mother feared he would be sick at Hampton and had asked me to find a place for him in Charleston; that I could not bear the idea of sending him to board with strangers, & that I should like to have him at home with me. She consented cheerfully, subject to Mr. Fourgeaud's approval, which has been given this morning. We are all very fond of children & Howell will be in good hands. He shall have a room to himself, and I will see what can be done to keep him from running behind with his studies. As soon as he comes to us, which will be on Wednesday, I will have his wardrobe overhauled by Mrs. F, and will get him whatever may be indispensable, & keep a rigid account thereof for your benefit. Now, my dear love! will you be satisfied about that boy? Of course he knows nothing of this yet; I will see him & his principal this afternoon.

Last night was a wretched night for me. I dont think I slept half an hour. In truth your trouble about Howell made me so nervous that I could not rest until I knew that every thing was settled. To: night I will sleep like a top.

There is one phrase in Miriam's letter which I must speak of, or I might cause you to think that I had given it my assent. She says, "He (I) does it all, *without one Hope.*" I have never said this to you, or to her. Sometimes I am right to despair, but never for very long. I cannot live without hope. I am not impatient, but hope I must have, that I may live. This was more than I meant to say just now, but I cannot bear the idea of seeming to sail under false colors. I love you, and I am doing what I can to win your love. That is the whole history. By the way, will you deliver a message for me and give me the answer?

Say to Miss Sarah Morgan that "the love I had for her when I parted from her at Hampton was weak; & barren, in comparison with the mighty love I bear her now." And ask her "what she thinks of it?"

Do, darling, cheer up. You are over: much affected by mental trouble. This matter of Howell's has set you back I know; but that is over now and I see no other shadow in the immediate future. Dont work too much! By the way, are you praying for Time to pass slowly with you, while I am praying that the Sun may "hurry up" so as to bring me to you soon? Surely I am not "bogey" for you. Give my love to your mother & Believe me

Yours always

F. W. Dawson

Charleston: July 23. [1873]

No 33

I felt too unwell to write to you yesterday and I am not much better to-day. The pains in my head & general weakness make it very hard for me to do more than keep up the compulsory routine of work. The letter of yours was printed to-day.[1] It is very nice. I wonder that you have improved so rapidly in style & manner. I wish you could compare your letters with those which other first class papers have. You would esteem yourself more highly. If you regard my wishes you will take entire rest from Augt 1st. I can say no more. Should I by any accident be unable to write to you for a few days, I will get Mr. Riordan to telegraph, & you must not allow any malady of mine to interfere with your visit to Miriam, & your future sojourn at Greenville. I have arranged every thing, and all that you will have to do will be to "drift with the stream," as you say you are fond of doing. Yesterday, I sent you a little roll of note paper which I hope will suffice you. It need not be used for me; for whom the plain editorial paper will do well enough so long as your fair hand has passed over it.

Yours always,
F.W. Dawson

1. "Style at the Springs: The Rush of Visitors to the Greenbrier White," July 23, 1873.

ↄᗺↄ

The following is Sarah's first surviving letter to Frank.

White Sulphur
July 25th [1873]

I never enjoyed such peace about Howell; but it is more than counter balanced by concern for you. I never dreamed of such an arrangement. I am ashamed to accept so many benefits from you, I who give only pain to all who love me. But what can I do? Shocking as it is to be forever exacting & never returning, I am not insensible to the mercy it is to my poor little boy to be in such tender hands. I cannot wish him to change, either for his sake or my own. But it grieves me to think of the perplexity & trouble you must have had at first, & of the effort it must have been to ask such a thing of Mrs. Fourgeaud. Pray thank her for mother, & me too. With your letter came a most lovely one from Ella. She expected the child in a few days & promised to do every thing in her power to save him from fever. Nothing could be more affectionate & sweet, but her alarming accounts of the prevalence of fever on the place made us rejoice that Howell should escape such certain illness. She said she would move to Columbia in August; & that the doctor feared Jimmy would have the fever.

It is impossible to tell you all I think of what you have done for Howell; I shall not attempt it. There are a few things to be suggested, however. Give yourself no concern about him, please. He stands in awe of you, & will not deliberately offend. If he should fail to show Mrs. Fourgeaud or any of you the respect I would exact, give yourself neither the tongue of men nor of angels,[1] borrow mine for awhile. One severe tone will suffice. I hope he will not require it. Send me the account of his expenses. I may be able to discharge the debt at once. So much for Howell! As if you were doing your simple duty, Howell was enjoying his right, & I, an unconcerned spectator washing my hands of the whole responsibility!

Ella's letter chiefly pleased me because she spoke so sweetly of you, & of your kindness to Jimmy. Who does not? Here is mother, moralizing on the other side of the room of the small trifles that can make perfect happiness, & of the rarity of happiness in the world. "It takes so little, that I wonder why I have never been happy these twelve years, until I remember I did not know Capt. Dawson until lately." That is genuine. And that is the man you would work to death, or devote to paralysis or softening of the brain! Stop! there are so many others who could better be spare[d]! People unfit to live, or tired of life. But you—you have been God's providence for two women at least. Whatever regret retrospection may suggest, remember that you have made two sad hearts to blossom like the rose. God be with you.

I mean to improve. Yesterday I ate my mutton not to obtain the ice-cream which depends on it, but because I wanted it! Some saw tomatoes in the vicinity disappeared about the same time, perhaps with a secret understanding with the mutton. At all events, when John offered the usual second installment of ice-cream, I shook my head so sadly that he hoped I did not feel "bad." But I did! Who would not, whose yearnings exceeded their capacity?

"Will I answer the message that you love that odious Sarah Morgan better than when you parted from her?" (The quotation is not strictly accurate, but is quite near enough the truth.) What answer can I give? "An ye talk blank verse, heaven help you!"[2]

It seemeth unto me that Miriam counts on a long sojourn for us at any point where her ladyship may choose to alight. It can only be two days at most. Christiansburg, or any other, would suit us. I laughed at her objections on account of the uninteresting walks or scenery. As though we were going for either! You will not be in the way in the least. Au contraire [On the contrary], I trust to your presence to save me from some painful cross questions. I dont like to answer anything about myself. When they ask here where I live, I tell them I have no idea!

Mother sends her love, but she is always doing that. She is looking better than you ever saw her. Her cheeks are puffed out, just as her heart is with content.

I'm *not* lovely. I declined standing in the group photographed on the piazza this morning pour causes [with cause]. Take care of yourself. That is the only thing I ask which you do not grant me.

Sarah Morgan.

I will write not later than Tuesday. Verily you must not send me any more paper. I do not mean to give you so many letters, & if I did, you know you would not mind how they were written. At least, so I judge.

1. "They ended parle, and both addressed for fight / Unspeakable; for who, though with the tongue / Of Angels, can relate, or to what things / Liken on earth conspicuous, that may lift / Human imagination to such highth / Of godlike power?" (John Milton, *Paradise Lost* [1674], book 6).

2. "Nay then, God be wi' you, an you talk in blank verse" (Shakespeare, *As You Like It*, 4.1).

Ↄↄↄ

Sarah to Frank

White Sulphur.
July 27th [1873]

I was greatly distressed by your letter of Wednesday, & waited anxiously for last night's mail, hoping to hear that you felt better. Imagine my disappointment when the gentleman who usually brings my mail offered me only a Graphic! He said the mail was so enormous that it could not be distributed until this morning. This morning I sent a servant, & received just what I deserved—nothing. The postmaster sent word that someone had already called for my letters. And it isn't true! for it is night nearly, & I have not yet found the culprit. The explanation is that the man thought his breakfast more urgent than my letters, & locked the office for his Sunday holiday before I could protest in person. So I am left to speculate as to your condition. I would have written yesterday, only there was no use of posting a letter until to-day. Is that the way you obey my entreaties? I beg you to take care of yourself, & you write back of your very serious threat of illness. Do you remember Mrs. Wragg who filled so many orders for beefsteak & potatoes that her head was buzzing & buzzing all the time? Now Mrs. Wragg was not a fascinating person, even with that charm. Why would you be like her? Is it not a sin to destroy such a head piece as yours? Et pour qui? Pour une in-grate![1] Ah no! not that, I hope.

But keep well, I implore. It hurts me to know that one so good & kind is suffering. I will not be defrauded of my journey to Christiansburg, besides! Indeed it will never be carried out without you—unless you dont want to come.

Last night there was a flutter in the ball-room, over the Richmond In-quirer with the account of Wednesday's ball.[2] How I thanked Heaven it was not the N & C, & how devotedly I resolved to avoid personalities that could subject me to such an ordeal. The ugliest girls were the most eager to seize the paper. I naturally enrolled myself among them, & flattered an idolizing mother by crossing the room to ask permission to judge for myself whether her daughter's dress was properly described. Entre nous [Between us], any accurate description would necessarily have been most *im*proper. I skipped her entirely, liking the girl too well to expose her, though she seemed to have no hesitation about it. You would not believe how ugly one fifth of those "beautiful" "lovely" "sprightly" etc. people are. Two of them are absolutely hideous. Ah! but they were delighted with that Inquirer man! So were nu-merous anti-admirers of theirs. Every one had sport, & some few, justice.

Dont write until you are quite well. And please get Mr. Riordan to lock you out of the office until you resolve not to work yourself to death. If you will be good, I will write to you often. Only three weeks! Isn't it dreadful, the way time flies? Isn't that rather too mean?

Sarah Morgan.

I am decidedly better these three days.

1. And for whom? For an ungrateful female!
2. "Greenbrier: White Sulphur Springs," *Richmond Inquirer,* July 26, 1873.

ఎꝩꞔ

Sarah to Frank

White Sulphur.

July 29th [1873]

Last night's mail, nor this morning's brought news of you; & your three lines of Friday, received yesterday morning, only confirm my fears that you are seriously indisposed. I know nothing but illness would keep you from writ-ing. But you promised that Mr. Riordan should let me know how you were, if you could not write yourself. I never knew you to fail keeping a promise, & I am still looking for a letter, & dreading a telegram saying you are worse! Still, you must not write until you are quite well. You need rest; already you have given me too much of your life. I wish I could tell you how much we are grieved about your illness, or how glad we would be to alleviate your sufferings. If you would only understand that even that apple of your eye—the N. & C.—is not worth the sacrifice of your life! Suppose it becomes the greatest & most valuable of papers; will its renown affect you in your grave? Will a few thousand more or less compensate your mother for your loss? I know I should never meet any one like you again. It would make a vast gap in my life. Think of that, if only my troubles can move you! I only send this shred to let you know that somebody is anxious & concerned. I hoped to tell you I was still improving; but a hot bath yesterday rather injured me. Still, I am ever so much better than I was a week ago. The removal of that Saturday terror has lifted a thousand pounds from my brain. I know I should not take advantage of your indulgence; but from the hour I decided to try it for a little while, my face commenced to fill out, to the surprise & *admiration* of every one, including myself. Those Saturdays fairly kill me. I do not know why they should, for they are mere moonshine. Perhaps moonshine is my substance. Certainly each article represents a large share of vitality which is not regained. The letters are nothing. The only trouble is to find something to say. I could spin something from within, as long as thought lasts; but that can be of no interest to the public. Some of the facts seem too hard, especially if I told the truth of the men here. I have been introduced to a score to whom I never bow, finding it impossible to distinguish them. A little widow rebuked me for it the other day, & I fancy my excuse was rather harsh, sweetly as I smiled in saying I meant well, but had never been able to distinguish horses, dogs or men. Considering the noble, brave, true men I know, that was mean, wasn't it? I frightened away an odious little Charlestonian who joined in an amusing discussion I was enjoying with a New York lady. He said some nonsense about the mutual advantage to be derived from constant intercourse between ladies & gentlemen. In another mood, or man, I should have said something still more trite. But the fear of further intimacy with him made me say that it was decidedly objectionable; that woman's proper sphere was to be in perfect subjection to man; & that I was satisfied that any intimate knowledge of that noble creature weakened the respect that might have been maintained in the abstract. He glared—he was silent—he moved off. Never has he since attempted intimacy! Forlorn as Salome;[1] I have "no

Hebrew boy to smile away my blame among the Hebrew mothers," or to suggest I am not made of spear points.[2]

I enclose some money for Howell. I hope he does not trouble you very much. Dont write. But I should like to hear you were well.

S. Morgan.

1. In the Bible, Salome was the daughter of Herod Philip and Herodias. She danced in exchange for the head of John the Baptist (Mark 6:21–27). Salome was also one of the women who witnessed the crucifixion of Jesus and visited his tomb (Mark 15:40–16:1).
2. "And I went mourning, 'No fair Hebrew boy / Shall smile away my maiden blame among / The Hebrew mothers'" (Alfred Tennyson, "A Dream of Fair Women," *Poems* [1842]). In this portion of the poem, Tennyson relates the story of Jephthah the Gileadite's daughter, who was sacrificed after her father promised to kill the first person who ran from the doorway of his home if he was victorious in battle (Judges 11).

Frank to Sarah

Charleston
July 30. 1873

37

I am very much obliged to you for your letter of Sunday which arrived this morning. You are kind and considerate; but it is not worth while to trouble about my frame of mind, or condition of body. If you loved me it would be very different. I tell you now, to relieve your mind, that you have not given me any reason to suppose that you do love me. You need not, therefore, be fearful of compromising yourself, as you are; nor need you send your own messages in your Mother's name. My thoughtfulness for you, such as it is, is the natural out: come of my love. Only those who love as I do can know what that thoughtfulness is worth to me. My poor child! what would it serve if Mr. Riordan did lock me out of the office? Perhaps it is a blessing that I have so much to do; sometimes it saves me from myself. I can drag along with my work, but it is hard to overcome the lassitude which almost prevents me from writing to you. The anxiety of this newspaper, in its several branches, is about as much as any one man can bear without losing his senses. Add to that another anxiety equally constant, & more torturing, & how can I expect to stand the two for long?

A truce to these things! I hope to see you soon; it seems very long to me. Please God! I shall leave Charleston to-day two weeks, & hope to meet you at the "Sweet"[1] on the following Saturday or Friday. All the necessary arrangements are made with Miriam, whom we shall meet in Lynchburg [Virginia] on Wednesday Aug 20, which allows time for going to Orange C.H. Let me know when you will go to the "Sweet", & please see to it that if any letters of mine should reach the "White" after your departure they will not fall into stranger hands.

Howell is well & happy. Mrs. Fourgeaud & Mr. F & Mr. Magrath[2] say I'm a brute to make him say any lessons in holy day time, but the child is quite willing to study. I think I will let him off every thing but arithmetic & French.

It is so good of you to tell me that you feel better these "three days." You know how much pleasure it gives me to hear of any improvement. I have set my heart on seeing you reasonably well. As for me, I am ready to be ill for ever if that will make you think of me & write to me. But your "Springs" letter is exquisite;[3] you could not have written it a month ago, because you were not as well then as you are now. It is the most symmetrical & polished letter you have ever written to us. I am very proud of you.

I will try to write you a few lines every day, but I fear that while I am in this case my letters will give you little pleasure. Indeed! I reproach myself for not pretending to be better than I am, so that I may not cloud your content. Only pray for me that the time may pass quickly; that I may soon be with you. Above all, believe that I never willingly say a word to pain you, & that I am tempted to tear up this letter for fear it should hurt you. Forgive me, if it does. I cannot write it over. My head is thick, & my limbs ache & my eyes are dim & my heart aches. Am I not a fit subject for a Morgan Hospital? "And men die! But not for Love!"[4] Perhaps!

Good: bye my blessed saint! To the last moment of my life I shall love you; for to lose you is to lose all that could make life precious to me. I kiss your hands, & remain (& I do like to write the words, which I scarce can see)

Yours always

F.W. Dawson

1. Sweet Chalybeate Springs (Monroe County, West Virginia), or Red Sweet, was located sixteen miles from White Sulphur Springs and was one of the "Springs of Virginia," a collection of resorts that included White Sulphur Springs, Blue Sulphur Springs (Greenbrier County, West Virginia), Red Sulphur Springs (Monroe County, West Virginia), and Salt Sulphur Springs (Monroe County, West Virginia). Each resort was reputed to offer different health benefits.

2. William Joy Magrath, lawyer and president of the South Carolina Railroad.

3. "Scenes at the Springs: Stray Leaves from the Volume of Humanity," July 30, 1873.

4. "Men have died from time to time, and worms have eaten them—but not for love" (Shakespeare, *As You Like It*, 4.1).

.)C.

Frank to Sarah

Charleston

Aug 1. [1873]

My darling:

One of my troubles I had barely mentioned to you. Mr. R has been compelled to leave his wife[1] finally & irrevocably, & the conduct which made this imperative made it necessary that his little girl[2] be put in safe hands. He is endeavoring to arrange things so that there shall be no public scandal, but the other side, being in the wrong, are very malignant, and at this writing it seems likely that he may have to appeal to the Courts for a divorce and for the custody of his children. This would be horrible for all of us, but it may come in spite of us. You can imagine how this, coming at such a time, upon the top of all my other perplexities, bothers me and helps to break me down. Be then as patient with me as you know how, no matter how snappish I may seem to be. It is not meant for you, dear!

You must have had a charming letter from Jem's wife, but I am growing suspicious. Cats have velvet paws, dont they? The very description of the danger of fever would suffice to prevent you from allowing Howell to go there whatever the apparent cordiality of the invitation, & the hint that Jem & his wife would go to live in Columbia in August would serve to cut you off from any thought of returning if you had it. And just at the same time that she wrote that to you her mother[3] wrote to Frank Trenholm's wife[4] to say that Jem and Ella would stay at Hampton throughout the Summer, & this, I hear, is confirmed by subsequent advices. This is a queer world! "Seems!" boy "Seems!" Dont think that I mind your saying that you are sorry that your time at the Springs is drawing to a close. I can understand your feeling perfectly. You are happy & at rest there & you do not know whether you will be either happy or at rest when you leave that "Happy Valley."

Riordan has just come in from the lawyer's & says that his wife has agreed to a quiet separation; the little girl to go to a school selected by him & approved of by Mrs. R & the younger child, a boy,[5] to remain with Mrs. R for the present, without prejudice. These were his propositions. I hope there will be no further hitch.

Good: bye: If you are sorry your happy time is drawing to a close, I am wild with the thought that my happy time is coming. Think of it! I shall leave Charleston in ten days. *Non intende?* (See Marryatt).[6] The article I ground out last week, will have to serve for to: morrow's Saturday.[7] You are off duty 'till you come back to S.C.

À bientôt [See you soon]

Yours always

F. W. Dawson

1. Mary Riordan, twenty-nine.
2. Rachel Riordan, six.
3. Eliza G. DeSaussure Burroughs. Mary Chesnut described Eliza as having "such a sweet face, such soft, kind, beautiful dark gray eyes" (Chesnut, *Civil War Diary*, 389).
4. Mary Elizabeth Burroughs Trenholm, Gabriella Burroughs Morgan's sister.
5. Bartholomew R. and Mary Riordan had two sons, James (b. 1868 or 1869) and William (b. 1869 or 1870).
6. Possibly a reference to a phrase in a work by Frederick Marryat (1792–1848), a naval officer who wrote a series of seafaring novels, or by his daughter, Florence Marryat (1837–99), who wrote *The Life and Letters of Captain Marryat* (1872) and *No Intentions: A Novel* (1875).
7. "Second-Hand Swains," August 2, 1873. In this piece, Frank argued that "if the object of marrying be a life-time of tranquil happiness, not a month of delirium, a second-hand swain is more desirable than the frantic youth of the salad period, who has just discovered that he possesses a heart." Frank declared that the title "second hand-swain" was a "patent of nobility; a token that the possessor is desperately in earnest."

༄ SEVEN ༅

The Correspondent

August 1873

Sarah Morgan began to recover from her illness less than a month after her arrival at the Springs. Dr. John Jennings Moorman, the resort's resident physician, would have attributed her improvement to the daily doses of springwater, which, he believed, was a proven and effective treatment for gastritis. Yet the Greenbrier resort did something far more profound for Sarah's battered sense of self. The company, the facilities, and the servants at "the White" provided Sarah with the opportunity to embrace her girlhood identity as a Baton Rouge aristocrat. Many old acquaintances from Louisiana had not seen Sarah and her mother since the Civil War and were unaware of the hardship and heartache of their subsequent experience. Consequently, Sarah was able to reinvent herself, abandoning the "useless," single, dependent persona that had characterized her life at Hampton in favor of a genteel and accomplished self, worthy of her wartime status as a proud Morgan.

༄༅

Sarah's newfound status was closely tied to her associations with other visitors at the Springs, and when friends began to gossip, she grew anxious and upset.

White Sulphur S.

August 1st [1873]

As I sat down to write, a singular conversation between a lady & gentleman just at my door threw me into a panic from which I cannot recover. Judge for yourself! The gentleman was describing his room-mate, a correspondent—editor perhaps—of some paper. He said he could no longer endure his fault-finding & general hatefulness, & had applied to Mr. Peyton to give him some more tolerable companion. Mr. Peyton told him "that was the way with those people. They paid less, & gave more trouble than all the rest. He had been over-run by them, & bothered to death. The only exception he had ever met with was a Southern young lady who corresponded with some paper, & her mother." "A *young* lady correspondent! you mean the mother!" his companion cried rather sharply. "No I dont, either. Mr. Peyton says she is *very* young. He says he just turned her loose when she came, & she never bothered him, & he never troubled her after. And he says she does her work splendidly, too." "Good gracious! Cant you find her out?" was the next thing that paralysed me. I have not an idea of what became of them afterwards. No escaped convict was ever more alarmed. The object of their curiosity was only six feet off, staring horror stricken at the back of their heads. I think I would be overwhelmed with shame if I was published.

These unhappy little bantlings of mine suggest an old occurrence in connection with Miss Alston,[1] who wished, you once told me, to know the author. I saw her name one morning on the book. That night, a crowd passed me in the parlor, all of them strange faces. I singled out Miss Alston instantly, though she had never been even described to me. The lady to whom I applied for confirmation was amazed. Was it not singular? Ever since, we meekly gaze at each other. I never made an advance in my life, save to Mrs. Jones. Perhaps Miss Alston was never moved even by a Mrs. Jones.

Do not think me capricious. I shall not go to the Old Sweet. However inconsiderable the expense, to me it would be very serious. The sum could be profitably invested a thousand times over, for either mother or Howell, to say nothing of myself. Orange C.H. & Miriam will be quite enough variety for me. Indeed I doubt the expediency of the first. But for mother, I would not include it in the journey. I purpose to leave here on such a day as you may specify. The hour I should prefer to be 6 A.M. That would bring us to Staunton at 11, A.M. Am I to take tickets to Orange C.H., or for Lynchburg at once? The trains often wait three or four hours at Staunton, if there are many passengers expected. There is no possibility of missing you. If we should, inquire for Mrs. Hiden[2] at Orange. George is buried in her garden. She will tell you what hotel to storm. If unpropitious fate should still frown, pursue us to Miriam. Should that fail, let us meet in heaven! C'est le semettre au calende Grec.[3]

I have all your letters, including 36. The one inclosed in that, I instantly burned; without comprehending, I must say, its object.[4] I never heard of any charge against him, save the general disreputable one of being an ultra Republican, which seems a euphemistic term for corruption & general dishonesty. I am so grieved about that unification meeting in N.O.[5] I know some hundred of the members—know them to be men of honor & true patriots. But I am compelled to doubt their perfect sincerity. They mean to give the negro any right he can extort, & to put it out of his power to obtain any thing approaching equality. As I foresaw the Liberal defeat from that barter & sale with despised Warmoth,[6] so I see the political ruin of these zealous men, who put their trust in their own astuteness, & trust to outwit sharpers.

Miriam has found the accommodations desired in Christiansburg. She wrote asking if she should engage the rooms, & concluded by saying I need not reply, as you were to decide the question with her. She still appears under the impression that it is to be a long visit. I shall repeat that it can only last a few days.

Ever since the "Saturday" incubus has been removed, I have improved visibly. You will find me rather more than natural, I hope. Wednesday I tossed my hair into a puzzle by sticking a pin wherever it fell on the head, which nearly cost me my nightly glass of milk. John said it was so "beautiful" he didn't know me; my hair "becomed" me so! Mother troubles me though. She has eaten nothing of any consequence for several days, & seems to have a slight fever from cold.

As nearly as I can judge, leaving Staunton at 11 A.M. we reach Gordonsville [Virginia] at 2 P.M. Orange is nine miles beyond. But I have studied myself into idiocy, endeavoring to understand the necessity of twelve hours delay before starting for it. I will try to obtain further information, & also "bother" Mr. Peyton about the bill!

S.M.

1. Possibly Helen Alston (b. 1845), the daughter of John Ashe Alston (1816–58) and Frances Alston, fifty-one. The family resided in Georgetown County, South Carolina.

2. Cordelia Hiden, sixty, of Montpeliso. Cordelia was married to Joseph Hiden (d. late 1868 or early 1869). Many Confederate soldiers were buried on the grounds of Montpeliso and later moved to Graham Cemetery, on another part of the farm.

3. That is to put it off indefinitely.

4. Frank explained in a later letter that he was referring to allegations surrounding Franklin J. Moses Jr. (1838–1906), the Republican governor of South Carolina, 1872–74 (Dawson to Morgan, August 4, 1873, Dawson Papers). There is no surviving evidence to explain why Sarah burned the letter, but she may have done so as a result of Frank's comments about Moses.

5. Louisiana's Unification movement was, as Eric Foner argues, an "alignment independent of the two existing parties that . . . made far greater concessions to blacks' aspirations than 'reform' coalitions in other states, not only pledging to guarantee their civil and political rights, but accepting the integration of schools and public accommodations and an equal division of offices between the races" (*Reconstruction*, 547).

6. Henry Clay Warmoth (1842–1931), Republican governor of Louisiana, 1868–72. He was impeached thirty-five days before the end of his term for his role in the fraudulent 1872 election.

꙳꙳꙳

Frank and Sarah had agreed months earlier that they would discuss the future of their relationship on August 5, 1873. The plan had been revised as a result of Sarah's trip to Virginia, but Frank wrote the following letter regarding this original plan.

Charleston S.C.

August 5. [ca. August 1] 1873

How was it that we came to attach so much importance to this day than to any another? It could have been understood if my lips were to have been sealed until the coming of this particular day; but those lips refuse to be sealed, & can no more refrain from telling their love for you & to you than they can cease to breathe the fragrant breath of life. The one will end with the other. Yet we did agree that this should be an eventful day "big with the fate," not of Cato and of Rome,[1] but of a very ordinary man & a very lovely woman. Then came the proposed trip to Virginia, and it was agreed, I think, that this day should be postponed. I do consider it; but, however much either of us may try to ignore it, the certainty is that sooner or later you must decide whether you can bear with me for always, and when, if you desert me, I must learn whether I can live without you. And, whenever the time comes, you will have means of judging that you could not have had six months ago. I think I may say that I have proved that my affection for you is not a mere fancy of a day, or a month, but the deep undying and ever: increasing love of a life: time. I have proved to you that I understand you, & that the greatest intimacy leads to no jarring between us. I have proved to you that even confirmed ill: health, which you dread, will only increase and intensify my tender care of you. I have proved to you that your people are my people, & that they can love me as warmly as I love them. These are things which very few men can say to any woman whom they ask in marriage, but I can say them to you, because you know this truth. I do not press you for any decision. There is time enough for that. I only wish, on this day of all days, to remind you of what time has done, and to repeat to you, solemnly, my vows of constant and unselfish love. And it makes me glad to know that, whether it be requited or not, you never doubt now the truth of my love for you. My one aim in life is to win your hand; that gained, I have gained all I wish for, more to me, indeed, than riches or public fame, or the honors most men crave.

Yours always
F.W. Dawson

1. "The dawn is overcast, the morning lowers, / And heavily in clouds brings on the day, / The great, the important day, big with the fate / Of Cato and of Rome" (Joseph Addison, *Cato* [1713], 1.1). Marcus Porcius Cato (95–46 B.C.) was a Roman statesman and opponent of Julius Caesar. Cato supported Pompey during the civil war and later moved to North Africa, where he took command of the city of Utica and continued his campaign against Caesar. Cato committed suicide after Caesar's victory at Thapsus.

ↄᗄↄↄ

Sarah to Frank

White Sulphur
August. 4th [1873]

Some way, Aug. 5th came on the 3rd for me. At least I opened yesterday a letter with that date. It was a *beautiful* letter. No answer was expected. Of that of July 30th, nothing need be said. I laughed at it heartily. My poor boy! You need not try to be cross with me. It has the most pitiful air imaginable. It reads "If you get angry, I'll go on my knees." Now how can I snarl at you? Would it not be equivalent to saying I want you at my feet forever? For if it made me happy, you know you would do it! God bless you for being a good, true man, & send you some good you do not dream of.

No. 40. has just come. I am greatly distressed for Mr. Riordan. She must be mad to give him such trouble. And you would run the risk of an unhappy marriage? The sooner the world turns Shaker,[1] the happier it will be. Divorce, or more terrible regret! I grow sick at the thought of what your friend must suffer. And death only can help him!

You anticipated me in your Second-handed Swains, & did it so well, that there is nothing left for me to say. I meditated one on a similar subject. I need not say I am abashed by your brilliancy. Indeed I think I must yield my peculiar province to you. You are far beyond me. I look like an idiot following.

There is no possibility of your letters falling in other hands. They come in thirty six hours. Any that arrive later, will be sent to me. You will already know my determination of not going to the "Sweet." To-morrow your letter should come, saying if you still purpose meeting us at Staunton. Miriam must be content with the briefest visit. I must get to work as speedily as possible.

My rest is improving me amazingly. It was all I needed. I do not quite indulge myself though, there are so many things to be attended to for mother, as well as myself. I will write Friday, if there is anything to be made of it. But I am steeped in mental & physical lethargy.

Mother is very unwell. So feeble, pale, & without appetite, that I am terrified at her condition. Like myself, she clings to this place as though she were taking leave of life & happiness.

I am so thankful, and enjoy such peace about Howell! You will never know what I owe you. I have long since ceased to reckon it. It is all briefly comprised in some "thoughtfulness" of Capt. Dawson. Mother sends you ever so much love, & tells you that only the hope of seeing you reconciles her to the idea of leaving here. I dare you to repeat that that is "my own message in my mother's name!" Will you take a "dare"? If you cannot, perhaps you can accept a choice paper of "needles"?

Good bye. Au revoir the 16th, since it must be so! Heigh ho!

S. Morgan.

Please give the enclosed paper to Howell, with my love.

1. Popular term to describe members of the United Society of Believers in Christ's Second Appearing. The movement was at its peak in the late 1820s, when there were eighteen Shaker communities in eight states. One of the movement's basic tenets was celibacy.

♋︎

Frank to Sarah

44

Charleston

Monday Night [August 4, 1873]

My dearest! This is to-morrow's letter begun to: night. Apart from the loss to you of the visit to the Sweet I am quite content to meet you at Staunton on Saturday morning as originally proposed. As I understand the railroad guide there is no waiting at Gordonsville at which point the train for Orange

CH makes close connection. My meeting you on Saturday depends however on Mr. Riordan's movement. He must make some instant disposition of his little girl, and will most likely go to Baltimore or elsewhere with her. As soon as he comes back I shall be free. [. . .]

It is a happy thing that the person whom you over heard said such sweet things about you. You have done your work splendidly, and you will find that when you return you will be able to write leading articles as easily as you write your letters. Indeed, the last ought to be easier, because there is no chance of tracing them to you. Of course I am delighted to hear that you continue to improve, but I hope that you do not abuse those unfortunate "Saturdays" so in order to prepare me for some forthcoming refusal to do any more work for the paper. *Is that what you mean?*

I am sorry your Mother does not improve. Would not that trip to the Sweet have been of vast service to her?

As to [Franklin J.] Moses [Jr.]! the articles to which I alluded in the N&C (& to which he refused) accused him of crimes to which robbery and general corruption are virtues.[1] I believe him to be guilty. As you say; that Louisiana movement is a blunder; who shall bid against radicals for negro votes. If we eat a spoonful of dirt they will cheerfully swallow a peck. I think the men honestly meant to do what they said; they would have tried it and failed as they deserved. Our Reform movement here was a very different thing.[2]

I enclose some matters that may amuse you.

Yours always

F. W. Dawson

1. The *News and Courier* published a series of articles on Moses during this period, mostly alluding to allegations of misconduct. See, for example, "Governor Moses and the Colleton Gazette," July 21, 1873; "Governor Moses: His Duty and the Duty of the People," July 22, 1873.
2. Frank was referring to the Union Reform Party of South Carolina, which campaigned for fair administration of the Fifteenth Amendment. In 1870, the party nominated Richard B. Carpenter for governor, but he lost the election to Radical candidate Robert Kingston Scott (1826–1900).

≈✺≈

Developments in Riordan's divorce proceedings made it imperative that the couple's daughter, Rachel, be placed at a boarding school. Frank sent an immediate dispatch to Sarah, hoping that she could convince his wartime friend, Hetty Cary Pegram, to accept Rachel at the Southern Home School in Baltimore, where Pegram was the principal.

Coming from the ball-room last night, I found your telegram under my door. I hardly read it through, before I started in search of Mrs. Pegram,[1] who had never been introduced to me. This morning, I have but a confused idea of your message. But then, I was so excited that I thought I did. I tried the parlor, walked up the hill to a distant cottage, then the piazzas, & at last found her at the ball-room window, & put the telegram in her hand, merely asking her to step aside a moment. She read it, glanced at the address, asked if it was my name, & then asked who Mr. Dawson was. I said she perhaps knew him as Capt. Dawson in Richmond. "English? Frank D.? He is a dear friend!" she exclaimed so prettily, that we both shook hands, in admiration of knowing such a person. I waived the discussion of your merits for an immediate reply. She called her mother[2] out, & we three retired to a quiet place. They were both doubtful, saying they had repeatedly refused children under half grown, & had only within a few days declined a young girl whose little sister of nine was made a condition. I was very much excited. Said all that was in my heart about Mr. Riordan, amazed them next by saying I never met him, but knew him through you, & of his perplexity about his little girl, through hear say. That it was imperative for family reasons that she should be placed in safe hands, & that you had probably recommended her as the best, as you were always befriending every one in trouble. They asked what was the "family" reason. I said I knew nothing, save that Mr. Riordan was bravely endeavoring to silence all scandal, & to make proper provisions for his family; but that there had been some talk of a separation. I added that nothing but their hesitation would have induced me to mention a matter which Mr. Riordan would never have published, & that I hoped they would not refer to it again, understanding how painful it must be to me to intimate that the child needed better protection than her mother's. They said they would hold it sacred, & added that but for that information, they must have declined breaking their rules. Old Mrs. Cary pressed my hand, & said "my dear, your friend could not have secured a better pleader. Let me talk it over with Mrs. Pegram to night, & at seven to morrow I think I can conscientiously promise to be a mother to the child." I could not sleep for excitement, & was wide awake when the reply came, which I sent instantly to the office. I have just left Mrs. Pegram. Of the child, she only said that Mr. Riordan might make any arrangement by correspondence; that she was deeply interested, & would do all in her power. The rest of the talk was chiefly of you, whom she seems to remember with great pleasure. They were anxious to know our connection. I told them I was one of the many you lived to serve, & that you had my child, to my great content. They said they could well understand how happy I must be, knowing he was in such keeping. If I said too much, I shall be grieved. But they thought I did not, & that less would have failed. I think you have made the best possible choice, since the poor little creature is doomed to boarding school. But that is a dreadful risk—one I should not expose any girl to, even if she was to grow up an Edistonian.[3] If I had any kind of a home, I would ask Mr. Riordan to trust her to me until he saw fit to remove her. Mother is painfully interested, & says it would be happiness to her to teach her & watch over her. Ah! what lovely lives people with homes might lead! We can only dream of it, while leading lives as selfish as others.

I imagine you may bring the child with you, to meet Mrs. Pegram who leaves on the 15th (Friday week.) If you preferred sending her here at once, tell Mr. Riordan I would be glad to take charge of her until Mrs. Pegram leaves. She would sleep with me, & never leave my sight until Mrs. Pegram goes. I make the suggestion having a dim recollection of "Springs" in your telegram, & fearing Mrs. Pegram did not understand that it was to be immediate.

My sympathies are painfully excited. I can think of nothing else, though I have been in an unprecedented whirl for thirty six hour. At breakfast, May Morse[4] was seated near me!! She knew me first, & was even more surprised than I, at our meeting. I told her of her "engagement" to one "Frank Warrington", English. In a few moments, she was quite wild about him, & ratified the engagement. I congratulate you. I do not know whether it was my assertion of your being the best reader, truest friend, most purely intellectual character, or fervent Catholic, that won her heart. At all events, she says I have the knack of finding out only perfect people, & of driving my friends frantic with jealousy. "How I envy you in all things!" she said. Poor May! She left me when I was only beloved, being myself rather more than indifferent to it. She has no idea of my subsequent experience, or of how gladly I would lay down life, rather than endure it again. I assured her that you would some day make your appearance, & ratify the vows your sponsor made "for you!"

Mother is wonderfully better to-day, & quite strong. It is altogether unaccountable.

I *have* been thinking of my bird, but dared not ask, thinking it might have died. I continue to dream of it.

I have seen the Richmond reporter, rolling his eyes around. Last night, Mrs. Deas frightened me asking why I did not write for the papers. Had I her mind, I would be too happy to attempt it, I said meekly. She said she was convinced I would excel. I said I dare not try. She entreated me to make the effort, & she would have it published either in Richmond or New York. I pleaded inability, but said I would like to try, just for fun, if she would keep it secret, & correct it. May I be forgiven for lying! [. . .]

Do you know Mr. Baskerville, of Richmond?[5] "Buried two wives, & wants to bury a third," as Mrs. Deas explained in stating his singular anxiety to be introduced to me. He sits by us at table.

Is all this to please you, or me? Adieu! I ache, but am still improving.

S.Morgan.

1. Hetty Cary Pegram (1836–92), a noted belle from Baltimore who married General John Pegram (1832–65) in 1865. John was killed less than three weeks after their wedding. Frank met Hetty in Richmond in June 1862. "I am staying at a very nice boarding house on Franklin St in this City," Frank wrote to his mother, "where the only other boarders are Miss Hetty Cary the celebrated Baltimore beauty, who is even more beautiful in her noble mind and chivalrous disposition than in her charming face, and her sister—equally amiable, but with rather too great a tendency to expand" (F. W. Dawson, *Reminiscences*, ed. Wiley, 144–45, 183).
2. Jane Margaret Cary (1809–1903).
3. Edisto Island, which is located forty miles southwest of Charleston. The Edisto planters, who grew long-staple sea island cotton, were extremely wealthy before the war, unlike Charleston's merchants and professionals. By the 1870s, however, the planters had lost the wealth they had invested in slaves and the means of recouping it. Charlestonians probably considered themselves intellectually and culturally superior to the Edistonians both before and after the war.
4. May Morse, a friend of Sarah's from Louisiana. During her visit to White Sulphur Springs, May was accompanied by her uncle, Alexander Porter Morse (1842–1921), a prominent Washington, D.C., lawyer.
5. Henry Embra Coleman Baskervill (1817–1900), a commission merchant who operated dry goods and grocery stores in Petersburg and Richmond, Virginia. During the Civil War he served as an aid to Major General William Wing Loring (1818–86). Baskervill was married three times: in 1846 to Isabella Alston Hamilton, in 1866 to Eugenia Buffington, and in 1876 to Margaret Humphries.

Frank was forced to delay his departure due to Riordan's trip to Baltimore and telegraphed Sarah to inform her of the change in plans.

45

Charleston Wednesday [August 6, 1873]

1 p.m.

Ma Bien Aimée [My Much Beloved]

I am awaiting anxiously your reply to my dispatch of last night; the more anxiously as I am rather worse than usual to-day. I cannot doubt that you will consent to stay; as you like the place, & as the few days extra will cost you nothing, and will enable you to describe one of the famous fancy balls, which comes off I believe on the 15th. All our arrangements will remain, as before, with the single difference that I shall meet you at Staunton on Saturday Aug 23 instead of Aug 16. I will, as soon as your dispatch comes write to Miriam to expect us in Lynchburg on Monday Aug 25, & also to the Peytons. The reason of the change is this: *Mrs.* R had agreed that the little girl should be put to school with Mrs. Pegram, but flatly refused to allow her to be taken to the Springs. The only alternative was to deliver the child to Mrs. Pegram in Balto where she expected to be on the 16th. Riordan will leave here on Wednesday the 13th, the day I expected to start, & will come back in time to allow me to meet you on the 23rd. I am fearfully disappointed, but of course I cheerfully put myself out of the question. The final separation is agreed upon and all the papers are signed. I cannot describe Riordan's thankfulness at Mrs. Pegram's dispatch. The words "I accept the charge" went right to his heart, & for it he thanks you, my darling! He told me this morning that he saw the finger of Providence in your presence at the "White", which enabled you to do what no other could have done any where, & you could not have done elsewhere. Lay that unction to your soul!

Do you tell me of your improved appearance and of the admiration which you inspire, to make me love you more? I do not say that I cannot; for I love you more dearly every day that passes. And what would I give to have seen your hair when it compelled the homage of your sable attendant! Are you going to arrange it so for me?

Your letter of to-day is the best *for the public* that you have written.[1] The pupil will soon give lessons in good taste to the professor. I have sent the Peytons some copies. Beware! I shall wait now for your dispatch. The storm last night must have blown down the wires. [. . .]

Yours always

F.W. Dawson

1. "Fashion at the Springs: The Belles of the White and Their Ducks of Dresses," August 6, 1873.

46

Charleston
August 7. [1873]

My beloved! You have made me feel so bright and strong by your sweet, sweet letter of Aug 4 that I hardly know how to contain myself. Laugh at me, darling, if you will for fearing to pain you. I confess I am not brave enough to give you cause for grief. And, whether you do or dont want me at your feet for ever, you know how supremely glad I am to be there, & you must bear the infliction as patiently as you can.

Do not take poor Riordan's case as an argument for you against me. If you married me, not loving me, & learned to hate me, you could not (nor could this world & the next make you) do what his unfortunate wife has done. Let us not speak of her; for only he who is without fault shall cast the first stone. As I have told you before I can compel you (by winning only) to love me, if you only allow yourself to think of marrying me. Before I had known you a month you dreamed that you had married me. It ought to be more than a dream now. You might run a risk (I dont think you would) but I should run none. Surely I have proved to you that my love is steadfast!

Revenons à nos moutons![1] I will not let you off those Saturday articles permanently. I am a base imitator. In what you think good in my articles you see the reflex of yourself!

And, my life! I am so delighted to hear you speak of a desire to get to "work as speedily as possible." I feared that you wanted to abandon us. And let me say here that (irrespective of that frantic wretch F.W.D) you need have no fear for the future, even after leaving the Happy Valley! I have carefully arranged it all for you, & all you have to do is jump into the boat and float with the tide. You pain me in what you say about your Mother. Do you give her brandy or is it all gone? I charge you, upon your love for your Mother whom I love so dearly, to write to me instantly whether your supply of Cognac is exhausted, that I may bring you more. You shall pay for it, if you want to! If you dont answer quick I shall send it anyhow.

Dont think Howell troubles us. I am deeply moved by your thankfulness, but, honestly, the child is dear to us all—a ray of sunshine in a very dark place. You speak of what you "owe me", my darling! Dont you know that one letter like that of to-day would repay me a thousand: fold for the labor of years. For your "dare!" I dont take it so. But unless I could think that it would be a great pleasure to *you* to see me again, I would not budge a foot to meet you. One must draw a line somewhere; no matter how head-over-ears in love you (that's me) may be. So it must not be, the 16th that I meet you. Another week in, Elysium is yours; & through no fault of mine, bien entendu [of course]! You dont like to come away, because of what may come "after." Fear not! the "after" shall not hurt *you*. Will you not kiss your dear Mother for me, & tell her how earnestly I pray God's blessing on you both.

Yours always

F.W. Dawson

1. Let us return to the subject.

ﮯﮯ

Sarah had traveled to White Sulphur Springs with Frank's promise that he would accompany her and her mother to Orange, where her brother George was buried. George Morgan had enlisted in the Confederate Army at the outbreak of the Civil War and served most of his time in Virginia. He died on January 12, 1864. Sarah later learned that "the physicians had mis-taken his malady which was inflammation of the bowels, and he had died from being treated for something else."[1] During her final weeks at White Sul-phur Springs, Sarah began to inquire about the exact location of George's grave. She believed that he had been buried on the grounds of Montpeliso, an estate owned by Cordelia Hiden and later by Robert Stanard.

White Sulphur August 8th [1873]

Peccavi![2] I try to do your bidding, but I am a miserable creature at best. Since my last, 42, 43, 44 have come. Now what will you do about it? Take them back? Or tell me you did not mean them?

I find I used to know Mr. Baskerville myself. Met him with Col. Trenholm in New York, where he dined with us when Jimmy was first married.[3] He tells me Mrs. Hiden sold her place near Orange C.H three years ago, & has moved he does not know where. He knows the Mr. Stannard who purchased it, & made some changes in the grounds.[4] Mother was painfully affected. He offered to write for me to ask if the grave had been spared, & where Mrs. Hi-den was to be found. This will take a week at least, I suppose. If there has been any desecration of his grave, mother had better not go there. Mrs. Hi-den we must see, if possible. I will let you know later.

As to remaining, of course I am glad to be here a few days longer. But having made up my mind to go, I should have been quite as ready to leave on the 16th, but for you. I know you have looked forward these two months to that homeward journey. Ruthless as I am, I am not quite bad enough to enjoy your disappointment. Besides, I want you at Lynchburg. There are two words for you, & a dozen for me. This is why I telegraphed back instantaneously that I would wait for the 23rd. If you change, I await your new orders. The expense to the News & Courier annoys me a little, but it is involuntary on my part, & I will try to keep it in good humor until I go. Apropos of the "Saturdays": you ask if my assertion that they injure me very sensibly is to be understood as the fore-runner of a refusal to do any more work. Nay verily! You know, "no song, no supper!" Mine earns breakfast & dinner in addition. I scarcely touch any of them, but it is reputable to have meals, you know, & my pen alone can earn them for me in future. Depend upon it, there is no service of the brain you can demand of me that I shall not be glad to give, even unto the whole of my kingdom.[5]

To me, you have been God's providence. I owe you my present lease of life, however long or short it may be. Mother says it is short. I do not care. I am content to endure it so long as God wills, & to work so long as He gives me strength. I am not very well just now. Yesterday mother insisted on a short walk, & returning, May Morse persuaded me to walk around the parlor. I was interested, & consequently forgot to rest until breathing suddenly became a severe effort. The pain still continues quite acute. I have had no appetite for several days, but still I am gay, gay. You will not know me, I think. O for a strawberry mask!

You do not know why you could not rest Sunday night? Mother & I can tell you: Howell was there! I hope you will never repeat the experiment. I am so thankful to you, & the kind friends you have secured my child. It is very sweet to me to feel such content about him. I never felt it before.

Mrs. Pegram will have your message to-night, when she returns from her trip to the Kanaw[h]a Falls [West Virginia]. A large party went down this morning. I am quite in love with her.

Judging by your telegram, I suppose your programme in this last letter is altered, & that Mr. Riordan is not to come here. I wish he would. I never felt so much for any one's sorrow, I think. A new commandment I write unto you—take care of yourself.

S.M.

And I know there is not a word here that you wish to know! But I am so worn out! I dare you to scold me when I whine.

1. S. M. Dawson, *Sarah Morgan*, 597–603.

2. When Sir Charles James Napier (1782–1853) conquered Sind in India in 1843, he is said to have sent a telegram with a single word, *Peccavi*, Latin for "I have sinned" (a pun on Sind). The line passed into common usage as fact, although it was actually made up by *Punch* for a cartoon on the subject.

3. Sarah Morgan diary, August 11, 1865, vol. 6, Dawson Papers.

4. Robert T. Stanard (1837–81) purchased Montpeliso from the Hidens in 1868.

5. "And he sware unto her, Whatsoever thou shalt ask of me, I will give it thee, unto the half of my kingdom" (Mark 6:23).

Frank to Sarah

47

Charleston

Friday [August 8, 1873]

Mr. Riordan desires me to say to you that "you have earned his gratitude as long as he lives." I can explain it to you. He knows, as I do, that only you could have brought Mrs. Pegram to make the answer that she did; & that only such an answer could have made it endurable to part from his child. Then you had, as I knew you would, the thoughtfulness to send a full account of what was said & done. I read so much as related to him to R; & you can imagine what a balm to him were Mrs. Cary's words that she would be a mother to the child. You did not say too much, because you said just what was needed to accomplish our purpose. I am sorrowfully glad that you have so won Mr. Riordan's interest in you. Should you ever screw your courage to the sticking: point of quarrelling with me you will still find in Mr. Riordan a true friend; a better friend in every way than I can be, because I pester you with words of love, & torment you in divers ways. It was very thoughtful of you to suggest that you would take charge of Rachel if you had a home (which you can have so easily.) The condition is with Mrs. Riordan that the child shall go to a boarding school; and she would not, I know, agree to a school known to be kept by friends of R or of me. How much less would she consent to put Rachel in your keeping; you who are my "other me." Mr. Riordan will make his will before he goes to Balto, and will leave me, I believe, his executor & guardian of his children. I have given him my word that if you marry me we will watch over his children as though they were "*yours* or *mine* or *ours*." That rests with you.

Dont you think that Hetty Cary must have been a little puzzled to know what was the connection between you & me? You could not speak of the "N & C", & you repudiate any other connection. And pray dont say any more of what you would do if you had "a home." It makes me too miserable to see you so reluctant to accept the goods the Gods provide.

I am almost sorry that you spoke of me to Miss Morse as you did, but as I shall never see her it makes little difference. Remember that *I* am not "perfect", & that I thank Heaven for it. Surely you have had enough of "perfect" people. I am sure that I never dream of calling any one perfect. It has always been my belief that a perfect person would be a most undesirable partner. As to this old project of yours I have only this to say: It would be as great a disappointment as any you have ever had if you could even think it possible for me to transfer my love to Miss Morse, or to any other woman, from you. *To think that I could, by any possibility, do it, or think of doing it, is to hold me guilty of base treachery, lying & deceit.* And you have not reached that point.

Of course you had rather die than endure your old experience again! I know it, but there is no argument in that against me. Has my love caused you pain? If it has not, why should it?

I am delighted to hear that your Mother is better. Dont forget to tell me whether the brandy is gone. "Sweet" is flourishing! Do write that letter for your friend. It will be such fun. I know that withered Baskerville very well by name & sight; & I confess that I am not afraid of him. If there is any one at the Springs whom I have cause to fear it is not any one that you name; just because if you cared for any one you would not mention the name to me until the time came for giving me a formal notification that my attentions were no longer desirable. But I dont fear any thing of the sort!

What a pretty Fatima[1] you would make. I marked on that letter that it was not to be opened until Aug 5; yet you open and read it on Aug 3. *Explain me this!* My comfort is that the letter was filled with expressions of love for you, & yet you say it was "beautiful."

Howell "fooled" several persons at home yesterday by asking them to read your letter to him. I have ordered him to write to you to-day. The little scamp coolly said to me last night that it would be "a good thing to send Saidy a letter like that which she sent him"; where I at once preached a sermon on the respect due by loving nephews to loving aunts. Good: bye: my heart of hearts &

Believe me
Yours always
F.W. Dawson

1. Fatima was the daughter of the prophet Muhammad and was regarded by Muslims as one of the Four Perfect Women.

Frank to Sarah

48

Charleston

August 9. 1873

My Beloved! I fear there is something a little underhanded in some questions which Frank Trenholm has just asked me. He came in, and said he wanted to know whether you and your mother were still in Virginia. I said Yes! "Are you sure?" "I am." "When will they leave there?" "Towards the end of the month." "Where are they going then?" "To Lynchburg, possibly, to see Mrs. Dupré." ["]How long will they remain there?" "I dont know!" Then he said: "Of course they will not go back to Hampton until the winter." I said "I presume not." He then said "Ella & Jem intend going to Columbia *in the winter.*" I may be mistaken, but I think that Ella has asked Frank to find out what your plans were, so that it might be made practically impossible for you to return to Hampton, if you had any idea of so doing. Dont think me uncharitable, but I feel instinctively that I am right. E M is "devilish sly."[1] Mark it! How glad I was the other day that Howell was not at Hampton; that is, if one sister is like the other. Howell was at Frank Trenholm's riding the baby in her carriage.[2] One of the boys came behind Howell, upset the carriage and threw the whole company in a confused heap on the ground with Howell *on top;* just like a Morgan! Enter Mrs. Frank Trenholm who says: "Howell! you bad boy! You are always at mischief. You have killed my child. Go! Go!! Go!!!" And he went—to Mrs. Fourgeaud, & told her the story, which has been told in the same words by an impartial unseen spectator. This was a week ago & Howell, like a little gentleman, has said he will never go there again until the unjust blame put upon him is removed. Mr. Magrath is fairly in love with him: at least Mrs. Magrath[3] says so. Yesterday Howell met in the street the diminutive Trenholms who bowed low, to which the haughty Morgan made no response, and recd a scolding from me for not acknowledging a courteous greeting. 'Tis a brave boy; although he dont write to you as he should. But the fiat is issued to-day "No letter; no dinner" & you will have a scrawl. I take him this afternoon to the Sullivan's Island [South Carolina] regatta. Entre nous [Between us] I had rather go to sleep, but a Father must not evade his responsibilities!

Do you know how you fascinate me? I am wildly in love with you, darling! & I think you begin to know it. You may well say that I would not, & could not, be cross with you. Only one thing can separate me from you, & you know what that is, dear. Never did any woman hold more important interest in one small hand than you do. And this is all àpropos of your simple word about that Aug 5 "love letter" which you impatiently opened on Aug 3? When you find that my love words are "beautiful" your heart must have softened, the least little bit, towards me.

Nothing from the Peytons about the bill. Do stir them up. I will write them to: morrow of your prolonged stay.

I did not need any "dare"! Without that I believed & knew that you will be as glad to see me as your mother will. I *dare* you to say anything sweeter than you have said! Will you take a dare!

Yours Always

F. W. Dawson

There must be a sympathy between thought & pen. However cramped my hand may be it is always easy to write "Yours always" & "I love you!"

1. "He's tough, ma'am,—tough is J.B.; tough and devilish sly" (Charles Dickens, *Dombey and Son* [1848]).
2. Helen Morgan Trenholm (b. 1871), the daughter of Francis Trenholm and Mary Elizabeth Burroughs Trenholm.
3. Selina Bollin Magrath, twenty-four, a cousin of the Fourgeauds.

⟨ℋ⟩

Frank to Sarah

50

Charleston

Monday Night

August 11. [1873]

My darling: I hope that Mr. Baskerville will be able to give you some positive information about your Brother's grave. I wrote myself to Mrs. Hiden, some time ago, and have no answer. Yet I do not fear that the grave has been disturbed; unless, for the removal of the remains to Hollywood in Richmond,[1] which is not likely. I feel confident that the best plan is to go to

Orange CH ourselves. I will, upon our arrival, go to work to find out the place and particulars, and any certainty that your dear Mother might have will not, in the way that we should communicate it, be worse than her present doubts & fears. Let the arrangement stand as it was; Baskerville notwithstanding.

You relieve me very much by saying that you will go on with your work, when you come back. I think you will be satisfied with the business propositions I shall submit to you.

You dare me to "scold" you, & I do it. What do you mean by exerting yourself so much as to suffer from fatigue for days? Miss Morse, I fairly hate. Why does she tempt you to walk more than is good for you? I hope so much, and pray so much for your improvement that I grow sick at heart when you tell me that you have set yourself back. Do be more careful of yourself. It is very difficult, darling, to reconcile your ardent thanks to me with the little care you sometimes take to derive as much benefit as possible from your trip. And tell your Mother that I shall not love her, if she tells you that your life will be short. Is she so anxious to see me utterly and hopelessly lost, that she insists on taking from me the only stay & support I have?

It was not Howell that kept me awake. He was as quiet as a lamb. I suppose he is too much afraid of me to kick. You ask me whether, now that I have received your letter about Miss Morse, I will take my letters back. No! dear. *Months ago* when you were trying to persuade me to marry Miss Fisher or Miss Morse or somebody else, you were as honestly in earnest as I was, at the same time, (or *earlier,* rather) in trying to make you marry some one who was not me. But that is all changed now. I could not advise you to do what would be doom me to a living death. Nor can you, knowing how I love you, sincerely urge me to marry Miss Any body else. Had I imagined that you could, I should never write as I do. I could not. It would dishonor myself. What a mockery to you my words of love would be if you dreamed that they could be transferred by proxy to your friend.

There is a great deal, as you suppose, that you have left unsaid, but you have a way of making your apology or what is not said the next best thing to saying it.

Good: night, darling girl;

Yours always

F. W. Dawson

I reopen this to beg you in your own way to implore Mrs. Pegram to be in Balto on Monday so that R can see her that day & leave the child. Unless that be done, so that he can start back on Tuesday, I shall miss my trip to Orange & Lynchburg with you & you know how I have lived on the hope of that. D

1. Hollywood Cemetery in Richmond, Virginia, the burial place for thousands of Confederate soldiers and generals as well as Confederate President Jefferson Davis (1808–89).

ঽℋℐ

Sarah to Frank

White Sulphur Springs
August. 12th [1873]

I am forever making mischief. And now I have broken up a regular Margery Daw romance. Did you ever read that clever little tale?[1] May & I went out yesterday for a happy morning under the trees. And it was happy, until she asked about Frank Warrington, & I admitted that he knew her name, while she did *not* know his altogether. She was really piqued, & called it a breach of confidence on my part. I had some trouble to reconcile her to myself, but she says she will never look at you! There is my romance spoiled, & you refused before proposing! The fine day became clouded for me. As for May, she is sweetness itself. She talked for hours of books & people, while I humbly listened, chanting to myself "breach of trust." Have you Dante Gabriel Rosetti's poems? Do bring them to me if you have. I told May only one thing could be more delightful to me than her recitation, & that would be to hear you read The Beautiful Damoiselle & Sister Helen.[2] I have caught the rhythm, scarcely remembering a word; & I can tell myself the whole story in thoughts perhaps a little stronger than Rosetti. I have your letters up to 28, just received. Howell did well in declining to visit there until the amende honorable [apology] is made. If he had heeded my warning, & his own painful Clermont experience, his visits would have been ceremonious & unfrequent. The other would have treated him worse. I saw it done with less foundation for flagrant injustice. I pray God neither he nor I will see it again. How can I thank you for your goodness to my child? I shall be made to suffer bitterly for having left him with you. But the blissful rest & security is worth the harshness which will be visited on me later. I am perfectly indifferent to the consequences, knowing the happiness that has come to the child.

As to the brandy, let me tell you quickly that mother has still a bottle left,

& that she takes it with the regularity, if not with the devotion, of a toper. Please dont send her any more. She could not possibly drink half of what is left, before we leave.

The most casual acquaintance stops me to congratulate me on my improvement. They all say it is incredible. Geo. Holmes[3] came two days ago, & scarcely knew me. The most singular part of it is that I do not, & cannot eat, after the first mouthful. And my poor tongue, content with being numb at the tip, has gone permanently asleep for a solid inch. The Silent Woman![4] What a natural phenomenon I shall be!

I have no doubt that Frank was deputed to ask those questions, & that all possible steps were long since taken to shut out all unpleasant objects. You alone have been ignorant. I, alas! know too much, God help me. It is quite natural, & certainly God's mercy. We dont see very well when our eyes are dim with tears, but He sees all the same, & I am just beginning to thank Him for pain while it still racks.

I have just come from Miss Alston, having just before heard of her illness. I thought she had gone ten days ago, & all this while she has been suffering acutely from an abscess in her ear. Ill, & away from home. That was introduction enough—for me. I took me & my chair & "Kenelm Chillingly"[5] to her room, where we were received in the most lovely manner, my chair decorously waiting outside until my visit was over. She seemed very glad to meet all of "us." We had not talked ten minutes when like a very lady, as she could not help being, she said "May I tell you a secret? I would not like to take an unfair advantage of you. Mr. Riordan told me in strict confidence that you wrote those letters from the Springs." I supposed I must have looked idiotic; but it felt very much like losing consciousness. She interpreted it as dismayed innocence, probably; for I was roused by her quiet, surprised tone "Has Mr. Riordan deceived me?" I burst out with "No! he could not deceive anybody! I did write them, but even my sisters do not know, with one exception." She commenced to assure me that she held it sacred herself, & of her intimacy with Mr. Riordan, when some one knocked at the door. I opened it for a lady, & in a few moments took leave, she asking me to return after dinner. Someway, I dont mind her knowing it; but at first, I nearly lost my senses. I like her very much.

"Withered Baskerville"! I dont like *that* sir! Look out! It is dangerous. Mrs. Pegram leaves Friday, & Mr. Riordan to-morrow, I presume. Only eleven happy days left me! I have neglected Miriam shamefully. You get all the letters that should go elsewhere; for I am always tired, & never deliberately fatigue myself, save for you. Mother sends her love ad infinitum. I opened that letter before maturity because I knew you would be disappointed if I did not. There now! I have often heard every word it contained, from the author's lips, sir. Be good, & Heaven will spare you even the ill you desire.

S.M.

1. Thomas Bailey Aldrich, *Marjorie Daw and Other People* (1873). In the book, to alleviate the depression of invalid John Flemming, Edward Delaney manufactures an accomplished fictional character named Marjorie Daw and incorporates her into his letters to make them lively and interesting. John is captivated by the fictional Marjorie and soon falls in love with her.
2. Dante Gabriel Rossetti, *Poems* (1870), which included "The Blessed Damozel" and "Sister Helen."
3. George Lee Holmes, thirty-five, a Charleston broker.
4. Ben Jonson, *Epicoene; or, The Silent Woman* (1609).
5. Edward George Earle Bulwer-Lytton, *Kenelm Chillingly: His Adventures and Opinions* (1873).

Frank to Sarah

51

Charleston
August 13. 1873

Ay di Me! This evening I was to have started on my trip to meet you; a trip beginning in rejoicing and ending, how? I have to wait a week more, and time lags. You are happy in waiting, and I am unhappy because I shall not see your dear face until Saturday week. Strangely enough I had a dream last night urging me to put my house in order, & in the dream, I was saying that I was doing it because I had been warned in a dream to do so. It would be a just retribution, perhaps, if the journey which was to give me new life were to give only eternal death. Don't say I am blue. I have just as much right to talk about dying as you have; and every time you tell me that your life will be short I want to cut my throat.

Riordan goes to Baltimore to-day, and I shall be very busy during his absence. You may expect a telegram from me on Wednesday at latest giving you the latest orders. I do not apprehend that there will be any change of programme.

I am tired of complimenting you upon your letters. They are the best written, this season, from any watering place. To: day's is a dainty thing; full of quiet humor & abounding in hits.[1] If you will only write editorials as you write the letters you will make the fortune of the N & C. You need not put on airs because you are writing leaders. Go at it as freely and naturally as you do at those letters, & you will make one of the freshest & most attractive newspaper men in the country. (How glad you are I did not say newspaper *women*) I knew that you had great capabilities & believed in your potentiality. Has not time proved me to be right?

Yours always
F. W. Dawson

1. "Belles at the Springs: Apples of Discord in the Virginia Eden," August 13, 1873.

ↀↀ

Frank to Sarah

53

Thursday Night [August 14, 1873]

I certainly did not expect to write to you again to day; but you have haunted me during every hour of the afternoon and evening so that I am forced to write to you, almost without knowing why. You have been so vividly before me that I was upon the point of speaking to you, & I saw you in a hundred different positions. I saw you as you have stood by the mantel at Hampton speaking to me; I saw you as you came on the gallery, with your blue sacque on, ready for a walk to the bending tree; I saw you as you lay on the lounge when I read to you, & as you lay cold & pale when I was striving to nurse you; I saw you as you bade me good: bye, when your Mother kissed me for you, on the day we parted at Hampton. Never before has your bodily presence seemed so palpable. Often your spirit has appeared to be with me; to-day it was both body & spirit. Why is this, darling? I should be alarmed; only that there was nothing of menace in your looks, & that only those scenes came to my eye which are dearest to my memory. All a disordered imagination, perhaps! But there have been so many strange coincidences in our knowledge of each other, so many presentiments which have been realized to the letter, that I cannot help wondering whether you were telling me good: bye to-day & why.

Humour me in this—(I have just been scared nearly out of my skin. I raised my head, & there was Howell! standing erect & motionless within two feet of me. Happily, *in the flesh!* He had come down to see the machinery. But imagine my feelings). Well, humour me so far as to write me just a word *as soon as you receive this* & tell me what has happened to you to-day. I shall have time to receive your letter before I start & Believe me

Yours always
F. W. Dawson

ໄ)ໄ

Sarah to Frank

White Sulphur
August 15th. [1873]

I have just telegraphed you of Mrs. Pegram's change of programme. She left this morning direct for Baltimore. Had I known Mr. Riordan's address, I would have telegraphed him. That, you can do. Then your plans can be carried out as you arranged. It would be rather hard to miss your journey. I see from 49 that you are ill. No.50 looks better, though forlorn enough. "Du courage! toujours du courage"—l'audace je n'aime pas.[1] Life does not last forever; after—comes peace. Mrs. Pegram & I sat last night more than half an hour, hand clasped in hand talking about that hereafter. I love her, & I think she feels the same for me, brief as our acquaintance has been. But for your telegram, I should never have known her. There is a new happiness I owe you.

Ah! but I am cross! Last night I told my first deliberate falsehood—told it with such nerve & success, that I read a long series of such achievements in the future. A lady told me she had been repeatedly informed within the last few days that I had written some very clever letters for a Southern paper. "Who has taken such a liberty with my name?" I asked. She said several people—she did not remember, but they were friends of mine. I told her no friend would make such a statement. She asked if I meant to deny it, I replied I did, most emphatically. She persisted it was a great compliment; I could not see it. My injured dignity pleaded successfully. She has the longest tongue in the world, & would have published it before sleeping, but for my denial. As it is, she will do the unpleasant work for me. The housekeeper's husband is a clerk here. He found it out, through your letters, probably, & confided the secret to her. She has imparted it to Miss Alston, & possibly to many others.

I presume he read your letters, for the housekeeper said "he read the letters in the clerks office, & my name was in them." I shall continue to resent the charge.

My dear Dr. Taylor is here. He was delighted at my improvement. I have made no complaints to him, but have accumulated quite a score. Imagine how I have improved! Miss Custis[2] has been one of those who long ago urged me to leave, & scared mother about my condition. Night before last she brushed against me, put up her glasses to see who it was, & exclaimed with genuine surprise "Mon Dieu! que vous avez embelli!"[3] The astonished look removed all sense of flattery.

I am dreadfully out of humor, & very reluctant to write the News letter which I am resolved shall accompany this. There is no time to lose, either. Mother is better, I think.

What are you doing yourself, to continue so unwell?

No letters to-day. Perhaps that made me cross. It is almost time to forgive that long-tongued woman & the rest

S.M.

Nothing but your anxiety would induce me to send this. The letter, I am unable to write. To-morrow it shall go, or Sunday.

1. Courage! Always courage. I don't like audacity.
2. Possibly a member of a famous Virginian family that included Martha Custis Washington (1731–1802), wife of President George Washington (1732–99), and Mary Randolph Custis Lee (1808–73), wife of Confederate General Robert E. Lee.
3. My God! How much better you look!

ﻬ

Frank to Sarah

56

Sunday Night [August 17, 1873]

A thousand thanks, darling, for your letter of the 15th, which is so much sweeter because you sent it off on account of my known anxiety about you. I write very hurriedly that you may not miss, through me, your daily letter.

I am very glad that you like Mrs. Pegram. Talk with her about the "Hereafter", dear! but remember that to do your whole duty in the present, is the preparation, sweet & fit, for the time to come. Mrs. Pegram is a noble example of devotion to duty, & a duty not very pleasant either.

Mr. R has received your dispatch; also, the one which you sent me & I forwarded. His plan was to see Mrs. P on Saturday, see his child to-day & to-morrow, & start back on Monday night so as to arrive here on Wednesday. I will telegraph you.

Dont think you owe Mrs. P's liking to me. You would have won her heart, somehow & somewhere.

Dont mind the impertinent curiosity of those gabbling women at the Springs. I wonder you have not been tormented before. They must respect you! Mrs. Chisolm[1] told me last night that both Geo Gibbes[2] & Geo Holmes told her *at the White* that you were our correspondent, & that every one nearly seemed to know it. I only tell you as you are so soon going away.

When you are next catechized, however, I would tell the person that her questions are impertinent, & you decline to answer them. That would be better, my love, than what you did.

Do have a talk with Dr. Taylor before you leave the Springs. I think he has treated you very cavalierly & his neglect in not writing might have done you serious harm.

You know so well how pleased I am to hear of your improvement, but I again thank you for telling me.

Do take your tickets from the White to Orange C.H. I shall take mine to that place.

Only three or four days more! And I have hardly time to breathe, I am so busy. How happy I shall be to start off to meet you, & how impatient to see you. I dont think I am really sick; only worn down with anxiety & work. You can make a new man of me. Won't you? Indeed you do give me "courage"; there is no danger of my being "audacious" with you, is there?

Kiss your Mother for me, and tell her I love her more than ever; only she ought not to allow you to sit out in the open air at night with nothing on your shoulder but a thin muslin dress. There's a scolding for her!

A Samedi [Until Saturday], my sweet love!

> & Believe me
> Yours always
> F.W. Dawson

Howell is well & happy.

1. Mary Chisolm (1835–1905), a neighbor of the Fourgeauds. Frank described Mary as "staunch and sincere" but admitted that she was "a grand old gossip." After learning of the Chisolms' plans to visit White Sulphur Springs, Frank warned, "Do not let her know anything that you are not willing to have printed in the New York Herald" (Dawson to Morgan, July 3, 1873, Dawson Papers).

2. George Evans Gibbes (1845–85), the son of Charleston merchant James Shool-
   bred Gibbes (1819–88) and Mary Evans.

Sarah to Frank

White Sulphur
August 17th [1873]

Mr. Baskerville has received an answer. There is no trace of the grave.
Mr. Stannard says he found none when he took possession eighteen months
after purchasing the place. But he consulted Mrs. Hiden who says she left it
in her garden, the headstone still standing. Mr. Stannard has kindly written
to the person who superintended the removal of the Confederate dead
around Orange, to Hollywood Cemetery. He assures us he will make every
effort to obtain some reliable information. Mother is inconsolable. I cannot
think it so hard, though it would have been a sad consolation to stand by his
resting place. I have never seen a face & form more beautiful than George's.
But his soul was more to me, & that I know where to find.[1]

Unless you direct otherwise, we will leave for Orange on Saturday. We
can at least find Mrs. Hiden.

I cannot doubt that my "official capacity" is freely whispered about. My
personal appearance is too strictly neutral to account for the attention I attract, wherever I go. I know my hair is the standing topic of conversation,
for I hear it discussed by every one, & receive innumerable appeals to display it, which I grimly decline. But all that is different from the new feature.
I see people pointing me out at dinner. Day before yesterday four tables had
me under inspection at once. I turned away from one group to the other half
wild, I fear; & in a silent attitude of denial of anything. I grow sick to see
men peeping at me over other people's shoulders, & hear them whisper
something inaudible, but which I choose to interpret "Correspondent." I
fancy it has been well published. Dr. Taylor has made a dozen allusions to it,
which I chose not to hear, even when he asked me if the correspondent of
the News could not gratify Miss Cram, who is crazy to see herself in print.[2]
Perhaps it had to be; but it makes me miserable. Miserable in Paradise! I am
only miserable about leaving it. This is my last Sunday. Where will we spend
the next? Do make yourself agreeable, I am afraid of what awaits me in the
outer world. I feel I shall leave my life here where I found it. And yet, I dont
care. Did you ever read as many contradictions? 51, & 52 are at hand. Thank

you for your thoughtful provision for Howell. I hope no such misfortune will occur, for I would prefer his remaining with Mrs. Fourgeaud. But you have certainly taken every precaution against every vicissitude which can befall man or woman. I will write to Howell later. I wish you would ask Mrs. Fourgeaud to make him write to me for whatever money he may need for necessary things. If you have room in your trunk, bring me a box of paper please. C.O.D., of course, or rather before, as you will have to keep it until we part.

Johnson[3] says we never do anything consciously for the last time, without feeling regret. I have this moment signed "Feu Follet" with intense reluctance to the most stupid letter of all.[4] I regret that it is last, more than I regret the stupid. If I improve, will you send me to Europe next summer? Modest eh? This is your very last letter—forever an ever? Amen. See then you look lovely when we meet. "I love not faded cheek nor hollow eye—"[5] possibly because rivals are objectionable.

S.M.

1. Sarah described her brother, George, in her Civil War diary. "How can I describe George?" she wrote. "By leaving his actions to speak for him, I expect, for I certainly cannot do him justice. As to personal appearance, Monseigneur is just of a nice size, and perfectly in proportion. A head that might serve as a model for an Apollo; hair of a beautiful chestnut, or brown, that *will* curl up in the most extraordinary shapes; blue eyes of a most wonderful size, which do terrific execution among the girls; a handsome nose that says 'Character' as plainly as though it were a posted bill; the prettiest mouth ever seen on man, [words lined through], these all serve to make up the 'personnel' of my amiable brother, who is certainly the most amiable, easy going, fiery, determined and patient man I ever knew" (S. M. Dawson, *Sarah Morgan*, 39).
2. Ida Balch Cram (1854–77), the daughter of Mary Boggs Cram (d. 1878) and Thomas Jefferson Cram (1804–83), a topographical engineer. In 1866 he was brevetted brigadier general and major general for his services during the Civil War. Sarah had gratified Ida Cram's wish, mentioning her in "Style at the Springs: The Rush of Visitors to the Greenbrier White," July 23, 1873.
3. Samuel Johnson (1709–84), an English author.
4. "Scandal at the Springs: 'Tell Me, My Heart, Can This Be Love?'" August 21, 1873.
5. "I love not hollow cheek or faded eye" (Alfred Tennyson, *The Princess* [1847]).

Frank to Sarah

Charleston
Wednesday [August 20, 1873]

You were sad, darling, in writing your letter of Sunday, which may, as you say, be your last letter to me, but need not, nevertheless, be your last letter to the newspaper you have adorned these many months. Nor have you written "Feu Follet" for the last time. The name is yours; & I hope to live to see it famous. Let it be endeared to you, at least, by the recollection of the circumstances under which it was given you. I do not wonder that you look with anxiety upon the future, but you will be more cheerful when you know my plans. Surely it will be as easy to care for you for years & years as for these past months; especially as you are now able to help yourself. Take home to yourself the words of "Feu Follet," & ask "whether old scores are not most effectively wiped out by a new departure; whose pure light shall cast a halo over even the bitter past."[1]

Do not be disheartened about your brother's grave. It will & shall be found. And if the remains have been really removed, I can do any thing with the Hollywood people.[2] I think they are there in Orange still. You & I will find them and save them from oblivion.

I dont wonder that you are looked at and talked about. No letters equal to yours have been written from the Springs this season (from any Springs) to even the biggest Northern papers. Think of that little lady! Please God! I shall see you on Saturday, & after? Of course you can go to Europe next year if you want to; only you would have to take me with you. I must close this & yet I would not, for when, & how, may I write to you again?

Riordan is back; in fine spirits. He writes to you to-day. Good: bye "my life, my Sweetness & my Hope"[3]

Yours always
F. W. Dawson

1. "Scandal at the Springs: 'Tell Me, My Heart, Can This Be Love?'" August 21, 1873.
2. Frank had been a secretary of the Hollywood Memorial Association, which maintained the graves of more than fifteen thousand Confederate soldiers (F. W. Dawson, *Reminiscences*, ed. Wiley, 162–63).
3. "Hail Mary! My Queen and my Mother! My Life, my sweetness and my hope" (St. John Eudes, *Salutation to Mary* [ca. 1500s]).

Carte-de-visite of Sarah Morgan, taken in New Orleans in 1863. On the back of the photograph, Sarah wrote, "Hold me upside down if you want [to] improve the picture—It is really better looking—don't hold it near as it looks coarse." Courtesy of Morgan Potts Goldbarth.

Francis Warrington Dawson, age twenty-two, Richmond, Virginia, 1862.
Courtesy of Rare Book, Manuscript, and Special Collections Library,
Duke University, Durham, North Carolina.

James Morris Morgan, Liverpool, 1863. Courtesy of Morgan Potts Goldbarth.

Sarah Fowler Morgan.
From Sarah Morgan
Dawson, *A Confederate Girl's
Diary*, ed. Warrington
Dawson (Boston: Houghton
Mifflin, 1913).

Miriam Morgan, n.d.
Courtesy of Morgan Potts
Goldbarth.

Charleston

Jan 15. 1873

My dear Miss Sarah;

I wrote you a long letter last night, but I was so miserable that I thought I had better sleep on it. This is the result — for better or for worse, in the words of a service which a lady never reads. I found my business in a very satisfactory condition, with mountains of dry work to be done. "Home," as it is called, is inexpressibly dreary. Enough of me!

I have sent you some New Orleans papers and to-day I have sent by Express the second volume of Middlemarch, the French Revolution, & Valerie Aylmer. What can I say of Middlemarch, except that I

Francis Warrington Dawson to Sarah Morgan, January 15, 1873. Courtesy of Rare Book, Manuscript, and Special Collections Library, Duke University, Durham, North Carolina.

I never enjoyed such peace about Howell, but it is more than counter balanced by concern for you. I never dreamed of such an arrangement. I am ashamed to accept so many benefits from you, I who give only pain to all who love me. But what can I do? Shocking as it is to be forever exacting & never returning I am not insensible to the mercy it is to my poor little boy to be in such tender hands. I cannot wish him to change, either for his sake or my own, But it grieves me to think of the perplexity & trouble you must have had at first, & of the effort it must have been to ask such a thing of Mrs Fourgeaud.

Sarah Morgan to Francis Warrington Dawson, July 25, 1873. Courtesy of Rare Book, Manuscript, and Special Collections Library, Duke University, Durham, North Carolina.

White Sulphur Springs. From *Harper's New Monthly Magazine*, August 1878.

Sarah Morgan Dawson, 1886. Courtesy of Rare Book, Manuscript, and Special Collections Library, Duke University, Durham, North Carolina.

Francis Warrington Dawson, 1888. Courtesy of Rare Book, Manuscript, and Special Collections Library, Duke University, Durham, North Carolina.

Offices of the *News and Courier*, Broad Street, Charleston, South Carolina.
Courtesy of Rare Book, Manuscript, and Special Collections Library, Duke
University, Durham, North Carolina.

♧ EIGHT ♧

Society
Editorials by Sarah Morgan

Sarah Morgan's trip to White Sulphur Springs allowed her to reacquaint her-self with the ritual and tradition of southern society. Like all members of her class, she recognized the importance of elite society, which marked out class boundaries, generated ties with families of similar status, and provided men and women with a public forum where they could display and affirm their gentility. Society encompassed both the formal and more casual aspects of elite life and included balls, parties, church activities, picnics, political social events, and fish fries. Society embodied leisure and culture, formality and fun.

Unlike most adolescent girls, Sarah had not eagerly anticipated her formal debut into society. Overcome by shyness, she dreaded the endless rounds of balls and parties that required her to dress in the most fashionable attire and exhibit her accomplishments and charm. "I am not fit for the world," she conceded, "we have no sympathy in common; it is torture to be thrown in contact with strangers. It turns me to a stiff iron rod, and if I un-bend, I only make a fool of myself." "I'd be satisfied to sit up stairs alone for-ever," she added.[1]

As an adult, Sarah remained ambivalent about society. While she loved to be surrounded by gentility and actively played her part in the daily festivi-ties at White Sulphur Springs, Sarah was keenly aware of the irony and hypocrisy that underscored elite southern culture. In her editorials, she wrote subtle and thought-provoking pieces on the harmful repercussions that she associated with "keeping up appearances." Ironically, Sarah pub-lished some of these articles while exalting the fine society in her Springs let-ters. Readers of the *News and Courier* were unaware that these contrasting viewpoints came from the same pen.

1. S. M. Dawson, *Sarah Morgan*, 558, 583.

Sarah Morgan began her foray into fashionable society with "Easter Devotions." In it, she argued that women's Easter-time commitment to gentility often took precedence over a spiritual contemplation of the "glories that lie beyond the tabernacle." Frank heralded Sarah's editorial as a resounding success. "Upon me the article had a marked effect," he declared, "the solemn cadence of the closing passages thrilled my very soul & thanks to it Easter day did seem to me a day of Rising."

Easter Devotions, April 12, 1873

For more than eighteen centuries Easter has been observed as a festival by all Christian nations. It is emphatically called Rising. A rising from the bondage of flesh to the spiritual life; from the conquered grave to immortality; from earth to a glorious heritage—undefiled, incorruptible and eternal.

The serious contemplation of these mysteries is left to persons of simple faith. Liberal ideas have modified the primitive celebration of Easter to suit larger views. The customs of by-gone ages can be typically represented, so as to meet the requirements of society, without becoming onerous, and without offending the aesthetic taste. Modern chimneys having superseded the ancient fireplaces, which were heaped over with fresh, green boughs in commemoration of Easter, we have transferred to our persons the decorations once restricted to blackened hearthstones. The transformation of leaves into drapery, is a suggestion as old as the Fall. Hiding the unsightly remains; throwing a pleasing veil over charred places; breathing joy, peace and beauty—what more appropriate adornment could be devised? One is hardly afraid of the exposure any mischievous gust of wind may make; so universal are the smoldering fire, the unlovely ashes, the vanity of vanities of life. To our simple ancestors the opportunity of personal display was denied. These Great Unwashed[1] were limited to a pair of leather breeches, donned for life and never changed. But Fashion and Religion are now more nearly allied. The worldly find it expedient to refrain from extravagance during a portion of the year. Professed free-thinkers adopt some of the observances of Lent, openly avowing that, considered as an economy, or as a regimen, it is a desirable practice. The pious and worldly are so commingled, that the young and unthinking often fail to distinguish between them. Mistaking the spirit of thanksgiving that animates the Church for the natural outburst of delight that follows release from distasteful restraint, a Spring Opening has been decided on as a mean term expressive of a common joy. The last commemorative days of the most awful period in a life human or divine, are spent in devising or making adornments for a festival which humanity would do well to observe by divesting itself of all ornaments, and losing itself in contemplating the glories that lie beyond the tabernacle.

To-morrow's sun will shine on tens of thousands in their freshest garb and most contented mood. Those who dress for the love of dress, will be rivalled by those who dress because others do. Meditation in a graveyard can afford no more solemn suggestion than a glance at the toilettes that will throng the churches. The prettiest costume will be the one whose preparation has occupied most time in these holy days. Who will care to claim it? Where wealth can gratify the taste, the anxiety of decision remains. Where poverty cramps the aspirations, what feverish toil may this Holy Week have witnessed! What efforts to secure success, where an exhausted purse can do no more! What secret envy, false pride, weariness and emptiness are illustrated in this flaunting display of Vanity Fair!

To-morrow's sun will herald the day of Rising. The discordant bells of wrangling faiths will unite in a carillon of gladness. None but Sandalphon, the angel of prayer, will be able to distinguish the humble Christian from the votary of Fashion. Together they will display their rival pretensions to taste in the sight of the congregation. The Golden Calf[2] in the midst of the people; the prophet descending the mount with the sacred tables of the law. To your tents, O Israel![3] There meditate on the garments that waxed not old in a pilgrimage of forty years, and which were then deemed fit to enter the Promised Land!

Even in things spiritual, the force of Fashion is strong enough to induce some innocently envious young souls to absent themselves from Easter services, because they lack the means of adding their mite to the general display of frill and furbelow. The strong-minded who will disregard the edict to-morrow, may still feel half ashamed of their modest dress. Conscious splendor will sail down the aisle apparently oblivious of admiration. Like the merchant's ship, bringing her goods from afar, there may yet be too much rigging for safety. The shabby genteel will shrink sensitively from observation, as though convicted of that unpardonable crime—bad taste resulting from poverty. Beauty in fresh attire will glance and sparkle, billowing through the narrow portal which hems it in. Pretty feet will trip down the stairs unabashed. Ugly ones will betray themselves by an exaggerated embarrassment. Callow youth will render itself odious, blocking up the pavement and involving itself in voluminous flounces. The full measure of its hatefulness will be expressed by its passing heedlessly six faultless toilettes, in its haste to attain a seventh. The slighted six will immediately pronounce that dress in bad taste, and declare those young men insufferable. One eye on Heaven, the other on flounces, gives a squint to the moral vision that mars the loveliest face.

Among animals, the male is always the most imposing, or most gaily be-dight. Why is the Spring Opening less imperative upon man than woman? In the fifteenth century both sexes wore robes embroidered, in gold, with Latin hymns or psalms. Both wore sleeves trailing the ground. Men rejoiced in one leg dressed in a boot, and the other cased in a stocking. Why this meek renunciation of a lawful prerogative? If decoration is an evidence of inward grace, why this clinging among men to a uniform which allows no display of personal differences?

It is a poor tree that spends its force in leaves and suckers. The husband-man looks for no fruit where he finds this evidence of misdirected vigor. Women are ever emulating men in undesirable and unattainable matters. When will the more exalted turn from the tyranny of Fashion and find hap-piness in things belonging to a higher sphere? Most persons believe in the perfectability of the human race. A disbeliever might devoutly pray for that consummation. In that more noble life, Fashion will be powerless over larger minds. Who is great enough to usher in the new dispensation? Who will stand forth, divested of the outer adornment of plaited hair and broi-dered garments, personifying the faith whose ornament is a meek and quiet spirit? Each in his degree feels the influence of this sacred festival. Few would acknowledge they were untouched by it. Yet in offering up praise and thanksgiving in anticipation of to-morrow, how few can say, "So would I make my preparation; thus would I be employed, if this were the Saturday night of the world, and to-morrow dawned on the Sabbath of Eternity!"

1. Artisans. Sir Walter Scott (1771–1832), Scottish novelist and poet, used the phrase in his writing.
2. Aaron made a golden calf when Moses was on Mount Sinai (Exodus 32).
3. 1 Kings 12:16

ဆာ

Like most elite young ladies, Sarah Morgan received comprehensive train-ing in music and the arts. She began to learn the piano but eventually gave it up in favor of the guitar. "Originally, I was said to have a talent for the piano, as well as Miriam," she remarked. "Sister and Miss Isabella said I

would make a better musician than she, having more patience and perse-
verance. However I took hardly six months lessons, to her ever so many
years, heard how well she played, got disgusted with myself, and gave up
the piano at fourteen, with spasmodic fits of playing every year or so."[1]

In the following article, Sarah commented on the "wasted" hours that
young women devoted to the piano when they could be more "profitably em-
ployed" attending to the myriad needs of the southern household. Like
many Confederate belles, Sarah's ornamental education had done little to
prepare her for a postwar world filled with poverty and hardship. Practical,
useful, life-sustaining skills, she noted, were now far more essential to elite
young ladies than was a genteel education in musical performance.

The Piano Plague, May 16, 1873

A decision has been rendered by a Parisian judge which is worthy to be made the cause of a universal jubilee. This Daniel[2] come to judgement affirms that even paying house rent, and owning a piano, does not justify any virtuoso in practicing chromatics and chords more than seven hours a day. Seventeen hours are allowed the neighbors to repair the injury done their nervous system, and by loss of sleep. It is only just that the "Tenant's Petition" should supersede the "Maiden's Prayer." The constant strumming of that dreary invocation will force every victimized auditor to clamor for its suppression.

Where musical talent exists, no pains are too great to secure its development. But the greatest and most general mistake is to cultivate a taste which only has being in a fond imagination. Hours are wasted at the piano which would be much more profitably employed in cooking or darning stockings. The piano is rarely a resource after marriage. It is only just that it should not be made an instrument of torture before that event. The Spartans cast out the weak, unpromising babies. Musical taste would be elevated if young performers were served in the same way.

Proficiency on the piano cannot be attained by practicing less than four hours a day. The French seven-hour law will thus limit every family to one good performer and one three-quarter one. O wise Judge! Remembering that the land is teeming with mediocrity, and with families of six-daughter power, how much is it to be regretted that there is but one tribunal in the world which gives lookers-on, and involuntary listeners, redress and protection!

1. S. M. Dawson, *Sarah Morgan*, 24.
2. A biblical prophet and figure in the Book of Daniel.

When Frank received the following letter from a socially inept adolescent girl, he requested that Sarah write a response. "You will feel for her," he commented on May 18, 1873. "Be careful not to be too hard on Charleston!" Sarah responded with a provocative piece on Charleston's "straightlaced Propriety."

The Sin of Being Natural, May 21, 1873

To the Editor—If, after reading this, you do not regard mine as a hopeless case, please give the desired information.

One of your editorials, a few weeks since,[1] was the means of opening my eyes to the name and nature of my *greatest* fault. Alas! I am too *natural*. I have struggled hard against this fearful crime, since my début into your dear, old, (proper) city; particularly since reading in your columns the dreadful consequences of acting as my heart directs—the displeasure of men. (For who, of our sex, *dare* regard their disapproval as naught?) Before seeing your opinion, I was foolish enough to imagine that these views were peculiar to the remarkably prim "set" in which my lot has placed me. But you are "the voice of the people" (at least *this* people.) In order that you may the better advise me, I will relate some of my sad experience.

The kind old lady who raised me was often heard to say that "he who could not raise a hearty laugh carried an uneasy conscience," and it was her delight to hear my laughter ring out clear and happy. But so changed are my surroundings now, that if in girlish glee one burst of laughter escapes my unlucky mouth, such looks of horror and dismal shakings of heads, such murmurs of "unrefined," "unladylike," greet me on every side, that all signs of mirth are quickly dispelled; and deeply chagrined, I solemnly resolve never again to be guilty of such unparalleled rudeness. But wo to me, I *cannot* suppress my evil nature, and often am called upon to undergo the same mortification. Again, if at an evening entertainment I indulge in dancing, when the music swells forth, my miserable nature *will* assert itself, my eyes sparkle, my cheeks tingle, and with a step far too buoyant to be "lady-like" (according to *Charleston* opinion) I skip lightly through the dance. Too happy now to note the lowering brows of the elder ladies, or the scornful glances of the younger ones, I give myself up to enjoyment, and for a few short hours am *perfectly natural*. But alas! the pleasure, sweet as it is, is too dearly bought. For hours, the next day, I am lectured kindly but sadly, and am informed that I have almost disgraced myself. With bitter tears and in deep humility, I repent of my crime, and shun all temptation until I think *the evil monster* is somewhat subdued. But I fear he is not yet conquered, for my hardest trial came a few days since.

I met with a most agreeable and companionable gentleman, (I say this in confidence,) and so vivacious and sparkling was his conversation that I forgot the dozen uncompromising eyes that were watching us, and glided into a most spirited argument, in which my opinions were freely expressed, nor did I refrain from retorting to his *jeux d'esprit* [mind games]. His eyes seemed to approve my conduct, and his manner encouraged me to converse without reserve. How *could* he deceive me so cruelly? They informed me, after his departure, that he was turning me into ridicule all the while, and that, undoubtedly, I had established a reputation of being extremely *fast*. Since then I have given up to despair.

Dear NEWS AND COURIER have pity on me, and show me how to overcome this awful sin. Believe me, I am not altogether base; for there is no discipline, however severe, that I will shrink from; if it but cure me of this unfortunate quality. With a crushing sense of my terrible shortcomings,

I am, yours most humbly,

A GEORGIA GIRL.

1. This may be a reference to Sarah's "'Flirtation': A Lecture to Flirts and an Incidental Indictment of the Courier for Coquetting," April 25, 1873.

さ℃と

Sarah's Response

Society and Propriety, May 24, 1873

The deplorable case of the "Georgia Girl," whose plaint we printed the other day, will touch every one whose life has not been utterly crushed by that annihilator of Nature—Propriety. Even culprits who have been reduced to the conventional standard of inanity, will recall the long, painful death to which their buoyant spirits were subjected by considerate friends. Man barely escapes infantile perils, when repression, censure, criticism and injustice seize him in the name of Propriety. The belief in the efficacy of depressing influences must have suggested the introduction of skeletons at Egyptian feasts. There are good people who estimate piety by its dismal effects. There are others who adopt this doctrine as they might subscribe to the Thirty-nine Articles;[1] caring little, and knowing less about them; only zealous to support orthodox views. Trivial ailments can ever find sympathy. It is only the death-in-life that young people suffer, which elicits no compassion. Natural impulse is a reproach to artificial refinement, and is consequently intolerable in society. Poor morality and fustian are afraid of any little rub which may expose them. People who are not sure of their social status are in constant dread of being reduced to their proper sphere. Internal laxity exacts most external propriety. Perfect innocence and conscious delicacy alone can afford to disregard the empty forms which replace the real substance. Surely the "Georgia Girl" will derive some comfort from these axioms.

For ourselves we confess to a preference for a laugh and

"Voice sweet and low; a marvellous good thing in woman."[2]

But time, thought, trouble and the kind offices of friends, will eventually reduce the most boisterous hilarity to a smile faint as the reflex of star-light. The "Georgia Girl" need not despair of outliving that defect of a healthy nature.

As to the sinful pleasure she takes in dancing, it is confined to a very brief period of life. Her vivacity need fear no censures save from those who have passed their first youth, and those who were not originally formed for the poetry of motion.

Touching the perfidy of man, we feel a natural hesitation in revealing all we know of him. He may be deceitful and wicked beyond imagination; but prudential considerations seal our lips. We can only venture on the general proposition that men are not all either scamps or scoffers. No doubt the tongue of a merry girl may carry her beyond the bounds of discretion, and that she will be encouraged in any display of folly. Yet she will never be aware of it, if her interlocutor is a gentleman. It takes sour old women to discover improprieties in innocent nonsense. With experience and opportunity an evil mind can convert a simple child into a wary old campaigner who sees two faces in every thing, and who wears two herself. In conclusion, we would entreat the "Georgia Girl" not to believe that Charleston is the sole abiding place of straight-laced Propriety. It prevails wherever society, after reaching a certain point of development, falls asleep. There are other places where generation succeeds generation likewise, while etiquette forbids disturbing the venerable slumberer.

A hundred years is the orthodox limit of enchanted sleep. It must soon be daybreak for the benighted regions. Then people will rub their eyes, and wonder how life can endure voluntary paralysis. Charleston's years may, however, be measured by those of the planet Saturn.[3] In that case there are two alternatives for the restless thrall of Propriety. The first is, to eschew Society; the second is, not to be born.

1. The Thirty-nine Articles of Religion are the foundation documents of the Church of England and were adopted by the Protestant Episcopal Church of America.
2. "Her voice was ever soft, / Gentle, and low, an excellent thing in woman" (Shakespeare, *King Lear*, 5.3).
3. Saturn's period of revolution is 291–92 years.

⁂

Sarah wrote one of her most acclaimed editorials on the hypocrisy of mourning rituals. The piece was written during her visit to White Sulphur Springs and was reprinted in edited form in the Boston Globe *on July 11, 1873.*

As Nancy Schoonmaker has noted, the Morgan family were inconsistent in their observation of mourning practices. When Henry and Judge Thomas Gibbes Morgan died in 1861, the Morgan women chose not to don the customary mourning attire or to suspend their visits to church. Their decision caused a sensation in Baton Rouge and prompted a severe backlash from their peers, who "went wild on the subject of our not going in mourning," Sarah wrote in May 1862, "their tender feelings were outraged at such a breech [sic] of propriety and decency, and of course we were not grieved at father's or Harry's death, if we did not wear black!"[1] Sarah and her mother did, however, wear black when Sarah's brothers, Gibbes and George, died in Confederate service in 1864. It is unclear why the Morgan women chose to revise their position. Sarah's editorial on mourning, in which she described the social customs as nothing more than a "doubtful tribute," indicates that her change in behavior may have been enforced by her half-brother, Philip Hicky Morgan, with whom she was living at the time.

Mourning, July 5, 1873

Mourning, as restricted to external decoration, is so universally regarded as a symbol of faith and respectability, that it is scarcely safe to question its use or abuse. And yet, to one who has observed its inconsistencies, it suggests some painful reflections on the tyranny of custom.

As a decree of fashion, Mourning reduces sacred woe to the dead level of heartless indifference. Like an imposing monument with a pompous epitaph, it may cover a mere sham after all. Hypocrisy finds in outer trappings an invaluable substitute for genuine grief. It is this desecration of the keenest anguish common to humanity, which makes Mourning odious to the generality of men who love truth as perfectly as they detest falsehood. Few, however, care to brave public opinion. Though rebels at heart, the majority meekly hold to popular prejudice, and enroll themselves for protection under the banner of desolation. There are mourners who wear scarlet within and bombazine without. These are the "bereaved" who have reason to send up paeons of thanksgiving for their deliverance. This is the travesty of woe which brings reproach on a garb originally signifying affliction. Sympathy is regulated by the width of the crape. If poverty or principle prohibits black in a family which has lost an idolized member, scandal and uncharitableness, seeking an unworthy motive, rend the breasts of the survivors, and scan with prying eyes the scarce closed grave.

One who is a shame and dishonor to his name may die, and the judicious assumption of black will secure public condolence and silence hostile criticism. Well may it be urged that Mourning is a "protection." As usual, protection is here extended to those who do not need it.

If anything could be sacred from the intrusion of Fashion, it would be reasonable to suppose that grief would be exempt. Yet it has become necessary to suffer its impertinences in the very presence of death. Before that awful warning against the vanities which perish, a lively disquisition on the styles and materials best adapted for a pantomime of woe can be maintained. In England the regular Mourning houses transact these painful but indispensable preliminaries. It is only necessary to mention the degree of relationship, and the period which has elapsed since the demise, to be provided with orthodox raiment. He who runs may read the obituary of the departed in the dress of the promenader. And yet is there any comparison between the loss of a bad husband and that of a devoted brother? Is not two years of crape a hard sentence for the first, when a year's mourning is thought an ample concession to the manes of the other? In France every degree of relationship and mourning has its prescribed costume. America alone ignores these laws. The anxiety to lighten the grim array breaks out in premature effervescence of jet, an exuberance of bugles, which rather detract from the idea of Mourning, but answer very well as Fashion.

If Mourning is symbolical of grief, is grief supposed to terminate with it?

Love and sorrow never die. Whoever has worn Mourning from genuine sentiment, knows the pain of discarding it. It is second only to the reluctance with which many persons assume it. To some it is like shutting the vault on a living soul. These find solace in inspecting their forbidden treasures in secret, pining for the day when they can display openly the toilettes they don for private edification alone. There are slaves of Fashion to whom the dead count as nothing; the necessity of wearing black is their sole regret. Mourning is not incompatible with actual resentment against one whose unreasonable demise cuts short the survivor's career of pleasure. The first appearance in Mourning is of immense moment to the bereaved, as well as to society in general. The verdict of "Becoming," or "Not Becoming," must then be delivered. Friends are as anxious to discuss it, as the subject is to hear the decision. It is unfortunate that there should be no possibility of putting aside Mourning without being censured. Having no regular standard, each judge expounds a private law. The culprit cannot escape conviction of indecorous haste; no matter how long the change is delayed. The transition state, too, is generally indescribably forlorn. No condition save that of a bride on the eve of marriage, can rival its shabby gentility. Mourner and bride, intent on new scenery and decorations, are not willing to waste time in embellishing the old ones.

Fashion, which rigidly enforces Mourning, does its best to soften its asperities. In our great, fashionable cities, it sanctions the use of private boxes jealously draped, whence private balls and masquerades can be witnessed by recently afflicted social devotees. In that modest privacy so admirably suited to their grief, some subdued king and queen of fashion sit enthroned in woe. The sparkle and splendor for a while denied them, pass in bewildering pageant before their tear dimmed eyes. "Ah!" sighs Madame, "if my husband had only lived till to-morrow!" Monsieur responds, "Ah! if my wife had not lingered until last week!" Peace! troubled souls. Within a little while you shall resume your natural sphere. The privilege to

> "Drag about the mockery of woe
> To midnight masquerade and public show,"[2]

is coeval with Mourning itself. If it were denied, the fashionable world would apostatize. Brunettes would turn Chinese, to affect yellow; or claim royal blood, to assume purple. Blondes would prove their Persian descent, in order to wear white; or Japanese, to secure a right to dress in indigo blue. Some might cry, "Am I not a man and a brother?" to the Creole negro,[3] for the sake of that "blue guinea," the *ne plus ultra* of colored desolation.

There is a potent spell in Mourning, surely. Worn for a lover, it secures a tangible husband before it need be doffed. Serious inconvenience occasionally arises from this singular fact. No. 2 can scarcely contemplate with satisfaction this trace of a pioneer in the unexplored regions of the beloved one's heart. The young lady cannot doff it suddenly, like Columbine in a pantomime.[4] Altogether it must be trying. But then, she who wears mourning for a lover, is sure of a husband; she who does not, must run the risk of having none. [N.B. Young ladies, under these circumstances, are unanimously in favor of wearing mourning.]

Natural feeling revolts against any prescribed expression or regulation of grief. In Boston and Philadelphia attention to these regulations is carried to a ludicrous extreme. Where ordinary people say that a family is in great affliction, Bostonians and Philadelphians say, "their very kitchen windows are bowed with black ribbon." The listener is expected to be struck silent with awe. But if the informant adds that for years the very sun has not been allowed to enter the house, a beaming expression of admiration is substituted. So much for folly! The gravest objection to the canons of Mourning is the expense they entail on people who cannot afford it. Families often deprive themselves of absolute necessaries to procure the requisite uniform. Half starved and overtasked, they pride themselves on paying that mark of respect to the dead, no matter what the sacrifice.

It is true that death obliterates all wrongs, and that some tender hearts faithfully mourn a tyrant. But until some distinction is made between the true and the false, Mourning must remain a doubtful tribute. There is some inconsistency in wearing it indiscriminately for the hardened sinner and the little child. Mourning either means something, or it means nothing. If something, it cannot be worn with too much circumspection. If it means nothing, it cannot be discarded too soon.

1. S. M. Dawson, *Sarah Morgan*, 72. See also Schoonmaker, "As Though It Were unto the Lord."
2. "And to bear about the mockery of woe / To midnight dances and the public show" (Alexander Pope, *Elegy to the Memory of an Unfortunate Lady* [1717], 57).
3. "Am I not a man and a brother?" appeared on a 1787 medallion by Josiah Wedgwood (1730–95) that showed a black man in chains with his knee on the ground and his hands uplifted. It became the seal of the Committee for the Abolition of the Slave Trade and was widely adopted as an icon of the antislavery movement.
4. Columbine and her suitor, Harlequin, were figures in the European commedia dell'arte.

*The luxury and refinement of West Virginia's White Sulphur Springs pro-
vided young ladies and gentlemen with an ideal environment for courting.
"A successful season at the springs," noted Charlene M. Boyer Lewis,
"often ended with a young couple returning home to plan a wedding."[1] As
parents and children both knew, courting at the Springs provided families
with the opportunity to affirm or enhance their status and honor through
marriage, thereby rebuilding the war-ravaged boundaries that defined the
southern elite and distinguished them from lower social orders.*

*As Sarah Morgan watched the fashionable spectacles that adorned the
White Sulphur ballroom, she began to contemplate the "dreary drama" of
marriage that followed the "sparkling" society "prologue." Convinced that
"the prettiest butterfly of Society does not wear well," Sarah wrote "The
World before Him, Where to Choose," a warning to men who would pay
"for hasty impulses with undying regret."*

"The World before Him, Where to Choose," July 26, 1873

Marriage is a *sine quâ non* with very young men. They know better, after a
while; but it is then generally too late for anything save regret. Society is the
garden where the world collects its butterflies for exhibition, and devotes itself to promoting their happiness and welfare. Matrimony is not the specified object; but it is too obvious to be more than tacitly ignored. The first
duty on emerging from the chrysalis state is to seek a Psyche[2] among the
flowers. Any insect with golden wings is supposed to be the destined one,
whose companionship will make life more perfect than a fairy tale. Well for
butterflies, whose existence is too brief to compass disappointment! But
man, with the life of a butterfly, pays for hasty impulses with undying regret.
The sooner he finds his Psyche, the longer the pang will last. The prettiest
butterfly of Society does not wear well, and its captor seems to live aeons
after perceiving it. Her colors come off; her wings droop; she refuses to soar;

> "Every touch that woos her stay,
> "But serves to break some charm away,"

and the lover must witness the transformation of what he loves, into that
which he does not love, without a murmur. Everything goes, but Psyche. She
threatens to linger forever, bereft of all that made her fair. She has nothing
more to fear from time, because there is nothing more for time to destroy.

Why should the dreary drama follow the sparkling prologue? Is there latent irony in the command, "Love one another," that the willing slave should be smitten hardest when he most zealously obeys? Society is the accredited field for successful marriages. Centuries of fiascoes cannot destroy its prestige. Presenting himself, as in duty bound, before the sole legitimate tribunal, has not each one the right to believe he will receive justice? The cruel verdict is returned, and the victim must accept it in silence. Pride only asks that the world shall make no comment, and resigns itself to suffer. Society continues to give pinchbeck in exchange for fine gold, and exacts a heavy premium in addition. Whoever has the means may make his purchase; but that which is most worthy of the purchaser is not always displayed to the public gaze. Cinderella's sisters dance in royal attire; but the maiden meet [meant] to be the bride of the prince must be diligently sought in unfrequented places. She may be familiar with kitchen, rats and pumpkins; but for her there is no transformation scene. She has not spirit enough to pine for the ball, and would probably present a very poor figure there. So many yards of illusion represent, for her, so many joints of mutton. She refuses to spend on the vanities of a night the sum that could purchase a comfort for any one else. And if the beneficent fairy would provide the paraphernalia, she would not expose papa and mamma to night air and draughts. While her sisters revel she is in the nursery with cross little brothers and sisters, or striving to cheer disheartened parents. She has no leisure for personal adornments, nor the means to adopt them. She is altogether uninteresting. But for the transformation of her rags to splendor, she must pass her life in obscurity like all the real Cinderellas of the world.

Nature, so beauteous in the wilds, is a sad failure in Society. The form of Venus[3] would not compare favorably with that of a skeleton, if the skeleton had the best dressmaker. Berenice, whose fabulous locks placed her among the constellations,[4] would suffer disadvantage from her glory in the hands of a hairdresser. The true artist asks nothing of nature save a well-molded skull, on which to found the fantastic structure. Lady Coventry,[5] the Miss Gunning whose marvellous complexion was the boast of London, and whose beauty attracted throngs of gazers, created the keenest disappointment in the French Court. By the side of a painted Du Barri[6] she sank into insignificance. Her pretensions to beauty were only admitted when she borrowed the paint pot of that delectable dame. Lord Coventry can almost be pardoned for the scene which followed at dinner, when to the scandal of the noble ladies he chased his wife around the table, swearing at the discovery, and rubbed her face clean with a napkin.

Modesty is made to look silly, underbred, and even ridiculous, contrasted with the assurance Society imparts. Erudition is put to shame by the magpie who can glibly rattle off three civil little nothings. There is not a charm of society which is not purchased by the sacrifice of some sweetness of home life. With a little attention to conventional rules, whoever mars a family circle could become instead an ornament to society, where pretence is everything and true merit nothing. Given a perfect toilet, crowned by the triumph of a hair dresser and the dazzled spectator gratuitously furnishes the rest. The ill temper which animates the eye, is hidden under the heavenly smile. In kissing the rose-cushioned hand, the lover has no suspicion of the forcible blow it has just administered to child or servant.

Ambitious men require wives who will reflect additional lustre on the career to which they dedicate themselves. Society alone offers such helpmeets. Alas! that it should be impossible to combine all perfections, and that the fairest form must often imply the absence of some more desirable quality! A faultless face outside of story books, seems incompatible with intellect. Perfect physical beauty is rarely combined with high moral tone. The suave manner and honeyed speech create an impression of insincerity while their flattery still intoxicates. But can this conviction lessen the value of such charms? Spiritual and intellectual excellence are tame and mean contrasted with beauty hollow as a Lorely's Fixed Star[7] sees Aurora Borealis[8] at a grand exhibition. In his exalted position he longs for some brilliant companion to illuminate his path. Dazzled by her coruscations, he claims her effulgence for his home, amid universal congratulations.

How she went out after the ceremony, and never revived save in spasmodic, imperceptible shimmers, poor Fixed Star dares not reveal. High above mortal sympathy he pursues his lonely way, mutely turning from all displays of succeeding Auroras, in memory of that poignant anguish. Fixed Star could a tale unfold, longer than Enke's comet,[9] and striking as much terror in the soul. But the secrets of Society must not be revealed; every one must purchase his own experience. Experience is the only possession of which man cannot be defrauded. The harder his fate, the more he has of it. The more he has, the less he needs it. It accumulates, but it cannot be bequeathed. Man profits by individual experience alone, and then, only when the urgent occasion for using it can never return. Whoever prizes the vanities of the world, must part with the best portion of his heart. Each one may hope to escape the penalty, but disappointment and unutterable sorrow are common to all who fall into the toils. "The world's mine oyster, which I, with sword, will open,"[10] is a faith peculiar to youth. How the sword is hacked and broken; how the fingers are cut and torn; how the oyster only opens to close fast on the bleeding stump; how the hungering soul dwells ever after "full in the sight of paradise, beholding heaven and feeling hell,"[11] remains to be recorded.

1. Lewis, *Ladies and Gentlemen*, 176.
2. In Greek myth, Psyche was the personification of the human soul. Eros fell in love with her.
3. In Roman myth, Venus was the goddess of love.
4. Berenice (ca. 273–221 B.C.) was a queen of Egypt and Cyrene who promised her hair to Venus and who was the inspiration for Berenice's Hair (Coma Berenices), a constellation in the northern sky.
5. Maria Gunning (1733–60), a celebrated Irish beauty who became the toast of London society and subsequently married the Earl of Coventry.
6. Jeanne Bécu, comtesse du Barry (1743–93), the mistress of King Louis XV (1710–74) of France.
7. A star so far from Earth that its position in the sky appears not to change.
8. The northern lights, a brilliant nighttime display in the far Northern Hemisphere.
9. A comet named after Johann Franz Encke (1791–1865), a German astronomer, that is visible every 3.3 years.
10. Shakespeare, *The Merry Wives of Windsor*, 2.2
11. Thomas Moore, "The Fire-Worshippers," *Lalla Rookh* (1817).

ॐ

Sarah Morgan's position at the News and Courier *required her to be both a society columnist and a social critic. After condemning the ostentatious display at Easter, Sarah shifted her focus to write a series of articles entitled "Fashion Gossip for Charleston Ladies." Here, she discussed stylish winter coats, the demise of lace collars, and plunging necklines.*

Out and About: Fashion Gossip for the Charleston Ladies, November 8, 1873

All persons who have a present or prospective interest in weddings or balls are notified that white kid gloves are no longer imperative. Pale shades of blue, rose, lavender, straw and pearl color are preferred, and three buttons take precedence over four or more. Much time and attention are now devoted to the

ADORNMENT OF THE THROAT,

whose beauty has too long been ignored and neglected. For many years linen collars disfigured the softest and roundest outline by their harsh precision and dead contrasts. The loveliest throats became merely sallow, ungainly cylinders. At last, after many generations, good taste prevails so far that some consideration is shown to throats. Where linen once disfigured beauties, lace and tulle now impart grace and softness to the least prepossessing women. Fashion is revelling in the invention of pretty ornaments for this new feature of attraction. Velvet ruffs, lined with white, pink or blue silk, with inner quillings of tulle or Brussels net, are seen everywhere. Neck ties can be worn at the base of these, the ends crossed or knotted in front, with a locket in place of a breastpin.

THE LAST NECKTIE

is a velvet ribbon an inch and a half wide, with ends embroidered in blue or scarlet bees, and finished with fine silk fringe. Others are of soft armure silk, brocaded in white. Scarfs of *crêpe de chine,* six inches wide, are worn around the throat, until furs become seasonable. Plain neckties are basted in shallow pleats, surmounted by a simple ruche of tulle or wash blonde. Another style of ruff or "round collar" is easily made. Black silk or velvet for the exterior is lined with silk of any color, run together on the wrong side. The strip is graduated from three or more inches in the middle to about one and a half at the ends. Turned on the right side, it is box-pleated in double or treble pleats down the centre. The top and bottom of every pleat are then tacked together, and form a succession of roses and hollow shells, revealing the colored lining and the inner ruff of tulle, which rests against the throat.

THE NILSSON COLLARET[1]

is both serviceable and attractive. A band of silk, edged on either side with Valenciennes, is cut to fit the back of the neck and pass down the front to the waist, strapped across the breast by two bows to hold it in place. Black lace scarfs around the neck held by scarlet bows are also quite effective. Black velvet vests, piped with silk and edged with lace, preserve or renovate dresses, offering a rare combination of style and economy.

are of soft twilled silk a foot wide. They are worn, too, on the left side of the back, passed through the large sash-buckles, which are now a full dress necessity. A steel anchor for this purpose, with belt, tackle and twelve buttons to match, can be bought for nine dollars.

1. A garment named for Christine Nilsson (1843–1921), a Swedish opera singer.

NINE

Politics

Editorials by Sarah Morgan

Sarah Morgan made her writing debut in the *Charleston News* with an editorial on politics. Ironically, "The New Andromeda," a passionate yet eloquent plea on behalf of the people of Louisiana, came from a woman who had always denounced women's political involvement, even in its mildest forms. During the Civil War, Sarah staunchly resisted the prevailing notion that women's interest in politics was a legitimate expression of patriotism. "I hate to hear women on political subjects," she declared. "They invariably make fools of themselves, and it sickens me to see half a dozen talking of what *they* would do, and what ought to be done; it gives me the greatest disgust, so I generally contrive to absent myself from such gatherings, as I seldom participate." Resolved that she had "too much respect for [her] father's memory to adopt so pitiful a warfare," Sarah used her diary as a medium for expressing her thoughts.[1]

The demands of newspaper work, however, compelled Sarah to educate herself on the turbulent and ever-changing political landscape. Frank sent her copies of the South Carolina and U.S. Constitutions and encouraged her to write on international issues. During 1873, Sarah wrote editorials on the Grant administration, Louisiana politics, woman suffrage, and contemporary political events in Spain and France. While she dismissed women's active participation in the American political system as "sheer nonsense," Sarah's role as a writer for the *News and Courier* required her to embrace her own political voice, even if she did so to denounce the right of other women to do the same.

1. S. M. Dawson, *Sarah Morgan*, 73–74, 121, 142–43.

Sarah's political editorials often addressed contemporary issues relating to women. In the following piece, she discussed the plight of the thousands of women compelled to earn a living in the defeated South. "Stitch! Stitch! Stitch!" highlighted the irony of extending patents for sewing machines when those women forced to take in piecework had become "rapidly dying slaves" of the "steel finger." Sarah took the title from Thomas Hood's "The Song of the Shirt" (1843):

> With fingers weary and worn,
> With eyelids heavy and red,
> A woman sat, in unwomanly rags,
> Plying her needle and thread—
> Stitch! stitch! stitch!
> In poverty, hunger and dirt,
> And still with a voice of dolorous pitch,
> She sang the "Song of the Shirt."

Stitch! Stitch! Stitch! April 10, 1873

It is said that the bill to extend the patents for Sewing Machines cost those interested in the monopoly about $1,500,000. The Credit Mobilier Investigation[1] is the only act of Congress more worthy of commendation than the defeat of this bill.

The actual cost of manufacturing the best Sewing Machine is only twelve dollars. Yet a Grover or Wheeler is thought cheap at $90, and $150 is a common price. Few of those who are compelled to sew for a living, can afford to purchase the best machine. The majority must content themselves with the more imperfect. And those who must, perforce, struggle for bread without mechanical assistance, labor under the additional disadvantage of reduced wages. No human hand can compete with the steel finger. No human industry can vie with its speed. Thousands of women are condemned to starve in the unequal contest—gaunt complement of the multitude of more rapidly dying slaves of the Machine. Statistics indicate that seven years is the full average life to be hoped for by those who use the machine constantly, as in the workshops. It is the old question of the advantage of Consumption with its slow progress, or Consumption with great strides. Each person may have a preference. But, if a Protective system is so necessary for machines, protection might well be extended to those now starved out of the hope of procuring such assistance. A "Ring," to entice the universal use of hemstitched handkerchiefs would give work to hundreds of thousands. It is true that the savages have not yet clamored for these articles. Indeed, in higher grades of civilization, their use is sometimes surprisingly rare. But Japan and China might be induced to renounce the small squares of paper so long in vogue, and thus give rise to a new industry.

Is it too much to hope for the protection of the working classes, until the patentees are rewarded in proportion to their own estimate of their deserts. "Public benefactors," who make a profit of thousands per cent., savor too much of Credit Mobilier disinterestedness to command public applause. It is time to break down every monopoly; and it is to be expected that Congress will remain obdurate, under the effort that will assuredly be made to induce it to reconsider the case of the suffering inventors.

1. An investigation into the corruption surrounding railroad development. Crédit Mobilier, Eric Foner explains, was "a dummy corporation formed by an inner ring of Union Pacific stockholders to oversee the line's government-assisted construction. Essentially a means by which the participants contracted with themselves, at an exorbitant profit, to build their own line, the arrangement was protected by the distribution of Crédit Mobilier shares to influential Congressmen" (*Reconstruction*, 468).

ↀↀↀ

Sarah Morgan wrote a small number of editorials and short pieces on the position of freedpeople in the postwar South. As a member of a slaveholding family, Sarah had grown up within a household where servants were an integral part of family life, helping to dress the ladies, fixing their rooms, doing the laundry, working the vegetable patch, fetching wood, and cooking dinner. Sarah did not question the legitimacy of the "peculiar institution" or the loyalty of the Morgan slaves, who, she believed, worked in the interests of the household and therefore accepted the elite ideology that governed relations between masters and slaves.

During the Civil War, Sarah clung to her antebellum notions of slavery, describing the conduct of her family's slaves as "beyond praise." "Five thousand negroes followed their Yankee brothers, from the town & neighborhood; but ours remained," she boasted. Still, Sarah could not ignore the ways in which the war had dismantled most master-slave relations. When she heard rumors that the Yankees had raided elite homes for clothing and given it to the contrabands, Sarah was outraged at the thought of her dresses "doing active duty on the sylph like form of some negro woman" while Sarah wore a patched dress and an old sunbonnet. "Wicked as it may seem, I would rather have all I own burned than in the possession of the negroes," she cried angrily. "Fancy my magenta organdie on a dark beauty! Bah! I think the sight would enrage me."[1]

In war and in defeat, Sarah maintained her belief that slaves and freedpeople were inherently childlike and could be used by whites for good or for evil. Under the watchful eye of the elite white South, she argued, blacks had assumed their rightful social position. But under the postwar rule of carpetbaggers and "fanatics," she argued that freedpeople had become nothing more than pawns in the northern quest to "degrade" the South.

Paradox, April 25, 1873

The material interests of the black race are so identified with those of the white that it is singular that any attempt should be made to divide them. It is still more remarkable to hear those who are professedly the best friends of the colored people dwell exclusively on the importance of their political status, neglecting all exposition of the greater benefits to be derived from honesty, industry and sobriety. The question seems to be, not what will help the colored man, but what will profit his quondam friend.

1. S. M. Dawson, *Sarah Morgan*, 250, 213, 215

Whites and Blacks, May 12, 1873

It is to be regretted that the Southerners and negroes, with interests so nearly identical, should be arrayed in opposition to each other by fanatics who are, openly or secretly, the enemies of both races. The best of the colored people, the few who are conspicuous for a love of justice and order, are ready to acknowledge that the Southerner is worthy of respect and trust. The Northern adventurers have proclaimed with wearying iteration that the negro is "a man and a brother."[1] And why? As a man, he is their political tool; as a brother, he can be defrauded and oppressed. Their aggressiveness is due to the selfish feeling that their own interests are superior to every consideration of law, justice and honor, and that their ends are cheaply gained at the cost of the public purity and private prosperity which, in theory, they hold so dear.

This has thrown the Southerners into a false position. They remain cold and indifferent, rather than seem to cringe to the weak instruments of cunning politicians. As the readiest protest against the apotheosis of the negro, the Southerners are tempted to declare that they will have no part or parcel with him. The degradation of the South is the sole object of the new cult; and the negro is too elated to perceive that he owes his deification not to his own merit, but to a bitter sectional animosity against a superior race. The natural disqualifications of the negro would exclude him from public life, if he were nothing more than a white man. His ignorance, not only of public interests but of the higher law, has led him to abuse power wherever it has been placed in his hands. Self-respect and the instinct of self-preservation have compelled the more enlightened race to deny the propriety or wisdom of continuing authority in such hands. Northern fanaticism flourishes at a distance which effectually precludes the possibility of understanding the strength and weakness of the negro. Its disciples, enjoying a perfect immunity from a degrading vassalage, encourage the worst members of the body politic to commit new excesses. Every remonstrance they brand as "disloyalty." Incendiary paragraphs inflame the passions, and the facts are distorted until the very negroes whom the romances are meant to benefit fail to recognize in them pages from their own brief history.

To be ruled by competent officials is the modest demand of the misrepresented and unrepresented South. To be governed not only by the worst of the blacks, but by the infinitely more degraded adventurer, is a slavery which far exceeds that from which the negroes were freed. It is unreasonable and unwise, if not a crime against Nature, to subject an enlightened race to the domination of a class who have not been fitted for the work of government by either birth or education. Incapacity is seated in high places, only to debase what is noble and good. Federal authority upholds the tyrannous oppression. If the bayonet were withdrawn and the "carpet-bagger" gone home, the intelligent whites would soon restore peace and fortune to the Polands of the South. At the same time, the colored people, freed from the cruel kindness of their Northern taskmasters, would find true happiness, and comfort for their families, in honest, hard work. They would be sure, moreover, that their earnings would not be filched from them by political assessments or extravagant taxation. The State governments would extend to every citizen the protection of equal and considerate legislation. For whites and for blacks the simple rule would prevail that none should hold public office unless qualified for the trust by experience, intelligence and integrity.

1. See chap. 8 for Josiah Wedgwood's medallion featuring this saying.

Sarah Morgan was never an ardent secessionist, nor did she believe in the sustainability of southern independence. Instead, she "quietly adopted father's views on political subjects, with out meddling with them." "I dont believe in Secession, but I do in Liberty," she declared in May 1862. "I want the South to conquer, dictate its own terms, and go back to the Union for I believe that apart, inevitable ruin awaits both."[1] When the South found itself unable to dictate its own terms, Sarah felt bitter and disillusioned by the conduct of the victorious North. In the following editorial, she questioned whether the upcoming U.S. centennial celebrations could indeed "wipe out" the old scores between North and South.

Wiping Out Old Scores, April 28, 1873

It is claimed that the approaching Centennial will serve to cement in closer bonds of affection the sister States so long alienated from each other. Where family disputes are inherited, and secretly cherished, it may be questioned whether any real charity or affection can be secured by outward demonstrations. *Savoir vivre* [Good breeding] compels those possessing it to treat with courtesy the most obnoxious persons, but it exacts no renunciation of private opinion, and, as we know on which side the prejudice lies, we cannot help thinking it more important that Northerners should visit the South than that the reconstructed Rebel should hurry across the river. Mahomet, however, will cheerily go to the mountain if the mountain will not come to him. There is no sulking about it.

For nearly a century each State has been persuaded that her individual arm is the shield of the Commonwealth. This is a glorious boast, if it can be admitted that others upheld it while the battle raged; but is an offensive pretension if it arrogates to itself the entire credit of a grand result. There is too much prejudice and narrow-mindedness in State relations. Each is but a link of a single chain. Whether the link be large or small, it cannot be subtracted without a solution of the continuity of the whole. By some unwritten law, the State which gives the country a man who does his duty, considers herself unrivalled, and is prone to taunt the others with her superiority. The most recent settler shares the heritage of that man's fame, with his actual descendents. Our "success," our "glory," our "achievements," reflect lustre on the humblest citizen.

> "If by your father's worth yours you rate,
>   Count me those only who are good and great."[2]

A strict analysis of personal claims to distinction would reduce us to a natural level, and give each an opportunity of proving, by future emulation, which State deserves precedence. If the Centennial can wipe out old scores, and serve as the inauguration of a new reign of toleration and Charity, the celebration will be the dawn of the true Golden Age, and will be fitly held in the City of Brotherly Love [Philadelphia].

1. S. M. Dawson, *Sarah Morgan*, 74.
2. "But by your fathers' worth if your's you rate, / Count me those only who were good and great" (Alexander Pope, *An Essay on Man: Epistle IV—Of the Nature and State of Man with Respect to Happiness* [1734]).

i⊃€i

Sarah Morgan never supported the administration of President Ulysses S. Grant, who held office from 1869 until 1877. She argued that his Republican politics had turned once prosperous Louisiana into the new southern Andromeda. Outraged by the rumors that Grant and his notoriously corrupt government were contemplating "a third term," Sarah called for legislative action to prevent the emergence of "a military dictatorship." The "soldier of fortune," she believed, would be far better off serving his "cabbage-beds in the West" than entertaining the possibility of another four long years as "the head of the land."

The Third Term, April 29, 1873

It is suggested that the proposed Western and Southern tour of the President indicates a design to curry public favor with the view of securing a nomination and election for the third time, which would be equivalent to enjoying the Presidential office for life. A military dictatorship is the next step. The country will then see what she has gained by giving her shoulder-strapped soldiery a dagger with which to stab her liberties to the heart. The Roman Republic perished in vain, if its example be so soon forgotten.

It will be admitted that Washington[1] as a man, was as irreproachable as General Grant, and that his services to his country were at least as great. Yet a grateful nation, styling him the father of his people, acquiesced in his refusal when offered a third term of office. No benefits he could have otherwise bestowed upon his country would have secured him as much honor as did his firm, unselfish rejection of the proffered prize. He has left an example which a loyal love of the country and an unswerving allegiance to the Constitution alike demand shall be scrupulously followed. It is no disparagement to the merit of General Grant that he should be invited to follow in the footsteps of his illustrious predecessor. If there is any truth in the report that the President is, by nature, incapable of refusing anything that is offered him, a consideration for this weak point of one who has so long been the head of the land should lead his warmest partisans to put the temptation out of his reach. The fortitude which enabled Americans to survive the loss of a Washington can give them the patience to endure the valedictory of General Grant when that unselfish soldier of fortune retires to his cabbage-beds in the West.

The United States may, in its zeal, have saddled itself, like Sinbad, with an Old Man of the Sea, who has no idea of vacating his comfortable perch.[2] Let the grizzled embracer have at least a chance to dismount. This can scarcely be done while Sinbad or the nation civilly protests that the burden is not the slightest inconvenience, and that its imposition for a life time, would, in the words of Mr. Toots, be "of no consequence whatever."[3]

1. George Washington (1732–99), American Revolutionary War general and first president of the United States (1789–97).
2. In the story of Sinbad the Sailor (*Arabian Nights*), the old man of the sea perched on Sinbad's shoulders and refused to let go.
3. Charles Dickens, *Dombey and Son* (1848).

᠅

While Sarah had discovered her own political voice, she used her editorial position to discredit the suffrage movement. Enfranchised women, she argued, "will triumphantly prove themselves capable of blundering as systematically as the average male voter."[1]

Suffrage-Shrieking, May 20, 1873

The Woman's Suffrage Association[2] has passed a resolution denouncing Gen. Grant as "ungrateful, a man to be feared and watched, and a dangerous foe to republican institutions." The failure to take some notice of the "dear creatures" in his inaugural address has brought this thunderbolt upon him.[3] In extenuation it might be pleaded that there are many important questions which Gen. Grant persistently ignores. But Miss Anthony & Co. feel that this woman suffrage affair is the one chord in the human heart which cannot be rudely touched without jarring the hand which trifles with it. The wild women have undoubtedly a modicum of influence, and by controlling others who are not so conspicuous, may yet revenge themselves by interfering with somebody's third term aspirations. Woman suffrage is, of course, sheer nonsense. But each maid and matron can command the vote of at least one man. Sensible men always defer to the wishes of their wives; or sensible women will conform to the opinions of their husbands, which comes to the same thing. A larger field is presented by the anxious lovers, who are figuratively on the "mourner's bench" waiting for "a change of heart."[4] Few of them would have the spirit to resist the political dictum of their charmers. Geese saved the capitol.[5] Recalcitrant females might, under Providence, be made the means of saving the American Republic.

Between the pedestal on which Mill[6] has exalted woman, and the idea of Liberty represented by Mesdames Woodhull and Claflin,[7] there is an abyss which can never be bridged over. The true position of woman begins to be fully understood. As soon as the menads presided over by Miss Anthony are disbanded, worthy women will find that a large sphere of practical usefulness is opened to them; one for which they are fitted. The ravings of dreamy fanatics only injure a cause which would be pushed to its legitimate results if the repulsive pretensions of the Anthonys and Stantons were withdrawn. Wrongs are proclaimed until Rights are forgotten. No one would deny to women the opportunity of self-support. The desire to open new channels, and to give them a fair compensation for their toil, grows in strength every day. But the denunciation of the President for not making sufficiently humble acknowledgements to the Woman's Suffrage Association, only add to the contempt and ridicule which that distinguished body has already fairly earned.

1. "Two Hundred and Fifty Dollars for a Vote," April 4, 1873.
2. The National Woman Suffrage Association was founded by Susan B. Anthony (1820–1906) and Elizabeth Cady Stanton (1815–1902) in 1869. The organization opposed the Fifteenth Amendment, which enfranchised ex-slaves but not women.
3. Sarah was probably referring to Elizabeth Cady Stanton's "To President Grant—Letter from Mrs. Stanton," which appeared in the *Woman's Journal* on March 29, 1873. In it she stated, "While congratulating you, Mr. President, on the wisdom and humanity of your 'inaugural address,' I would remind you that in making many generous pledges to three classes of oppressed citizens, namely, laborers, negroes, and Indians, you forget to mention the 20,000,000 disfranchised women who are classed in all the State Constitutions with idiots, lunatics, paupers and criminals."

4. Sarah drew on rhetoric often used at revival meetings. People sat on a mourner's bench to repent their sins and learn the plan of salvation from the Bible.

5. In Roman legend, honking geese first alerted the Romans to the Gauls' attack on Rome in 390 B.C.

6. John Stuart Mill, *The Subjection of Women* (1869). Mill likened the condition of women to slavery and called for an end to political, legal, educational, and social frameworks that subordinated women.

7. Victoria Claflin Woodhull (1838–1927), a radical and suffragette, who declared herself a presidential candidate in 1870; and her sister, Tennessee Claflin (1846–1923). The two women launched the highly controversial *Woodhull and Claflin's Weekly* in 1870.

A Greenville Sojourn

September–October 1873

In August 1873, Frank made his proposed trip to Virginia. After accompanying Sarah and her mother to Orange, he secured the Morgan women temporary accommodations at Mary Williams Ware's boardinghouse in Greenville, South Carolina.

Sarah's sojourn in Greenville marked a time of transition for her and her mother. After months of work and careful consideration, she made definite plans to leave Hampton and set up her own home in Charleston. Frank was delighted by the news and consulted with Sarah on accommodation, servants, linen, and tableware as he made arrangements for her imminent arrival. In Greenville, Sarah began to reassess Howell's academic future and petitioned longtime friend George Trenholm for a scholarship for her nephew. She also agonized over her relationship with Frank, once again entreating him to think of her "only as a sister or a friend," not as his future wife. The news devastated Frank, who had returned from his trip to Virginia "more than ever determined to make [him]self worthy of [her] love." Overwhelmed by a financial crisis that threatened to destroy the *News and Courier,* Frank slipped into depression, condemned, as he remarked to Sarah, to "pass through it all without an affectionate word from any one, and, at a time, when the conviction has reached me that all my labor to win your love has been miserably in vain."

ꜱ

Frank's despondency was in stark contrast to the feelings of hope he possessed on his way home from Greenville. Forced to wait in Columbia for hours after the derailment of a train, he wrote to Sarah, recommitting himself to the task of winning her hand in marriage.

Columbia: Saturday
Midnight [September 6, 1873]

My Sweet Love;

The engine of the train from Columbia ran off the track this morning, and so delayed our train that we did not arrive here until between 10 & 11 to-night, too late for the Charleston train. I go down by the train at 5.30 a.m. "Sais tu que" [Know that] I am content at the delay which allows me to write to you so soon to thank you for your parting words (some of them unspoken), to assure you of my love, & to entreat you to bear a brave heart for my sake as I will do for yours? My sleeping and waking thoughts last night were of you, & my last moments in Greenville this morning (even as the shrill whistle sounded) were devoted to new vows of faithfulness to all my promises, and to prayers for your happiness which, also, is mine. At that moment you were, I trust, sound asleep, taking the rest you sadly need.

Jemmie was in town to-day, but I did not see him as he had gone out an hour or so before my arrival. I am told that his Mill is about finished, that he has a splendid new buggy, that he has taken three stalls at the coming State Fair, & that his cotton is so fine that he wants to take down a lot of caterpillars to thin it out. Certainly there is here no evidence of want of funds at Hampton to do whatever is desired to be done.

You may rely on my sending Howell to you by Tuesday's night train, so as to arrive at G on Wednesday evening.

In the cars to day I had ample time for introspection and retrospection; you were not there to catechise me, sweet child! so I cross examined myself. I have marked out my general plan of action for business affairs, and I shall tell you every thing without apologising for doing it. And what of your darling self? Only this! I know that I love you better than I ever loved you before, because I am more than ever before determined to make myself worthy of your love, which I hope to win to be the crown of my life & yours too, sweetest! I know that I have been and am unworthy of you, but with your two hands you have lifted me up, & with your face, shining as that of an angel, you have inspired me with the purpose to be as good & true as you would have me. I may stumble by the way, but you shall again raise me up & be my guide & comforter and more than friend. I owe you more than you could ever owe me; for you have done for me what no other woman could do, & I have only done what a score of others could have done had they chosen to do it. Look on me & know that yours is no longer a useless life. A soul is in your keeping, & an aching head & hungry heart are yours to encourage and make content. Be cheerful as you would have me to be & remember that no private or public cares can daunt me while you can tell me that you do your best to regain your health & strength.

Note the letters in the Graphic on Low: necked dresses. Can you not write something about it as soon as you finish "Facilis Descensus"?[1] Take your own line, I had rather be guided by your pure heart in such a matter than by any society talk or opinion. Send down as soon as ready. You shall have plenty of subjects to suit you.

And now, my life, Good Night. I kiss your fair hands & am

Yours always
F. W. Dawson

1. "Heart-Breaking," September 13, 1873.

After taking a short respite from her Saturday editorials, Sarah returned to her work with vigor and determination. Her first piece was entitled "Heart-Breaking," an editorial that, she admitted, could be read as an "exposeé" into her relationship with Frank. "The suffering resulting from honest love, however mistaken or unappreciated, is not in vain," she wrote. "It has its purpose for educating and developing the soul for a higher life. If earth denies its fruition, its perfection will be found beyond." Frank was delighted with her work and declared that it was a sign of her "soul's awakening" after years of sorrow and affliction.

Sarah to Frank

Greenville. September. 8th 1873

Here beginneth Vol. 10th of our correspondence! Master Shylock will naturally require his pound of flesh first of all. Here it is, still warm & palpitating. Knowing you read my words to you before looking at those for the public, let me beg you to read this "Heart-breaking" as if there was no me in the world. If you look at [it] as an exposeé, you will be justly shocked & disgusted. I dreaded making it what it could have been, for that reason. But I know scores of people who would be benefited by a little sympathy. The girl for whom this was written is one of the many. Once, I could have escaped the refinement of martyrdom by some such little help. Dont throw it aside judging it only by me or you. Of course, in the abstract, you are the best judge. Of myself, I would bury every word I might could would or should write. Especially about the weather![1] What can I make of it? I tremble at the prospect. Yet I mean to do my best. I will work hard & faithfully, indeed I will.

We are as delighted with everybody, as everybody is delighted with us. It would be impossible to be more pleasantly situated. The one possible bane to my enjoyment keeps out of sight—Mrs. Ware's son.[2] I hear him mildly subdued in adjacent rooms, but never yet have been incommoded by his presence. His mother apologises for him, saying he is very modest & retiring. I sent word I was, also. Sweet sympathy of kindred minds!

Every body is in love with you—except, of course—! I hear your praise chanted at every turn, & sing as sweetly as any one, myself. Mrs. Green breaks out at stated intervals with "Such sweet ways! Such beautiful teeth, my dear! Such pretty hair! And his expressive eyes beam with intelligence! He just worships you! Now you wont mind telling an old lady like me that it's a match, will you?" I tell her I would not, if it were only true; but that I never voluntarily throw away a friend, especially without having the chance. The old lady cannot exactly untangle the thread, so she vaguely shakes her head, & impiously "hopes the Lord will change my heart." The heart is all right & good enough, if it only had a little life & feeling. I think there is a leak in it, & all the feeling ran in my back. It *will not* rest. It aches more & more, & wakes me up to remind me of it. Last night it fancied sleep, but mother did not; so she kept me awake moaning. She did not even feel badly, which did make it seem hard. You have made me so selfish, I think more of such trifles than I used to. I told her I would tell you she would not let me sleep, hoping to scare her into good behavior to-night. For it is a wretched preparation for work, & brings out more pains than ideas. I promised to tell you exactly how I was. In a nutshell, the truth is I am not well. But it is a lovely cool, rainy day, & I shall [be] better if it will only put an end to the heat. And you? Taking care of the head as well as the heart, I trust, & both growing more noble, tender & pure for the whole world, as well as for me. I trust to you to say something clever to Mrs. Fourgeaud for me. Would you believe that this Monday, after twelve, I have not yet spoken to Mrs. Ware of Howell? I will go at once however. But how I shrink from everything, good, bad, or indifferent!

S.M.

Do not send my "salary" until I write for it. That will be safest & best. Call the article anything you please.

1. "Weather-Wisdom," September 15, 1873.
2. Mary Williams Jones Ware (1815 or 1816–85) was the owner and operator of a boardinghouse on Pendleton Road in Greenville. She was the widow of Thomas Edwin Ware (b. 1806), a planter and politician who served in the House of Representatives between 1840 and 1847 and the state Senate between 1848 and 1864. He was found guilty of murdering his sixty-four-year-old father-in-law, Adam Jones, in 1853, but was pardoned by Governor John Laurence Manning (1816–89) after serving just one week of his sentence. Sarah was referring to Mary Ware's grandson, possibly Irvin F. Ware (b.1872 or 1873), the son of Thomas Ware, twenty-three, and Lucy Foote Ware, nineteen, with whom Mary was living in 1880.

Frank to Sarah

2.

Charleston
Monday [September 8, 1873]

My darling! I frankly confess that I am awfully blue, and disheartened to-day. I hope to work out of it in a day or two. I know that I can, and will, if I have some cheering news from you. Business is tolerably good; but money matters are awfully mixed, and when you see me again I shall have more grey hairs than ever. I should like you to help me personally by allowing me, if I need it, to sell the City stock of yours which I have so as to repay myself that little sum. Mark me! I can do without it; but I thought that you would prefer to help me as far as you could. Mr. R agrees with me that you can do more for us and for yourself in Charleston than in any other place. You must certainly come down by the middle of October; I do so want you. They are kind enough in Rutledge Avenue but it is no "home" for me, as I would understand "home." Mr. Magrath seems to be in love with Howell, and has, I believe, promised him a free pass to Greenville. Is it not kind? I fear, however, that Howell has been persuaded by Mrs. Chisolm and our folks that he had much better remain with you than return to school; that he will learn more with you & the rest. This may be true, but these good people dont know the circumstances. My own advice to you is: Send Howell back to School at the opening of the session, & if you are not better satisfied, and in better circumstances, next Spring you can send him to another school or return him to his Mother. This is the best that I can think of. You cannot as at present circumstances, keep him with you for long & unless you return him to School he must be sent to his Mother. Let us wait & hope! You can look after him in Chn and give him and yourself one more chance. I warn you, in advance, that you must take with several grains of salt what he now says about the School. He has reversed his opinions entirely in two weeks; influenced doubtless by what has been said to him. Assez [Enough]! Howell starts to: morrow night. I have written to Mr. Bollin[1] to look after him in Columbia.

Sweet Heaven! how dreary this place is to me! Do tell me, if you can, that you are better & that you are more cheerful. Give my love to your Mother &

Believe me
My poor darling,
Yours always
F. W. Dawson

1. Charles J. Bollin, fifty-two, of Columbia was an employee of the South Carolina Railroad.

ﻞﻟ

Frank to Sarah

4

Charleston
Tuesday Evening [September 9, 1873]

My sweet Love!

In an hour's time Howell will start—to see you, while I remain behind to mourn her who is my only hope. A truce to these thoughts—you must be so tired of them.

I send you by Express to-night the "needle instrument" with full instructions.[1] It goes by the same train as Howell. The hat rack which I have put in Howell's trunk is to save you from living in your trunks. I have taken the liberty to send you a bottle of claret for your Mother, & two bottles of sherry for yourself. Please, dearest, take some of the sherry every day to oblige me. I send you the handkerchiefs you lent me, & the little box you can put them in. What a lot of "I sends." So much & so little. So little in themselves, and so much, because of the love of which they are the poor emblems.

And I send you good news. Col Trenholm, whom I saw this morning, and whom I told in general of your tour, said he would be in Greenville (I presume on his way to Batesville [South Carolina]) in about a week, & would see you. How glad you will be; and I am glad for your sake, though I had much rather go myself.

No letter from Miriam yet! Unless one comes soon I shall begin to think she has forgotten me. What a slander to say such a thing—even in jest.

In the little box with the "needles" you will find a letter from some one who loves you too devotedly, perhaps, for your comfort. I put it there to decoy you to send for the box as soon as possible; but I think they will deliver it to: morrow night.

Send me some good news about your sweet, sweet self. My head aches very drearily, & so would my heart, if it were not in your keeping with all the rest of what is worth having in

Yours always

F. W. Dawson

I have lent Howell my big cape to keep him warm. I do not use it. Time enough to return it when you come.

1. This device was for Sarah's back. It consisted of a panel of needles that were applied to the spinal area (Dawson to Morgan, September 9, 1873 [additional letter], Dawson Papers).

ℒꝐℯↄ

Frank to Sarah

No.6

Charleston

Wednesday Night [September 10, 1873]

My darling! Although I write to you often I really write very little. Half of my letters are made up of complainings and grumblings. But I have just carefully read "Broken Hearts", and you shall have an old-fashioned lecture thereupon; while I am fresh from the furnace. In the first place, nothing that you could have said would have disgusted me. Talk out your thoughts. In that way you can do most public good. Only they who have learned can teach. Your life shall be made a lesson and an Evangel. And, in that you do good to others, good shall come to you when you least expect it. I give you carte-blanche in writing more confidently than ever before; because there is a better tone in your articles—the unconscious expression of the new birth which is dawning for you as it has dawned for me. Already, as you know, the bitterness of your death is past. Perhaps the change may be expressed thus: A year ago you were dead, & content to remain so. Now you regret that you died, and wonder whether there can be a resurrection. You are feeling the chastening & softening influence of affliction—the stone age is nearly over. Is it not sweet that Love should heal the hurt which Love gave? "Similia similibus curantur."[1] That Love which might break the heart that was whole, shall join together, and make whole, the heart that is broken. The scar will remain; but a scar which is nor shame nor reproach—only the emblem of a stab which was unlooked for, & pierced the deeper because of the openness with which the defenceless breast was exposed to the hand which gave it! In your very complaining of physical pain, my beloved, is a sign of your soul's awakening. And the same is found in your new willingness to live. While to live was to suffer death was craved. As soon as there is a gleam of hope & comfort, living becomes desirable. Even if you were peevish, as you never are, I should take it as an evidence that you were mending in health. Who so fretful as those recovering from severe illness? Out of temper—out of danger. And surely you would not desire to avenge yourself on those who made you miserable, by fastening years of woe upon one who has proved that you can live, and can have, in this life, a rational and lasting happiness, as different from the old frenzy as is the calm light of Hesperus[2] from the lightning's lurid glare. Say, if you will, that I bother you, and do not understand you. I flatter myself that I know you better than you know yourself. My Cupidon[3] is not blind, darling! Certainly, I will not allow you to fall back again into the slough, without using remonstrance & entreaty, & exhausting prayer, in the endeavor to prevent it. I have done! For a while you have lifted me out of myself, & back I fall to the vexations of a lonely life. Amen! Tell me, at least, that you can read what I have written. My fist is very shakey to-night.

I forgot to tell you that the "needles" answer the same purpose as a blister, and act more quickly. Be cautious!

You will soon have your *"Heaven"! William* Trenholm told me to-day that he would go to Greenville next week. *N.B.* This is joke; not jealousy. Only I wish I could go as his substitute.

And why, my love, did you forget your catechism? Do you think that my love for you has ceased to grow? That Mrs. Green was right in saying that I worship you. I loved you enough before I met you at Staunton & you know how much there was in the intimacy of those two weeks to make me love you more & more. The more you raise the curtains the more I see in you to reverence, & even worship. Do I not love you as mature man loves mature woman & as mother loves her child besides? My poor darling! would that you were with me now to be comforted & cheered. Once more then, darling, let me bid you know me to be

Yours always

F. W. Dawson

1. Like things are cured by like. Dr. Samuel Hahnemann (1755–1843) based his science of homeopathy on this principle, which later became a motto for the profession.
2. Hesperus is Venus in its appearance as an evening star.
3. In Roman mythology, the god of erotic love.

᠄᠊ᡭᢳᡭ᠊᠄

Sarah to Frank

Greenville. September. 10th [1873]

By all means, sell the City Stock. You are perfectly right in supposing I would be glad to assist you. I should not only be glad, but very much relieved of some great fears that beset me besides. Remember you are not to send my "salary" until I ask for it. When you are at leisure, make out a careful list of my indebtedness.

I have just received the telegram concerning Howell, also your second letter. I am greatly concerned about the child & his prospects. I cannot make up my mind to write to Mr. Trenholm. If I could speak to him I would do it very frankly. In a letter I must either appear obsequious or arrogant—neither of which is natural to me, or agreeable. I am satisfied that some unjust representations have been made of me, & I am not willing to exculpate myself at the price of accusing others. Fortunately, I believe the Lord directs all results. If it is best for Howell, he will be taken from me. I have grave fears that I am not a good mother. "Good" generally means weak, does it not? And I often assure him I could kill him if it was right, & for his own advantage. Medea! Par paranthèse [By way of parenthesis]—how much responsibility should fall on Jason? I should punish him for every wrong she did, if I was Rhadamanthus.[1]

Your Columbia letter came last night. While rejoicing sincerely to hear of Jimmy's prosperity, it struck a chill to my heart. I do not believe he has a friend in Columbia, or knows one there who would refrain from doing him a wrong openly or secretly. I know what his most devoted friends have said of him, & can scarcely expect others to be more reticent. He delights in being thought extravagant & wealthy; not perceiving the reproach it would be if it were so. Nothing could injure him more in the opinion of persons worthy of respect, & he is too blind to perceive anything beyond the envy of fools. My heart is so heavy, that I scarcely think a balloon could raise it from its place of great depression.

Your "Meteorology" has been altogether boiled to pieces. Neither the Eclectic, nor the author would suspect any connection. If it is insipid, pray forgive me. I threw in Herodotus & St. Medar for reasoning. The record was kept by my cousin, as I have already told you. Mr. Herodotus' opinion I read years ago for myself.[2]

This is a bad way of cheering you, is it not? I do not know when I have more keenly felt that the world is all hollow, & its bread only saw dust. But I have no right to tell the bread purveyor about it.

We rejoice heartily at being with Mrs. Ware who makes me a simple declaration of love at stated intervals through the day. She says you are the only person who ever made her change her mind. She did not mean to take us, & now she thanks you for having secured her such charming inmates in her family. Mother continues well. I am getting on reasonably enough. Send me some work. I have lost the faculty of selecting, except for Saturdays. God keep you a good child.

S.M.

1. In Greek myth, Rhadamanthus was the son of Zeus and Europa. After his death, he became a judge of the underworld.
2. "Weather-Wisdom," September 15, 1873, addressed the ways in which "social, commercial, agricultural, financial, marine and sanitary interests" were connected with the weather. Sarah wrote about Herodotus's theory of the overflow of the Nile and of the "popular belief that if it rains on St. Medard's day, the 7th of June, it will rain on forty consecutive days." Sarah was wrong, however; St. Medard's day is June 8.

☙❦❧
Frank to Sarah

No 7

Charleston S.C.
September 12. 1873.

Your letter of the 10th arrived this morning. My dear, dear, child! I fear that I am causing your depression by telling you of my business troubles, and I will henceforth strive to make every thing couleur-de-rose [rose colored]. Indeed! I owe it to you to devise some manner of making you well, in mind and body. That is the least atonement I can make for the pains I have caused, and is only a poor return for the good you have done me.

I am glad that Howell arrived safely. You need not be in perplexity about him. He shall either go back to school or remain with you as you choose. I have told you what *I* think best, but what *you* think best shall be done. Mr. Trenholm is almost sure to see you in G. Why not write, and say you are there, and that you would like to see him when he comes in from Batesville, which he will do as soon as Wm Trenholm arrives. He is only staying at Batesville until W. L. T, who is going North, arrives. In the mean while try to be cheerful.

I cannot reconcile your trust in God with your doubts & fears for the future, and think it must be due to the fact that you do not realise that He only helps those who help themselves. For instance, if you, by inaction, avoid a talk with Mr. Trenholm, you may make it impracticable for Howell to come back to school, and in that case you, & not the Almighty, will have decided the question. My idea is to pray for Light & do what you deem best, *but do something,* and leave the rest with Our Father. But, my darling, if you cant do any thing, I will be the worker for you. Only have faith in God and confidence in me.

I send your week's pay in registered letter. Mrs. Ware will probably require, next week, payment in advance of the balance of the month ($25) and you would not have the money. Your pay will be sent each friday. *When you come here you can strip yourself of your last dollar,* because you will be under my eye. Until then you must be kept in funds!

Dont blame Jem. I have two business letters from him, and he is evidently very tight in money matters. He is, I fear, a very poor man of business. What I cannot excuse is the denial of kind words & affectionate demeanor. These cost nothing. How much happier you would be, if you knew that he, with a love like yours for him, was ready to share his much or little with you. Would not the crust be moistened by joyful tears? However we must all act after our natures, & our duty as well as inclination towards him is to do the best we can for him, to shield him and save him as far as possible. At the same time he shall not interfere with any plan which is necessary to your happiness.

I will make up your account; it is a small affair now that the sale of the city stock to-day wipes out the $60 lent you.

Do not be alarmed if the needles cause an eruption or some other irritation of the skin. That is to be looked for.

Sweet is getting on finely, and will be an accomplished singer by the time that I hand him to his beloved mistress.

The article on the weather is excellent. You have assimilated the whole thing which was what I wanted. I have sent some subjects & will send more as they come up.

I am very glad that Mrs. Ware likes you. Draw a lesson from it. I only gave you the opportunity which you improved. Apply that to your ideas of Providence, and it will change the current of your thoughts. God gives opportunities, as He has given them you, & if you do not turn them to account the responsibility is yours not His.

My dear Love if I only knew what to say to brighten your path, & lighten your load. My only power is my love for you, & that may, I fear, become a burden to you. If so, tell me so, &, though I love you better than ever, no word of love shall come from me. May God help us both.

Yours always
F. W. Dawson

≈✵≈

Frank to Sarah

No 8

Charleston S.C.
September 13. 1873.

Chère Ange [Dear Angel]! I spoke to Mrs. Fourgeaud this morning about Howell's board. She spoke of him very kindly, almost lovingly, and said she could not think of accepting any payment for "the few days" he was with us. I told her that this was what I had expected her to say; but that I had asked the question, at your request; although you felt that money alone, could never express your gratitude for her kindness to the child. We miss Howell very much; particularly Mr. Magrath who had made quite a pet of him, as was shown conclusively by his volunteering to give him a ticket, and by the telegram to you. My opinion of the child is pretty well fixed: *His future depends upon the character of the influence exerted over him during the next four years, which influence can be exercised as well while he is in school, and in vacation, as when at home:* I think you are the fittest person I know to manage a boy of his character; the very firmness and moral rigidity which you think hurtful are precisely what he needs. Like a fast horse he will make splendid time if a strong and skillful hand hold the reins; but give him his head, or turn him loose, and he will soon smash himself to pieces. I see in him the material of an able upright man, who may make a name for himself and will certainly lead a useful life; that is, if the next four years are properly directed. I do not say this to make it harder for you to send him to his mother. My idea is, as you know, that you need not do any thing of the sort. He can come back to School, and you, being here, can watch over him. The uniform will be a small matter which I can provide. Surely you would not take from Mr. Trenholm what you would refuse from me. If my love for you is to make me powerless to serve you, it must be to you more of a bane than a benison. Moreover I have not so many pleasures that I can afford to abandon any that I have.

I send you some New Orleans papers in which you may find something about the yellow fever panic in Shreveport [Louisiana]. If your sister[1] is still there you will naturally be anxious about her. I enclose you a paragraph about our social articles from a leading Philadelphia paper. I hope the News & Courier reaches you regularly; if so, say nothing about it—I dont want you to waste your words to me on purely routine things.

I think that Howell left some of his clothes here, after all, shall I send them up?

We are advertising for rooms for you & have already found two desirable places; where you can have two furnished rooms, with use of parlor if needed, for from 20 to 25 dols a month. Please say at once, as these things take some time to arrange, whether you authorize me to engage and prepare rooms for you from (say) Oct 5 or 10, & tell me whether you have any bed linen &c or any other things, or whether you require every thing (except board) to be provided for you: say, also, whether you need servant's room and kitchen. Tell me what you want & what you can afford to pay, and you may rely on my finding a pleasant place. Your personal income will be $20 a week.

Let me know about this immediately; there is no time to lose. Good: bye, my darling girl, take good care of your sweet self:

Yours always
F. W. Dawson

---

1. Eliza Ann Morgan LaNoue (Lilly) (1833–1917) married John Charles LaNoue (1826–90) in 1851. The Episcopalian Morgans opposed the marriage on religious grounds because John was Catholic, so the couple eloped. Many of Sarah's relatives remained in Louisiana after the war.

Sarah to Frank

Greenville September. 14th [1873]

I know not where to begin in my list of acknowledgements, but suppose the safe arrival of my child should be the first. As to thanking you or your household, that I can never do. I am very, very glad to have him with me, & he seems more than glad himself. Your cloak will be cared for. He says he would have suffered severely without it. He only explained about the key yesterday, & as the mail only goes to-morrow, I am compelled to subject you still longer to the inconvenience of doing without it. For all the "I sends" I am much obliged. It would be impossible to enumerate them, but they are very visible "in my mind's eye, Horatio,"[1] as I write.

Mother is lost in admiration of les petite soin [the little attentions] which she truly says were never surpassed, or rather never were equalled. While selfishly receiving such devotion, I am truly grieved to see you think so much more of my comfort than of your own. Think of me only as a sister & friend, & measuring yourself by that standard, ask yourself if it is right to do for me what you would not do for any other. It frightens me to see how your whole soul is absorbed in this matter. What will you do when you find the clay? Believe me, there is much of it. For the first time in my life I hailed the "rack" with joy—Alas! & alas! was ever a promise of good fulfilled? Behold me without a peg on which to hang my hope![2] Human flesh alone has the privilege of having nails driven in it. Wall paper & doors are exempt. It is more of a rack to me lying on the chair, than you could believe. I pack & unpack my trunks for every article civilized Christian, & literary life can demand. There is not a tack to support a ruffle, even. I am growing very weary of the severe labor. It will retard the effect of the "needles."

My son, glad as I am to have the needles, you must have a little scolding. I fear they are expensive. And people in my circumstances have no right to try extravagant restoratives when inexpensive ones may answer as well. I am looking as harsh as possible, & mean this to be very severe. Let me know the price. Then I will decide just how inexorable I should be.

I am not doing my duty. Worse still, I cannot. Lethargy of mind & body possesses me. Last night, ten hours of sleep was my modest share. It could have been twelve, if they had let me alone. Day after day last week I spent bolt upright, pen in hand, striving to seize an idea. Not one came, I was so tired & achey. I tried to give you a legitimate little speech on Cremation.

Instead, I wrote myself out on the horrors of funeral preparations.[3] It is a nondescript failure, but is more of a "Saturday" than was intended. Do send me every day topics or "boil downs", as current events would grow stale before they could be returned. I have spent days gaping at Eugénie[4] without result. Nothing comes of it. What will you think of me? And I am so anxious to work! Dont give me up yet.

Yesterday Mr. Trenholm & Cellie[5] came to see us. He was most lovely to me. I had no chance to speak of Howell's affair. He said he would come back Tuesday, on his way to Charleston. Then I will try to speak, if he gives me any chance.

I rejoice that the money pressure is over. Do get speedily out of debt. Are you taking care of that head? Nothing from Miriam, save a card from [Alcée] Louis [Dupré] dated 6th saying they were to be in Brattleboro [Vermont] in a few hours & he was to leave for Norfolk [Virginia] by sea, last Tuesday.

S. M.

Letters received, 7th I know to be at Mr. Stradley's[6] since last night; but the clerk denies it, to keep the Sabbath holy—with a story.

1. Shakespeare, *Hamlet*, 1.2.
2. Sarah had been prohibited from hanging a hook on the back of her door for the needles rack or her clothes.
3. "Dust to Dust!" October 4, 1873.
4. Sarah was probably trying to write a piece on the French Empress Eugénie (1826–1920), consort of Napoleon III (1808–73).
5. Celestine Robertson Trenholm (1851–79), the daughter of George and Anna Trenholm who married Derrill H. McCollough in 1874.
6. Samuel Stradley, thirty-nine, a merchant.

Sarah to Frank

Greenville,

September 15th [1873]

I have just received No 7th. The pious clerk was not bad enough to keep it until Tuesday, to make his denial yesterday seem true. With it came one from Jimmy. Short, troubled, & sad, asking when he was to expect us. I have written saying I would like to spend a week with him to consult about Charleston.

It is sunset, & I have only ceased writing to eat dinner. Since early morning I have been at work. I have overtasked myself, not liking to write without sending some proof that I am trying to do my duty, however poor the result. The necessity of writing to-day, is to tell you I would prefer leaving Greenville on the 5th October. A week, or perhaps two at Hampton or Columbia would make it time for Charleston any way. It is best for us to be "settled" as mother says, at once. This is decidedly expensive. I am aghast at hearing that Howell is valued at $25.00 per month. Mrs. Ware's sister[1] prescribes it. I said I had never heard of such a thing. She asked then $5.00 a week, just what I pay for myself. I gave my last earthly cent with a royal indifference, but with the most abject feeling at heart. This is still further increased by the conviction that we are all looked on as pensioners, instead of assistants. The family is very large, & naturally costs more than we do. Mrs. Ware is very lovely to us, but I am hurt to find her sister is at liberty to fleece me. The charge for "furnishing" Howell's room is absurd, as the child has simply an old mattress on the floor. As to tables, my back is broken writing on my knee. Isn't this cross? I forgot to tell you last week that Mrs. Irving[2] had engaged board for us, from Miss Alston's letter. Every luxury of home, table, & carriage thrown in for twenty dollars a month. She came to urge us to change, but we could not. If I can be in Charleston; I would rather have it arranged to have my own servant. Then mother can have just what she likes for dinner. One room for a bedroom, one for a sitting room, & one small kitchen would suit us perfectly. The difficulty would be to find that however plainly furnished. Since you *must* know domestic details, cooks in small families serve as laundresses also. Qu'en dites vous [What do you say]? Indeed I am very anxious to go to work, & to reduce my expenses. Two things I seem bent on not doing.

Do send me some every day subjects. Howell is waiting for this to go to the office, & to inquire for that registered letter. I must say he interferes sadly with my writing. He never leaves my side except when I insist, & then he never stops asking questions at a distance. School in some form is an imperative necessity. I will speak tomorrow, if possible. Tell me all about your business. What else was woman made for? You will see I have another opinion in this article, for which you are to find a name. "Blue" nor "Simplicity" will answer.[3]

I hope you are well.

S.M.

I have mislaid my bands. Emptying each trunk does not reveal them. So you must be shocked at this substitute.

1. Sarah was referring to Louise Bolling, fifty-four, Mary Ware's sister-in-law. Mary was an only child.
2. L. H. Irvine, a widow who was a boarder at Mays House, located on Main Street in Greenville.
3. "Blue Birds," October 18, 1873, a piece on people who suffer from the blues.

Frank to Sarah

10

Charleston
Tuesday September 16. [1873]

The best news you give me in your letter of Sunday is that you sleep so long and well. Continue that, & you must improve; sleep is better than medicine. I gave Howell (they were put in his desk) two brass screw hooks to hang "the rack" on. They can be put in the door, while nails cannot. Find them, put them up, & save yourself more unpacking.

Do not fret yourself about the writing. You are doing quite enough. We are satisfied, & I dont expect you to be satisfied with any thing that you do. A more distrustful person of herself I never knew, & you have little reason for it. Make a digest of the Saturday Review article enclosed; we want to show impartially what that able & iconoclastic paper think of the struggles of the day; the other article can be worked in with it, if I can find it in time.[1]

I am glad that Mr. Trenholm was so kind. You will probably see him soon.

Is it not sad news from Memphis about the fever. I fear that it will hurt the Appeal very much.[2]

You need not fear that while you live I shall give you up. We are not prone to give up our one thing worth living for.

I did not say that the money pressure was over it has only just begun.

In your letter you say: "I am grieved to see that you think more of my comfort than of your own. *Think of me only as a sister and friend*, &, measuring yourself by that standard, ask yourself if it is right to do for me what you would not do for any other. It frightens me to see how your whole soul is absorbed in this matter. What will you do when you find the clay &c." My presentments about you seldom deceive me; hence my saying yesterday how much to me a few words from you would have been. I was prepared since Sunday for what you say, & my answer was ready. If I thought of you as a sister, or as a friend, I should treat you very differently; if I could think of you so, I should have done it long ago. I will try to grieve you & appal you no more. If I cant (as I cannot) love you less than I do, I can certainly refrain from saying any thing about it. My letters shall be such a brother or friend would write. What my future may be, God knows. The less said of it the better.

F. W. Dawson

1. Sarah's scrapbook indicates that she never wrote this article.
2. Frank was probably referring to the *Commercial Appeal*, a Memphis newspaper. Sarah later wrote two pieces on the yellow fever outbreaks in Memphis and in Shreveport, Louisiana; see "Faith and Works," October 20, 1873; "The Heroes of the Epidemic," October 28, 1873.

ℐℭℎ

Sarah to Frank

Greenville September. 16th [1873]

Here are letters enough already this week, to forgive that line to Mrs. Fourgeaud! But why should a word from me be worth more just now? Has gold gone up? Tell me all about it! Instead of telling me all about myself, let me know a little of you and of your affairs. Unless you had a "warning" Monday night, never claim to have a spiritual affinity or subtle connection with me! Dr. Moorman's prediction that any over-exertion of mind or body would result in proportionate suffering, seems correct. Any unusually expressive cries of anguish you may have heard from nine to ten that evening, were undoubtedly uttered by me. I suppressed all active demonstrations then, but the pain has never quite ceased. Yesterday the result was a slight fever, which still continues. It does not interfere with my duties, however. I am up, & going about as usual.

The enclosed may be even more objectionable than I think it.[1] But I do hope you will look favorably on the suggestion, if you disapprove the form. I agree with Mrs. Bristed of N. Y.,[2] who said she never saw anything like the toddy proclivities of South Carolina women. Only she called it whisky drinking. Elle appele un chat, un chat.[3] Every casual visitor remarks it freely. Why ignore it? You will see I place it vaguely, & specify the two places North where several eminent physicians assured me it was almost universal. I do not mean to apply it personally to any place. But if a vice is practiced why should it be ignored? If it exists, exposure may repress it. If it does not exist, no one can take offence at something clearly not applicable to them. Count for yourself how many women you know who have either died of chloroform, or live to take it.

Mr. Trenholm did not come yesterday. Waiting probably for Col. Trenholm. Registered letter received, but I cannot feel I have quite earned the money yet. Letters include No. 9. I am delighted at what you have done about the rooms, & would like to see particulars. Of location, price, etc, you are of course the best judge. I told you I wished the expense to be as reasonable as is consistent with mother's comfort. I have a thousand means of employing every dollar I can earn. I have silver forks & spoons, & five linen sheets. The latter I fear are scarcely serviceable. That is my entire store for housekeeping—in S.C.

No servants' room will be required, as they generally stipulate staying elsewhere. Bed-room, sitting room & kitchen would be a principality.

If it would cost less to board in a family which would not expect to bring its knitting & spend the morning, let us have that. I want privacy above all things though. It is a shame to leave you such a task; but what can I do? If I was there, I would be unable to see to it myself. It would be a privilege to ask you to decide for me. But if you dread the task as I do, any temporary arrangement will answer. Whatever you say or decline saying will be duly appreciated & weighed.

Thanks for Howell's forgotten clothes which came safely.

Lillie says the fever kills in twenty four hours. She is awaiting it very bravely, & without the least fear. Mother is much more concerned. I have carefully kept the papers from her. This letter yesterday was her first intimation. Nothing from Miriam. But what of you? Tell us the trouble. To be good is to be happy. Miserable sinners that we are! Let us have your "experience", brother Frank.

S.M.

1. "Tippling," September 23, 1873, an editorial on the "toddy proclivities" of American women. "Fashionable physicians who are well able to judge say that tippling, as the habit of women of high social standing, prevails to an alarming degree in New York, Washington and other cities, both North and South," she wrote. "Ill-health is saddled with the responsibility for the pernicious practice; but half the sickness which is complained of results from drinking, or is aggravated by it."

2. Grace Sedgwick Bristed (1833–97), the second wife of writer Charles Astor Bristed (1820–74). The Bristeds were members of one of the leading families of

New York and were distant relations of the Morgans, who were extremely proud of the familial tie. "In those days the family connection [to the Bristeds] unto the fortieth remove was considered a sacred relation," remarked James Morris Morgan (*Recollections*, 260–61).

3. Calls a cat a cat, meaning to speak frankly.

Frank to Sarah

11

Charleston:
Wednesday September 17. [1873]

Excuse this paper;[1] I can write more quickly on this than on the other. For some days I have been unwell, and to-day I can hardly hold my head up. In truth I have not taken what rest I might have had. My only relief is in incessant labor, but the flesh is weaker than the troubled spirit.

I am very sorry that you are in the hands of the Philistines, but you must grin and bear it. The charge for Howell is a huge swindle. I ought to have hunted up Mrs. Irving before going elsewhere; it seems to me that I always leave something undone, as in not telling you I had sent the hooks for the rack. For Heaven's sake, do not work too hard. I have now two articles of yours which will certainly carry us on to Tuesday or Wednesday. To: morrow I will send you some more subjects.

I am glad that you agree that Howell must go to School. The plan of going to Hampton is excellent. It will look better & be better than coming directly here. And I can see you at Hampton, cant I?

You must enlighten me on all the domestic details or how can I house you? You can have two rooms in Beaufain St, plainly furnished, for $22 a month. They are large, with windows on three sides; communicate with each other and have separate doors on the landing; between the two rooms are closets which will serve for wood &c. You would have the use of a parlor. The house is old; but clean & handsome; one square from the tune of the street cars. Rooms on the second floor. I will try to find out to-day whether you cant have accommodations for a servant. Do you want the landlady to supply bed and table linen, china, cooking utensils &c. I must know this. There is another place at $25, but the rooms are on the 3rd floor and the ups & downs would be too much for you, I fear. Pitch your work aside for a day and give me precise and definite instructions. I want to know at once, as it will take some time to get the rooms ready. One other set are to be looked at.

Consider it settled that you leave Greenville on the morning of Oct 5. & go direct to Columbia and thence to Hampton. Remember your ticket will take you & your Mother free, & Howell's will bring him to *Charleston,* so *he* will not have to give up his ticket at Columbia.

Write to the "Graphic" people and tell them to send your paper from Oct 5 to Box 92—Charleston S.C.

I shall be really angry with you if you only write to me when you have something to send the office. That is a poor compliment to pay any one; as it is, you say you dont like to write to me without sending something for the paper, & I dont like to feel that you only write when you do so officially.

Nothing from Miriam. I have written to Col Dupre for news of her.

Yours always

F.W. Dawson

PS I reopen this to ask whether you are determined to come to Charleston; or, whether you will be governed absolutely by what Jemmy advises. To stay at Hampton is to die; to come to Charleston is to live for your Mother & Howell. I do not think that Jemmy will object to any thing that you wish & I recommend, but he may. And the best way is, therefore, to resolve to come; peacefully if you can, forcibly if you must. What say you?

I like the "funeral" article; shall print it in a day or two. Go on in the same way & win you must.

D

1. This letter was written on editorial paper.

ⅈ꘎ⅈ

Sarah to Frank

Greenville September. 19th [1873]

I suppose it is fated that I should pain you to the last. I protest that my will is not in the matter. Knowing how readily you are wounded I strive to avoid grieving one who has been unfailing in his love & consideration for me. Common humanity would forbid it. A man would say the devil's in it. Not being permitted to use strong language, I can only say I cannot account for it at all. I read over that letter—something unusual—impelled by a vague apprehension. Convinced that the fear was unfounded, I dispatched both letter & concern, feeling sure you would be just to yourself as well as to me. Well! we have three weeks more for misunderstandings! We will scarcely keep it up face to face? But three weeks to any one in your condition of mind or health, is unending. Write that you mean to take all the rest possible, & that you will take as much care of yourself as if you valued body & soul as much as a hair of my head. The fulfillment of that promise would secure health an[d] enjoyment to some one whose comfort & peace of mind are matters of great import to me. I too have been ill. No respite however brief since Monday. Yesterday I was in bed, fairly vanquished, when Mr. Trenholm sent his carriage with a request that I would dine at the hotel with him. Jairus' daughter[1] could not have astonished the family more than I, coming out equipped for the ride. Mr. Trenholm was as lovely as he ever was to me. After dinner, without preamble I made my few remarks. I said it had pained me to appear in a false position, & to seem to make a convenience of him merely for caprice. That I could not explain the matter to him, but only wished to set it clear for the future. Here he said that he had himself offered me the scholarship for Howell, & had been glad when it was finally accepted. I was comfortable enough then; but I reminded him that I had not considered it as permanent, having expressly written that I hoped to have the house sold before this.[2] He took up the parable most sweetly, & assured me he earnestly desired it to be regarded as final. That the opportunity offered was not one to be neglected even by a wealthy boy. Howell's future was assured, if he remained there. A scholarship at Yale, or a dozen other colleges would be secured for him when he was prepared to enter, & he advised that the child should return at once & be urged to study seriously. I accepted the advice very simply, and with many sweet words from him, the interview ended. He directed me to notify Mr. Porter[3] at once, which is already ready for the mail. Nothing was said that I could wish to recall.

But business! There is one momentous question about lodgings you may feel a delicacy about asking. "Are there any babies in the house?" O if we *could* find a place where their shrieks do not rend sleep from the eyelids![4] Saturday was my last rest, & this is Friday! The week has been devoted to Mrs. Ware's grandson in the adjoining room. Yesterday, to obtain a respite, his mother went to the country without him. Consequently poor overtasked Mrs. Ware, mother & I, have been awake the entire night, with the same prospect for several nights to come for her, & for two weeks yet for us unhappy next door neighbors! To look at me in my forlorn condition, any one would take me for the mother of twins at least. I am just in that frame of mind which would make me take a prominent part in a massacre of innocents. Incessant suffering exhausts me until I could fall asleep standing. Just as I flatter myself sleep is near, shriek on shriek jerks me upright trembling in nervous terror. Unless the child or I takes chloroform, I will develop a case of brain fever. I cannot ask to be moved up-stairs without giving offence, or becoming liable to extras of unheard of magnitude, prescribed by Mrs. Bowlin, but I am really desperate. I should like to stipulate for the absence of babies from the next domicile. But I suppose there is no law human or divine by which I could prevent their entrance in the family circle later; so what is the use? Bed-bugs & babies seem the sine quâ non of life. I know not which is sweeter, no! not I! Still, I give bed bugs the preference until babies can be lawfully dispersed by a dose of corrosive sublimate too.

Does this not out-Herod Herod?[5]

But business! It is customary to supply towels, sheets, & bed-clothes generally, as part of furnished rooms. As to tablecloths etc; it would be better to buy them, unless the small amount of china, etc could be rented from the lady at so much per month. One bed-room & one sitting room would be amply sufficient, with a small kitchen. Our "wants" are very few indeed. But it does seem too much to impose on you. Would it not be easier to inquire about board in some quiet place, where we could take our time about the other? I cannot make the estimate just now; but it appears to me the suite of apartments you propose would prove far more expensive than boarding. Otherwise, it would be very desirable. I am rather used to discomfort, & really care for nothing but sleep at night, which is persistently denied me. What some people lack in one torment, they make up in another. The B.B.Bs are my bête-noir.

As to opposition from Jimmy, I do not expect it. He, as well as Ella advised Summerville [South Carolina]. A few miles beyond could scarcely be prohibited. He will probably answer that he has no advice to give, & I can do as I please.

Cease all reproach about the screws. Howell delivered them three minutes after arriving. A friend of the family cautioned us against using them, & we assume had official authority for doing so. But for that avatar of Satan in the next room, I should be quite happy. I have learned the secret of blessed Thomas à Becket:[6] "Resign all, & thou shall have all." My books lie on the floor, & I restrict myself to the dress which happens to be thrown across the chair. I have made a resolution not to pick up the extra one which will slip off. You will see for yourself that my worn knees are resting. I write on the back of a book held loosely in one hand up in the air, while my poor back does only the hourly work of breaking itself over trunk excavations in search of the indispensable. Who would not live & be happy? A roar, certainly not of approbation, comes from that small fiend. Verily if I had the appliances, there would be a case of suspended animation in a boy two years of age, until *somebody* could get half an hour's sleep! Failing that, I should be much soothed if allowed to relieve my over wrought nerves by thrashing him or his mother uninterruptedly for a day or so. Are you not afraid of such a vixen? Only be good, & take care of yourself.

S.M.

I shall hardly be able to write again before Monday or perhaps even Tuesday. We will meet at Hampton when we are about leaving for Charleston. Unless you decline.

Mother is greatly in favor of the Beaufain St. house, & thinks it expressly designed for us, especially when Miriam comes. I doubt Miriam's participation in Charleston festivities.

Dont put too much stress on my opinions to day, but do as you think best. I have not a clear view except on the horrors of sleeplessness. I like you opinion best—about house selecting, that is to say.

1. Jesus raised Jairus's daughter from the dead (Mark 5:22–43).
2. Sarah was referring to the family home on Church Street in Baton Rouge. In 1874, James Morris Morgan wrote to Frank Dawson and commented that the house was "in a general state of dilapidation" and would not fetch more than "$1000 to $1200" (J. M. Morgan to Dawson, March 31, 1874, Dawson Papers).
3. Reverend Anthony Toomer Porter (1828–1902), rector of the Home and School of the Holy Communion Institute in Charleston. During the Civil War he worked as a chaplain for the Confederate army, returning to Charleston in 1864 to take charge of the Holy Communion Church. After the war, he established the school.
4. Sarah made similar remarks in her Civil War diary. When dreaming of her perfect home, she described "a place where a child's cry is not heard!" "Is there such a paradise as that would be, in store for me?" she mused (S. M. Dawson, *Sarah Morgan*, 548).
5. In an attempt to kill Jesus, Herod ordered the killing of all children in Bethlehem under the age of two (Matthew 2:16).
6. Saint Thomas à Becket (1118–70), archbishop of Canterbury and martyr.

*After visiting Sarah in Virginia, Miriam Morgan Dupré had traveled
north to Canada. Frank urged Sarah to consider joining her sister in an
effort to improve her health, which had deteriorated rapidly as a result of the
"shrieking" infant.*

13.

Charleston S.C.
September 19. 1873

The enclosed letter from Miriam reached me last night & I thought it best to
send it to you at once, as I could do so without any violation of confidence.
It appears to have been seven days on the road. The news it contains will delight you. It is a pity that you did not go with Miriam, and it is not too late.
Say that you will go, and you can make your own conditions. I will not even
see you before you go, if you think that it will make it easier for you to accept
my proposition. Understand me! I make no conditions, whatever. You could
go as free & as freely as you would go to Hampton. I can afford the luxury
of doing good, & God only gave me the power that I might exercise it. Say
that you will go, and I will write to Miriam for the particulars, & send you off
as soon as you can get ready, & as I said without even wishing you Bon Voyage! except on paper. You exert yourself too much. How dare you, in face of
Dr. Moorman's warning? I did not know that you were ill on Monday night;
I think there was a good reason for it, but I will, as you bid me, be careful
never to claim again that I have "a spiritual affinity or subtle connection"
with you. I pray, with all my heart, that you may be perfectly well by the time
that this reaches you. Remember that I can make use of "Funerals" as a Saturday, so you have one article to your credit and can take some rest, which
you evidently require. I suppose that you write half the day, & patch & darn
for Howell the other half. I will not trust myself to say what I think of such
suicidal behavior.

I am very much obliged to you for the kind way in which you express your
willingness to be governed by my counsel in making your arrangements for
Charleston. Your letter confirms my opinion that you had better, as advised
in my letter of yesterday, board here for two weeks or four, and decide afterwards where to remain permanently. I do not wish or expect you to run about
& look after things. Your part will be to come here, & consider and decide
upon the propositions about housekeeping which I will submit. You will be a

Queen with despotic authority over one very loyal subject. Nothing that I can do for you is a trouble to me. My only trouble is when I want to do something, & dont see how. Incessant action is my life, while it lasts; that life belongs to you, & you need not fear to make demands upon what is your own.

I will carefully read and ponder what you say about tippling. I only know of one woman who takes chloroform, & of only one woman who died from its effects. I do not know even one female tippler: but then I see so little, & talk with no one.

I agree with you that it would cost less to board in a family than to "room: keep." But I shall have figures & facts to submit before you will find it necessary to decide, &, if you will do the wisest thing in your life, & go to Canada, we need not talk about board in Charleston until you two & my sweet sister Miriam come here in December. She asked me for a long letter; I have already sent her 12 pages! Lord help her!

I am watching carefully for any news of Mrs. Lanoue, & am very glad that she has so far escaped. The worst is over.

Give my love to your Mother.

Yours always
F. W. Dawson

✥

Frank to Sarah

14

Charleston
Saturday September 20 [1873]

I have read your article on "Toddying" which I will print on Monday. The only fault in it, is the same one fault which I find in nearly everything you write: viz, your disposition to make sweeping general statements, which are not, as you will see, borne out by the facts. For example, many women do resort to whisky in every emergency, but all women do not; again, some women are fools, but all are not. And there is as much harm done by indiscriminate praise as by indiscriminate censure. You have seen very few of the many types of humanity; you have not known either the best or the worst. It is necessary, therefore, to pass beyond the sphere of your own knowledge, & remember that there are other worlds than ours. I suppress, as far as I can, any expression in your articles of the broad criticism or condition of which

I speak, but it is better that you should know for yourself what to do. In condemning or praising any act, or mode of life or thought, I would always direct myself to those who do so, or live so, or think so; & you can always show that the force of example leads to the spread of whatever is strikingly good or bad in those to whom we look as examples. Thus, you will hit your mark, without treading on innocent toes. I have taken the liberty of speaking to you frankly about this, because of my great anxiety to see your work be made to be beyond reproach. Please take my criticisms with this excuse. One can't forget the Arch Bishop of Grenada, of whom you have doubtless heard, although you have not, I think, read Gil Blas.[1]

Please send me back Miriam's letter, when you have read it. There was a gale here last night; & an accident on the S.C.RR to-day delays the mails.

Yours always
F. W. Dawson

1. Alain René Le Sage, *Gil Blas de Santillane* (1715–35). In the book, the archbishop of Grenada aspired to be known as a great orator and asked his confidante, Gil Blas, to inform the archbishop if his sermons failed to reach the standard he had set for himself. When Gil Blas did so, however, he was fired by the archbishop.

Ↄℭↄ

Frank to Sarah

16

Charleston Monday Night [September 22, 1873]
Your note of the 19th did not reach me until this evening, too late to send off a letter to-night, so that this will not come into your hands until Wednesday night.

I am deeply distressed that the crying child should cause you so much pain, and cost you so much of the rest you sadly need. All my schemes, you see, go wrong! I think, however, that you allow yourself to be imposed on. You pay a good price, & you are entitled to quiet and reasonable accommodations. Were I in Greenville, you should have what hooks & pegs you want in a few minutes, and you should have a room where the howls of that brat would not be heard, or Mrs. & Miss Morgan would change quarters before sunset. Dont forget that your board is $45 a month, & that you have paid $20 on a/c, so that $25, more, whenever paid, will cover the entire month.

The news about Mr. Trenholm is lovely. Tact is one of his strong points, and he charmingly saved you the necessity of making painful explanations. Take his advice, & send Howell at once. The school opens on Oct 1st, does it not? And the marks, which determine the prizes, count from that date, & there is, therefore, no way to make up for lost days.

You will have seen ere this that, in the matter of Charleston, I have proposed just what you suggest; viz, to take a quiet place in a boarding house, & determine, when here, whether to take furnished rooms, or to continue to board. Let it be so. I will send you, to Hampton, the particulars of such answers to an advt I will put in as may seem most likely to please you. I enclose a curious advertisement about your "Life Awakener" of which you tell me nothing.[1] Is it one more added to the long list of my failures?

About you & me! I do not think there is any misunderstanding; certainly, not on my side. You told me honestly, as you have told me often, that you desired, above all things, that I might love you as brothers are supposed to love their sisters; so that you might be (what Miriam is) a loving sister to me. Holding that opinion & having that wish, I felt, & feel, that any affectionate words and phrases of mine—expressing a mighty love that will only die when I die—must be painful to you, as an evidence that your wish could not be gratified, and as a reminder that I was asking from you what you could not bestow. My duty clearly was, to suppress everything beyond what a brother would say, & I do it. If I cannot love you less than I do, I can, somehow or other, keep my mouth shut about it. You ask me about myself and my affairs. My answer is a simple one: We gladly share our joys with those whom we love, and multiply our joys in so dividing them; but our *sorrows we share only with those who love us.* I could not have been forced into this position at a worse time; had I picked over every day & hour since I have known you. What would I give, if I could only be with Miriam for an hour or two to-night.

Never for a moment had I thought that you dreamed of saying anything that would pain me. You were uttering, unconsciously perhaps, your earnest wish. A woman who loved me would, with equal unconsciousness of the reason, have instinctively avoided any such words. As you know, I did believe that you loved me. I do not believe so now. That letter did the business. Why! I could find indications of the same want in you of a love like mine even in the carefully written letter which I received to-day. Do not blame yourself for not saying what is not in you to say. *I* do not. You can count on me always, everywhere & anyhow, as you know. There is no change in me, except that my pride will not allow me to speak as I spoke before. May the God of the Fatherless prevent the dark waters from closing over your fair head, as they close to-night over me.

Yours always
F. W. Dawson

1. Frank is referring to the "needles instrument" for Sarah's back.

ℒℂℛ

Sarah to Frank

Greenville. September 24th. [1873]
Familiar as I am with your self-sacrifice & tender forethought, I am still really touched anew by your Canada suggestion. Of course you know my answer. It is scarcely necessary to repeat that even as your wife I would not take such an unfair advantage of one who never gives a thought to himself. Your constant attention can make me very selfish about my personal comfort; but it can scarcely render me insensible to the reproach of accepting all, & returning nothing, to the most generous & truest man I ever knew. I too believe God gave you the power of doing good, in order that you may use it wisely, & freely. I agree that St. Catherine's [Ontario, Canada] would restore me, also. But I really do not see how it would be possible for you to do for me more than you have done, unless I was your wife. To make the proposed scheme practicable, would require the assistance of a minister, & the necessary presence of the gentleman who proposes to absent himself. You lose sight of yourself completely in your desire to secure my health & comfort. It is necessary to demonstrate the dangers to which you expose yourself, & to extend a little of the mercy & protection you have ever bestowed on me. A little rest, & a gleam of happiness would restore me to health anywhere. I may see the possibility of such a thing, but God surely will not send it to me save in death. I am being educated through suffering, & hope to graduate some day. His blessing can never rest on me until this wrong is atoned for; & I am powerless.

Col. Trenholm came yesterday, & talked of you with affection & kindness which made me very glad. He says you are a "splendid fellow;" "goodness itself." He was much pleased with the house & its surroundings, & admired your taste & skill in securing the place for us. So do I, feeling really an affection for Mrs. Ware & her family. The two I cannot tolerate are her sister-in-law (whom I have never seen) & her grandson whom I never cease to hear. No sleep yet, save in disjointed atoms at long intervals. Last night I amused myself in counting how often I was disturbed. The assaults on my sleep & happiness numbered fifteen! It was the tenth night of that boy's orgies. I am utterly broken down, & quite as ill as I was at Hampton. At daylight every morning he is supplied with stones to amuse him. These he throws against the door between us until we go to breakfast. Only then he is removed. His mother is left to sleep for the rest of the day, & he soon follows her example. Meanwhile, I work all day, & tremble as night approaches. Without consulting any one, I have determined to sleep in the parlor to night on a blanket. I cannot endure it much longer. I look as though I had been ill for a month.

I am glad of your proposition in regard to boarding. If you know of any place in a private family where neither babies nor bed-bugs are considered necessary for happiness & health, it is more than likely we will remain permanently. Packing is too hard on me. I do not object to any other inconvenience, than the treble Bs, & I have a nervous dread of moving. So I should be glad to go at once, if it were possible to a place where we *could* remain. Do as you please, however. I am anxious to spare you some little trouble, having plenty more to give you. I am so glad to go to Charleston, that I feel sure it will either be denied me, or will be filled with regret & bitterness after. It is preposterous to suppose I could have more than a temporary lull in my gay pilgrimage. I had a whole summer of reconciliation with life. It is time to renew the strife. I know this will vex you. But to my experience, it is as true as death.

In the Secular Prophets enclosed, I wish you would notice Heine's prophecy about the fortifications around Paris. Were they traced by Thiers, or Napoleon?[1] I followed the Review, but question the fact. The article can be still more reduced by striking out the allusion to the war prophecies & Gen. Toomb's Bunker Hill anticipation.[2]

Thank you for looking so carefully for news of Lillie. We have no late news, but I have seen nothing like the name of La Noue yet.

Mother is still devoted to your memory. She sighs & wishes I could see what a wise thing it would be to leave instantly for Canada. Not unless I could *marry* you, of course; but then—Here she sighs again, leaving me to infer that the wisdom of imposing on you by giving you an invalid to nurse, signifies that highly desirable condition of wisdom & respectability yclept marriage.

Are you taking care of yourself? Only 13 received. The mail failed this morning. Nothing later than Friday's paper.

S.M.

1. Louis Adolphe Thiers (1797–1877) was the first president of the French Republic after the fall of Napoleon III. In "Secular Prophets," October 7, 1873, Sarah wrote, "The poet Heine would be accredited with divine inspiration, had he been less notoriously profligate and irreligious. He predicted the German war, and German victory. He prophesied that the line of fortifications Thiers was then building around Paris would draw on it a great hostile army, and would crush the city as if rampart and bastion were a contracting iron shroud." This article was based on an article of the same name that appeared in the *Saturday Review of Politics, Literature, Science and Art,* August 9, 1873, 171–73.

2. Frank rejected Sarah's suggestion. Sarah wrote, "From the beginning of the last war to its close, they [prophesies] were innumerable. The most conspicuous failure was that of the Georgian General who was to call the roll of his slaves from the summit of Bunker Hill. Otherwise, they were generally correct. The very demagogues of Secession predicted its end." In this piece, Sarah was referring to Robert Toombs (1810–85), Confederate secretary of state in 1861 and a brigadier general during the Civil War.

ईु&ी

Frank to Sarah

19

Charleston

September 25 [1873]

Picture it! I have had my likeness taken five times in these two days. You will remember that I promised it to you in Greenville, and I was determined that nothing should stand in the way of it. The five pictures run from bad to worse, but I will pick out the two types, which seem to be best and send them, as soon as completed, and you shall take your choice. The particular picture (each one was a distinct setting) that you may choose is to be yours to keep, for your very own, and no one shall even have a copy of it without your permission. I want to spare you the annoyance of feeling, as we generally do with photographs, that 11 or 23 other persons have a picture of our friend which is identical with our own. Any unfortunates must satisfy themselves with copies of the styles that you reject. Mr. Magrath told me this morning that he would give me a new pass for you & Mrs. Morgan from Greenville to

Charleston; this is a saving to you of about $24! I mean you will have a new pass, instead of the one I gave you. Howell is already provided for.

I do not forget your boarding house. By the time that you are at Hampton I will send you full particulars of the nicest places that can be found. Letters very rare; like angels' visits. Your last was dated Sept 18. To-day is Sept 25. Dont worry about any thing but your social articles 'till after Wednesday; until which time we must run election matters.[1]

Yours always

F W Dawson

1. Charleston was holding municipal elections for mayor and aldermen.

ↄↄℭↄ

Frank to Sarah

No 20

Charleston

Thursday Night [September 25, 1873]

Your letter came too late (that of the 24th) for answer earlier in the day. I do not appreciate the force of your reasoning about the Canada trip; and it would have been a mockery, you know, to make the offer, *if I could have been sure that you would be so unwise as to refuse it.* You cut the ground from under your own feet. I implored you to go as my wife; you declined. You admitted that to accompany Miriam would restore your health, and you say that you think so still, and that you believe that God gave me the power of doing good, in order that I might use the power wisely & freely. Your one objection was that you did not wish to marry me. I know now that you do not. The only way to use my power, then, freely & well is to send you without the marriage. And by your refusing to go you put aside an opportunity of recovering your health, and at the same time prevent me from doing the work which Providence gave me to do. I only proposed not to see you before your departure, in order to save you from embarrassment, and to spare you the danger that, from an unnecessary feeling of gratitude, you might do or say on impulse what your sober second thought would not approve of. I tell you once more that I have given up all hope, and that I expect nothing whatever from you. And as you are the only person for whom I care to do anything, or even shall do anything, you do me an injury by refusing to consent to what I propose for you. It is very strange that you should allow Mr. Trenholm to take entire charge of Howell for years & years, and should deny me the opportunity of making you well, & of putting you in a position which will enable you to do your work better than ever. It is just as much within my means to send you to Canada as it is for Mr. Trenholm to take Howell. I could not do the latter; I can do the former. My offer is a standing one and you will, in accepting it, be no more indebted to me than to the man in the moon. Again, you say "a little rest and a gleam of happiness would restore you to health anywhere." How dare you refuse then the opportunities of rest and happiness which God gives you? How dare you assume that you are always to suffer, when, of your free will, you refuse to escape from suffering? Do you not see how much of your suffering is made lasting by your good nature? You should not have stayed a day with Mrs. Ware, & that shrieking fiend. Indeed, you do need a strong arm to direct you & to direct you aright. One half of your womanhood was passed in leaning on an arm which led you to misery, & you propose, for the remaining half to reject every arm that is offered you. You dont love me; why not love somebody else. The object is not to make A or B happy, but to make you happy. To make the whole alphabet unhappy & yourself wretched is flying in the face of Providence. Please dont think me impertinent in saying this; I do not mean to be so.

I am deeply grieved that you are so ill. It was my doing. But I beg you to believe that you shall give your Charleston boarding house a full trial before you make any long engagement. I think I know where you can be well fixed; but I advertise also; see News & Courier of Friday.[1] You could come at once, but for your proposed visit to Hampton. If any thing should turn up, to prevent that visit, telegraph me (the cost will be small) and you can come in two or three days at latest. You have reason, of course, to find disappointment in everything. But you will come to Charleston, and will be more pleasantly situated here than in any other place since you left Orleans. You dont know how much can be done for you, when you are within reach. During the winter you will have many friends here. They will give you pleasure & I will give you work; I mean, in carrying out your wishes in regard to your domestic & other arrangements. Your articles will have to lie over a day or two on acct of the election. I am glad Wm Trenholm spoke kindly of me; it is more than I have always done of him. Thiers built the Paris fortifications. Pray tell your dear Mother not to pester you about marrying me. You have convinced me that you will not; and she should not tempt you to think that I am only working for that. I take what I can get, which is—Nothing! Pray excuse this scrawl. I have been writing so many hours that my hand almost refuses to do its office.

Yours always

F. W. Dawson

1. This advertisement, which appeared in the *News and Courier* on September 26, 1873, read, "Wanted by two ladies, quiet and pleasant board. The western part of the City, and a family where there are no other boarders will be preferred."

૮ૹૣૼૣ

Sarah to Frank

Greenville September 26. [1873]

I feel very much like a child chastised for the first time by an indulgent mother. The justice or injustice of the proceeding depends on the opinion of the two parties, & on the very different points of view from which they contemplate the innocence or wickedness of the act which lead to it. Judged by your self-sacrifice & unparalleled devotion, I seem a monster to myself. God knows. You have however chosen a keen instrument to inflict condign punishment, in refusing to confide your troubles to me. Who has the right, if not I? What else have I ever asked of you? True, if I had been framed to petition, I would have had no scope to use the task, with your tender care forever on the alert as it has been. Your joys you can share with whom you will. You could scarcely meet a man on the street too dull or too selfish to smile with you. It was only what no one else would care to have, that I asked for. I know you to be in trouble. It gives me great concern. I ventured to express it meekly, & am quietly told it is none of my business. It is very true. But it is not usual to spurn any evidence of kind feeling one forlorn being may shew to another. Kindness is not common enough to be repelled so coldly. Heaven knows that when I met you, I did not believe it existed. I see now as clearly as then, that the more intimate the relations, the more mythical it becomes. It is only the one you trust who ever strikes. Have I not told you that the certainty of that would enable me to bear the loneliest, hardest solitary life?

I presume I have no right to ask if the New York failures have affected the paper; but I hope the panic will be arrested.

Your needles only begin to prove themselves. I first thought them a failure, but waited to give them a fair chance. The back is very, very much stronger. It is that unhappy mucus membrane which is worse than ever, suffocating me & refusing to be touched. The needles are at work on it, but their stitches mend nothing as yet. The fabric is apparently worn out. The slight fever I have daily seems to preceed from there.

Not hearing from Jimmy, I have written again to say we will arrive on the 6th. I might as well pay the difference here, as there; for mother dreads the fever at Hampton. Last year the doctor would not let us go until November. I have asked Ella to suggest some one to whom I could write to make arrangements to board in town for a few days. I do not know but that they have moved, themselves. If Hampton is as unhealthy as it is represented, it would be rash, to say the least, to seek the fever.

Are we not to meet you there, the day before we leave Columbia? I was surprised to hear you would "send" the advertizements. What trouble I give you!

I had no paper from the 18th, until this morning when one of the 23rd came. From what you said, there must be one article at least of mine published before Tippling. Will you send it, please, for my record?

Last night the shrieker had me up but twice. I gained a pound from that first pretence of peace. Mother forbade my escape to the parlor, afraid of being left alone in the room.

Thank you gratefully for the lecture on composition. I feel my defects very plainly, but cannot remedy them as well. Indeed but for your gentle teaching & great patience, I could never do anything at all. Your telegram has just astonished me. Indeed, if you will be extravagant, I must learn to complain less. A telegram to ensure my rest! Common as it is, I am still startled anew by your spendthrift ways. Malheureusement [Unfortunately], I cannot sleep in the day. It has never happened to me save at the White Sulphur, & in case of fever when very ill. Yesterday I spent hours in striving to obtain it. But I have already told you how well I feel to-day.

Do send me some short topics. I find none. I wanted to do something for poor Mr. Stokes & his unjust imprisonment,[1] but I had only the data furnished by women, & was afraid to trust implicitly to that.

Can we not agree to a truce until I leave Columbia? It pains me unutterably to seem forever cruel—especially when I feel so much for you.

Mother sends much love.

God bless & help you, my poor boy,

S.M.

---

1. Sarah is referring to the third retrial of Edward Stokes for the January 1872 murder of James Fisk. The retrial commenced in October 1873. For a description of the trial, see "The Verdict," *New York Times*, October 30, 1873.

Frank to Sarah

21

Charleston

Friday [September 26, 1873]

I can only send you a very few words. Several of the Charleston banks suspended payment this morning, & there is almost a panic in the City. The Trenholms are safe, so far.

I telegraphed you this morning to sleep in the day to make up for wakefulness at night. We are full of Editorial matter, about the Crisis[1] and the Election until Thursday. You need not send before that time. But if you were here you could write about it every day.

I think I have already found a nice boarding house for you in a private family.

Yours always

F. W. Dawson

1. As the financial crisis worsened, Sarah wrote an editorial on what women could do to help their men through hard times. In this piece, she advocated a conservative role for women, insisting that ladies could make the greatest difference by observing "domestic reform and economy" ("Woman's Work," November 19, 1873).

Frank to Sarah

23

Sunday Night [September 28, 1873]

I have just received your letter, and have telegraphed you that, unless you hear formally from Jimmy, you had better come direct to Charleston where quarters will be ready for you, or remain a week longer at Greenville. It is certainly dangerous to go to Hampton. Telegraph me what you will do, and I will be ready to meet you at the depot in Charleston upon your arrival here &, will take you to whatever place I have decided on—there are several in view. But you must telegraph me from Greenville (if you determine to come direct to Charleston) the day *before* you start, at least; and if you go to stay in Columbia let me know at once from there when you may be expected here.

I am very very glad that the needles seem to do some good; I began to think that everything I touched would fail. As soon as possible I will send you some subject-matter, and I will try to hunt up the missing papers tomorrow.

I am sorry that the course which you have compelled me to take has caused you any annoyance; I do not see why it should. As long as I thought you loved me you shared in every thing that I had. Your only right was through the love that I believed that you felt. As soon as you, by your letters, broke the back which was already bended, I could not, for the life of me, write as I had done before; nor can I now. Do not let us discuss a matter which is exceedingly painful to me. I dont suppose that St. Lawrence would have cared to discuss the relative merits of different patterns of gridirons[1] & I am much more of a devil than a saint in these days.

I grant you that you have never asked anything of me; it was necessary. I can divine pretty well what you need, & my only pleasure in life is doing it. Only, until you see some diminution in my watchful care & tender consideration, do not doubt my love for you. My conduct now is the best proof of the unselfishness of my love.

I dont know that I shall see you before you come down; I should like to but we might only disagree.

Yours always
F. W. Dawson

1. St. Lawrence (d. 258), a martyr of the Roman Catholic Church, is often depicted with the gridiron on which he was roasted to death.

≈ↄᏇↄ≈

Frank to Sarah

Charleston

Late, Sunday Night [September 28, 1873]

I have written to you already and mailed the letter, but so anxious am I that I write again. I cannot believe that you, Sarah! would willfully pain me; I know that you would not do it; but, Sweet Heaven! what could be more exquisitely cruel than to say as you do to me: "Heaven knows that when I met you, I did not believe that kindness existed. I see now as clearly as then that the more intimate the relations the more mythical it becomes. It is only the one you trust that ever strikes." How can you say such things? Can you say that I have failed in kindness to you? Have you not repelled me in every imaginable way? Am I not eating my heart out, rather than speak words of love to a woman who does not love me? Am I not surrounding you with every protection, moral and physical, that I can devise; did I not do what I did to save you not me; and yet you tell me, in effect, that I have taught you that the better I know you the more pain you suffer through me? Is this, grievous or just? But two wrongs do not make a right. When I see you, you shall tell me in what I have sinned agt you, and I will ask your pardon; & if your conscience tells you that you are in the wrong, I will ask you to forgive me for making you think so. If this will not do, tell me what will. I have denied you nothing that you have asked me, and I answer your question briefly about the failures. Had there been no financial crisis I should, as I told you, have had a fearful month's work. As it is, I am fighting desperately from day to day to avert the protesting of our notes, which, as you know, would be commercial disgrace &, as I feel, personal dishonour. At 2 oclock each afternoon I can see my way to 9 oclock the next morning. How long it will last, or how it will end, I know not. What I do know is that I have to pass through it all without an affectionate word from any one, and, at a time, when the conviction has reached me that all my labor to win your love has been miserably in vain. What wonder that I despair; what wonder that, if it were not for the loss then of the power to serve you, I should let the whole thing go by default. Have I been mistaken in you? If you are deaf to every other appeal, can you be deaf to a pitiful cry like this? Generosity can not be dead in you. [. . .]

Monday [September 29, 1873]
I have been all the morning looking for quarters, and have engaged you a suite of rooms—sitting room, bed-room, & pantry on the ground floor, with servants room for a ridiculously small price. They will be scantily furnished, but better than Hampton. The house is in Pitt St, about 4 squares from Howell's school, in a large garden—you have the entire floor. I have telegraphed to know if you will come on Tuesday night. You can help me in my work and perhaps save me from a complete collapse. So come! The likeness is finished, but it is so big that I will not trouble you with it till you come.

Yours always
F. W. Dawson

(over) Your dispatch is received. Thank you, my sweet, sweet, Love! As usual, with me, you have won. Expect me, or a telegram, at the Columbia

Hotel. I should be there Tuesday morning and meet you at breakfast; the telegram will meet you on Monday p.m.

Yours more than ever

F. W. Dawson

ᒉᗷᒋ

Sarah to Frank

Greenville. October 1st [1873]

No! we will not disagree when we meet! We will live like two doves, when divested of the pecking proclivities inherent in pen & ink. All false perceptions come from using one side of the brain exclusively. Call in the right side, & you will see that there is a more natural interpretation to the oracle I last uttered, than the charitable one you suggest. Do you not see that the more you love me, the more I readily wound you? Not because I design it, but because your very love renders you more susceptible to pain? If you did not love me, could word of mine grieve you? You only illustrate my belief more forcibly in crying out under your self-devised torture.

I rejoice over the description of our future abiding place. It is far better than I dared hope. Mother is in bliss. A few moments after closing Sunday's letter, I received your 19 & 20, with one from Jimmy. His was brief, & troubled. He stated that they had moved to town, & said he would advise me not to go to Hampton, though of course I could do as I pleased. He asked when he was to go to the dépôt for us. At that very time, he must have received my letter to Ella, saying I presumed she had moved, & asking her to suggest a place where we could board for a week just to see them, as mother feared Hampton. On receiving your telegram, I wrote Jimmy that my presence in Charleston was necessary on Tuesday evening, & as that would leave us no leisure to see him, we had changed our departure from this place to the 4th instead of the 6th. He could expect us Saturday night, unless he wrote before some better suggestion. I greatly fear he is in some distress not easily removed. I object to the Hotel, memories of my last night there being still rife. Miss Percival[1] might accommodate us; but I prepare for the worst. If the hotel is to be my fate, I would leave at the earliest possible moment. This will be my last letter. But if you have any change to make, address me in Columbia. I hope you will join us. I should like to take the early train from C., in order to arrive in the evening.

I meant to correct your impression that Howell was to be provided for by

Mr. Trenholm. Before I could do so, I was mortified yesterday by a postal card from Mr. Porter, saying Mr. Trenholm had never offered him to support the child, & asking if I understood he was to call on him for that purpose. I replied instantly that Howell was *totally* dependent on me, & that I had nothing; but that whatever books or clothing he needed would be supplied by my own exertions, & that Mr. Trenholm had simply offered him a scholarship. I enclosed the card & my reply to Mr. Trenholm. I told him what he never suspected—that I worked for the support of my small family, & while I was glad of the chance, I could incur no rash expenses; that I did not clearly understand Mr. Porter, but if he meant the child's board or tuition, I could not pay it, though I could give him all the books & clothing he could need. The only surprise to Mr. Trenholm will be the assertion that neither my brothers nor sisters do anything for their mother. He can only infer that, however, for I did not say it, true as it is. People-in-law are solely responsible, if there is any reproach in the fact. For myself, I think it perfectly just & natural. The surprise to me, is that Mr. Trenholm should not have stated his position to Mr. Porter. The humiliation is the postal card limp & greasy from much handling, which was a week on the road to accommodate all who chose to inspect it. To Mr. Porter I stated I would take no further steps about the child's return until I should speak with him myself. To Mr. Trenholm, I announced my arrival next Tuesday evening. So you see that Howell's fate still hangs in a very doubtful balance. I shall not mind this, provided it settles the vexed question permanently. I told Mr. T. I was sorry to annoy him any further, but that I felt I could not be too frank, for the sake of all concerned.

Your larger photograph is perfect. The smaller almost-profile, is only a resemblance, & one not flattering. The expression of the first is almost too vivid. I have never seen it as intense on paper—unless in writing. I hope the other one is as good. Mother is already laying main forte [claim] on these.

The Vampire child continues his nightly debauch. His conduct is not to be described. Never have even *I* dreamed of such infant horrors. Providence has occasionally intervened after a long siege, & has sent me or the baby on an airing; but it is nearly three weeks since I last slept for one hour unmolested. From twelve to four I have the certainty of pandemonium nightly. I rejoice to say his health is beginning to give way. I trust his voice will go first. Last night I heard his mother shake him soundly & tell him he was not fit to live. It soothed both the boy & myself. We simultaneously fell in a sweet slumber. A hour after when the air was rent by the screams so necessary to our life & happiness, kind Heaven put it in that mother's heart to plant one firm blow—& we fell asleep again. I feel like a daisy from intervals of sleep amounting to five hour altogether. I owe it to my own ingenuity, for I told the mother yesterday that the child was looking dreadfully, that he had every indication of nervous fever, & unless she could break him of his habits before it set in, he certainly must succumb. I had a "for-true" anecdote about my bad niece ready for her, in which only a miracle saved the child. I count the days before my deliverance. But for him, I should be glad to remain. Keep a brave heart, & all will be well. I will *not* have the paper fail, & you go to protest. La reine l'a dit.

A dimanche, ou lundi, ou mardi, comme vous voudrez.[2]

S.M.

21, 22, 23, 24 received.

Just heard from Shreveport. Sept. 21st, my pet nephew, Morgan,[3] was recovering, & quite out of danger. All the rest were well. Some kind neighbor had taken the younger ones. And yet, I am not satisfied!

1. Charlotte M. Percival (1816–99) operated a boardinghouse in Columbia after the Civil War.
2. The queen has said it. Till Sunday, or Monday, or Tuesday as you will.
3. Gibbes Morgan LaNoue (1855–96), the son of John Charles LaNoue and Eliza Ann Morgan LaNoue.

Sarah and Mrs. Morgan arrived in Charleston in October 1873. The move marked a turning point in Sarah's relationship with Frank. Between October 1873 and January 1874, she reconsidered Frank's proposal, and she finally consented to become his wife. The couple married at Gadsden House on January 27, 1874.[1]

Frank and Sarah's marriage was an equal partnership, framed by love and mutual respect. "He rarely if ever took a decisive step in his public career without first requesting her opinion, by which he was frequently inspired," recalled their son, Warrington, "and he had the constant advantage, night and day, of asking her to remind him of some quotation, who said this or that and in what circumstances. Her encyclopedic mind, unerringly accurate and always able to cite a passage in any book she had read, was never at fault." Frank fondly—and appropriately—referred to Sarah as "his walking encyclopedia," and "this pseudonym so lovingly given by her husband, was," according to Howell Morgan, "taken up by the people of Charleston, and followed her long after her husband was killed . . . and her children were grown."[2]

In March 1874, Sarah's mother died after a long illness. Sarah and Frank's first child, Ethel, was born in November. "If it had been possible for us to be happier," Sarah declared, "I should say she makes us so." The couple had two more children, Warrington, born on September 27, 1878, and Philip Hicky, born on February 9, 1881. Philip died at six months of age.[3]

Howell Morgan received a scholarship from the Trenholm family and was educated at Charleston's Home and School of the Holy Communion Institute until 1875, when he returned to his mother in Louisiana. Sarah maintained a close relationship with Howell and encouraged him to be worthy of his proud and distinguished heritage. "[If you] could only know something of the name you inherit, I am sure you would strive to be worthy to be called by it," Sarah lectured her adolescent nephew. "There is no royal blood as pure as ours, there is none that can be traced as far back. 'A long line of brave gentlemen and women with unstained names' it was said two hundred years ago. It is only right that we should appreciate a heritage so few can boast, and above all strive to be worthy of it."[4]

Sarah set the same high standards for her children, who were educated at the finest academies in Charleston and Europe. She idolized Ethel, describing her as "the belle of Charleston, and the most beautiful girl, as well as the most popular one that ever was known." Still, there was no doubt that Warrington, who bore a striking resemblance to his father, was her most beloved child. "Her *Son*," noted Sarah's sister, Lavinia, "came first and above all else in the world." When Warrington exhibited an interest in writing, Frank joked that Sarah would be unsatisfied if he grew up to become "the poet laureate of South Carolina. Nothing less than the United States, and all the rest of mankind would content you." Concerned that his wife was a little "too ambitious" for their children, Frank took pains to assure Sarah that personal goodness ranked far above public success. He was actively involved in his children's lives, so much so that "every one with whom he was thrown, soon felt and realized that what he lived for principally was . . . his wife, and his children at home." "Romping, practical joking, story-telling, and table conversation" became the staples of Dawson family life.[5]

Sarah's familial and domestic responsibilities at 43 Bull Street were skillfully balanced with her writing commitments to the *News and Courier*. After her marriage to Frank, she published numerous book reviews but largely abandoned her editorial writing, which she had always regarded as a burden on her health and well-being. Sarah's influence on the editorial content of the *News and Courier* cannot, however, be overestimated. Frank often consulted with her on the direction of the newspaper, and editorials on women and work published as late as 1879 are reminiscent of Sarah's earlier editorials on the same issue.[6]

Frank Dawson continued to use his newspaper to champion his vision for South Carolina. Although he was an influential member of the Democratic Party, his liberal-democratic position often put him at loggerheads with the party's more radical elements. In the 1870s, Frank earned the animosity of some of Charleston's most prominent citizens when he favored a fusion alliance with Republican governor Daniel Chamberlain over the radicalism of the straight-out movement. Frank's steadfast commitment to this unpopular position hurt the *News and Courier* financially and prompted criticism of the paper's one-eyed editorial policy, which many Charlestonians believed did not reflect the views of the people it claimed to represent. The bitter affair culminated in the establishment of the *Journal of Commerce*, which sought to redress the *News and Courier*'s "monopoly" on Charleston's newspaper readership.[7]

Frank Dawson was no stranger to controversy, but his reputation behind the political scene earned him influence and respect among his peers. He lobbied fiercely against the widespread practice of dueling, and in 1883 Pope Leo XIII knighted Frank in the Order of St. Gregory as a result of his efforts to secure the passage of antidueling legislation. Throughout his career he also worked tirelessly for the industrial development of South Carolina, opposed "efforts to restrict immigration, resented any discrimination based on a man's religion, rebuked the nation for its shabby treatment of the Indian, [and] fought zealously for Irish home rule." He emerged as a key player in Grover Cleveland's 1884 presidential campaign and was appointed vice president of the American Free Trade Association in 1885. In that year, he also edited and published *Our Women in the War*, which chronicled the experiences of Confederate women during the Civil War.[8]

Frank Dawson's life was cut short on March 12, 1889, when he was shot dead during an altercation with Dr. Thomas McDow. Frank had suspected a liaison between McDow and the Dawsons' governess, Marie Hélène Burdayron, and confronted the doctor. McDow later testified about what happened next: "Here it is in a nutshell," he said. "Captain Dawson entered my office and knocked me down with a cane. I got up and he was about to strike me again when I shot him." As Frank slumped to the floor, an excited McDow was left to confront his now dubious fate. Fearing jail or a lynch mob, the doctor dug a shallow grave under his stairwell in an attempt to hide the body. When a patrolman knocked on his door to investigate reports of a disturbance, McDow knew the game was up. Almost three hours after the shooting, he surrendered himself to the authorities. He was later acquitted of all charges after a jury accepted his plea of self-defense.[9]

Sarah never recovered from Frank's death or what she always regarded as the supreme injustice of McDow's trial. "What justice, law or common decency prevail in the state of South Carolina?" she wrote bitterly. "Twenty-three years of such unselfish and heroic labor was never before bestowed on an unworthy people! And the reward—defamation and persecution through life, and crucifixion after death." Financially dependent on the dividends on her *News and Courier* stock, Sarah was outraged to learn that the newspaper's commercial success did not translate into remuneration for its shareholders. Rudolph Siegling had previously become Frank's partner when Riordan moved to New York to work as a cotton commission merchant. Convinced that Siegling was responsible for the mismanagement of the paper, Sarah spent months campaigning for her entitlements. In a letter to all stockholders, Sarah called for collective action against the administrators. "The paper is prosperous; it is without a rival; and yet the Stock holders are assured that their Stock is worthless," she wrote indignantly. "There must be some reason for this; and I suggest that it is due, in great part, to extravagance in the administration of its affairs generally, in the employment of superfluous and inefficient assistants, in the payment of exaggerated and unnecessary salaries to some of those employed, and to extravagant and unjustifiable expenditure for alleged 'betterments' and 'improvements' of the property. . . . I call particular attention to the fact that Genl Siegling assigns to himself and receives from us $3,000.00 per annum for administering a property common to us all." Sarah's virulent petition went unheeded, and she was finally forced to concede defeat. Siegling's position, while less than generous, fell within the rule of law.[10]

Embittered and disillusioned, Sarah found solace in her family and her writing. She wrote a biographical entry on Frank for the *National Cyclopedia of American Biography,* followed by numerous short stories and articles. In 1892–93, Sarah published her first work, *Round about Marriage,* which was a translation of *Autour du Mariage,* by Gyp. In 1895, she followed this effort with a fictional piece titled "A Tragedy of South Carolina," which appeared in *Cosmopolitan.* The story, which created a sensation in Charleston, followed the demise of a whiskey-drinking planter who murdered two poor white neighbors for letting their pigs run through his cotton field.[11]

After the death of her sister, Miriam Dupré, in 1898 and Ethel's marriage to New York lawyer Herbert Barry, Sarah moved to Paris to live with Warrington, who was a writer and agent for the U.S. government. In 1903, she published *Les Aventures de Jeannot Lapin,* a French version of the Brer Rabbit stories. In 1907, she published "Les Prisonniers," a French translation of Mary Cholmondeley's *Prisoners.* While enjoying the fruits of her literary success, Sarah also found some peace and solace in Paris. "I love most to remember her in the broad tree-shaded avenues of Versailles," Warrington wrote, "where, dreaming of a distant tragic past, she found ever new strength to meet the present."[12]

Sarah revisited her personal papers only a few times before her death. On July 23, 1896, she wrote an extended entry at the end of her last journal. "How merciful God is in making our paths straight, and choosing for us what is the very best for our souls!" she wrote. "What an awful life mine would have been—if not for his [Frank's] love—his adoration—his unceasing care! How I thank God for his life—yea! for his death! It was a fit crown for my hero. He would have asked nothing better than to die doing his duty—in defense of a helpless woman." In Paris, on January 27, 1906, she reopened the same book to commemorate her marriage. "Thirty-two years ago today—only it was a Tuesday—1874 Jan 27th—we were married. Nearly seventeen years, I have been alone. 'My beloved is mine, and I am His, and Love is Stronger than Death.'"[13]

Sarah Morgan Dawson died in Paris on May 5, 1909, at the age of sixty-seven. She is buried next to Frank in the St. Lawrence Cemetery in Charleston, South Carolina.

1. *News and Courier,* January 29, 1874.
2. Warrington Dawson typescript, Dawson Papers; Howell Morgan memoir, Sarah Morgan Dawson and Family Papers.
3. On Sarah Fowler Morgan's death, see *News and Courier,* March 11, 1874; Sarah Morgan Dawson to Lydia Carter Morgan, March 7, 1875, in Breed, "Sarah Morgan Dawson," 66. On the birth of the Dawson children and family life, see Clark, *Francis Warrington Dawson,* 26–30.
4. Sarah Morgan Dawson to Howell Morgan, May 23, 1880, in Breed, "Sarah Morgan Dawson," 68.
5. Sarah Morgan Dawson to Howell Morgan, January 11, 1895, in ibid., 75; Lavinia Drum to Warrington Dawson, June 23, 1909, in Clark, *Francis Warrington Dawson,* 29; Frank Dawson to Sarah Morgan Dawson, October 23, 1886, in Breed, "Sarah Morgan Dawson," 68; Frank Dawson to Sarah Morgan Dawson, November 23, 1886, and Augustine Smythe to Sarah Morgan Dawson, March 16, 1889, in Clark, *Francis Warrington Dawson,* 29, 28.
6. Sarah Morgan Dawson scrapbook, 1853–82, Dawson Papers. See, for example, "Only a Woman," *News and Courier,* March 29, 1879: "Around us on every side there are opportunities to employ women. The men, however, have no intention of making way for them. They pooh-pooh the suggestion that a woman will make a useful clerk or book-keeper, as competent a telegrapher, as nimble a type-setter and as deft an exhibitor of muslins and laces as the male Carolinian. They slam the door in the woman's face. They deny her, whenever they can, the blessed privilege of being independent, though it must be admitted that they will unhesitatingly give her their seat in a car, lend her an umbrella, or put themselves to direct inconvenience in buttoning her glove or picking up her handkerchief. What is pleasant to themselves they permit; what is useful to her they prohibit."
7. Clark, *Francis Warrington Dawson,* 34–69.

8. See Logan, "Francis W. Dawson," 190–213; Wyatt-Brown, *Shaping,* 277–79; Clark, *Francis Warrington Dawson,* 101.

9. Peck, "1889," 76. See also Logan, "Francis W. Dawson," 311–21; Clark, *Francis Warrington Dawson,* 215–32.

10. Sarah Morgan Dawson to James C. Hemphill, September 23, 1889, and Sarah Morgan Dawson to Mr. Willis, April 3, 1890, in Davis, "Sarah Morgan Dawson," 76, 77; Clark, *Francis Warrington Dawson,* 230; Sarah Morgan Dawson to *News and Courier* bondholders, 1890, in Breed, "Sarah Morgan Dawson," 72.

11. See "Francis Warrington Dawson," in *National Cyclopedia of American Biography* (New York: J. T. White, 1904), 12:441; "Francis Warrington Dawson" and "Sarah (Ida Fowler) Morgan Dawson," in *National Cyclopedia of American Biography* (New York: J. T. White, 1933), 23:300–301. Sarah's draft of this piece in the Dawson Papers contains a scathing attack on the people of South Carolina.

12. *National Cyclopedia* [1933], 300–301; S. M. Dawson, *Confederate Girl's Diary* (1913), xx.

13. Sarah Morgan diary, July 23, 1896, January 27, 1906, vol. 5, Dawson Papers.

APPENDIX

Sarah Morgan's Articles and Editorials, 1873

This list contains all identifiable editorials and articles written by Sarah Morgan in 1873.

Charleston News

March 5	The New Andromeda
March 10	The Use and Abuse of Widows
March 13	A Booth to Let In Vanity Fair
March 15	Old Maids!
March 17	"Killing No Murder"
March 19	The Economic Aspect of Widows
March 19	The Maiden All for Lorne
March 20	Charity Begins at Home
March 21	Marrying a Deceased Wife's Sister
March 22	Bachelors and Widowers
March 26	Remember!
March 29	Young Couples
April 1	April Fool
April 2	The Property of Married Women
April 4	Two Hundred and Fifty Dollars for a Vote
April 4	Liberty of Conscience in Japan

Charleston News and Courier

April 7	Mothers-in-Law
April 8	The Convenient Plea of Insanity
April 10	Stitch! Stitch! Stitch!
April 12	Easter Devotions
April 15	Work for Women
April 16	The Fight for the Crown
April 16	The Parting Words of Adolphe Monod
April 21	The Cant of Common Sense
April 24	Personal Good Works

April 25	"Flirtation": A Lecture to Flirts and an Incidental Indictment of the Courier for Coquetting
April 25	The Courage of Despair
April 25	Paradox
April 28	Wiping Out Old Scores
April 29	The Third Term
May 7	Present Takers and Present Makers
May 8	The Tichborne Case
May 10	Very Young America
May 12	Whites and Blacks
May 16	Khiva
May 16	The Piano Plague
May 17	Bores
May 19	Blue Laws in 1873
May 20	Suffrage-Shrieking
May 22	Euthanasia
May 24	Society and Propriety
May 31	The Last "Herald" Sensation
June 2	The Way to the Water
June 3	Conscience
June 7	Who Knows?
June 14	Calling Names!
June 21	Age
June 26	The Eden of the South: Summer at the White Sulphur Springs
June 28	Long Engagements
July 1	Beauty and the Beast: A Tale of the White Sulphur Springs
July 5	Mourning
July 9	A Summer Idyll: The Poetry and Prose of Life at the Springs
July 12	Brothers versus Sisters
July 16	A Season at the Springs: The White Sulphur in Full Blast—A Happy Company
July 23	Style at the Springs: The Rush of Visitors to the Greenbrier White
July 26	"The World before Him, Where to Choose"
July 30	Scenes at the Springs: Stray Leaves from the Volume of Humanity
August 6	Fashion at the Springs: The Belles of the White and Their Ducks of Dresses
August 13	Belles at the Springs: Apples of Discord in the Virginia Eden
August 21	Scandal at the Springs: "Tell Me, My Heart, Can This Be Love?"
September 13	Heart-Breaking
September 15	Weather-Wisdom
September 20	The Natural History of Woman
September 23	Tippling
October 4	Dust to Dust!
October 7	Secular Prophets

October 11	"What Is Truth?"
October 11	Spare the Trees
October 13	Twelve Hundred a Year
October 15	A Domestic Revolution
October 18	Pocket Money
October 18	Blue Birds
October 20	Faith and Works
October 21	The Greatest Plague in Life!
October 22	Out at Interest
October 23	The Fall Fashions
October 25	Very Small Talk
October 28	The Heroes of the Epidemic
November 1	Parlor and Promenade: The Fall Fashions for Charleston
November 3	Brains
November 5	Where Doctors Differ!
November 8	Friends
November 8	Out and About: Fashion Gossip for the Charleston Ladies
November 8	Monarchy or Republic in France
November 14	Pictures
November 15	Domestic Economy: Fashion Notes for Charleston Ladies
November 19	Woman's Work
November 21	Talk without Tongue
November 22	Affectation
November 25	The Clerks of the Weather
November 26	The Widow and Orphan
November 27	Thanksgiving
November 28	A National Tea-Party
November 29	Early Birds
December 2	Returning Thanks!
December 3	Sparing the Rod!
December 9	"Go to the Ant, Thou Sluggard!"
December 12	A Good Suggestion
December 13	Confidential

Sarah noted that she had published two other "columns on fashion" that do not appear in her scrapbook, but many articles on that subject appeared during this period, and hers cannot be identified.

BIBLIOGRAPHY

Manuscript Collections

Francis Warrington Dawson I and II Papers, Rare Book, Manuscript, and Special Collections Library, Duke University, Durham, North Carolina.

Sarah Morgan Dawson and Family Papers (boxed with Brunot-Duchein Family Papers), Louisiana and Lower Mississippi Valley Collections, Hill Memorial Library, Louisiana State University, Baton Rouge.

Works by Francis Warrington Dawson

Reminiscences of Confederate Service, 1861–1865. Charleston: News and Courier Book Presses, 1882.

Reminiscences of Confederate Service, 1861–1865. Ed. Bell I. Wiley. Baton Rouge: Louisiana State University Press, 1980.

"Our Women in the War": The Lives They Lived; The Deaths They Died. Ed. Francis Warrington Dawson. Charleston: News and Courier Book Presses, 1885.

Works by Sarah Morgan Dawson

Les Aventures de Jeannot Lapin. Paris: Hachette, 1903.

A Confederate Girl's Diary. Intro. Warrington Dawson. Boston: Houghton Mifflin, 1913.

A Confederate Girl's Diary. Intro. Warrington Dawson. Ed. James I. Robertson Jr. Bloomington: Indiana University Press, 1960; Westport, Conn.: Greenwood Press, 1972.

"Francis Warrington Dawson." In *National Cyclopedia of American Biography*, 12:441. New York: James T. White, 1904.

"Les Prisonniers." *La Revue Hebdomadaire*. 1907.

Round about Marriage. 1892–93.

Sarah Morgan: The Civil War Diary of a Southern Woman. Ed. Charles East. New York: Simon and Schuster, 1992. Reprint of *The Civil War Diary of Sarah Morgan*. Athens: University of Georgia Press, 1991.

"A Tragedy of South Carolina." *Cosmopolitan*, October 1895, 53–62.

Other Works

Berend, Zsuzsa. "'The Best or None!' Spinsterhood in Nineteenth-Century New England." *Journal of Social History* 33 (summer 2000): 935–57.

Breed, Charlotte Telford. "Sarah Morgan Dawson: From Confederate Girl to New Woman." Master's thesis, University of North Carolina at Chapel Hill, 1981.

Broussard, Joyce Linda. "Female Solitaires: Women Alone in the Lifeworld of Mid-Century Natchez, Mississippi, 1850–1880." Ph.D. diss., University of Southern California, 1998.

Burton, Orville Vernon. *In My Father's House Are Many Mansions: Family and Community in Edgefield, South Carolina.* Chapel Hill: University of North Carolina Press, 1985.

Cann, Katherine D. "A Most Awful and Insoluble Mystery: The Writing Career of Sarah Morgan Dawson." *Proceedings of the South Carolina Historical Association* (1990): 75–86.

Carter, Christine Jacobson. "Southern Single Blessedness: Unmarried Women in Savannah and Charleston, 1800–1865." Ph.D. diss., Emory University, 2001.

Cashin, Joan E., ed. *Our Common Affairs: Texts from Women in the Old South.* Baltimore: Johns Hopkins University Press, 1996.

Censer, Jane Turner. "A Changing World of Work: North Carolina Elite Women, 1865–1895." *North Carolina Historical Review* 73 (January 1996): 28–55.

Chambers-Schiller, Lee Virginia. *Liberty, a Better Husband: Single Women in America: The Generations of 1780–1840.* New Haven: Yale University Press, 1984.

Chesnut, Mary Boykin Miller. *Mary Chesnut's Civil War.* Ed. C. Vann Woodward. New Haven: Yale University Press, 1981.

Clark, E. Culpepper. "Sarah Morgan and Francis Dawson: Raising the Woman Question in Reconstruction South Carolina." *South Carolina Historical Magazine* 81 (January 1980): 8–23.

———. *Francis Warrington Dawson and the Politics of Restoration: South Carolina, 1874–1889.* University: University of Alabama Press, 1980.

Conte, Robert S. *The History of the Greenbrier: America's Resort.* 2d ed. Charleston, W.Va.: Pictorial Histories Publishing, 2000.

Crow, Terrell Armistead, and Mary Moulton Barden, eds. *Live Your Own Life: The Family Papers of Mary Bayard Clarke, 1854–1886.* Columbia: University of South Carolina Press, 2003.

Davis, Mary Katherine. "Sarah Morgan Dawson: A Renunciation of Southern Society." Master's thesis, University of North Carolina at Chapel Hill, 1970.

Edwards, Laura F. *Gendered Strife and Confusion: The Political Culture of Reconstruction.* Urbana: University of Illinois Press, 1997.

———. *Scarlett Doesn't Live Here Anymore: Southern Women in the Civil War Era.* Urbana: University of Illinois Press, 2000.

Farnham, Christie Anne. *The Education of the Southern Belle: Higher Education and Student Socialization in the Antebellum South.* New York: New York University Press, 1994.

Faust, Drew Gilpin. *Mothers of Invention: Women of the Slaveholding South in the American Civil War.* Chapel Hill: University of North Carolina Press, 1996.

Foner, Eric. *Reconstruction: America's Unfinished Revolution, 1863–1877.* New York: Harper and Row, 1988.

Gross, Jennifer Lynn. "'Good Angels': Confederate Widowhood in Virginia." In *Southern Families at War: Loyalty and Conflict in the Civil War South*, ed. Catherine Clinton, 133–54. New York: Oxford University Press, 2000.

Jabour, Anya. "'Grown Girls, Highly Cultivated': Female Education in an Antebellum Southern Family." *Journal of Southern History* 64 (February 1998): 23–64.

Jones, Anne Goodwyn. *Tomorrow Is Another Day: The Woman Writer in the South, 1859–1936.* Baton Rouge: Louisiana State University Press, 1981.

Juncker, Clara. "Behind Confederate Lines: Sarah Morgan Dawson." *Southern Quarterly* 30 (fall 1991): 7–18.

Kelley, Mary. *Private Woman, Public Stage: Literary Domesticity in Nineteenth-Century America.* New York: Oxford University Press, 1984.

Lebsock, Suzanne. "Radical Reconstruction and the Property Rights of Southern Women," *Journal of Southern History* 43 (May 1977): 195–216.

———. *The Free Women of Petersburg: Status and Culture in a Southern Town, 1784–1860.* New York: Norton, 1984.

Lewis, Charlene M. Boyer. *Ladies and Gentlemen on Display: Planter Society at the Virginia Springs, 1790–1860.* Charlottesville: University Press of Virginia, 2001.

Logan, Samuel Frank. "Francis W. Dawson, 1840–1889: South Carolina Editor." Master's thesis, Duke University, 1947.

———. "Francis Warrington Dawson, 1840–1889: South Carolina Editor." *Proceedings of the South Carolina Historical Association* 2 (1952): 13–28.

Massey, Mary Elizabeth. *Bonnet Brigades.* New York: Knopf, 1966.

McAlexander, Hubert Horton. *The Prodigal Daughter: A Biography of Sherwood Bonner.* Baton Rouge: Louisiana State University Press, 1981.

Morgan, James Morris. *Recollections of a Rebel Reefer.* Boston: Houghton Mifflin, 1917.

O'Brien, Michael, ed. *An Evening When Alone: Four Journals of Single Women in the South, 1827–67.* Charlottesville: University Press of Virginia for the Southern Texts Society, 1993.

Peck, Thomas K. "1889: The Killing of Captain Dawson." In *Charleston Murders*, ed. Beatrice St. Julien Ravenel, 71–107. New York: Duell, Sloan, and Pearce, 1947.

Peterson, M. Jeanne. *Family, Love, and Work in the Lives of Victorian Gentlewomen.* Bloomington: Indiana University Press, 1989.

Rable, George C. *Civil Wars: Women and the Crisis of Southern Nationalism.* Urbana: University of Illinois Press, 1989.

Reeks, Joseph. "A Catholic Soldier." *The Month* 66 (1889): 273–78.

Roberts, Giselle. *The Confederate Belle.* Columbia: University of Missouri Press, 2003.

Sass, Herbert Ravenel. *Outspoken: 150 Years of the News and Courier.* Columbia: University of South Carolina Press, 1953.

Schoonmaker, Nancy Gray. "As Though It Were unto the Lord: Sarah Morgan Dawson and Nineteenth-Century Southern Mourning." Master's thesis, University of North Carolina at Chapel Hill, 2001.

Schuler, Kathryn Reinhart. "Women in Public Affairs in Louisiana during Reconstruction." *Louisiana Historical Quarterly* 19 (July 1936): 696–701.

Scott, Anne Firor. *The Southern Lady: From Pedestal to Politics, 1830–1930.* Chicago: University of Chicago Press, 1970.

Simkins, Francis Butler, and James Welch Patton. *The Women of the Confederacy.* Richmond, N.Y.: Garrett and Massie, 1936.

Smith-Rosenberg, Carroll. "The Female World of Love and Ritual: Relations between Women in Nineteenth-Century America." *Signs: A Journal of Women in Culture and Society* 1 (fall 1975): 1–29.

Stevenson, Brenda E. *Life in Black and White: Family and Community in the Slave South.* New York: Oxford University Press, 1996.

Stowe, Steven M. *Intimacy and Power in the Old South: Ritual in the Lives of the Planters.* Baltimore: Johns Hopkins University Press, 1987.

Weiner, Marli F. *Mistresses and Slaves: Plantation Women in South Carolina, 1830–80.* Urbana: University of Illinois Press, 1998.

Whites, LeeAnn. *The Civil War as a Crisis in Gender: Augusta, Georgia, 1860–1890.* Athens: University of Georgia Press, 1995.

Wyatt-Brown, Bertram. *The Shaping of Southern Culture: Honor, Grace, and War, 1760s–1880s.* Chapel Hill: University of North Carolina Press, 2001.

INDEX

Note: FWD = Francis Warrington Dawson; SM = Sarah Ida Fowler Morgan

Committee for the Abolition of the Slave Trade, 190n3

Comprehensive Pronouncing and Explanatory Dictionary of the English Language (Worcester), 24n1

Conrad, Charles Magill, 133

Consultation of Physicians (Hogarth), 22n3

"Convenient Plea of Insanity, The" (SM), xxxv

Corcoran, William Wilson, 133

Corday, Charlotte, 56

Cosmopolitan, 252

Courier. See *Charleston Courier*

courtship: SM on, 191–94

Cram, Ida Balch, 176

Cram, Mary Boggs, 177n2

Cram, Thomas Jefferson, 177n2

Crédit Mobilier investigation: SM on, 198

CSS *Nashville* (ship), xxiv–xxvi

Custis (Springs guest), 174

Danton, Georges-Jacques, 25n1

Darling, Grace, 56

Darling, William, 59n5

Darwin, Charles, 43n4, 74n3

Davis, Jefferson, 169n1

Dawson, Ethel (daughter). See Barry, Ethel Dawson

Dawson, Francis Warrington: early life of, xxiv; military service of, xxiv–xxvii, 110; journalistic career of, xxvii–xxix; membership of, in societies, xxix, 31; marriage of, to V. Fourgeaud, xxix, 6n4; living arrangements of, at Fourgeauds', 2, 10, 12, 15, 211; relies on guidance from SM, xxx, 2–3, 6–7, 8, 9, 10, 13, 15, 16, 25, 37, 208–9; proposes to SM, 10, 23, 49, 153; espouses spiritual connection with SM, xxx, 4–5, 14, 97, 172, 231; proposes trip to Provence, 10, 14, 16; advises SM on writing, xlv–xlvi, 26–27, 28, 38, 41, 42–43, 46, 48, 93, 103, 106, 109–10,

113, 117, 127, 128, 156, 172, 209, 223, 232–33; encourages SM's writing, xxxiv, 20, 23, 24, 26, 27–28, 39–40, 41, 92, 94, 96, 103, 104, 105, 116, 123, 125, 137, 140–41, 147, 160, 172, 178, 213; depression of, xlv, 10, 95, 115–16, 172, 211, 213–14; ill health of, 135, 140, 143–44, 145, 147, 175, 207, 226; on SM's depression, 40, 47, 91, 92, 94, 98, 104, 107–8, 109, 115–16, 140, 239; on H. Morgan, 31, 44, 49–50, 92, 103, 161, 211–12, 217, 218–19; as guardian of B. Riordan's children, 164; friendship of, with M. Dupré, 213, 232, 234; financial troubles of, 207, 211, 216, 244; marriage of, to SM, 249; children of, 249–50; political interests of, 250–51; made Knight of St. Gregory, 251; murder of, 251

Dawson, Philip Hicky (son), 249

Dawson, Sarah Ida Fowler Morgan. See Morgan, Sarah Ida Fowler

Dawson, Virginia Fourgeaud, xxix, xxx, 1, 5, 12, 22. See also Dawson, Francis Warrington; mourning practices

Dawson, Warrington (son), 249, 250

Dawson, William A. (uncle), xxv

Deas (Springs guest), 159

De l'Allemagne (de Staël), 70n5

de Lamartine, Alphonse, 3n3

Delphine (de Staël), 70n5

Democratic Party, 60; FWD's involvement in, xxix, 250–51; "straight-out" movement in, 136n4, 250–51

DeSaussure, Daniel Louis, 30n3, 136n3

DeSaussure, Douglas Blanding, 134, 135

DeSaussure, Frances Martin, 136n3

DeSaussure, Martha Lamar Stark, 136n3

DeSaussure, William Ford, 8n2

Dickens, Charles, 3n3, 13n3, 27n1, 53, 204n3

Dickinson, Susan, 34

Divine Comedy, The (Dante), 18n3

Morgan, Sarah Hunt Fowler (*continued*)
xlvi, 222, 225, 245, 249; ill health of,
38, 116, 152, 155, 156, 161, 169–70;
death of, 249. *See also* Hampton

Morgan, Sarah Ida Fowler: historiogra-
phy on, xxxvii, xlixn53; Civil War
diary of, xv; early life of, xvii–xix; life
of, during Civil War, xix–xxii, 55, 66,
75, 78, 82, 179, 182–83, 187, 197, 199–
200, 202, 230n4; and buggy accident,
xxi; depression of, xxii, 10, 40, 43, 49,
91, 92, 94, 104, 107–8, 109, 115–16,
140, 216; ill health of, xix, xxxvi–
xxxvii, xlii, 28–29, 38, 44, 91, 94, 97–
98, 106–8, 113, 137, 138, 145, 163, 168,
210, 224, 228–29, 236; as guardian of
H. Morgan, xxii, xxiii, xxiv, 3n5, 43–
44, 71, 78, 91, 139–40, 141–42, 146,
155, 210, 215, 231; relationship of, with
J. Morgan, xxxiii, 71, 81–86, 98, 126,
136, 215–16, 217, 227, 229; relationship
of, with G. Burroughs Morgan, 19, 82,
83, 169, 170; discourages FWD's love,
xxxi, xlv, 4, 8, 116, 220; refuses FWD's
proposals, 10, 11n1, 49, 207; financial
status of, xxii, xxxiii, 19, 26, 33, 38, 41,
97, 100, 128, 217, 219, 225, 246, 251–
52; on writing career, xxxiv, xliii, 19,
27, 39, 47, 91, 109–10, 113, 145, 152,
154, 163, 220–21, 222, 241; secrecy of,
about career, xxxii, xxxiii, xliii–xliv,
27, 41, 45, 46, 99, 109, 112, 170; public
comments on published work of, xli–
xlii, 26, 28, 40–41, 47, 52, 53, 72, 127,
151; advises FWD on business, 13, 17,
41; as Feu Follet, 112, 118–22, 129–33,
178; friendship of, with H. Pegram,
xliv, 156–58, 163, 173, 174; searches for
G. Morgan's grave, 162, 167–68, 176;
visit of, with M. Dupré, 123, 138, 141,
142, 147, 151, 152, 155, 166; secures
scholarship for H. Morgan, 207, 215,
217, 221, 228, 234, 245–46; marriage
of, to FWD, 249; children of, 249–50;

career of, after marriage, 250, 252; and
FWD's murder, 251; death of, 253

Morgan, Thomas Gibbes, Jr. (brother),
xviii, xx, xxi, 3n5, 78; military service
of, xix; death of, xxii, xxxi, 81, 187

Morgan, Thomas Gibbes, Sr. (father),
xvii, xviii, xix, xxxi, 125, 187

Morse, Alexander Porter, 159n4

Morse, May, 158, 163, 165, 168, 169

Moses, Franklin J., Jr., 151–52, 156

motherhood. *See* women

"Mothers-in-Law" (SM), xxxv, 36n2, 37

Mount St. Mary's College, xxviii

"Mourning" (SM), xxxv, 137n1, 187–90

mourning practices: in Boston, 190; in
England, 188; in France, 188; of FWD,
xxx, 1, 5, 12, 22; SM on, 187–90; of SM,
187; in Philadelphia, 190

Mrs. Winslow's Soothing Syrup, 73

Mystery of Edwin Drood, The, (Dickens),
13n3

Napier, Charles James, 164n2

Napoleon I (emperor of France), 67

Napoleon III (emperor of France), 236

Nation, The, xxxv, 22, 25

*National Cyclopedia of American Biogra-
phy,* 252

National Woman Suffrage Association:
SM on, 204–5

"Natural History of Woman, The" (SM),
xxxvii, 52, 67–70

"New Andromeda, The" (SM), xxxii,
xxxv, xxxvi, 20–22, 23, 128, 197

Newman, John Henry Cardinal, 81n3

New Orleans, La.: Morgan family life in,
xvii–xviii; Union occupation of, xx;
Unification Movement in, 152

New Orleans Delta, xxviii

New Orleans Picayune, xxxiii, 61

News. See Charleston News

*News and Courier. See Charleston News
and Courier*

New York, N.Y.: FWD's business trip to, 16

"Very Young America" (SM), 12n4, 46n2, 71, 79–81
Victoria (queen of England), 27n4

Wagner, Richard, 122
Walpole, Horace, 76
Ware, Irvin F., 210, 228, 230, 233, 236, 239, 241, 246–47
Ware, Lucy Foote, 210, 228, 236, 246–47
Ware, Mary Williams Jones: boarding house of, xliv, 207, 217, 239; familial relationships of, 210, 223n1; friendship of, with SM, 216, 218, 222, 235
Ware, Thomas, 211n2
Ware, Thomas Edwin, 211n2
Warmoth, Henry Clay, 152, 153n6
Washington, George, 174n2, 203
Washington, Martha Custis, 174n2
"Way to the Water, The" (SM), 103n3
"Weather-Wisdom" (SM), 211n1, 216n2, 218
Webster, Noah, 24n1
Wedgwood, Josiah, 190n3, 201n1
Whaley, Mitchell, and Clancy, 128n1
Whites, LeeAnn, xvi
"Whites and Blacks" (SM), xxxvi, 200–201
White Sulphur Springs, W.Va.: FWD organizes SM's trip to, xlii, 91, 99–102, 104; and elite society, xlii–xliii, 100, 112, 122, 128–33, 144, 150, 191; health benefits of, xlii, 91, 97, 119, 120, 150; SM's description of, xlii–xliii, 118–22; SM as object of gossip at, xliii–xliv, 150–51, 159, 170, 173–74, 175, 176, 178
Willington, Aaron S., 33
"Wiping Out Old Scores" (SM), 43n1, 48, 202–3
Woman's Journal, 205n3

"Woman's Work" (SM), 242n1
women: FWD on, 10–11; and domestic ideal, xvi, xxiii, xxxii, xxxiii, xxxix, xl, xli, xlv, xlvi, 19, 100; and employment, xvii, xxxii–xxxiii; SM on, and age, xxxviii–xxxix, 63–66; SM on, and employment, xl–xli, 61–63, 198–99; SM on, and fashion, 40, 180–82, 188–89, 194–96; SM on, and friendship, 86–87; SM on, and intelligence, 67–70; SM on, as mothers, 56, 67, 78–81; SM on, and property rights, 60–61; SM on single, xxxvii–xli, 55–59; SM on, and tippling, 224–25; SM on, as widows, xxxix, 26, 53–55, 56, 59–60; and reciprocity, xviii–xix, xxiii, xxxi; and republican motherhood, 80; and watershed debate, xv–xvi; as writers, xxxii–xxxiii. See also education; suffrage
Wood, Benjamin, xxviii, 11
Woodhull, Victoria Claflin, 205
Worcester, Joseph Emerson, 24n1
"Work for Women" (SM), xxxvii, xl–xli, 32n5, 52, 61–63
"World before Him, Where to Choose, The" (SM), 191–94
Worsham, John, 133
Wragg, Mrs., 143

Yeadon, Richard, 33
yellow fever: in South Carolina, 139, 141, 241, 242; in Louisiana, 219, 224n2, 225, 232, 236, 247; in Tennessee, 223
"Young Couples" (SM), 34n3, 71, 75–78

Zaragoza, Augustina, 57
Zimmer, Lewis, 51n2
Zimmer, Lewis Lee, 51
Zimmer, Virginia, 51n2

The Publications of the Southern Texts Society

Books published by the University of Georgia Press

A DuBose Heyward Reader
Edited and with an Introduction by James M. Hutchisson

To Find My Own Peace: Grace King in Her Journals, 1886–1910
Edited by Melissa Walker Heidari

The Correspondence of Sarah Morgan and Francis Warrington Dawson,
with Selected Editorials Written by Sarah Morgan for the
Charleston News and Courier
Edited by Giselle Roberts